KATYN
1940

If it be the case that a monstrous crime has been committed by a foreign government – albeit a friendly one – and that we, for however valid reasons, have been obliged to behave as if the deed was not theirs, may it not be that we now stand in danger of bemusing not only others but ourselves? … We ought, maybe, to ask ourselves how, consistent with the necessities of our relations with the Soviet Government, the voice of our political conscience is to be kept up to concert pitch. It may be that the answer lies, for the moment, only in something to be done inside our own hearts and minds where we are masters. Here at any rate we can make a compensatory contribution – a reaffirmation of our allegiance to truth and justice and compassion.

Owen O'Malley

KATYN 1940

The Documentary Evidence of the West's Betrayal

EUGENIA MARESCH

SPELLMOUNT

Dedication

To my life-long friend and mentor, prelate Lt Zdzisław Peszkowski, survivor of Kozielsk camp, who in 1944 became a Scout leader to thousands of Polish refugee children – myself included – and to Dr Zdzisław Jagodziński, historian, librarian and first editor of the Katyn bibliography, my courageous friend and colleague; both now departed, without ever seeing the fruits of their inspiration.

Front of jacket: Big Ben, Wartime London. (Franklin D. Roosevelt Library ARC 195565)

Back of jacket: Unveiling of the Katyn monument, Gunnersbury Cemetery, London. (PISM Bednarski collection)

First published 2010
by Spellmount, an imprint of
The History Press
The Mill, Brimscombe Port
Stroud, Gloucestershire, GL5 2QG
www.thehistorypress.co.uk

British Library Cataloguing in Publication Data.
A catalogue record for this book is available from the British Library.

ISBN 978 0 7524 5535 8

Typesetting and origination by The History Press
Printed in India, Aegean Offset
Manufacturing managed by Jellyfish Print Solutions Ltd

CONTENTS

0
100 miles
0
100 kms
Baltic Sea
LATVIA
LITHUANIA
Niemen
Königsberg
Danzig
'Wolf's Lair'
EAST PRUSSIA
(GERMANY)
Wilno
Minsk
Grodno
GERMANY
Białystok
WESTERN
BYELORUSSIA
Narew
Treblinka
Vistula
Poznań
Chelmno
Warsaw
Bug
Pinsk
P O L A N D
Łódż
Sobibor
Lublin
Majdanek
Radom
Oder
GERMANY
Belzec
Vistula
WESTERN
UKRAINE
Lwów
Auschwitz
Kraków
PROTECTORATE
OF BOHEMIA
& MORAVIA
Dniester
SLOVAKIA
HUNGARY
ROMANIA
Occupied Poland, 1939–1944
Poland, 1939
Frontiers, 1939
Incorporated into the Reich
General Government
Soviet occupied until June 1941
Extermination camps

ACKNOWLEDGEMENTS

Grateful acknowledgements are made to various archives for permission to reprint previously published material as well as those documents recently declassified, upon which the bulk of this book is based. In particular the National Archives at Kew, the Polish Institute and Sikorski Museum, custodian of surviving records of the Polish government-in-exile based in London. Besides referring to the relevant official histories I have also drawn freely on recent publications by authors from Poland and these are acknowledged in the endnotes.

Debts of gratitude are owed to the personnel of the Polish Institute and Sikorski Museum, and the Polish Underground Movement Study Trust, the National Archives in Poland, the Central Military Archives and the Council for Defence of Memory, Strife and Martyrdom in Warsaw, for their support and encouragement.

Thanks are due to my family, friends and colleagues, amongst them Andrzej Suchcitz, whose counsel I have sought on many occasions, and to David List, especially for his meticulous eye for detail, whose critical reading of the typescript resulted in rational re-examination.

Appreciation is expressed to those who allowed me to use photographs from their family albums. All credits are noted in the captions to those libraries and institutions that provided images.

chapter one

DRANG NACH OSTEN AND PRISONERS OF WAR

Seventy years ago, Hitler's quest for domination of Eastern Europe continued with a blistering attack on Poland on 1 September 1939. Seventeen days later, Stalin 'plunged the knife in Poland's back', as agreed by both tyrants on 23 August 1939. The German Foreign Minister Joachim von Ribbentrop and the Soviet Commissar for Foreign Affairs Vyacheslav Molotov signed the German-Soviet Non-Aggression Pact, which contained a Secret Supplementary Protocol dealing with territorial allocations. Initially, boundaries had been along the rivers Narew, Wisła and San, but after the formal German-Soviet Treaty of Friendship and Borders, signed in September, they settled on the Pisa, Narew, Bug and San. The new boundary stretched roughly east of Białystok, through Brześć Litewski (Brest Litovsk) to the west of Lwów (Lviv, Lvov), a south-eastern Polish fortress, which for centuries had withstood the invasion of Turkish and Tartar hordes. The Soviet strategy was to create two fronts: the Belorussian heading from Smolensk and the Ukrainian from Kiev, enabling a swift destruction of the Polish regular army divisions and some 24 Frontier Defence Corps (*KOP, Korpus Obrony Pogranicza*) stationed on the Polish borders. Under the guise of 'rescuers' of the Ukrainian and Belorussian minorities, the Red Army overran the eastern territories of Poland, always known as Kresy, inhabited by 12 million people – in just twelve days.

On 18 September 1939 the two aggressors met to discuss further political cooperation; a communiqué was signed, declaring that the sovereignty of Poland had been 'disestablished'. The demarcation line was confirmed and the new territorial sphere of influence endorsed. As early as 19 September 1939, Lavrenty Beria,[1] People's Commissar of Internal Affairs, head of the Secret Police the *NKVD* (*Narodny Komissariat Vnutrennikh Del*) by order No.0308, had created a separate directorate of the *UPV* (*Upravlenie po Delam Voennoplennykh)* – an authority to administer wartime operations of the *NKVD,* primarily to deal with prisoners of war (PoW) headed by Major Pyotr Soprunenko.[2]

On 2 December 1939, Beria produced another official note for Stalin's[3] approval, which was endorsed by the Politburo of the Communist Central Committee on 4 December – to organize four mass deportations of Polish civilians to the wilderness of Siberia and other Soviet Republics. In 1940–1941, according to émigré sources, at least 980,000 were deported; incomplete statistics, gathered to date from *GULag's NKVD* documents, show only 316,000. These were combatants of the 1920 war with their families, landowners, police and civil servants, 'enemies of communism and counter-revolutionaries', destined for hard labour and death.

December was also a month of intensive consultations between Germany and Russia on the subject of the massive prisoner problem. Three joint meetings of the security services the *UPV* and the Gestapo for *RSHA,* the Reich Central Security Office (*Reichsicherheitshauptamt*), were held to discuss the possibility of territorial exchange of the PoWs as well as relocation of forced labour to *GULags* in the USSR and concentration camps in Germany. It is possible that the fate of some 15,000 Poles detained in Soviet camps and over 7,000 kept in prisons was decided at one of these three meetings, Lwów in October 1939, Kraków in January 1940 and Zakopane in March 1940. It is as yet unknown, due to lack of documentation, if this treachery is analogous to, or part of, the German 'pacification action', the *Aktion AB* (*Ausserordentliche Befriedungsaktion*), designed not only to stop any resistance by the people but also to exterminate Polish leaders and the elite, which was planned by the *Generalgouvernment* in early 1940 and reached its height from May to July. *Aktion AB* was sanctioned by Adolf Hitler and carried out by *Generalgouverneur* Hans Frank, Governor General of the occupied part of Poland, with its seat in Kraków and acting *SS-Obergruppenfuhrer,* head of the Nazi Security Service in Poland, ably assisted by Friedrich W. Kruger and others.

Soon after one of those secret meetings, the *NKVD* started to compile a list of their captives with full particulars as well as addresses of their families, including those under the German occupation. By February 1940, Soprunenko had sent to his superior Beria detailed proposals on the 'clearing out' (*rozgruzky*) of PoW camps at Kozelsk and Starobelsk. He categorised the prisoners as those too ill (about 300), and those who were residents of the western region of Poland whose guilt could not be proven (about 500); these were to be sent home.

'Special procedures' were to be applied to those who were 'hardened, irremediable enemies of Soviet power': officers, police, landowners, lawyers, doctors, clergy and political activists. They were to suffer the 'supreme punishment' by shooting, without prior call to face the charges in any court. Stalin and others of the Politburo duly signed the order presented to them by Beria on 5th March 1940. The executions were to start in early April and last till May 1940.[4]

'Operation Barbarossa', the German invasion of the Soviet Union in June 1941, put an end to the volatile Nazi-Soviet Pact. For Poland it offered the opportunity to ally with the Soviets, albeit reluctantly and with British inducement. General Władysław Sikorski,[5] Prime Minister of the Polish government in exile and Commander-in-

Chief of the Polish Armed Forces, with the Soviet Ambassador Ivan Maisky, signed a Pact in London on 30 July 1941. It was an uneasy alliance, but had one important military outcome, as it allowed the raising of a Polish Army on USSR territory made up of deported prisoners. The agreement stated that all Polish citizens held in the USSR were to be released on 'amnesty' – an irrational term as no war had been declared between Poland and the Soviet Union. The Polish government-in-exile did not argue, perhaps they considered it as a 'face saving' gesture to the Soviets. The pre-war border issue was provisionally settled by an ambiguous statement: 'The Government of the Union of Soviet Republics recognizes that the Soviet-German Treaties of 1939 relative to territorial changes in Poland, have lost their validity.'

The release of men from prisons, PoW camps and forced labour *GULags* started in September. By October 1941, it was clear that the majority of army officers were missing and there was no news of them. After repeated enquiries, which remained unanswered, Molotov and Stalin finally maintained that 'all officers were released.' The Poles had good reason to disbelieve them but were powerless to do anything about it.

A Top Secret report of those detained by the *NKVD*[6] was prepared by Captain Pyotr Fedotov, head of 2ed Administration of the *NKVD* for his superior Soprunenko and handed to Stalin on the day he met with Sikorski and General Władysław Anders,[7] Commander of the newly formed Polish Army in the USSR, on 3 December in Moscow. This most secret report indicated that the total number of prisoners of war captured by the Red Army was 130,242: some 42,400 were conscripted into the Red Army and a similar number, 42,492, were exchanged with Germany. Only 25,115 soldiers were released to join the Polish Army formation centres. 1,901 were rejected by the army or handed over to the German Embassy, some were invalided out, or counted as runaways, or were dead. Most importantly, Fedotov's report included a reference to 15,131 men 'disposed of in April-May 1940 by the 1st Special Department', which surely indicates the officers of Kozelsk, Ostashkov and Starobelsk camps. Stalin avoided mentioning these during the Kremlin meeting. A much later document reveals that in March 1959, Aleksandr Shelepin, head of the *KGB* wrote a note for Nikita Khrushchev, 1st Secretary of the Communist Party and head of state, putting the figure at 14,552, which is generally accepted as a more probable number of those massacred from the three camps. Fedotov's report brings the total – alive and dead – to 257,186. Again, by Western calculations, based on archival sources, about 250,000 is the more likely figure.

Absolute silence over the existence of these 'missing' prisoners baffled the British Military Mission in Moscow. Brigadier Colin McVean Gubbins, one-time member of the British Military Mission to Poland in 1939 and later head of the SOE (Special Operations Executive), was also concerned about the strength of the Polish forces, with the core of the military men missing or imprisoned. SOE's aim was to foster resistance movements in Western Europe. Although the distance and geographical position of Poland made the task difficult, SOE did have a Polish Section, responsible for clandestine operations. They used the secure communication facilities of

Oddział VI, the Special Operations Bureau of the Polish General Staff headed by Staff Lt Colonel Michał Protasewicz in London. It is through him that signals from the Home Army – *AK* (*Armia Krajowa*) were analysed, translated and distributed to various Departments, including the British.

Lieutenant General Mason MacFarlane's Report

The British Cabinet Office already knew of the Polish plight through successive British Ambassadors, Sir Stafford Cripps (till December 1941) and later Sir Archibald Clark Kerr, as well as from No.30 Military Mission in Moscow, headed by Lieutenant General Noel Mason MacFarlane,[8] who despatched his reports regularly to Major General Francis Davidson, Director of Military Intelligence (DMI) at the War Office. One 'personal for DMI' report, dated 7 August 1941, expressed his fears about the situation and unwittingly indicated a stance for the British Government to take. His words were prophetic:

> I am frankly terribly worried about this Russo-Polish business. I see innumerable snags ahead. I won't mention Polish BBC gaffs because they are too blatantly deplorable to merit further attention except that they MUST be stopped.
>
> We are going to find ourselves being pulled in as mediators in a situation which holds promise of developing in the most awkward way. I only hope the business won't sow a lot of discord.
>
> What is going to happen when the Poles find out the number of Poles who have been 'lost' since 1939 is clearly an awkward one to answer. What will the British Press want to say when they find out? *We've got to keep out of the affair as much as we can, and when we do intervene we must remember that Russia can help us to beat Hitler, and not Poland.*[9] [Author's italics]

Mason MacFarlane also advised the FO that Captain Józef Czapski,[10] a plenipotentiary to General Anders, had raised the question of the missing officers during his first meeting with the *NKVD*. He was kept in the corridor for five hours and sent home with nothing. MacFarlane advised Czapski to deal directly with Vsevolod Merkulov,[11] Deputy Commissar to Beria involved with PoWs, or alternatively, to go through General Georgy S. Zhukov, Chief of the *NKVD*, who was in charge of the affairs of the Polish Army in Russia and was on good terms with Anders. Mason MacFarlane despatched a 'Most Secret/Private/Most Immediate' cipher to the War Office, telling them that the Polish goverment were anxious to invite Zhukov to London for discussions. 'Zhukov is a very big noise, second only to Beria, a prominent figure in Russian secret organisations and has Stalin's ear.'[12]

MacFarlane was sympathetic towards Czapski and invited him to the British Embassy to write up his report, which he eventually submitted to the Russians and gave a copy to Mason MacFarlane, who in turn sent it to the War Office and Foreign Office. Frank Roberts, First Secretary of the Central Department of the FO[13] made a cryptic remark that the whole affair was very odd and underlined Polish suspicions of the Soviet government.[14]

The SOE had a desk officer in Moscow who reported regularly to London on the predicament of the Poles in the Soviet Union. The first report, which SOE received from the Poles dated 1 November 1941, came from Buzuluk USSR, one of several centres where soldiers flocked in anticipation of joining the Polish army; others were at Tatischev, Totskoe and Kuibyshev. In accordance with the 1941 Soviet-Polish agreement, they were being released from prisons and forced labour camps scattered throughout the vast Soviet empire. The report by Lieutenant Bronisław Młynarski[15] was intended for the Polish government-in-exile based in London. A copy was sent to Professor Stanisław Kot,[16] the Polish Ambassador to the USSR (1941–1942) who was temporarily in Kuibyshev, after being evacuated from Moscow with the Diplomatic corps.

Kot had set up an agency, the function of which was to gather information on Poles who were still in Soviet detention. It was staffed by a group of officers recently released, among them Professor Wiktor Sukiennicki.[17] Armed with their testimony, Kot would intervene with the Soviet authorities, sometimes not directly informing Anders, who acted similarly. This caused a great deal of friction between them as both claimed primacy of responsibility for the missing. Within the newly formed Polish army in the USSR, Anders had set up *Biuro Dokumentów* run by Lt Adam Telmany and Lt Gen Kazimierz Ryziński, which was moved to Jerusalem and in 1944 to Rome. By then it was reorganised and renamed *Biuro Studiów* (Research Bureau) headed by historian Zdzisław Stahl.[18]

After leaving his post as Ambassador to Russia, Kot became the Minister of State for the Middle East and was in charge of *Centrum Informacji* of the Ministry of Information and Documentation, which continued to collate information gathered by *Biuro Dokumentów.*

One of the most important reports – which clearly indicated the journey and final destination of the last deportation of the Polish officers from Kozelsk – was not amongst Kot's papers. Although not being able to identify the place as Gnezdovo station, the witness saw the prisoners being unloaded from prisoner's freight cars at a siding on 30 April 1940 and taken away in groups by a bus with blacked out windows. It would return at intervals to pick up the others and take them to a place he thought must be nearby. This secret observation came from Lt Stanisław Swianiewicz,[19] Professor of Economics at Wilno University, who was the only one to be separated from the others at Gnezdovo. He was taken to Smolensk prison and from there eventually to Moscow for a trial and sentence of eight years hard labour in Komi District. Swianiewicz was not aware that he was so close to the place of the massacre. In April 1942, he was released from *GULag* (*Glavnoe Upravlenie Lagernie*) forced labour camp and eventually reached Kuibyshev to tell the tale. He wrote a short report on 28 May 1942 for Brigadier General Romuald Wolikowski, Military Attaché, which is reproduced below.

It still remains a mystery why this vital information did not reach Mason MacFarlane or the Polish government-in-exile any sooner. Was it the fault of an incompetent individual, who failed to register the statement from a civilian witness on the list of officers, or simply forgot to pass the information to the appropriate authorities?

Similarly, Młynarski's report does not indicate Gnezdovo as a possible place of evacuation for prisoners, but it contained first-hand information on the missing Polish officers and gave precise dates and number of prisoners in each of the three camps who had been mysteriously evacuated to an unknown destination in April and May of 1940. Młynarski asked for help from the British and American governments to impress upon the Russians the need to indicate the whereabouts of these people and to recover them. Historically, Czapski's concise report, written almost at the same time, tends to overshadow Młynarski's important document.

Lieutenant Bronisław Młynarski's Report

Strength of Starobelsk camp

The first batch of prisoners arrived at the camp on 30 IX 1939. About 5,000 other ranks were removed from the camp during October. The winding up of the camp commenced on 5 IV 1940, when the strength amounted to about 3,920, including the sections reserved for Generals and Colonels. This also included over 30 civilians (mostly judges and Government officials) and about 30 officer cadets. The remainder were officers, of whom half were professionals. This included 8 Generals, over 100 Colonels and Lieutenant Colonels, about 230 Majors, about 1,000 Captains, about 2,500 subalterns and about 380 medical officers.

Two other camps, which existed at the same time, were at Kozelsk and Ostashkov. Their strength when wound up on 6 IV 1940 was: Kozelsk about 5,000 men including 4,500 army officers; and Ostashkov about 6,570 men, including 384 Field Police, frontier guards and prison guard officers.

Liquidation of Starobelsk camp

The first group of 195 men were sent from the camp on 5 IV 1940. The Soviet Commandant, Colonel [Aleksandr] Berezhkov and the Commissar [Mikhail] Kirshin, after reading the nominal roll of those to be sent away, declared officially that the camp was to be wound up and its inmates were to be sent to distribution centres from which they were to be repatriated to their domiciles on both sides of the German-Russian frontier. Groups of from 65 to 240 men were sent out daily from the 5th to the 26th of April inclusive, a further group of 200 was sent away on 2 V 1940 and small groups left on the 9th, 11th and 12th May. I left on 12 V 1940 with a group of 16 men. About 10 officers then remained in addition to a few sick officers who were under treatment in the local hospital.

Special groups

After reading a list of about 150 names on 25 IV 1940, the Soviet official declared that he would now read a special roll of 63 names of persons who were to be kept absolutely separate from the rest, during the evacuation of the camp. He repeated this several times, very emphatically. This caused much anxiety in the camp, as no reason for this order was apparent.

Camp at Pavlishchev Bor (near Yukhnov)

After five days of travel, during which we were subjected to the most brutal treatment, the group of 16 to which I belonged arrived at Pavlishchev Bor; the Commandant received us quite well. Here we met the 'special group' of 63 men mentioned above. There were thus 79 officers from Starobelsk, including some cadets. If, to this number, we add those officers who were removed from Starobelsk during the first period of our internment there, namely General [Chesław] Jarnuszkiewicz, Colonel [Adam] Koc, Lt Colonel [Jan] Giełgud-Axentowicz, Colonel A[ntoni] Szymanski, Major [Rev. Franciszek] Tyczkowski and Lt W[ładysław] Evert and others it is 85 out of a total number of 3,020, i.e. about 2% of the former strength of these camps.

Griazovets camp (near Vologda)

After about a month the entire camp strength of about 400 was transferred to Griazovets, where they remained from June 1940 until they were liberated. Their living conditions during this period were quite satisfactory. They were joined on 2 VII 1940 by a group of 1,250 officers and other ranks, who had until then been interned in Lithuania, Latvia and Estonia.

Conclusions

Two conclusions may be drawn today, from the results of our investigations and from that fact that no word has reached us from over 8,000 officers and many thousands of other ranks who had been interned in Russia. These are:

1. That the Griazovets camp was the only camp existing in Russia for the Polish PoWs after June 1940 and was probably especially created in order to be able to produce a certain number of representative Polish prisoners of all categories, should the need arise at any time.
2. The declaration that they were returned to German-occupied Poland is completely false as nothing is known of them in that part of Poland. Moreover, about half of the prisoners had their homes in Russian-occupied Poland and no word has been received of their fate either.

Since we cannot believe that the Soviet Government does not intend loyally to fulfil the conditions of its agreement with the Polish Government, we can only think that the non-liberation of these prisoners is due solely to technical and administrative difficulties. Should this be the case, could not the Soviet authorities at least inform us of the whereabouts of these men, in order to permit us with the help of the British and American Governments and people to devise some means of rescuing them?

Bronisław Młynarski
Buzuluk, 1 XI 1941

Captain Józef Czapski's Report

Memorandum on the missing Polish prisoners of war, formerly interned at Starobelsk, Kozelsk and Ostashkov.

The prisoners of war who were interned at these camps from 1939 to April 1940, and who numbered 15,000, including 8,700 officers, have not reported to the Polish authorities, nor do these know anything of their present whereabouts, except for 400–500 persons, or about 3% of the total number of the internees of these three camps, who were released in 1941 from Griazovets near Vologda or from various prisons, after a year's imprisonment.

Camp No.1 at Starobelsk

Parties of prisoners arrived here during the period 30 IX 1939 to 1 XI 1939. The winding up of the camp began on 5 IV 1940, when the strength was 3,920, including 8 Generals, over 100 Colonels, about 250 Majors, 1,000 Captains, 2,500 Subalterns, 30 Cadets and 50 civilians. Over half of the officers were professional soldiers and the prisoners included 380 doctors and many university professors.

Camp No.2 at Kozelsk

The strength on the day of liquidation (3 IV 1940) was about 5,000, including 4,500 officers of various ranks and services.

Camp [No.3] at Ostashkov

The strength at the time of liquidation was 6,570, including 380 officers.

Liquidation of Starobelsk camp

The first group of 195 persons was sent away on 5 IV 1940. The Soviet Commandant [Aleksandr] Berezhkov, [in charge of the camp] and the Commissar [Mikhail] Kirshin, [who 'cleared out' the camp] officially assured the prisoners that they would be sent to a distribution centre from whence they would be taken to their domiciles in German and Soviet-occupied Poland. We know with absolute certainty from numerous letters received from Poland during the winter of 1940-41 that up till now, not one of the former internees of the three camps in question has returned to his home in Poland. Up to 26 IV

1940 inclusive groups from 65 to 240 persons were sent from the camp. On 25 IV 1940 a group of over 100 persons were instructed to get ready to leave, after that a special roll of 63 names was read; these persons were to constitute a separate group during the march to the railway station.

The next party of 200 left the camp on 2 V 1940 and the remaining prisoners left in small groups on May 8th, 11th, and 12th. The last group was sent to Pavlishchev Bor (Smolensk district), where they joined the special group of 63 sent from Starobelsk on 25 IV 1940. There were thus 79 officers from Starobelsk at this camp and they were released from Griazovets in 1941. In addition seven officers who had been taken from Starobelsk to various prisons were released. The total number accounted for is thus 86, being just over 2% of the total strength of 3,920.

Liquidation of the Kozelsk and Ostashkov camps

This was effected in a similar way. The camp at Pavlishchev Bor contained 200 officers from Kozelsk and about 120 persons from Ostashkov; these figures represent about 2% of the respective strength of these camps.

Griazovets camp

After a month's stay at Pavlishchev Bor, the inmates, numbering about 400, were transferred to Griazovets near Vologda. To this camp were also sent 1,250 officers and other ranks who had previously been interned in the Baltic Republics and who had been kept as internees (not prisoners of war) in no.2 camp at Kozelsk, from the autumn of 1940 to the summer of 1941.

The Griazovets camp is the only camp containing a majority of Polish Army officers known to us to have existed in the USSR from June 1940 to September 1941. Practically the entire strength of this camp is now part of the Polish Army in the USSR.

Six months have now elapsed since an amnesty was proclaimed for all Polish prisoners of war and other prisoners on 12 VIII 1941. Since that date, a steady stream of officers and other ranks of the Polish Army have been reporting to their H.Q. from various camps and prisons. In spite of the proclamation of this amnesty, notwithstanding the categorical promise that our prisoners of war would be released, made by the Chairman of the Council of People's Commissars, M. Stalin to H.E. [His Excellency] Ambassador Kot on 14 XI 1941 and in spite of the categorical order given by Stalin in the presence of Generals Sikorski and Anders on 3 XII 1941, that the former inmates of the camps in question should be sought out and released, not one of them has yet returned (with the exception of the Griazovetz group). Nor has any communication as yet been received from any of these prisoners.

Interrogation of thousands of prisoners released from very numerous prisons and camps has not elicited any trustworthy information as to the location or fate of these prisoners, except for reports received at second hand. These are:

a. Six to twelve thousand officers and NCOs were sent to Kolyma via Bukhta Nakhodka in 1940.
b. Over 5,000 officers were sent to the mines of Franz Joseph Land.
c. That they were sent to Novaia Zemlia, Kamtchatka and Tchukotka; that during the summer of 1941, 630 officers from Kozelsk were working 180 kilometres distant from 'Piostroy Dzesva', that 150 men in officers' uniforms were seen to the North of the Soava River, near Gari, that Polish officer PoWs were taken in huge barges drawn by tugs (1,700–2,000 men per barge) to the Northern Islands and that three such barges sank in the Barents Sea.

Not one of these reports has been confirmed, although those suggesting Kolyma and Northern Islands seem to us to be the most probable.

We know how carefully the registration of each prisoner was conducted, and how the dossier of each prisoner, complete with questionnaires, interrogations, photographs, etc., was kept in a special file and we know with what meticulous care all the records were kept by the *NKVD*. We cannot for these reasons believe that the present location of 15,000 prisoners, including over 8,000 officers, is not known to the higher authorities of the *NKVD*.

In view of the solemn promise made by M. Stalin, and of his categorical order that the fate of the prisoners should be elucidated, may we not hope that we shall be informed of the present whereabouts of our comrades, or, if they are no longer alive, at least that we should be told where they died and in what circumstances they lost their lives.

Number of officers missing:

Total strength of Prisoners of War at Starobelsk on 5 IV 1940 (excluding 30 cadets and 50 civilians)	3,820
Total strength of the Kozelsk camp on 6 IV 1940 was 5,000 (including officers)	4,500
Total strength of Ostashkov camp on 6 IV 1940 was 6,570 (including officers)	380
Total	8,700
Reported to the Polish Army from Griazovets and various prisons	500
Total missing officers from Starobelsk, Kozelsk and Ostashkov	8,200

All of the present officers of the Polish Army in the U.S.S.R. on 1 I 1942, numbering about 2,300, are ex-internees from the Baltic countries, but are, with the exception of the above mentioned 500, not ex-prisoners of war.

It is impossible for us to present an exact estimate of the number of such prisoners still missing, excluding the case of the three officer camps under discussion. In accordance with the decision made by M. Stalin and General Sikorski, the

> strength of our Army in the U.S.S.R. has been increased. As a result the need for these officers is being felt increasingly urgently, the more so as these were our most highly qualified military specialists.
>
> Moscow, 2 February 1942

Czapski would not have known that amongst the 4,500 prisoners at Kozielsk – which held four generals, one admiral, about 100 colonels and lieutenant colonels, 300 majors, 1,000 captains, 2,500 lieutenants and second lieutenants and over 500 sergeants – that there was one woman officer, Second Lieutenant of the Polish Air Force, pilot Janina Lewandowska, daughter of General [Józef] Dowbór-Muśnicki. She had married pilot instructor Lt Col Mieczysław Lewandowski in the summer of 1939. He managed to reach France, then England, to serve as an RAF pilot. She was shot down over Russian territory in September 1939 while in action and was taken to Kozelsk camp. According to statements of those who survived, she had a separate room and was often castigated by the *NKVD* guards for attending forbidden religious meetings. Her two airmen friends, with whom she was in close touch, were on an earlier list of the condemned to be evacuated into the unknown and she confronted the guards beseeching them to take her as well. A few days later, dressed in male uniform, pilot Janina Lewandowska joined her dead friends in the Katyn woods.[20]

With Czapski's report, which was probably translated at the British Embassy, Mason MacFarlane transmitted his own 'Most Secret' observations to Major General Davidson in London, about the missing officers:[21]

> There is not the slightest doubt that the *NKVD* must know what has happened to these Poles as the most detailed nominal rolls and information are kept up at every concentration camp and prison ... I am in close touch with Czapski but propose to keep us out entirely of this business, which is a purely Polish-Russian affair ...
>
> The *NKVD* is clearly going back on the categorical assurances given by Stalin to Sikorski. My personal opinion is that nothing short of a personal communication from Sikorski to Stalin will produce results. I send you this only to keep you and COS [Chiefs of Staff] in the picture. The question is a domestic one between the Poles and Russians and I don't think we ought to get mixed up in it.

The Foreign Office Comments

Others in the Cabinet and Foreign Office quickly picked up this argument. The obstacle lay, amongst other issues, with an unwillingness to help Ambassador Kot, who, while asking Clark Kerr for intervention, was known to have openly criticised the Anglo-Soviet Treaty, which was obviously detrimental to Poland's future.

In consequence, the War Office advised Clark Kerr not to be too accommodating toward the Polish Ambassador. Frank Roberts, head of the Central Department grudgingly gave his support, while others declared that supporting the Poles would not make much difference – except to irritate the Russians. And on top of that, Kot had been talking 'poisonous stuff' about the Anglo-Soviet Treaty. Prior to being seen by Anthony Eden,[22] the Secretary of State for Foreign Affairs and Sir Alexander Cadogan,[23] the Permanent Under Secretary of State, had the last word: they should not link the two matters but base the refusal on the grounds that the British government could not exert sufficient influence on the Russians. Eden agreed and annotated with his usual red ink: 'Yes, let Kot see the link, rather than point it out to him.' On May 1942, Sir William Strang,[24] the Acting Under Secretary of State, Central Department of the FO, sent Ambassador Sir Archibald Clark Kerr an 'immediate decipher yourself signal' with just that advice:

> I should prefer you not to intervene in this Russo-Polish question. Our intervention might only serve to irritate the Soviet Government. You should base your refusal on this ground and on our inability at present to exert sufficient influence with the Soviet Government but without directly connecting the two questions, you may be able to let your Polish colleague see that he is unlikely to obtain much satisfaction on this issue while he continues to criticise the Anglo-Soviet negotiations so openly.[25]

The British, in spite of opportunities to do so, did not raise the matter again, while the Polish government remained unable to elicit the truth from the Russians without British assistance.

Lieutenant Colonel Leslie Hulls' report

The three reports written for the War Office by British Liaison Officer Lieutenant Colonel Leslie R. Hulls[26] have survived. The first, dated 18 June 1942, was sent from Yangi-Yul, a place near Tashkent, the HQ of the Polish Army in Uzbekistan. The other two came from Quisil Ribat, dated 29 October and 3 December 1942. Hulls had witnessed the miserable condition of the Polish Army and pleaded with the British military authorities to put pressure upon Stalin to adhere to the agreement and release the rest of the missing officers.

Hulls must have written a number of reports to the Military Intelligence Department of the War Office. The follow-up briefs indicate that Hulls' personal experience and knowledge of the Russians were ignored. The subject of his report of 3 December 1942 can be verified by the Soviet documents released between 1992 and 1997 to the Polish Committee of Military Archivists in Warsaw.[27] Hulls' verbatim reports are difficult to follow owing to their peculiar grammatical structure. In the interest of clarity some of his grammar and vocabulary has been amended; but the tone and factual content has not.

Polish Soviet Relations

The Soviet note to the Polish Government dated 31.X.1942 regarding the military agreement and the refusal of the Soviet Government of a further recruitment in Russia.

1. Said document deals with two questions:

a. It intends to show the good will of the Soviet Government towards Poland concerning the military agreement of August 14 1941.

b. It intends to justify the refusal of the Soviet Government of further recruitment of Polish soldiers in Russia.

There is little truth in this document and in general it gives a completely false picture of the situation.

Notwithstanding its length, the contents of the Soviet note can be brought down to this one statement: the Poles have refused to send the 5th Division to the Russian-German front, in consequence of which the Soviet Government now refuses to allow a further recruitment of Polish soldiers in Russia. Although at this point, the Note mentions loosely the Polish Army and 'Polish Division' there was no question whatever of any other division besides the 5th, which was to get ready to go to the front. The 6th Division which was to be formed had, not even for training purposes, neither motorized vehicles, nor artillery, nor was it in possession of machine-guns or with liaison and engineering implements (I state it here on the basis of my personal observations). In connection with the above, the Soviet General Staff had communicated to the Polish Staff in September 1941 that the situation on the front did not allow for the equipping of a second Polish Division. Stalin had promised to settle this in December 1941, but in spite of this, up to the summer of 1942 the situation had not altered.

In my position as an independent observer who has been a witness to all these events, I try to represent all that has happened in the light of truth and with objectivity. In brief, the whole question can be summarised as follows.

The Polish-Soviet agreement of July had been completed by a military agreement on August 14 1941. The basis of this agreement was that a Polish Army was to be created in Russia, the recruitment of said army was to be made among the Polish officers and soldiers deported and imprisoned in Russia. The strength of the army had not been defined and thus the affirmation contained in the Soviet note that said army was to consist of 30 thousand men is not true. There has been no mention, either in writing or in any other form, of such a question being asked. The manpower of the army had been defined for the first time during General Sikorski's visit to Moscow in December 1941 and had been already then been fixed as 96,000, 25,000 more were to be transferred to the

British Empire and ... there would have been more manpower suitable for military service; the figure of 96,000 was to be increased with a further division of 11,000 men.

Officers and soldiers started presenting themselves in September. In December about 40,000 were called and enlisted in the ranks, in March 1942 the figure of 70,000 had been reached. In February, the Army, with the aim of avoiding the consequences of the winter, had been transferred from the Samarkanda region to Uzbekistan. The soldiers were located in cells in a temperature of 45 degrees below zero. As I have already mentioned, these people were coming to the Army from prisons and penitentiary camps. They never had been treated as prisoners of war, as a consequence of which they came out of prison with damaged health.

For an army at this stage of organization, the food rations were inadequate, even for a healthy man, and so the problem of restoring the sick soldiers to health was pressing up to the last moment, until the evacuation of the Army from Russia.

A number of food rations had been sent from England through Archangelsk and were being used for supplementary feeding of the sick, of the convalescents and for those employed in heavy work. Exhaustion caused by denutrition [sic] and lack of vitamins amounted to 14%. It was a common occurrence for soldiers during night manoeuvres to be returned to their quarters because they were afflicted by nyctalopis [sic; nyctalopia, night blindness].

Armament and Equipment

In the beginning, England and the US had undertaken the task of equipping the Polish army on the condition that the troops would be transferred to a place where the said task would be convenient and easy. One thought at the time was India; the Soviet Government did not give its consent for the army to leave Russia. The Russians agreed then to equip two infantry divisions, while the English continued to attempt to equip and arm the whole of the rest of the Army.

In the spring of 1942, the Russians had partially armed one division, the 5th. Still, the armament was greatly lacking, there was a deficiency in particular of motorised vehicles, machine guns, mortars, anti aircraft batteries and tanks. The whole artillery was limited to just 16 field guns. The armament specification of the 5th Division is herewith included. The remaining divisions and the Army as a whole were, rifles excepted, quite without arms. The uniforms had been sent from England.

The Soviet Government in their note insist on the fact that the Polish Command ... has not prepared to a level of readiness one division by the date of 1.X.1941. No Soviet Staff officer had ever declared seriously that it was possible to form even one division for that date. Whether this had been previously established or not, is an irrelevant question as the responsibility in this regard is borne by both parties. The Russians on their side had not furnished the armament, neither for the date of X.1941 nor six months later, but nobody can blame them for it, considering the conditions and the general situation. As to the Poles, considering the fact that the first soldiers started arriving only in September they were certainly not in a postion to organize a division for 1.X.1941. In the Soviet note pt 3, this aspect of the question is only partially acknowledged.

The fact that six months later the 5th Division was still unarmed and unprepared for the fighting, can be explained only and exclusively by the lack of armament, for which the responsibility falls upon the Soviet Government.

In February 1942 the Soviet authorities proposed to General Anders sending to the front the first two divisions when their armament was completed. The General refused to send these units to the front without previously training them to handle the arms that they were to use.

Referring again to the Soviet note:

Pt.1 underlines that the Soviet Government showed the maximum good will and energy in forming a Polish army in Russia. On the contrary, the soldiers came out of the penitentiary camps in rags and were without clothes until the uniforms arrived from England. The food rations were quite insufficient in quantity and quality. (Russia in that period was only after eight months into the war). The authorities were refusing all information concerning the locations of officers and soldiers. Considerable numbers of Polish officers have not been found. Those imprisoned in Kozelsk, Starobelsk and Ostaszkowo [Ostashkov] simply disappeared without any trace (8,300 altogether). Nobody has heard of any of them since 1940 and notwithstanding the promise given personally by Stalin to General Sikorski and General Anders, the fate of these officers remained a complete mystery.

Pt.2 underlines the friendly attitude of the Soviet Government in their consenting to fix the number of the Polish soldiers at 96,000. Why this is alluded as a positive point, for the Soviets remains quite incomprehensible. It was the desire of the Poles to fight again and in consequence to organise the greatest possible army. This was to the advantage not only of Russia but also of all the Allied nations.

Pt. 3 underlines the difficulties of provisions and the measures taken to increase the rations of the fighting soldiers at the expense of the non-combatants. The Polish Army has of course been defined as being in the second category. The Note continues, stating that it has been decided to diminish the number of rations for the Polish army to to 44,000, the remaining troops, requested by the Polish Government, are to be evacuated to Persia. Nobody intends to contest the decision of the Soviet Government to consider the Polish army as non-fighting, but leaving 30,000 soldiers without food rations could have only one result, namely said detachments would have to be transferred to another place where they would be fed and equipped.

The remaining part of the said paragraph is completely false and would not convince anyone. Concerning the second evacuation to Persia, it should be remembered that for four months the Soviet Government steadily refused to accede to this evacuation, although on their part, literally nothing had been done to arm the remaining 44,000. The Soviet authorities even went so far as to inform our [No.30] Military Mission in Moscow that the evacuation bases at Pahlevi [port] in northern Persia should be shut down as no further evacuation would take place (telegram addressed to Troopers at the Military Mission in Moscow No 6132 dated 30VI 1942).

The Soviet authorities were not able to give any justification for their refusal to transfer the Polish army to a place where the troops could have been armed and equipped. As it was becoming increasingly obvious to all the Allies that this solution was the only possible one, we decided to become involved. Quite unexpectedly, on 27 July, without any explanations, the Soviet Government consented to the evacuation.

Pt. 4. The Polish Government, whilst considering it impossible to restore the Polish soldiers in Russia to a state of physical fitness and to equip and arm them, was now making an effort to transfer these troops to a place where all this could be done. In this endeavour the Polish Government wanted to help the Allies. The Polish Government was following, to the best of its understanding, the intentions of the Polish Soviet agreement: 'the creation of a Polish army to fight by the side of Russia and of the Allies against Germany' (see pt.1 of the Soviet note).

The question of further recruitment in Russia

The refusal demonstrates the disposition of the Soviet Government towards Poland. This refusal is expressed clearly in the Soviet note. It is contrary to the interests of the Allies. It is difficult to believe that not sending one Polish infantry division of 11,000 soldiers (even if said division were fully prepared for fighting) to the Russian front could become the cause of an international misunderstanding, as is actually the case.

If anyone is unconvinced, I stress the point again:

a. Did the Soviet Government attach any real importance to the immediate forwarding of the 5th Division to the front?

b. Was the 5th Division effectively armed and equipped?

It will perhaps be sufficient to quote here some of the conversation between General Anders and Stalin that took place on the 18. III. 1942: discussion of the matter of reducing the quantity of food rations (the Soviet Government had fixed the limit of rations to 20,000 soldiers) and of transferring half of the army to Persia, a logical consequence of that reduction, and lastly, on the matter of the part to be played by the remaining army in Russia. Stalin in conclusion said: 'All right, I consent to assign 44,000 rations. This quantity will be sufficient for three divisions. You will have time enough for drilling, we do not insist on your speedy appearance on the front. It will be better for you to start when we are nearer the Polish frontiers. You should have the honour to enter Polish land first.'

At the end of the conversation, General Anders said to Stalin: 'To save time I should like to discuss all the technical details with General [Aleksei] Panfilov if you authorise him to do this.' Stalin replied 'Good, these matters will be settled by General Panfilov.' On the next day, that is 19 March, General Anders met with General Panfilov (Head of the Russian General Staff) and during the discussion on the evacuation and on the equipment of the troops remaining in Russia, General Panfilov said 'Tomorrow we will arrange for the completion of the armament of the 5th Division and the furnishing of arms also to the 6th Division.'

Pt. 5. I hope that in the name of truth the above facts are sufficient to frustrate the attempt made in the Soviet note to give a completely false picture …

One could ask here what is behind this attitude of the Soviet Government. As already underlined in my previous reports, the Soviet Government had never fulfilled the agreement signed with Poland, neither from the military point of view nor in those matters that concern the civilian population. Far from helping in the formation of a strong Polish Army, the Soviet Government tended to divide it. In the first place the initial 70,000 have been divided in two parts. When such a situation could no longer be maintained, the Soviet Government cut away a great number of Polish soldiers from the Army in Iraq.

There are no reasons to refuse these soldiers the opportunity to enlist in the army. On the contrary the Polish army needs them badly and the Polish Government demands them. In this matter the Polish Government looks for our help.

L R Hulls

Professor Stanisław Swianiewicz' Declaration

From the beginning of November 1939 until 29 April 1940, I was a prisoner of war in Kozelsk camp. From the beginning of April, the camp was slowly liquidated by removing groups of people 200 to 300 strong to an unknown destination. The camp authorities tantalised us for some time that soon we were to be sent home. The group I was assigned to was the last one to leave.

On 29 IV 1940, we were loaded into railway carriages adapted to carry prisoners [*Stolypinki*].[28] The walls were covered with messages, something like: 'returning home is a lie, they are taking us to another camp.' In the morning of 30 IV 1940, we passed Smolensk, and a dozen or so kilometres beyond Smolensk we stopped. It appeared that we were to detrain. Presently an *NKVD* officer came in with information that I was to be taken out of the convoy and placed separately in another railway compartment. From the narrow top slit of the compartment I could observe the area, which was well guarded by the *NKVD*. My compatriots were unloaded and put into buses with blackened windows. The bus would return empty to pick up others after an interval of about half an hour. From this scene I gathered that my colleagues were being taken to another camp not far from the railway station. After this movement of men had finished, I was taken separately by car to Smolensk prison and soon afterwards I was transported to Moscow.

From that moment I have lost all contact with my comrades in distress with whom I stayed in Kozelsk camp, with one exception, that is in February 1941 while in Butyrki prison in Moscow, I met Captain [Janusz J.] Makarczyński of *DOK* (*Dowództwo Okręgu Korpusu Lublin* - General Staff, Lublin Corps), who was deported from Kozelsk camp on his own, as far as I remember, before April 1940.

During my stay in various prisons and *GULags,* I used to hear fragments of information about the Polish PoWs in Northern Russia:

1. Towards the end of 1940, in the Lubyanka prison, a Russian prisoner had told me that previously, he met and sat in prison with a Polish NCO who was brought from Komi *GULag*, where in 1940, he worked on road repairs and said that conditions were bearable.
2. In March 1941 I met another Russian from Kotlas camp, who in the summer of 1940 worked in Uhta in the Komi region, extracting radium. He too, saw a large group of about 200 PoWs, marching in a northeastern direction. He was told that all of them were Polish officers.
3. While staying in various camps and *GULag* posts north of Kniazpogost between March and April 1942, I have seen small groups of soldiers in uniform near a railway station at Josser but the guards did not allow us to make contact. By the style of some uniforms, I gather there must have been some Poles amongst the officers and men marching to work; another guard has confirmed it. At a place called Ropcha, 8 kilometres north of Josser station, there was a hospital belonging to Sievzeldorlag district, where sick people from the camps were sent. There was a cemetery with Polish graves nearby, showing clearly the names and ranks of the dead. This particular PoW camp was closed down in the summer of 1941.
4. In February 1942, at the 14 Ustvim *GULag* while in hospital, I was told by another Russian that in the summer of 1940, he was doing hard labour in the region of Murmansk and saw large movements of Polish soldiers. I was told the life in these camps was exceptionally hard and by observations it can be assumed that they were Polish officers.

Stanisław Swianiewicz[29]
Kuibyshev, 28 May 1942

Notes

1 Lavrenty Beria (1899–1953) in 1939 Commissar General of the Internal Security NKVD (*Narodny Komissariat Vnutennikh Diel*) of the USSR, member of the Politburo and a close friend of Stalin. He was instrumental in submission of a resolution on 5 March 1940 to shoot the Polish PoWs. After Stalins' death Beria was charged with 'anti state' crimes and was executed on 23 December 1953.

2 Pyotr Karpovich Soprunenko (1908-1992) Soviet Security official *NKVD,* close to Beria, head of PoW administration (1939–1944). Supervised 'clearing out' of the three camps. In 1990, identified as a witness to the massacre.

3 Joseph Stalin (Iosif Vassarionovich Dzhugashvili) (1879–1953). Born in Georgia, member of Lenin's Bolshevik Party (1903-1917), party bureaucrat and Soviet leader (1928-1953). Introduced wholesale purges and crimes against his own people, created the GULags; responsible for the massacres of the Polish PoWs. Considered by the Russians as a man of steel, who led them to victory and domination over Eastern Europe; denounced by his accomplice Khrushchev in 1956 and by the last president of the USSR, Mikhail Gorbachev, in 1990.

4 Katyn. *Dokumenty Zbrodni, Jeńcy nie wypowiedzianej wojny, 23 sierpień 1939 – 5 marca 1940* (Katyn, Documents of Crime, Prisoners of Undeclared War, 23 August 1939 – 5 March 1940), published jointly by *Naczelna Dyrekcja Archiwów Państwowych* (Directorate of The National Archives) in Warsaw and The National Archival Services of Russian Federation GARF (*Gosudarstvenny Arkhiv Rossiiskoi Federatsii*) and the Central Security Service Archives of the Russian Federation FSB RF (*Federalnaia Slusba Bezopasnosti Federatsii Rossiiskoi*) in Moscow. Editorial Committee under Aleksander Gieysztor and Rudolf Pikhoia, editorial work Wojciech Materski, Natalia Lebedeva and others. Warsaw 1995, Vol I, p.7-55, docs. 188, 216; Vol II docs. 87, 95; Vol III doc68; Vol IV docs. 197, 207, 208, 212, 221. Translated copies of the *NKVD* documents in four volumes, selected by the Russian and Polish historians between 1993 and 2005.

5 Władysław Sikorski (1881–1943). Polish General and statesman, took part in 1920 War of Independence against the Bolsheviks, Chief of General Staff, Premier and War Minister till 1925. Spent thirteen years in opposition. In 1939 escaped the German invasion via Rumania to France, formed a government in Paris, after its fall moved to GB together with armed forces, set up a coalition government in exile as its Prime Minister and Commander in chief. Died in plane crash off Gibraltar, 4 July 1943.

6 *Katyn Dokumenty Zbrodni*... Vol III document 217, Fedotov report 3 December 1941.

7 Władysław Anders (1892-1970), General, served as a young officer in the Tsarist army during the First World War, later joined the Polish Army and fought in 1920 War of Independence against the Russians. In 1939 commanded a cavalry brigade, wounded and taken prisoner by the Russians and held at Lubyanka prison in Moscow. Released after the Soviet-Polish Agreement of 14 August 1941. Commander of a newly formed Polish Army in USSR from thousands of Poles released from Russian imprisonment. Commander in Chief of 2 Polish Corps (under command of the British Eighth Army) who led the Poles to victory at the battle of Monte Cassino in Italy. After the Polish Forces were disbanded in 1946, remained in exile as a prominent leader of the 'free' Poles. Wrote memoirs, *Bez Ostatniego Rozdziału* (Without the Last Chapter) 1949.

8 Frank Noel Mason MacFarlane (1889–1953) Lt Gen. RA, served in Africa and India, Staff Capt. WWI, Afghan War 1919, GSO1 in India 1922-5, Staff officer 1928–30 in India, Military Attaché Budapest 1931–5, Vienna, Berne then Berlin 1937–39, Head of Military Mission in Moscow 1941–2, Governor of Gibraltar 1942–44, Chief Commissioner of Allied Control Commission in Italy 1944, awarded *Polonia Restituta* 1st class, retired 1945, became an MP.

9 TNA WO 32 /15548, a self-typed report by Lt Gen Mason MacFarlane, head of 30 Military Mission in Moscow, dated 7 August 1941.

10 Józef Czapski (1896–1993) Cavalry Captain in reserve, 8 Lancers Division, born and raised in Moscow of aristocratic family, accomplished painter who studied in Paris, survivor of Starobelsk camp. After the war published among other pieces *Wspomnienia Starobielskie* (Starobelsk reminiscences) Rome 1945 and *Na nieludzkiej ziemi* (Inhuman Land) Paris 1949.

11 Vselevod Nikolaevich Merkulov (1895–1953). Soviet Security official, aide to Beria specialising in cruel interrogation, member of Troika appointed 5 March 1940, to exterminate the Polish officers. In charge of 'clearing out' the three camps. Arrested with Beria and executed in 1953. Named with Beria in 1990 as responsible for murdering the Polish PoWs in 1940.

12 TNA HS 4 /243 Most Secret cipher telegram sent from No. 30 Military Mission in Moscow to the War Office DMI, MIL 681, 8 September 1941.

13 Frank Kenyon Roberts (1907-1998), started his diplomatic career as Third Secretary in the FO in 1930, served in Paris 1932, Cairo 1935, transferred to the FO in 1937; First Secretary in 1940, acted as Chargé d' Affaires in Czechoslovakia; war years in FO as Head of Central Department, Chargé d' Affaires in Moscow 1945–7; Principle Private Secretary, Assistant Under Secretary of State in 1949; High Commissioner for India in 1951, Deputy Under Secretary of State German Affairs; Ambassador in Moscow 1960–2 and Bonn 1963–8. Knighted. *Dealing with Dictators*, autobiography published 1991.

14 TNA FO 371/31083 C 4529/19/55. Translation of Captain Józef Czapski's memorandum on missing Polish officers dated 2 II 1942. Mr H. Lacy Baggallay, acting Counsellor, British Embassy, who despatched the report to Anthony Eden at the FO, questioned the number of the missing men, believing that a far greater number of Polish prisoners of war had been sent to the extreme north-east of Siberia than originally suggested by Czapski in his 2 February report.

15 TNA HS 4/199 report to GOC (General Officer Commanding) Polish Army in Buzuluk Soviet Russia 1 November 1941, by Lt Bronisław Młynarski (1899-1971) Lieutenant, adjutant to Senior Officers in Starobelsk camp: Major S. Zaleski, Major K. Niewiarowski and Major L. Chrystowski successively. The report deals with missing Polish officers from PoW camps, especially Starobelsk, where he was interned from 30 IX 1939 to 12 V 1940. Part of Młynarski's report was incorporated in 'Facts and Documents' compiled in 1946, p 64. After the war settled in America, where he wrote his memoirs *W niewoli sowieckiej* (In Soviet Captivity), Gryf publication London 1974.

16 Professor Stanisław Kot (1885-1975) History Professor at Jagiellonian University, politician, in 1941–2 Polish Ambassador in Moscow. After the war, at odds with the Polish Government-in-exile, a forlorn figure, died in London. Published *Listy z Rosji do Gen. Sikorskiego* (Letters from Russia to General Sikorski) London 1956.

17 Wiktor Sukiennicki (1901–1983) Professor of Law at the University of Stefan Batory in pre-war Wilno, Lieutenant in reserves, deported by the Soviets to Siberia, joined the Polish Army in USSR, called upon by Ambassador Kot to set up an Agency to record the whereabouts of the Polish prisoners from depositions made by those who survived; Author of many publications, the relevant one is *Wspomnienia i Relacje* (Reminiscences and Statements) published in *Zeszyty Historyczne,* 1982.

18 Zdzisław Stahl (1891-1987) economist, journalist and politician, 1930–1935 and again in 1938 member of the Polish *Sejm* (Parliament) representing National Party. Arrested and deported to *GULag* by the *NKVD*, in 1941 joined the Polish Army, engaged as Head of *Biuro Studiów* of 2 Corps, working on Katyn papers.

19 Stanisław Swianiewicz (1900–1997) Professor of Economics, born in Dyneburg, Latvia, before the Revolution studied at Moscow and Wilno Universities, Head of the East European Institute, expert in the political economy of the Soviets, published *Lenin as Economist* and *Political Economy of Hitler's Germany*. In 1939, Lieutenant 85 Infantry

Division, taken prisoner by the Russians, kept at Kozelsk camp till 30 April 1940, taken to Lubyanka and Butyrki prisons, sentenced to eight years hard labour. In 1942 released from *GULag* at the intervention of Ambassador Kot, whom he joined in Kuibyshev. Despatched to the Middle East, to join a Research Bureau in Jerusalem with the task of preparing projects for the expected Peace Congress after the war. Stayed in Great Britain as a political émigré, lectured at the Polish University College in London, then a Fellow in International Studies at the London School of Economics. In 1963 Professor at St Mary's University, Halifax Canada and Notre Dame University USA. In 1965 Oxford University Press published his outstanding work *Forced Labour and Economic Development*. In 1989 published his memoirs *W cieniu Katynia* (In the Shadow of Katyn). Swianiewicz suggests that the meaning of *Koze Gory* is not Goat's Hill, but Slanting Hills – *Kose gory*.

20 *Zbrodnia katyńska w świetle dokumentów* (Katyn massacre in the light of documents) Gryf publication, London 1962 p.30. The story is based on recollections of Dr Wacław Mucho who survived Kozelsk.

21 TNA FO 371/31078 C 1370/19/55 and WO 208/1735A secure signal from Moscow to the DMI, War Office ML 2706, dated 1942 February 3, 12.54 hours; C 1786/19/55, another secure signal ML 2971 dated 1942 February 12 15.46 hours.

22 Anthony Robert Eden (1897–1977) Conservative Member of House of Commons 1923–1957; Under Secretary of State at FO 1931-1933, Foreign Secretary in Chamberlain's Government. Minister for Dominions in 1939; War Minister May 1940; December 1940 to July 1945 Foreign Secretary; in 1945 Co-Chairman of UN Founding Conference in San Francisco; Foreign Secretary again in 1951–5, Prime Minister 1955–1957, resigned, Earl of Avon 1961, Member of the House of Lords.

23 Alexander Cadogan (1884–1968) Attaché in Istanbul 1909, Third Secretary in the FO in 1910, posted to Vienna in 1913–4, in FO between 1914–1919 as First Secretary, Private Secretary to Permanent Under Secretary of State 1919–1920, Acting Counsellor in FO 1928, KCMG in 1934; Envoy then Plenipotentiary Ambassador to Peking 1934–5, Deputy Under Secretary of State 1936, promoted to Permanent Under Secretary of State 1938–1946; 1946–1950 Permanent Representative to the United Nations Organisation in New York, retired 1950.

24 William Strang (1893–1978) MBE in 1918, Third Secretary in the FO, posted to Belgrade, Second Secretary attached to Anglo-Soviet Conference in 1924, First Secretary in 1925, acting Chargé d' Affaires, Counsellor in Moscow 1930–1933; knew Serbo-Croat and Russian. CMG in 1932 and CB in 1939, Acting Assistant Under Secretary of State, KCMG in 1943; Joint Permanent Under Secretary of State; Political Advisor to Commander in Chief of British Forces of Occupation in Germany in 1945; General Secretary 1947, appointed Permanent Under Secretary of State 1949.

25 TNA, FO 371/31083 C 4929/19/55 secure signal, 1942 May 12 No. 731, 'Immediate' 1942 May 19 12.35 hours from FO to Kuibyshev.

26 Leslie R. Hulls (N N) Lt Col Gordon Highlanders, RNVR in 1917, Captain in 1920, MC, fought in the Caucasus during the Russian Revolution and knew the language. Commissioned in 1939 by Regular Army Emergency. Temporary Major in February 1941, Acting Lt Col in July 1941 as a Liaison Officer to General Anders with the Polish forces in Russia and Iraq. Accused of having too much influence over Anders, General Sikorski requested his relief in April 1943, but later retracted his charges. Hulls was not allowed to return to his post. In July 1943 Hulls was temporarily seconded to the Allied Liaison Directorate of the War Office and took a Civil Affairs course. In March 1944, he was still involved with evacuation of refugees including Poles. His superior Lt Gen F. G. Beaumont Nesbitt of the DMI considered him best qualified for the job.

27 TNA FO 371/97632 AU 1661/26, three typed copies of confidential reports written by Lt Col Hulls and sent via Military Attaché in Cairo to the War Office, dated Yangi-Jul

18 June 1942, the other two came from Qisil Rabat 29 October 1942 and 3 December 1942. Yangi-Jul copy with slight variations is also in WO 208/1735A C11048/152/G; Hulls' reports were accurate and can easily be compared with the Russian documents of the time, acquired from the State Archives by the Polish Committee of historians and archivists of the CAW Central Military Archives in Warsaw between 1992 and 1997. Kol. WKA (*Wojskowa Komisja Archiwalna* – Military Archives Committee) Syg. VIII.800.26/ 1 to 12.

28 Pyotr Stolypin (1862-1911) Russian Minister of Internal Affairs, was instrumental in repressing the revolutionary reactions of 1905–1907; assassinated in Kiev. Movement of thousands of prisoners required suitable transportation and passenger coaches with compartments were specially adapted for this purpose and nicknamed *Stolypinki*. The compartments had no windows and up to 14 people would be crammed in. The entrance had a reinforced iron grate, which could be opened only from the outside. There were small observation windows only on the corridor side, where armed guards were strategically positioned. In post Revolution times, such wagons were frequently seen coupled onto the normal passenger trains.

29 Translation by EM.

chapter two

KATYN 1943

From 11 April 1943, the German radio service *'Trans-ocean'* started to broadcast the discovery of Polish mass graves in the Katyn woods, near Smolensk. Although suspected, but never consciously accepted by the Polish people, it was devastating news, which actually reached a world audience on 13 April 1943 on the German Home Service. The Confidential Annex of the War Cabinet meeting held on 13 April did not record the shocking news, but concentrated on Eden's report of his meeting with President Roosevelt, who had asked him if Russia wanted to communise all Europe after the war. To which Eden replied that he did not think so, but 'one of the best ways of avoiding this was to keep on good terms with Russia'. Roosevelt was decisive about the prolonged wrangle on the subject of the Curzon Line. He assumed that if Poland took over Eastern Prussia and Silesia, she ought to be satisfied and accept the Line as the boundary with Russia:

> Let the United States and Russia settle between themselves what they regard as fair terms and then with the help of the British, try to persuade the Poles to accept the settlement.[1]

On 15 April, Prime Minister Winston Churchill invited General Władysław Sikorski, together with Ambassador Edward Raczyński,[2] to lunch; also present were Eden and Cadogan. The main purpose of the meeting was to discuss the newly proposed boundaries. It was also an occasion for Churchill to raise the subject of Katyn. He warned the Poles not to be drawn by the German provocation. On 19 April the War Cabinet discussed the Katyn massacre, with an attempt by Eden 'to persuade the Poles to treat this as a German propaganda designed to sow discord between the Allies'.

Apparently Lieutenant General Marian Kukiel,[3] Minister of Defence of the Polish government, issued a long communiqué directly to the press, ending with a statement that the Polish government would be approaching the International Red Cross to take charge of the Katyn investigation. The same day, during lunch given by Eden to the Foreign Ministers of the Allied countries, Raczyński in passing mentioned that a reply was to be made regarding the accusations, to which Eden and Cadogan expressed the view that the reply should throw doubt on the German story. Roberts confirms this in his hand-written note – 'The Poles did I believe mention the matter casually at lunch, but this could hardly be described as consultation.'[4] The subject was raised again in Parliament. Viscount Cranborne speaking for the Government stated that the Polish government took this decision without communicating beforehand with Owen O'Malley,[5] the British Ambassador to the Polish government-in-exile.

The Polish Council of Ministers met on 17 April to announce on the 19th that instructions had been sent to the *PCK, Polski Czerwony Krzyż* (Polish Red Cross) Delegate Stanisław Radziwiłł in Geneva asking the ICRC (International Committee of the Red Cross) to take charge of the investigation of the graves. Almost simultaneously, on 17 April, the Germans delivered a similar note to the ICRC. The Soviets interpreted this as collusion against them by the Poles and the Germans. On the same date, *The Times* of London published an article about the Katyn discovery and General Kukiel's letter to the ICRC. Once the subject was in the public domain, Sikorski had to issue another statement quickly, condemning German hypocrisy as they were continually committing similar crimes against humanity.

Churchill signalled Stalin on 10 May 1943, full of apologies and assured him that the Polish press would be disciplined in the future. As regards the invitation to the ICRC, he stated that 'the Poles did not tell us what they were going to do and so we could not warn them against the peril of the course which they proposed to take.'

The Polish Army in the East, by now training in Iraq, took the news badly. On 21 April, two days before Good Friday, a Requiem Mass was said for the dead officers as well as for those thousands who had perished from hunger, illness and those who had been killed as a result of the German invasion. After the Mass, General Anders, Commander of the Polish Army in the USSR spoke from his heart.[6]

General Anders' Speech

> No other Nation had to suffer tragedy like the Poles, who in 1939 took to arms in defence of their freedom. We were the only ones who in 1939 fought with the Germans, and for that, to receive a dagger in our backs from the Soviets. It took great responsibility, sacrifice and strength, which the nation had gathered throughout hundreds of generations, not to give in. That is why our nation still lives and fights without respite in foreign lands. Our huge sacrifice in this war, unknown to the rest of the world, cannot be counted as chivalrous combat, because a large number of victims were murdered or tortured to death or died from illness, hunger or the harsh climate. I feel that today, our brothers are with us in spirit. Soldiers! When you stand in readiness for war, remember to do your duty, because standing behind each of you are the souls of our departed. They are

also Poles, whose duty falls onto you. I believe that justice will always prevail and our Polish cause, which is so righteous and fair, must triumph. I believe that our nation has always been and will be great if only for its sufferings and its hardened spirit. I know that with great effort we shall secure the Poland that we dreamed of, while we stayed in prisons and camps; our desire for vengeance at long last would be taken. This is why, today, while praying for our colleagues, brothers, sisters and children, who are no more – we pledge them, that we shall discharge this obligation on their behalf. In our long march to Poland, when we reach the borders, a signal will sound 'Poles to arms!' and people will come to us and those who have passed away will support us and induce us to greater deeds, for the glory and might of Poland.

Ambassador O'Malley's Involvement with Katyn

There is no doubt that all the relevant documentation on the missing officers as well as the official and non-official reports on the massacre itself, came from Polish sources. The British Ambassador to the Polish government, Owen O'Malley, wrote a striking despatch 51, on 24 May 1943.[7] Based on a Polish signal from 'Kalina' Gen. Stefan Rowecki, Commander of the *AK*, it included a transcribed report of Dr Adam Schebesta, chief medical officer and one of the *PCK* members who went to Katyn to inspect the graves. It reveals the state of the graves and possible number of the dead, their documents and diaries, all ending in April 1940. O'Malley refers to this report as 'unauthorised', it should be treated as most secret and should not be referred to by the British. Presumably he got it from Lt Col Michał Protasewicz, head of *Oddział VI*, the Polish Special Operations Bureau of the Polish General staff. Somehow a sentence on the German bullets found in the graves, marked *GECO*, was erased from the English version, with dire consequences, as O'Malley, who took on the challenge of Katyn with the FO, was ignorant of this while preparing his second report.

O'Malley's despatch with attachments was read successively by the senior Foreign Office staff, amongst them: Sir William Strang, Sir Orme Sargent,[8] Sir Alexander Cadogan, Frank Roberts, and eventually by Denis Allen.[9] The Foreign Secretary Anthony Eden passed it over to Churchill, who after reading it wanted to know if the despatch had been sent to the King and the President – not the President, Eden replied, as he considered it to be 'pretty explosive and in some respects prejudicial'. Eden feared that 'if it fell into unauthorised hands then the reaction on the relations with Russia would be serious'. Nevertheless, Churchill sent a copy of O'Malley's despatch to President Theodore Roosevelt on 13 August 1943 with a note that the first two pages were 'grim' but it was a well written story; and he asked for its return! Denis Allen, the geographical desk officer at the FO, as well as Sir Alexander Cadogan expressed their opinions, which would shape Katyn's course.

British Embassy to Poland
45 Lowndes Square S.W.1
(No. 51)
(15/192/43) May 24th 1943.

Sir,
My despatch No.43 of April 30th, dwelt on the probability that no confederation in Eastern Europe could play an effective part in European politics unless it were affiliated to the Soviet Government, and suggested that so long as the policy of this Government was as enigmatic as it now is, it would be inconsistent with British interests that Russia should enjoy a sphere of influence extending from Danzing [Gdańsk] to the Aegean and Adriatic Seas. The suppression of the Comintern on May 20th may be considered to have brought to an end what was in the past the most objectionable phase of Soviet foreign policy and to entitle the Soviet Government to be regarded less distrustfully than formerly.[10] It is not, then, without hesitation that I address this further despatch to you which also gives grounds for misgivings about the character and policy of the present rulers in Russia.

2. We do not know for certain who murdered a lot of Polish officers in the forest of Katyn in April and May 1940, but this at least is already clear, that it was the scene of terrible events which will live long in the memory of the Polish nation. Accordingly, I shall try to describe how this affair looks to my Polish friends and acquaintances of whom many had brothers and sons and lovers among those known to have been taken off just three years ago from the prison camps at Kozielsk, Starobielsk and Ostashkov to an uncertain destination: how it looks, for instance, to General Sikorski, who there lost Captain [Jan] Fuhrman, his former ADC and close personal friend; to M. [Kajetan] Morawski, who lost a brother-in-law called Zoltowski [Adam Żółtowski] and a nephew; or to M. [Lt Col Adam] Zaleski, who lost a brother and two cousins. (See Annex I).

3. The number of Polish prisoners taken by the Russian armies when they invaded Poland in September 1939 was about 180,000, including police and gendarmerie and a certain number of civilian officials. The total number of army officers was around about 15,000. At the beginning of 1940 there were in the three camps named above round about nine or ten thousand officers and six thousand other ranks, policemen and civil officials. Less public reference has been made to these 6,000 than to the 10,000 officers, not because the Polish Government are less indignant about the disappearance of other ranks than about the disappearance of officers, or were less insistent in enquiries for them, but because the need of officers to command the Polish troops recruited in Russia was more urgent than the need to increase the total ration strength

of the Polish army. There is no reason to suppose that these 6,000 other ranks, police and civilians were treated by the Soviet Government differently to the officers and mystery covers the fate of all. For the sake of simplicity however, I shall write in this despatch only of the missing officers without specific reference to other ranks, to police prisoners or to civilians. Of the 10,000 officers, only some 3 or 4,000 were regular officers. The remainder were reserve officers who in peace time earned their living, many with distinction, in the professions, in business and so on.

4. In March of 1940 word went around the camps at Kozelsk, Starobelsk and Ostashkov that under orders from Moscow the prisoners were to be moved to camps where conditions would be more agreeable, and that they might look forward to eventual release. All were cheered by the prospect of a change from the rigours which prisoners must endure to the hazards and vicissitudes of relative freedom in Soviet or German territory. Even their captors seemed to wish the prisoners well who were now daily entrained in parties of 50 to 350 for the place at which, so they hoped, the formalities of their discharge would be completed. As each prisoner was listed for transfer, all the usual particulars about him were re-checked and re-registered. Fresh fingerprints were taken. The prisoners were inoculated afresh and certificates of inoculation furnished to them. Sometimes the prisoners' Polish documents were taken away, but in many such cases these were returned before departure. All were furnished with rations for the journey, and, as a mark of special regard, the sandwiches furnished to senior officers were wrapped in clean white paper – a commodity seldom seen anywhere in Russia. Anticipations of a better future were clouded only by the fact that 400 or 500 Poles had been listed for further detention, first at Pavlishchev Bor and eventually at Griazovets. These were, as it turned out later, to be the only known survivors of the lost legion, and some of them are in England now; but at the time, although no principle could be discovered on which they had been selected, they supposed they had been condemned to a further period of captivity; and some even feared that they have been chosen out for execution.

5. Our information about these events is derived for the most part from those routed to Griazovets, all of whom were released in 1941 and some of whom – notably M. Komarnicki, the Polish Minister for Justice, are now in England.

6. Entrainment of the 10,000 officers from the three camps went on all through April and the first half of May, and the lorries, lined with cheerful faces, which took them from camp to station, were in fact the last that was ever seen of them alive by any witness to whom we have access. Until the revelations made by the Germans broadcast of April 12th 1943, and apart from a few words let drop at the time by the prison guards, only the testimony of scribbling on the railway

wagons in which they were transported affords any indication of their destination. The same wagons seem to have done a shuttle service between Kozelsk and the detraining station; and on these some of the first parties to be transported had scratched the words: 'Don't believe that we are going home', and the news that their destination had turned out to be a small station near Smolensk. These messages were noticed when the vans returned to Smolensk station, and had been reported to us by prisoners at Kozelsk, who were later sent to Griazovets.

7. But though of positive indications as to what subsequently happened to the 10,000 officers there was none until the grave at Katyn was opened, there is now available a good deal of negative evidence, the cumulative effect of which is to throw serious doubt on Russian disclaimers of responsibility for the massacre. **(See also my despatch No.52 Secret of today's date).**

8. In the first place, there is the evidence to be derived from the prisoner's correspondence in respect to which information has been furnished by officers' families in Poland, by the officers now with the Polish army in the Middle East, and by the Polish Red Cross Society. Up till the end of March 1940, large numbers of letters had been despatched, which were later received by their relatives, from the officers confined at Kozelsk, Starobelsk and Ostashkov; whereas no letters from any of them (excepting from the 400 moved to Griazovets) have been received by anybody, which had been despatched subsequent to that date. The Germans overran Smolensk in July 1941, and there is no easy answer to the question why, if any of the 10,000 had been alive between the end of May 1940 and July 1941, none of them ever succeeded in getting any word through to their families.

9. In the second place there is the evidence of the correspondence between the Soviet Government and the Polish Government. The first request for information about the missing 10,000 was made by Minister Kot to Wyshinsky [Andrei Vyshinsky][11] Deputy Foreign Minister on October 6th, 1941. On December 3rd, 1941, General Sikorski backed up his enquiry with a list of 3,845 names of officers included among them. General Anders furnished the Soviet Government with a further list of 800 names on March 8th 1942. Enquiries about the fate of the 10,000 were made again and again to the Russian Government verbally and in writing by General Sikorski, M. Kot, M. [Tadeusz] Romer [Ambassadors to Russia 1942–43], Count Raczyński [Foreign Affairs] and General Anders, between October 1941 and April 1943. The Polish Red Cross between August and October 1940 sent no less than 500 questionnaires about individual officers to the Russian Government. To none of all these enquiries extending over a period of two-and-a-half years was a single positive answer of any kind ever returned. The enquirers were told

either that the officers had been released, or that 'perhaps they are already in Germany', or that 'no information' of their whereabouts was available, or (M. Molotov to M. Kot, October 1941) that complete lists of the prisoners were available and that they would all be delivered to the Polish authorities 'dead or alive'. But it is incredible that if any of the 10,000 were released, not one of them has ever appeared again anywhere, and it is almost equally incredible, if they were not released, that not one of them should have escaped subsequent to May 1940 and reported himself to the Polish authorities in Russia or Persia. That the Russian authorities should have said of any Polish officer in Soviet jurisdiction that they had 'no information' also provokes incredulity; for it is notorious that the *NKVD* collect and record the movements of individuals with the most meticulous care.

10. In the third place there is evidence of those who have visited the grave: first, a Polish commission including among others, doctors, journalists and members of the Polish Assistance Committee, a former president of the Polish Academy of Literature and a representative of the Mayor of Warsaw; secondly, another Polish commission which included priests, doctors and representatives of the Polish Red Cross Society; thirdly, an international commission of criminologists and pathologists of which the personnel is given in **Annex II**. The Report of this Commission forms **Annex III** to this despatch, and the reports of the two Polish commissions add little to it. Several hundred identifications have been established. All this evidence would normally be highly suspect since inspections took place under German auspices and the results reached us through German broadcasts. (For reasons reported separately in **my secret despatch 52 of today's date**) There are fair grounds for presuming that the German broadcasts accurately represented the findings of the Commissions, that the Commissions' findings were at any rate in some respects well founded, and that the grounds were sound on which at any rate some of the identifications were made.

11. In the fourth place there is the fact that a mass execution of officer prisoners would be inconsistent with what we know of the German army. The German army has committed innumerable brutalities, but the murder by them of prisoners of war, even of Poles, is rare. Had the German authorities ever had these 10,000 Polish officers in their hands we can be sure that they would have placed some or all of them in the camps in Germany already allotted to Polish prisoners, while the 6,000 other ranks, policemen and civil officials would have been put to forced labour. In such a case the Polish authorities would in the course of two years certainly have got in touch with some of the prisoners; but in fact none of the men from Kozelsk, Starobelsk or Ostashkov have ever been heard of from Germany.

12. Finally there is the evidence to be derived from the confusion, which characterises explanations elicited from or volunteered by the Soviet Government. Between August 1941 and April 12th, 1943, when the Germans announced the discovery of the grave at Katyn the Russian Government had, among other excuses, maintained that all Polish officers taken prisoner in 1939 had been released. On the other hand, in conversation with the Polish Ambassador, a Russian official who had drunk more than was good for him, once referred to the disposal of these officers as 'a tragic error'. On April 16th, immediately after the German announcement, the Soviet Information Bureau in Moscow suggested that the Germans were misrepresenting as victims of Russian barbarity skeletons dug up by archaeologists at Gniezdowo [Gnezdovo], which lies next door to Katyn. On April 26th, M. Molotov in a note to the Polish Ambassador in Moscow said that the bodies at Katyn were those of Poles who had at one time been prisoners of the Russians but had subsequently been captured by the Germans in their advance at Smolensk in July 1941 and had been murdered then by them. On a later occasion, and when the German broadcasts gave reason to think that some bodies were sufficiently well preserved to be identifiable, the Russian Government put forward a statement that the Polish officers had been captured by the Germans in July 1941, had been employed upon construction work, and had only been murdered shortly before the German 'discovery' was announced. This confusion cannot easily be understood except on the assumption that the Russian Government had something to hide.

13. The cumulative effect of this evidence is, as I said earlier, to throw serious doubt on Russian disclaimers of responsibility for a massacre. Such doubts are not diminished by rumours which have been current during the last two and a half years that some of the inmates of Kozelsk, Starobelsk and Ostashkov had been transported towards Kolyma, Franz Joseph Land or Novaya Zemlya, some or all of these being killed en route. It may be that this was so, and it may be that some less number than ten thousand odd were destroyed and buried at Katyn; but whether the massacre occurred (if it did occur) in one place or two places or three places, naturally makes no difference to Polish sentiments. These will accordingly be described without reference to the uncertainty, which exists as to the exact number of victims buried near Smolensk.

14. With all that precedes in mind it is comprehensible that the relatives and fellow-officers of the men who disappeared should have concluded that these had in fact been murdered by their Russian captors and should picture their last hours – somewhat as follows – with bitter distress. The picture is a composite one to which knowledge of the district, the German broadcasts, experience of Russian methods and the reports of the visitors to the grave have all contributed, but it is not so much an evidentially established description of events as a reconstruction

in the light of the evidence – sometimes partial and obviously defective – of what may have happened. But it – or something like it – is what most Poles believe to have happened, and what I myself, in the light of all the evidence such as it is, incline to think happened. Many months or years may elapse before the truth is known, but because in the meantime curiosity is unsatisfied and judgement in suspense, we cannot even if we would – and much less can Poles – make our thoughts and feelings unresponsive to the dreadful probabilities of the case.

15. Smolensk lies some 20 kilometres from the spot where the common graves were discovered. It has two stations and in or near the town the main lines from Moscow to Warsaw and Riga to Orel cross and re-cross each other. Some fifteen kilometres to the west of Smolensk stands the unimportant station of Gnezdovo, and it is but a short mile from Gnezdovo to a place known locally as *Kozlinaya Gora* or 'the Hill of Goats'. The district of Katyn, in which this little hill stands, is covered with primeval forest, which has been allowed to go to rack and ruin. The forest is mostly coniferous, but the pine trees are interspersed here and there with hardwoods and scrub. The month of April normally brings spring to this part of the country, and by early May the trees are green; but the winter of 1939–40 had been the hardest on record, and when the first parties from Kozelsk arrived on April 8th, there would still have been occasional patches of snow in deep shade, and of course, much mud on the rough road from the station to the Hill of Goats. At Gnezdovo the prison vans from Kozelsk, Starobelsk and Ostashkov discharged their passengers into a barbed wire cage surrounded by a strong force of Russian soldiers, and the preparations made here for their reception must have filled most of the Polish officers with disquiet, and some indeed with dismay who remembered that the forest of Katyn had been used by the Bolsheviks in 1919 as a convenient place for killing of many Tzarist officers. For such was the case, and a Pole now in London, Janusz Laskowski[12] tells me that when he was eleven years old he had to listen every evening to an account of his day's work from one of the executioners, Afanaziev, who was billeted in his mother's house. From the cage, the prisoners were taken in lorries along a country road to the Hill of Goats, and it must have been when they were unloaded from the lorries, that their hands were bound and that dismay gave way to despair. If a man struggled, it seems that the executioner threw his coat over his head, tying it round his neck and leading him hooded to the pit's edge, for in many cases a body was found to be thus hooded and the coat to have been pierced by a bullet where it covered the base of the skull. But those who went quietly to their death must have seen a monstrous sight. In the broad deep pit, their comrades lay, packed closely round the edge, head to feet, like sardines in a tin, but in the middle of the grave disposed less orderly. Up and down on the bodies the executioners tramped, hauling the dead bodies about and treading in the blood like butchers in a stockyard. When it was all over and the last shot

had been fired and the last Polish head been punctured, the butchers – perhaps trained in youth to husbandry – seem to have turned their hands to one of the most innocent of occupations: smoothing the clods and planting little conifers all over what had been a shambles. It was of course, rather late in the year for transplanting young trees, but not too late; for the sap was beginning to run in the young Scots pines when, three years later, the Polish representatives visited the site.

16. The climate and the conifers are not without significance. The climate of Smolensk accounts for the fact that, though the Germans first got wind of the existence of the mass graves in the autumn of 1942, it was only in April of 1943 that they published to the world an account of what had been unearthed. The explanation is surely this: not that the Germans propagandists had chosen a politically opportune moment for their revelations, but that during the winter, the ground at Smolensk is frozen so hard that it would have been impossible to uncover corpses without dynamite or such other violent means as would have destroyed the possibility of identifying dead bodies. The winter of 1942–43 was exceptionally mild and the German authorities probably got to work as soon as the soil was sufficiently soft. The little conifers also deserve more attention than they have received. In the first place they are presumptive evidence of Russian guilt; for, considering the conditions under which the German army advanced through Smolensk in July 1941, in full expectation of early and complete victory, it is most unlikely, if the Polish officers had been murdered by Germans and not Russians, that the Germans would have bothered to cover up their victims' graves with young trees. In the second place, one of these young trees under examination by a competent botanist would reveal beyond any possibility of doubt whether it had last been transplanted in May 1940 or some time subsequent to July 1941. Perhaps this test of Russian veracity will presently be made.

17. The political background against which the events described in paragraph 15 are viewed by Poles, is by contrast a matter of undisputed history, including as it does, all the long story of partitions, rebellions and repressions, the Russo-Polish war of 1919–20, the mutual suspicions which this left behind it, the unannounced invasion of Poland by Russia in September 1939, the subsequent occupation of half Poland by Russia and the carrying into captivity of some million and a half of its inhabitants. Most recently comes the virtual annexation of the occupied eastern parts of Poland, the refusal of the Russian Government to recognise as Polish citizens the inhabitants of the occupied districts, the suppression of relief organisations for Poles in Russia and the persecution of Poles refusing to change their own for Russian nationality. When Poles learned that in addition to all these misfortunes, round about 10,000 men of the best breeding stock in Poland had (according to Russian accounts) been either dispersed and 'lost' somewhere

in the Soviet Union or else abandoned to the advancing German armies, or had (according to German accounts) been found to have been murdered by the Russians, many of them naturally concluded (though I do not here give it as my own conclusions) that the Soviet Government's intention had been to destroy the very foundations upon which their own Poland could be rebuilt. This sinister political intention imputed by Poles to Russia poisoned the wound and enhanced the sufferings of a nation already outraged and dismayed by the conduct of the Soviet Government. Some Poles remembering Lenin's attitude to the holocausts of 1917 and subsequent years, and probing the dark recesses of Stalin's mind when he took (if take he did) the dreadful decision, compare disciple with master. Lenin would have broken apart the heads of ten thousand Polish officers with the insouciance of a monkey cracking walnuts. Did corpses pitching into a common grave with the precision of machines coming off a production belt similarly satisfy a nature habituated to manipulate blood and lives with uncompassionate detachment? Some at any rate so interpret Stalin's mind. 'These men are no use to us,' they imagine him as saying: 'in fact they are a nuisance and a danger. Here is elite of talent; here is valour and a hostile purpose. These stallions must not live to sire a herd of hostile Christian thoroughbreds. Many of the brood-mares have already have been sold to Siberian peasants and the camel-pullers of Kazakhstan. Their foals and yearlings can be broken to Communist harness. Rid me of this stud farm altogether and send all this turbulent bloodstock to the knacker's.'

18. The men who were taken to Katyn are dead and their death is a serious loss to Poland. Nevertheless, unless the Russians are cleared of the presumption of guilt, the moral repercussions in Poland, in the other occupied countries and in England of the massacre of Polish officers may well have more enduring results than the massacre itself; and this aspect of things, therefore, deserves attention. As I have as yet seen no reliable reports on public feeling in Poland and German-occupied Europe, my comments will relate only to our own reaction to the uncovering of the graves.

19. This despatch is not primarily concerned with the reaction of the British public, press or Parliament, who are not in such a good position as His Majesty's Government to form an opinion as to what actually happened. We ourselves, on the other hand, who have access to all the available information, though we can draw no final conclusions on vital matters of fact, have a considerable body of circumstantial evidence at our disposal, and I think most of us are more than half convinced that a large number of Polish officers were indeed murdered by the Russian authority and that it is indeed their bodies (as well, maybe, as other bodies) which have been unearthed. This being so, I am impelled to examine the effect on myself of the facts and allegations and to adjust my

mind to the shocking probabilities of the case. Since the Polish Government is in London and since the affair has been handled directly by yourself and the Prime Minister with General Sikorski and Count Raczyński, it may seem redundant for me to comment on it, as I should naturally do were the Polish Government and I both abroad; but though all important conversations have been between Ministers and leaders of the Polish Government, my contacts have doubtless been more numerous than yours during the last few weeks with Poles of all kinds and they have possibly spoken to me with less reservation than to yourself. I hope therefore I may, without impertinence, submit to you the reflections which follow.

20. In handling the publicity side of the Katyn affair, we have been constrained by the urgent need for cordial relations with the Soviet Government to appear to appraise the evidence with more hesitation and leniency than we should do in forming a common sense judgement on events occurring in normal times or in the ordinary course of our private lives; we have been obliged to appear to distort the normal and healthy operation of our intellectual and moral judgments; we have been obliged to give undue prominence to the tactlessness or impulsiveness of Poles, to restrain the Poles from putting their case clearly before the public, to discourage any attempt by the public and the press to probe the ugly story to the bottom. In general we have been obliged to deflect attention from possibilities which in the ordinary affairs of life, would cry to high heaven for elucidation and to withhold the full measure of solicitude which, in other circumstances, would be shown to acquaintances situated as a large number of Poles now are. We have in fact perforce used the good name of England like the murderers used the little conifers to cover up a massacre; and, in view of the immense importance of an appearance of Allied unity and of the heroic resistance of Russia to Germany, few will think that any other course would have been wise or right.

21. This dislocation between the public attitude and our private feelings we may know to be deliberate and inevitable; but at the same time, we may, perhaps, wonder whether, by representing to others something less than the whole truth so far as we know it, and something less than the probabilities so far as they seem to us probable, we are not incurring a risk of what – not to put a fine point on it – might darken our vision and take the edge off our moral sensibility. If so, how is this risk to be avoided?

22. At first sight it seems that nothing less appropriate to a political despatch than a discourse upon morals can be imagined; but yet, as we look at the changing nature of the international world of today, it seems, that morals and international politics are becoming more and more closely involved with each other. This

proposition has important consequences; but since it is not universally accepted I hope the following remarks in support of it are not out of place.

23. Nobody doubts that morals now enter into the domestic politics of the United Kingdom, but it was not always so. There was a time when the acts of the Government in London were less often the fruit of consultation and compromise in the general interests of all than of the ascendancy of one class or group of citizens who had been temporarily successful in the domestic arena. It was the realisation of the interdependence of all classes and groups of the population of England, Scotland and Wales, which discouraged the play of intestine power politics and set the welfare of all above the advantage of the strong. Similar causes are producing similar results in the relations of states to each other. 'During the last four centuries of our modern era' writes Professor [Albert] Pollard[13] 'the last word in political organisation has been the nation; but now that the world is being unified by science and culture' the conception of the nation state as the largest group in which human being are organically associated with each other is being superseded by the conception of a larger, it may be of a European or indeed of a world-wide unity: and 'the nation is taking its place as the bridge, the half-way house, between the individual and the human family.' Europe, and indeed the world, is in the process of integrating themselves and 'the men and women of Britain' as you said at Maryland, 'are alive to the fact that they live in one world with their neighbours.' This being so, it would be strange if the same movement towards the coalescence of smaller into larger groups which brought about the infiltration of morals into domestic politics were not also now bringing about the infiltration of morals into international politics. This, in fact, it seems to many of us is exactly what is happening, and is why as the late M [James] Headlam-Morley[14] said: 'what in the international sphere is morally indefensible generally turns out in the long run to have been politically inept.' It is surely the case that many of the political troubles of neighbouring countries and some of our own have in the past arisen, because they and we were incapable of seeing this or unwilling to admit it.

24. If, then, morals have become involved with international politics, if it be the case that a monstrous crime has been committed by a foreign government – albeit a friendly one – and that we, for however valid reasons, have been obliged to behave as if the deed was not theirs, may it not be that we now stand in danger of bemusing, not only others but ourselves: of falling as Mr [John] Winant[15] said recently at Birmingham, under St Paul's curse on those who can see cruelty 'and burn not'? If so, and since no remedy can be found in the early alteration of our public attitude towards the Katyn affair, we ought, maybe, to ask ourselves how, consistently with the necessities of our relations with the Soviet Government, the voice of our political conscience is to be kept up to concert pitch. It may

be that the answer lies, for the moment, only in something to be done inside our own hearts and minds where we are masters. Here at any rate we can make a compensatory contribution – a reaffirmation of our allegiance to truth and justice and compassion. If we do this we shall at least be predisposing ourselves to the exercise of a right judgement on those half political half moral questions (such as the fate of the Polish deportees now in Russia) which will confront us both elsewhere and more particularly in respect to Polish-Russian relations as the war pursues its course and draws to its end; and so, if the facts about the Katyn massacre turn out to be as most of us incline to think, shall we vindicate the spirit of these brave unlucky men and justify the living to the dead.

I have the honour to be, with the highest respect Sir
Your most obedient, humble Servant
Owen O'Malley

Annex I (paragraph 2)
A list of 49 names and the ranks of missing officers, passed to O'Malley by his Polish contacts.[16] [Not reproduced]

Annex II (paragraph 10)
List of personnel composing the Commission of criminologists and pathologists.

Dr [Reimond] Spoleers, Professor of Opthalmology at the University of Ghent.
Dr [Vladimir] Markov, Instructor in Forensic Medicine and Criminology at the University of Sofia
Dr [Helge] Tramsen, Assistant Professor of Anatomy at the Institute for Forensic Medicine in Copenhagen.
Dr [Arno] Saxen, Professor of Pathological Anatomy at the University in Copenhagen.
Dr [Vincenzo] Palmieri, Professor of Forensic Medicine and Criminology at the University of Naples.
Dr [Edward] Miloslavich, Professor of Forensic Medicine and Criminology at the University of Agram.
Dr [H. M.] de Burlet, Professor of Anatomy at the University of Troningen.
Dr [Francisek] Hajek, Professor of Forensic Medicine and Criminology in Prague.
Dr [Alex] Birkle, Coroner of the Rumanian Ministry of Justice and First Assistant at the Institute of Forensic Medicine and Criminology in Bucharest.
Dr [Francois] Naville, Professor of Forensic Medicine at the University of Geneva.
Dr [Francisek] Subik, Professor of Pathological Anatomy at the University of Bratislava and head of the Public Health Service of Slovakia.

Dr [Ferenc] Orsós, Professor of Forensic Medicine and Criminology at the University of Budapest.
Dr [Gerhard] Buhtz, Professor of Forensic Medicine and Criminology at the University of Breslau.
Dr Costedoat Medical Inspector

Enclosure

Despatch No. 52 Most Secret, 24 May 1943[17]
1. At the foot of a hillock is the 'L' shape mass grave, which has been completely opened up. Its dimensions are: 16 x 26 x 6 metres. The bodies of the murdered men have been carefully arranged in from 9 to 12 layers, one on the top of another, each layer with the heads laid in opposite directions. The uniforms, notes in the pockets, passports and decorations are well preserved. The skin, hair and tendons have remained in such a good state that in order to carry out the trepanning it was necessary to cut under the skin and tendons. The faces were however unrecognisable.
2. Perpendicular to the first grave is a second mass grave, which up to now has only been partially opened up. Its dimensions are 14 x 16 metres. All the bodies in this grave have the hands tied behind them with a plait of string: in some cases the mouths have been gagged with handkerchiefs or rags: in some the head has been wrapped round with the skirts of an overcoat.
3. Up to now 906 bodies have been extracted, 76 per cent of which have been identified on the strength of passports, letters etc found on them.
4. It is presumed that in the two graves together there lie the bodies of from 2,500 to 4,000 officers: in only a few cases are they reserve officers in civilian dress.
5. Twelve persons, including one doctor and three non-commissioned officers of an ambulance unit, were present on behalf of the Polish Red Cross when the graves were opened up, the bodies identified and the documents found on them collected.
6. A characteristic feature is that nothing except watches has been removed from the murdered men: notebooks, money and papers are still in their pockets: sometimes rings are still on the fingers.
7. All the bodies have a bullet wound in the back of the skull. The representatives of the Polish Red Cross who were present at the exhumation took pains to collect the bullets extracted from the heads of the murdered men, the revolver shells and ammunition lying in the mass graves as well as the cords with which the hands of the murdered men had been tied. The entire material found was sent to the Polish Red Cross in Warsaw for Dr. Gorczycki. [**All bullets are of 7.65 calibre, shells bear inscription Geco, and the ropes are of twisted variety**. Sentence omitted]

8. In the presence of the author of this report, there was taken from the clothing of Major Solski a diary written up to April 21st. The writer of the diary stated that from Kozelsk they were taken in prison vans to their destination, then taken to Smolensk where they spent the night: reveille was sounded at 4 a.m. and they were placed in prison motor cars. At a clearing in the forest they were turned out of the motorcars and at 6.30 taken to some buildings there, they were told to give up their jewellery and watches. At this point the diary ends.
9. Under the supervision of the German authorities the Delegate of the Polish Red Cross is carrying out the exhumation and autopsies, besides collecting the papers. He has moreover established private contact with the local population. Whenever the body is identified a small tablet with a Red Cross number is attached to the bones. Afterwards all the bodies are put into a freshly dug, common grave. All of the officers identified were from Kozelsk with the exception of one from Starobelsk.
10. The clearing in the forest at Katyn covers several square kilometres: on it there used to be *NKVD* rest houses. The local civilian population states that in March and April 1940 one transport of Polish officers to the number of from 200 to 300 used to arrive every day.

Annex III (paragraph 10)

***Katyn Wood*: Text of Protocol: Berlin**

The report of the International Commission of scientists on the examination of mass graves at Katyn Wood in the main section reads as follows:

From the 28th April to the 30th April 1943, a Commission composed of leading representatives of forensic medicine at European Universities and other prominent University professors of medicine have conducted a thorough scientific examination of the mass graves of Polish officers in Katyn wood.

The discovery of those mass graves, which was recently brought to the attention of the German authorities, prompted Reich's Chief Health Officer, Dr [Leonard] Conte, to invite experts from various European countries to inspect the Katyn site in order thus to contribute to the clarification of this unique case. Members of the Commission personally heard the testimonies of several Russian native witnesses who, among others, confirmed that during the months of March and April, 1940, almost daily big railway transports with Polish officers arrived at the station of Gnesdovo, near Katyn, where the Polish officers alighted and were then transported in a prisoners motor van to Katyn wood and were not seen again; The Commission further took cognisance of the discoveries and facts thus far established and inspected objects of circumstantial evidence.

Accordingly, up to 30th April 1943, 982 bodies were exhumed, of which approximately 70 per cent have been identified, while papers found on others must first be subjected to careful preliminary treatment before they can be used for identification. Bodies exhumed prior to the commission's arrival were all inspected, and a considerable number were dissected by Professor Buhty [Buhtz] and his assistants. Up to today seven mass graves have been opened, the biggest of which is estimated to contain the bodies of 2,000 Polish officers. Members of the Commission personally dissected nine corpses and submitted numerous specially selected cases to post-mortem.

In all cases, bullets entered the nape. In the majority of cases only one bullet was fired. Two bullets were fired only rarely and only one case was found where three bullets had been fired into the nape. All the bullets were fired from pistols of less than 8 mm calibre. The spot where the bullets penetrated leads to the assumption that the shot was fired with the muzzle pressed against the nape or from the closest range. The surprising regularity of the wounds ...permits the assumption that experienced hands fired shots. Numerous bodies revealed a similar method of tying the hands; and in some cases stabs from four-edged bayonets were found on bodies and clothes. The method of tying is similar to that found on the bodies of Russian civilians that were earlier exhumed in Katyn Forest. The assumption is justified that a ricocheted bullet first killed one officer, then went into the body of one already dead in the pit – the shootings apparently being made in ditches to avoid having the bodies transported to graves.

The mass graves are situated in clearings in the forest, the ground being completely levelled off and planted with young pines. The mass graves were dug in undulating terrain, which consists of pure sand in terraces, the lowest going down as far as the ground water. Bodies lay, practically without exception, face down, closely side by side and in layers one above the other, clearly ledged methodically at the sides of pits and more irregularly in the centre.

The uniforms of the exhumed bodies, according to the unanimous opinion of the commission, were, especially with regard to buttons, rank insignia, decorations, form of boots, etc., undoubtedly Polish. They had winter wear. Frequently furs, leather coats, knitted vests and typical Polish officers' caps have been found. Only a few bodies were those of other ranks. One body was that of a priest. The measurements of the clothes correspond with the measurements of the wearer. No watches or rings were found on the bodies, although from the exact date and time found in entries in several diaries, the owners must have had these objects up to their last days, even hours. Comments found on bodies – diaries, correspondence, newspapers are from the period of the autumn of 1939 to March and April 1940. The last hitherto established date is that of a Russian newspaper of 22 April 1940.

There were varying degrees of decomposition of the bodies, differing according to the position of the bodies within the grave and their juxtaposition to each other. A large number of skulls were examined for changes, which according to the experiences of Professor Orsoa [Orsós], are of great importance for the determination of the time of death. These changes consisted of various layers of calcareous tuft-like incrustation on the surface of the already loamy brain matter. Such changes are not to be observed on bodies that have been interred for less than three years. But this change was observed to a marked degree on the skull of the body No. 526, which was found with a surface layer in one big mass grave.

Second Secretary Denis Allen's Opinion

[...] This is useful, and the material is skilfully assembled. On the evidence available it is, I think not difficult to share his conclusion that at any rate a strong presumption exists that the Russians were responsible. In the next five paragraphs, Mr O'Malley embarks upon what he admits is a 'sometimes partial and obviously defective' reconstruction of what may have happened at Katyn, leading up to a final ghoulish vision of Stalin condemning the Poles to the knacker's yard. This passage seems to serve no other purpose than to arouse anti-Soviet passions and prejudices in the reader's mind. Mr O'Malley then applies himself to the question of how such passions and prejudices may best be turned to account. By way of a devious argument about the infiltration of morals into international politics he recommends, while recognising the present necessity of avoiding public accusations of our Russian Allies, that we should at least redress the balance in our own minds and in all our future dealings with the Soviet Government, refuse to forget the Soviet crime of Katyn. Our future dealings with the Russians should in fact be governed by the moral necessity of 'vindicating the spirit of those brave, unlucky men and justifying the living to the dead'. In effect, Mr O'Malley urges that we should follow the example, which the Poles themselves are unhappily so prone to offer us and in our diplomacy allow our heads to be governed by our hearts. The minutes on Mr O'Malley's earlier despatch suggest that this is the one thing above all to be avoided at any rate in our dealings with Soviet Russia.

Frank Roberts agreed with Allen's scrutiny of the despatch and added that it was an awkward matter when an ally such as Russia was opened to accusations of this kind. According to him, to improve the conduct of the Soviets, there was nothing else to do but to aim at improving Anglo-Soviet relations. However, he was for the distribution of O'Malley's despatch to the King and War Cabinet, selected paragraphs 1 to 13 only, adding: 'I cannot help feeling that subsequent imaginative reconstruction of the scene in paragraphs 14 to 17, and more particularly paragraph 17, and moral observations in paragraphs 19 to 24 cast very little light upon this problem and merely leaves the reader with the impression that Mr O'Malley is working up the maximum prejudice against the Soviet Union.' Sir William Strang and Sir Orme Sargent were for the uncut version. As should be clear to all, points 18 to 21 were truly remarkable and carried straightforward arguments. Significantly, O' Malley's implicit proposal of a scientific test of 'Russian veracity' at point 16, was nowhere remarked upon by any other FO analyst, until pounced upon in his usual inimitable style by Winston Churchill.

Sir Alexander Cadogan, Permanent Under Secretary of State, a quintessential diplomat, expressed his thoughts pragmatically. He knew that the evidence could not possibly change Britain's course of action or policy; but here is no doubt the moral side of the report affected him profoundly:

Sir Alexander Cadogan's Remarks

> This is very disturbing. I confess that in cowardly fashion, I had rather turned my head away from the scene at Katyn – for fear of what I should find there.
>
> There may be evidence that we do not know of, that may point in another direction. But on the evidence that we have, it is difficult to escape from the presumption of Russian guilt.
>
> This of course raises terrible problems, but I think no one has pointed out that on the purely moral plane, these are not new. How many thousands of its own citizens has the Soviet regime butchered? And I don't know that the blood of a Pole cries louder to Heaven than that of a Russian. But we have perforce welcomed the Russians as Allies and have set ourselves to work with them in war and peace.
>
> The ominous thing about this incident is the ultimate political repercussion. How, if Russian crime is established, can we expect Poles to live amicably, side by side with Russians for generations to come? I fear there is no answer to that question. The other disturbing thought is that we may eventually, by agreement and in collaboration with Russians, proceed to the trial and perhaps execution of Axis 'war criminals' while condemning this atrocity. I confess I shall find that extremely difficult to swallow.
>
> However, quite clearly for the moment, there is nothing to be done. As to what circulation we give to this explosive material, I find it difficult to make up my mind. Of course it would be only honest to circulate it. But as we know (all admit) that the knowledge of this evidence cannot affect our course of action or policy, is there any advantage in exposing more individuals then necessary to the spiritual conflict that a reading of this despatch excites.[18]

The same sentiments were recorded in Cadogan's private diary on Friday 18 June 1944.[19] Indeed, his advice of not exposing people to the arguments over the responsibility for the killing at Katyn and keeping all as secret as humanly possible, was accepted by the Foreign Office.

O'Malley's despatch in its full version may not be known by the latest generations of scholars, hence the decision to include it in this publication. Although addressed to and clearly read by Eden, there is no sign of his evaluation of the report, bar one – a hand written, astonishing comment, referring to O'Malley's third paragraph, not about Katyn but the need for officers to command Polish troops recruited in Russia. 'This is simply not so. There is a vast surplus of Polish officers here and General S [Sikorski] has often lamented to me about this problem.' Churchill's reaction was totally different as described earlier. Be that as it may, O'Malley's report to the War Cabinet was truly shocking and unimpeachable at the same time – for his pains he paid a price – he had to adhere to official statements of the Foreign Office even when well into retirement.

Diplomatic Dilemmas and Attitudes

The British War Cabinet had discussed the problem of Polish-Soviet relations on three occasions, on 12, 19 and 27 April 1943.[20] Churchill spoke about Molotov's recently presented diplomatic note from Stalin and about the decision of the Soviet government to sever diplomatic relations with the Polish government in London. Its consequences bothered the Cabinet and the Prime Minister, who later advised his counterpart Sikorski, that the Poles should ignore what has happened at Katyn, what mattered now was to improve relations with the USSR and to get the Polish troops and their families out of Russia. A Most Secret telegram from Churchill was sent to Stalin dated 28 April, asking him to act 'in a spirit of magnanimity' and let the rest of the Polish forces in the USSR and their dependants depart to Persia (now Iran). In the afternoon of 29 April, the War Cabinet had before them a modified text of the announcement issued by the Polish government, which the Secretary of State had shown to the Soviet Ambassador during the meeting that morning. Other matters such as the 1939 frontiers were raised, but the general view of the Cabinet was that 'It might be necessary to reach a settlement on this question before the end of the war.' It was agreed that the Polish Press communiqué was to be toned down. The Ministry of Information was to ensure that the British and Polish press did not canvass over the Russo-Polish quarrel or take sides on Katyn. The minutes note Churchill's great displeasure:

> No Government, which had accepted our hospitality, had any right to publish articles of a character which conflicted with the general policy of the United Nations and which would create difficulties for this Government. Nor should any of these Governments use the broadcast in a way, which would have the same results.

The heart of the matter lay elsewhere. Churchill was afraid that Stalin might insist on changes in the Polish government-in-exile, getting rid of Sikorski as Premier, or even wanting to set up his own alternative political authority for Poland and raise the question of boundaries now, rather than after the war. As it turned out, Stalin had his way on all three issues.[21]

The Foreign Office did not entirely rely on the Polish memoranda and secret reports; they had their own sources of information, chiefly from their Military Missions and Ambassadorial despatches. As part of hushing up the killings, the British diplomats abroad received hints from the FO how to subdue the Katyn issue and what discretion was to be shown towards the Russians while interacting with Polish colleagues, regardless of the protocol. The story is rather amusing but it reflects the Foreign Office *dictum* of the time, when Katyn was beyond the pale. The British Ambassador in Turkey, Sir Hughe Knatchbull-Hugesson, distanced himself from the Poles at several diplomatic gatherings by ignoring the Polish Ambassador Michał Sokolnicki and his wife, constantly offering his arm to the wife of the Soviet Ambassador Sergei Vinogradov. Lawrence Steinhardt, the American Ambassador in Turkey, whose restrained distance was far beyond the accepted norm, showed a similar attitude towards the Polish ambassadorial couple. Sokolnicki informed Sikorski of this pro-Russian atmosphere, but the latter's tragic death at Gibraltar prevented the issue being raised with Eden. It must have annoyed the Poles considerably, especially as Poland was the first ally and had diplomatic priorities as well legitimate grievance with Stalin.[22]

An interesting new German document has revealed that Franz von Papen, head of the German spy network in Ankara, during Sokolnicki's time was approached by influential Polish and American V men with a request to provide anti-soviet material from Poland to put before President Theodore Roosevelt, who in the course of negotiations with Stalin, was reported to be 'fully taken in by the latter'. Apparently, the document states that items of correspondence were interchanged, following von Papen's request.[23]

German Secure Signals – *Auswartiges Amt*

On reading these freely accessible wartime documents, one realises how completely factual was some of the so called 'German propaganda material' which was transmitted from Berlin to all diplomatic posts.[24] A decryption of a German re-ciphered text dated 22 May 1943, intended as diplomatic conversation matter, was read by the British Intelligence staff and probably disregarded. It stated that:

> The discovery of mass graves of Polish officers near Smolensk has caused an extraordinary sensation in world opinion and particularly in Polish émigré circles. Both the German Red Cross and the Polish émigré Government in London referred the matter to the International Red Cross and asked that a delegation should be sent to investigate; but the Soviet Government, whose relations with the Polish émigré Government had for some time been very strained, principally on account of the question of Poland's eastern frontier, used the opportunity to make capital for their own view that Eastern Poland belong to the Soviet Union and also to disembarrass themselves of the uncomfortable

Sikorski Government, they therefore broke off diplomatic relations with the Polish émigré Government on 25th April 1943.

Against this resounding success of German propaganda the Soviets had nothing to offer but fairy tales about 'archaeological grave discoveries' and the lie, which has been refuted by official documents, foreign journalists and neutral medico-legal authorities, that the Germans had murdered the Polish officers. The British and North American Governments recognised that the rupture of relations between the Soviet Union and the Polish émigré Government would have undesirable consequences, not only for Poland's relationship to the Soviet Union, but also for their own, and further, that in view of the Atlantic Charter, the effect on the smaller States would not be favourable; they therefore set themselves to work at once and make vigorous efforts to put an end to the conflict. As a result the Polish émigré Government published a declaration, which was moderate in tone though its content was intransigent. It avoided the question of the International Red Cross being called on, but emphasised the integrity and unqualified sovereign rights of the Polish Republic and referred to the Polish-Soviet agreements of 30th July 1941 and 4th December 1941; it also repeated earlier demands that the Poles now in the Soviet Union should be released and that action to help them should be continued.

Further mediation was rendered difficult because in the first place it was impossible to accede to the Polish point of view on the real question at issue, namely the eastern frontier of Poland, without giving up one's own, further, because the British Government had already admitted the Soviet ambitions on Eastern Poland and finally, because the Soviet Government saw no kind of ground for renouncing its claims. These efforts produced nothing but ambiguous observation by Stalin in a letter to *The Times* correspondent and Sikorski's declaration on the subject and these made no change in the fundamental attitude of the two parties. Vyshinsky's aggressive pronouncement to representatives of the British and North American Press, criticised the Polish Government for evacuating the Polish army from the Soviet Union, also on the ground of espionage by Polish officials, and also for approving the attempt of a group of Polish communists to organise a 'Polish Division' in the Soviet Union, but this rather complicated the position and provoked in England and North America a feeling of bitter disillusion. The Polish-Soviet conflict is a splendid example of the differences, which exist between the Allies. The behaviour of the Soviet Government proves that its object is the bolshevisation of Poland and indeed of Europe, and further that it is still pursuing its claim to the immediate hegemony of eastern and south-eastern Europe, and that when the Polish and other émigré Governments in London entertain hopes of effective support from England and the United States, those hopes are a complete illusion.

Steengracht
[Gustav Adolf von Moyland]

SOE Interests in Katyn

The Polish Section of SOE, 'MP' (the cryptic designation for clandestine operations organisation), unwittingly became involved in the Katyn affair towards the end of April, as the news of the unearthed mass graves filtered through by radio messages from Warsaw. A memorandum entitled 'Katyn and After' was compiled for the Foreign Office and PWE (Political Warfare Executive) desks and must have been read by the political department of SOE and approved by its head, Major General Colin McVean Gubbins. Curiously, there is no sign of the report being read or used for briefs by the EE&R Department (East European and Russian) of the FO. The report is long and covers political issues, such as: the significance of the massacre for Poland and the western democracies, what the object of the massacre was, why the Soviets broke relations with the Poles and how all this affects SOE.[25]

The memorandum suggested that the news of finding the missing Polish officers did not surprise the London Poles - they almost expected it. What astonished them was that the dead bodies re-appeared so dramatically, and after being convinced of the truth of the German allegation, they were then compelled by the British to maintain silence about the massacre. It describes the Polish attitude towards the Western Allies as 'almost childlike faith in the honesty of purpose'. The memo writer suggested that the Poles simply did not believe that Britain and the US would abandon them to the mercy of Russia. But the reason for the massacre had to be based on past and future Soviet ambitions. The Soviets hoped to dominate Eastern Europe, especially Poland, hence perhaps the social makeup of the Katyn victims – officials, military men, administrators, teachers, political leaders, doctors, lawyers, academics, writers and priests, who were an obstacle to their domination and had to be eliminated. This is however a simplistic view of Stalin's motives to exterminate the elite of the Polish nation; the lack of documentation defying reasoning.

The main concern of SOE seems to be about those who were left behind in Poland, the *AK (Armia Krajowa)* Home Army, who were determined to survive by planning a general uprising, when the Western front was deemed close enough .The SOE document 'Katyn and After' refers to the possible clash in pointing out the Soviet anger at Sikorski bringing in the Red Cross.

> The Soviet reaction to the announcement is not convincing. The suggestion first made was apparently that the Germans were trying to pretend that prehistoric remains known to be in this area were those of Polish officers. The second explanation was that Polish PoWs had been engaged on construction work in this area in 1941 when they were over-run by the Germans and massacred, and that the Germans were now accusing the Soviets of this crime. The third suggestion is that they were captured in 1941 and were only massacred recently, which would account for the good state of preservation of the bodies. General Sikorski's action in asking for the Red Cross investigation

> has been violently condemned by the Soviets, which now suggest that General Sikorski and Hitler have concocted the whole matter as a frame-up. The balance of the evidence available appears to be that the German report is substantially correct.

Another report entitled 'German Propaganda' originated in Poland and was subsequently edited by the Polish Ministry of Internal Affairs in London. The report was circulated within departments, including PWE (Political Warfare Executive) and SIS (Secret Intelligence Service) whose head, known as 'C', requested an extra copy, thus expressing an interest.

Notes

1 TNA CAB 65/34, minutes of the War Cabinet meeting, confidential Annex, 13 April 1943.
2 Edward Raczyński (1891-1993) Polish diplomat, representative at the League of Nations 1932–1934, Ambassador to Britain 1934–1945, acting Foreign Minister 1940–1943. Prominent émigré politician in London.
3 Marian Kukiel (1885–1973) General, politician and military historian; veteran of the Polish Legions and the Polish-Soviet war 1919–1920. Between the wars Professor at the Jagiellonian University. Joined the Sikorski government as Minister of Defence.
4 TNA FO 371/34577 C 5947, hand-written note by Frank Roberts with minutes by Alexander Cadogan and Anthony Eden regarding suggestions as to how to avoid an embarrassing reply in Parliament.
5 Owen St Clair O'Malley (1887–1974) Entered Diplomatic Service in 1911, served in China 1925 and Yugoslavia; FO between 1933–1937, Minister Plenipotentiary to Mexico 1937–1938, British Embassy in Spain 1938–1939, Chargé d'Affaires in Budapest 1939-1941; Ambassador to the Polish government in exile in London 1941-1945, knighted 1943; after the war Ambassador to Portugal 1945–1947, retired in 1947; published historical articles and autobiography *The Phantom Caravan*, 1954.
6 Polish Institute and Sikorski Museum (PISM) KOL 12/16d, signal No. 2592 from Baghdad to the Polish Ministry of Defence in London 14 IV1943. Translation by EM.
7 TNA FO 371/ 34577 C6160/258/55 a typescript of nine pages, despatch no 51, written by O'Malley 24 May 1943 with additional annexes and enclosures no 52; SPP *Studium Polski Podziemnej* (Polish Underground Movement Study Trust) A.7.1.1.deciphered signal sent 13 May 1943; FO 688/31/9 C6160/G; PREM 3/353.
8 Orme Sargent (1884–1962) Third Secretary FO 1911, Second Secretary in Berne 1917 First Secretary and Peace Delegate to Paris in 1919; Deputy Assistant Under Secretary of State posted to Paris, made CMG in 1925, Counsellor at FO 1926; Assistant Under Secretary of State 1933, CB 1936, KCMG 1937, promoted to Deputy Under Secretary of State in 1939; Permanent Under Secretary of State 1946, made KCB in 1947, GCMG in 1948, retired in 1949.
9 William Denis Allen (1910-1987) Third Secretary in the FO 1934, on Far East staff, Chargé d'Affaires in Chunking 1942, FO during war time, First Secretary 1944, transferred to Washington in 1946, back in London head of German Political Department until 1949, Counsellor 1949–1953, made CMG 1950, Ambassador in Ankara till 1963, Deputy Under Secretary of State to 1967, retired in 1968. The quote is from FO 371/34577 C 6160/258/55.
10 At a Presidium meeting of 8 June 1943, it was decided to dissolve the Comintern, an International worker's organisation, as of 10 June 1943.

11 Andrey Vyshinsky (1883–1954) politician, lawyer, from 1935–39 Procurator General of the USSR, from 1949–53 Minister of Foreign Affairs and a Delegate to the United Nations Organisation.

12 Janusz Laskowski, born in 1908 near Smolensk, knew Katyn woods well, where he often cycled as a boy. A journalist of Socialist convictions, editor of pre-war *Iskra* (A spark) and *Kurier Wileński* (Wilno's Courier), released from Russia with the Polish Army in 1942. War correspondent and one of the editors of clandestine Radio Unit *Świt* (Dawn) engaged in black propaganda broadcasts 1943–44. In 1946 sent to Nuremberg to report on the Katyn trial. He was also instrumental in tracking down Herr Germandt in Germany, who in 1941 was posted to Katyn. Germandt's interview is recorded later.

13 Albert Frederick Pollard (1869–1948) constitutional historian at the University of London 1903, served on the Government Committee on the League of Nations, visiting Professor in Canada and USA, founder and Director of the Institute of Historical Research until 1939, contributed to the Dictionary of National Biography, wrote articles on parliamentary history for the English Historical Review.

14 James Headlam-Morley (1863–1929), historical adviser to the propaganda department in 1917 and the FO until 1928. Took part in negotiations at the Paris Peace Conference, (Treaty of Versailles), 28 June 1919.

15 John G. Winant, American Ambassador in London.

16 TNA FO 688/31/9 enclosure I in O'Malley's despatch No. 51 of May 24 1943. The list contains 49 names and rank of missing officers, as well as names of relatives in the UK.

17 TNA FO 371/34577/ C6161 C6160/258/55 Secure Signal 1943 May 15, from the underground organisation in Warsaw. Unauthorised copy obtained by O'Malley from his 'contacts' without prior knowledge of the Polish government- in-exile and asked by O'Malley to be treated as 'particularly secret'; SPP *Studium Polski Podziemnej* (Polish Underground Movement Trust) in London, ref. A.7.1.1. The original signal in Polish L.dz. 2290/tjn 43, Radiogram No. 779, Wanda 6, 13 5 43, deciphered 14 5 43 1030, despatched by 'Kalina' (Gen. Stefan Rowecki, head of AK) indicating the source of information as Dr Adam Schebesta of the PCK. In point 7 of the report, a sentence was intentionally omitted in translation by Lt Col Protasewicz, head of *Oddział VI*' (the VI Bureau), before being passed onto O'Malley; as indicated, it should have read 'All bullets are of 7.65 calibre, shells bear inscription Geco, the ropes are of twisted variety'.

18 TNA FO 371/34577 C.6160/258/55 refers to the report from Ambassador O'Malley about the disappearance of the Polish officers. Contains remarks and comments by FO officials including Sir Alexander Cadogan.

19 *The Diaries of Sir Alexander Cadogan O.M. 1938-1945*, edited by David Dilks, Cassell 1971, pp 520-528.

20 TNA CAB 65/34 Minutes of the War Cabinet 59 meeting 27 April 194; on the agenda Russo-Polish Relations; present at the meeting: W. Churchill PM, C. Attlee Secretary of State for Dominions, A. Eden Secretary of State for Foreign Affairs, E. Bevin, Minister of Labour and National Service, Sir Alexander Cadogan, Permanent Under- Secretary of State for Foreign Affairs, the three Chiefs of Staff, and many others.

21 Tehran Conference December 1943. The United States and Great Britain agreed with the USSR that the Polish boundary should go as far as the river Oder and the eastern boundary to run according to the Curzon Line. Stalin got his way with Eden and Churchill, who declared that 'Russia had to have security in the west.'

22 Michał Sokolnicki *Dziennik Ankarski 1939–1943* (Ankara Diary 1939–1943) London 1965, pp 503–547. Photograph of Madame Sokolnicka, Robin Hankey and Geoffrey Shaw originates from the book.

23 TNA GFM 33/403 No 262328 German Foreign Ministry Inland II g Collection entitled '*Geheime Reichssachen*' 1944 Vol. XV (box 3) dated 9 January 1944.

24 TNA HW 12/288 'Most Secret' German secure signal 117825,1943 May 22, transmitted via machine encryption, deciphered and translated by GCHQ and distributed in nine copies, entitled 'Russo-Polish Dispute – German Version' by the analysts at Berkeley St London. It was intercepted on 15 May 1943; GFM 33/2525, E 424331-2, shows original German text, nr Multex 459 dated 15th May 1943, sender Geheim Schrieber on Berlin to Berne link and signed by the Permanent Under Secretary Steengracht.

25 TNA HS 4/137 'Katyn and After', typescript carbon copy of a memorandum dated 21 April 1943, sent to L/S (Political Liaison Section, cryptic designation for GSOII) to Major T. G. Roche RA, Intelligence Division of SOE by 'MPX' (Major Richard Truszkowski 1897–1988), an SOE desk officer GSO II, who got to know the Russians during a previous posting to Russia. Truszkowski was born in the UK of Polish parents who were political exiles. Studied Chemistry, first in England then in Poland. During WW I served in France and then with the North Russia Expeditionary Force. At the outbreak of WW 2, joined the British Military Mission in Warsaw. Served again in Russia, France and Middle East. Awarded *Krzyż Walecznych,* the Polish Cross of Valour in 1943. The file also contains a comprehensive report entitled 'German Propaganda', edited by the Polish Ministry of Internal Affairs in London, which attracted more attention from the Secret Intelligence Service (SIS), than the memorandum.

chapter three

CRIME SCENE REPORTS

Throughout April and May 1943, the *AK* (Home Army) despatched secure signals to the Polish government in London. The first four were picked up by *Oddział VI,* the Polish Special Operations Bureau of the Polish General Staff, headed by Lt Col Michał Protasewicz on 19 and 26 April, 15 and 27 May 1943, respectively.[1] Signals on 10 and 15 April covered the first two visits to Katyn by a group of Poles, who, after their return to Warsaw, were in agreement with the German statement, but probably not with the total of the dead, which they guessed. The following secure signal of 15 May, to which O'Malley referred, has been covered earlier. However, there are serious implications regarding the *GECO* rounds, which need clarification.

As already mentioned, the first information about the spent cartridge cases was brought to Warsaw by the first group of Poles who, after their visit to Katyn, met with *Herrn* Heinrich, a German official from the *Propagandaamt*, who immediately informed Hans Frank the *Gouvernergeneral* resident in Kraków. At the Nuremberg Trials on 2 July 1946, the Soviet Prosecutor Nikolai Smirnov produced Heinrich's Teletype of 3 May 1943, sent to *Herrn Oberverwaltungsrat* Weirauch, claiming the Americans had offered the document to him.[2] It read:

> Urgent, to be delivered at once. Secret. Part of the Polish Red Cross returned yesterday from Katyn. The employees of the Polish Red Cross have brought with them the cartridge cases, which were used in shooting the victims of Katyn. It appears that these are German munitions. The calibre is 7.65, they are from the firm Geco. Letter follows. Heinrich.

The same Polish source had sent a report to the *AK* Command, which reached London belatedly on 15 May 1943. It contained a sentence about the *GECO* rounds which was erased from the translated version passed to O'Malley, presumably by Protasewicz, who must have been alarmed by it, as it undermined the theory that the perpetrators were the Soviets, whose culpability was confirmed by all the other evidence. Dr Buhts' report, which was part of the *Amtliches Material* on Katyn published in Berlin 1943, admitted that *GECO* ammunition from Gustav Genschow & Co, near Karlsruhe, was used for the executions; and that the retrieved bullets from the graves indicated manufacture dates between 1922 and 1931. This ammunition was exported in large quantities to Poland, the Baltic States and to Russia before the war. The War Office on this matter should, have briefed the British War Crimes Executive (BWCE). No wonder the Soviet statement at the Trials dumfounded the British lawyers, as reflected in Phillimore's reports: 'The Russians had much the best of the argument and rightly so.' The FO Research Department (FORD) analysis of the Soviet report of 1944, refers to this subject again, quoting an obscure statement by the War Office that 'the Russians are not known to use 7.65 mm pistols, but the German officers and police, widely use it – though, it is not a regular army weapon.' These manipulations of crucial facts, brings us to the real issue, was it relevant to the case? The Soviets well knew they could not rest their case solely on the *GECO* ammunition as evidence against the Germans.

The inflow of secure signals that reached London indicated to the Allies that in spite of the Soviets' refusal to accede to the formal request by the International Committee of the Red Cross to inspect the mass graves, the Germans had started a propaganda campaign by bringing groups of people, German and foreign, to witness the exhumation. More importantly, they expected the arrival of an international committee of pathologists from twelve neutral countries[3] to give a verdict on the massacre. A team of Polish professionals under the auspices of the Polish *PCK* arrived in stages as early as 15 April 1943, while the Allied PoWs, mostly British and American, arrived involuntarily a month later, in early May 1943.

The outcome of these frequent visits to Katyn generated a number of vital additional and supplementary reports and depositions. Some were technical in nature and these can be traced in various publications: Professor Gerhard Buhtz's *Amtliches Material zum Massenmord von Katyn,* Berlin 1943, which includes the official medical report of the International Committee under Dr Leonard Conte; The *PCK* reports written by Mr Kazimierz Skarżyński,[4] General Secretary of the *PCK,* who incorporated Jerzy Wodzinowski's report marked C, with technical drawings, into his 1943 all inclusive *PCK* report; and lastly, Dr Marian Wodziński's[5] pathology report, which became the backbone of *Facts and Documents concerning Polish Prisoners of War captured by the USSR during the 1939 Campaign*. It was circulated in a limited edition in 1946[6] and later incorporated in part in the first edition *Zbrodnia Katyńska w świetle dokumentów* (Katyn massacre in the light of documents) originally written and edited by Józef Mackiewecz.[7]

Towards the end of 1945 and the beginning of 1946, in expectation of these reports being used in evidence at the International Military Tribunal at Nuremberg, they were updated with additional accounts, like the circumstantial evidence of Ferdynand Goetel,[8] a Warsaw literary figure, who was the first to visit Katyn and produced an initial verbal report for Skarżyński, who also visited Katyn on 16 April and subsequently passed his official *PCK* statement destined for Geneva through the Polish government in London.

There was also a striking deposition made on 31 May 1945 by Ivan Krivozertsev, a Belorussian peasant who informed the Germans about the whereabouts of the burials of the Polish officers. Krivozertsev was the most important witness, who had lived nearby and observed activities in the Katyn area. In September 1943 Krivozertsev joined the retreating German troops and worked on Berlin's railway lines. In 1945, he looked for asylum from the 1st Polish Armoured Division stationed near Wilhelmshaven. He was interrogated and sent to Italy, where he was temporarily assigned to the Red Cross section, which enabled him eventually to come to Britain with the Polish 2 Corps in 1946. Krivozertcev gave his story to Goetel, who wrote it down, ending it by saying that Katyn was constantly on his mind and that he lived for the moment when he would be able to testify before judge and jury. On arrival in Britain, he was given a new name and sadly, owing to his drinking habit, he moved from place to place, uncontrolled by the Polish or British security services. Krivozertsev, the principal witness of the massacre, was found dead in the tranquil English countryside of Gloucestershire in 1947.

Another curious recollection comes from *Herr* Germandt, a former German medical orderly – one would have thought, a reliable witness of the discovery of the grave, who, like Krivozertsev, was alive but not called upon at the Nuremberg Trials or any other subsequent enquiry. His interesting and little known story follows in a later chapter.

Last, but not least, are the American and British PoWs, who were taken to Katyn in early May 1943, and produced 'Top Secret' informative reports. The background story of their visit is recorded in Lt Col John Van Vliet's deposition, re-written in 1950 for the Congressional Hearings of 1952. Both reports were routinely classified by virtue of their content and method of collection and therefore unavailable to the Hearings.

It is interesting to compare the accounts of the meeting of two medical men at Katyn, the Polish Doctor Wodziński and the British Army Medical Officer Captain Stanley Gilder. Their recollections differ slightly, which is understandable. Controversial passages are here underlined for ease of extraction from the maze of other information. Notice should be given to Gilder's references to PoW Colonel Frank Stevenson, who was with them and who in 1952 was willing to make a deposition for the US Select Committee. The British authorities did not take up his offer on the American's behalf! The relevant FO file indicates that in 1952 he was living in Durban and was willing to stand as a witness for the USA Congressional Investigation Committee, and bring with him important material on Katyn. The FO officials did not contact him further and the Congressmen went home unaware of Stevenson's potential testimony.

The archives at the Polish Institute and Sikorski Museum, together with the National Archives, hold numerous reports of different dates and lengths. It would be impractical to include them all here as many of them overlap in content and detail. Therefore, for comparison of facts, a selection has been made of the most significant material, previously unpublished, documented in 1945–1946.

Stanisław Wójcik's MI 19 Interrogation

The FO was aware of many visits to Katyn and reports were available not only through the Poles but the British 'Royal Patriotic School' in Wandsworth, London's screening centre for all incoming foreigners to be interrogated by MI 19 (Military Intelligence branch primarily concerned with debriefing PoWs). On 29 May 1944, Stanisław Wójcik who had direct knowledge of the Katyn massacre [9] had arrived in the UK via Norway and Sweden. MI 19 graded his information C (Z), which meant not a very reliable source of unknown veracity.

Stanisław Wójcik was born in Pustelnik in Poland on 4 July 1924. He was registered with the *Arbeitsamt* (labour office) as a welder in late 1940 and managed to avoid being sent to Germany owing to his father's black market dealings. He bribed the Germans with food. Germany's drive for labour was intensified in 1942 and Wójcik thought his fate would be kinder if this time he volunteered for work. He turned up at 11 Wiejska Street, Warsaw in January 1943 for a job with the German company *IMO*. With a team of workers he was assigned a plumbing job in a newly constructed field laundry for German troops at Smolensk. By that time, German propaganda was in full swing and many people were obliged to visit the graves. On Sunday 18 July 1943, Wójcik with five other Poles, twenty Germans and three Russian women set off in a truck for Katyn, a journey of about 7 km. According to Wójcik, they saw two dug up graves in a sandy hillock, the first, he was told, contained some 2,000–3,000 Polish officers, the second around 2,000 officers and NCOs and the third grave, which was soon to be opened, allegedly held more bodies than either of the first two. The account of the murders was described to them in German and translated into Polish by a bilingual factory foreman.

According to the German guide, after about 90 Poles had been shot by three Russians, one of them an airman, the latter then shot the other two in order to preserve the secret of the killings. After interrogation when he disclosed his part in the massacre the Russian airman was later also shot dead.

The papers and letters found on the bodies were read out to them because they were not allowed to view them or touch the bodies. They saw a display of Polish coins. The Germans did not call the local people to witness this, although the farm hands were quite near the vicinity. Wójcik noted that the stench was awful and it made him sick for two days. He thought the decomposition was advanced and the killings must have been done when the Russians were in the area, that is, before the German occupation. The MI 19 interrogator noted that, as regards corpse decomposition, Wójcik would have had no idea how rapidly such disintegration progresses. In conclusion, the interrogator noted that Wójcik said the Germans made no attempt to engage the Poles in a crusade of vengeance against the Bolsheviks. They had simply said in effect: 'Here are the graves containing your murdered compatriots, here are the facts, draw your own conclusion as to which policy to follow.' When the group left Katyn, they were convinced that the Russians had committed this terrible crime.

Ferdynand Goetel's Recollections

Ferdinand Goetel, a well-known writer and chairman of the Polish *PEN* Club, found himself in difficult and controversial circumstances when he decided to go to Katyn with the first group of five Poles, on 10 April 1943, to inspect the burial site. He reported the findings directly to the *PCK* (Polish Red Cross) in Warsaw and to the Polish Underground authorities. It also appeared in *Biuletyn Informacyjny* as an open letter, in consequence of which the Polish communist press castigated him as a Nazi collaborator. He had to lie low and towards the end of 1945, living under the communists, he decided to escape from Poland to join the Polish Army, still stationed in Italy. He repeated his earlier testimony on oath to the Military Court attached to the forces in 1943.[10] Goetel was engaged by the *Biuro Informacji i Propagandy* (Department of Information and Propaganda), primarily to gather further statements from Polish soldiers who had been in Soviet camps or from eyewitnesses like Krivozertsev, whose recollections follow Goetel's, below.[11]

In the first days of April 1943, I was telephoned by Władysław Zyglarski, the Secretary of the Association of Writers and Journalists, and during the German occupation, one of the members of the so-called Literary Committee of the *RGO* [*Rada Główna Opiekuńcza* – Council for Social Welfare], that I am keenly sought after by Dr [Karl] Grundmann from the *Propaganda Abteilung* [Propaganda Unit] …

Realising that something new had happened, I went to see Grundmann that afternoon. He informed me that not far from Smolensk in a place called Kozie Góry [Koze Gory], German military intelligence had discovered large communal graves, where Polish officers are buried. They started to open the graves, which gave unusual results. There must be several thousands of victims. The German authorities were greatly moved by this site and intended to support the Polish delegation by giving them assistance and not demanding from them any declarations, which might be used for German propaganda.

I was taken aback with the news, which immediately suggested to me that Koze Gory might hold the mystery of Polish prisoners of war in Kozelsk, Starobelsk and Ostashkov camps. I thought a while and asked Grundmann why he didn't turn to the *PCK* with this problem, which is a fitting institution, with its rules and its significant standing among the Polish community. Grundmann agreed, but pointed to certain considerations, which made co-operation between that institution and Germany very difficult and pointed out they were probably well known to me.

Actually, I knew of the attitude of the Germans towards the *PCK*, which was the only remaining organisation in the General Gouvernment [*Generalgouvernment*], which represented the remnants of sovereignty of the Polish State. Guarded by international law, it resisted many attempts by the

Germans to liquidate it. As a result, it scarcely formally existed and was reduced to caring for the 1939 casualties.

Realising that the *PCK* might be strengthened by the news from Koze Gory – if it was true – I agreed on condition that if I decided to go to Katyn, I would make a report to the *PCK*. Before then I wanted to know who was taking part in the delegation. Grundmann declared that representatives of the Warsaw Council of *RGO*, city councillors and representatives of the judiciary and clergy were invited. I was going to see them all tomorrow morning at an informative conference in *Propagandaamt* and departure would be in three days time by plane. I then declared that in these circumstances I agreed to take part, provided it was understood that my judgement about what I was about to see would not be bound by anything, I was acting as a Polish spokesman, I did not intend to keep secret what I was about to see in Koze Gory, and I would share my observations with the Polish community through every means possible. Grundmann accepted my conditions.

On leaving Grundmann, I hastily sought contacts for consultations with the Underground [*AK*] organisations he mentioned. I was a member of the *Obóz Polski Walczącej (OPW)* [Political group of Fighting Poland] and the editor of *Nurt*. I did not have direct contact with my superior Julian Piasecki. His contact 'Koral' was to see me in few days time so I took the option of contacting Marian Buczkowski who lived near me and through his contact with 'Marta' I managed to pass ae message about my talks with Grundmann to 'Hubert' [Koral, Marta and Hubert codenames], the head of propaganda for the Warsaw District *BIP* [*Biuro Informacji i Propagandy* of *AK, Armia Krajowa* – Bureau of Information and Propaganda, Home Army]. According to Buczkowski, 'Hubert' ignored my account, suggesting that 'the Germans were bluffing Goetel,' nonetheless, he gave permission for me to go, and requested a report after my return.

I telephoned [Julian] Kulski, President of Warsaw and Machnicki, Chairman of the *RGO* and they did not deny that a trip was also offered to them, however they had showed some lack of interest, perhaps due to their apprehension. Theirs and 'Hubert's' standpoint had annoyed me somewhat. The automatic dislike for any kind of initiative shown by the Germans did not seem warranted in this case. I knew that Katyn would be painful and fearful for all who touched it. Whatever we were about to see, the German or Bolshevik attacks were awaiting us. We had a foretaste of the latter in Warsaw.

At the next day's sitting at *'Propagandaamt'*, I met the town deputies in person: Dr Kip [Emil Kipa] and Director [Władysław] Zawistowski, Kulski excused himself due to being busy. Warsaw's *RGO* was represented by Director Machnicki and [Stanisław] Wachowiak, the clergy by Reverend [Zygmunt] Kozubski, and the judiciary by someone unknown to me. Besides them there were a few others, whose names I do not remember. There was also Emil Skiwski the writer, whom Dr Gundmann did not mention to me.

Grundmann repeated the same story about Koze Gory with more details, and then read a list of names asking each if they were agreeable to go. The Rev. Kozubski excused himself, having a dislike of travelling by plane and his superior [Bishop Antoni W.] Szlagowski was unwell. Similarly Wachowiak and Machnicki, who proposed substitutes for the *RGO* and the City as Dr Kip could not come either. As regards representation of the judiciary, its chairman was seriously ill and someone else would be sent directly to the airport. As far as I remember, Rev. Kozubski for the clergy gave a similar declaration. (Neither of the delegates turned up at the airport).

The following day [10 April] at the airport, I met two doctors, one from the Warsaw City Council the other from *RGO*, additionally, Emil Skiwski and a few photographers. There was no official press present but a man introduced himself as the editor of a newspaper from Lublin. There was Edward Seyfried, Director of the Executive Committee of the *RGO*, as well as [Frederich, Wilhelm] Ohlenbusch, chief of German *Propaganda Amt* in General Gouvernment, he was assisted by a German and a cameraman in uniform, all of them arrived by plane from Kraków. Additionally, another Pole turned up from Radio Kraków, who introduced himself as Wąsowicz [Władysław Kawecki].

We arrived at Smolensk about noon. In the afternoon, assisted by the Germans, we toured the city. In the evening in the officer's mess we were introduced to three officers from the Propaganda Section of the Smolensk Army; two Lieutenants and one Captain. Lieutenant [Gregor] Slovenzik, of the reserve, [*Oberleutnant* Gregor Slovenzik was attached to the propaganda service in *Heeresgruppe Mitte* in Smolensk], was born in Vienna, supposedly a journalist by profession, the second was a sculptor from Innsbruck. Listening to our conversation was a Lieutenant from the *Geheimpolizei*; I expect it was Foss [*Leutnant* Ludvig Voss, *Geheime Feldpolizei sekretar, GFP Gruppe 570*], of whom I learned later.

OLt Slovenzik gave us a more accurate version of Katyn, he showed us photographs of the woods, the corpses and the documents found on them. There were a few things worth examining. ... The trail to the graves was found by *Feldpolizei*, who questioned the local people living near Koze Gory, which was part of the large Katyn woods, stretching along the Dnieper River and the main road running from Smolensk to Vitebsk. The local people maintained that for a long time Koze Gory was guarded by the *NKVD* as it was used as a place of execution, and that many thousands of Polish officers were shot and buried there in mass graves. Apparently, the Polish workers in the *Organisation Todt* [12] later found these graves. They inspected one excavated spot in the ground, and finding the statements of the locals to be true, erected a wooden cross, of which only a photograph exists, the cross must have disappeared when the first large excavations began. In any case, it served as a guide where to start the works. When asked if they had traced the Polish workers, they said no.

The second story, which is more interesting than the first, was that Slovenzik, who presented the events of Katyn in such dramatic terms from the Polish point of view – did not know where these massacred officers came from! He only knew from the locals that transports with officers arrived from Smolensk. He already had in his possession postcards and letters found on the corpses, so he was baffled why the address of Kozelsk appeared on them. I told him what I knew about the prison camps at Starobelsk, Ostashkov and Kozelsk, while keenly observing his reaction. His reaction was animated and made the impression on me that Slovenzik had learned something from us. This was also the only moment during our conversation that Slovenzik made notes. After our conversation had ended, I heard him sharing the news with Ohlenbusch and other Germans. I believe Voss was not in the mess at the time.

The following morning, we went to Koze Gory by car. We stopped in the woods and alighted near a long excavated ditch. The ditch was probably the length of the whole grave and to its bottom but not taking its whole width, as was shown by the arms, legs and heads left at the sides. The cross section indicated that the bodies were put in neat rows, one upon the other. The mass grave on the incline of the hill contained dry soil at the top and a mixture of clay and sand at the bottom, wet due to the water table. Nearby, we saw the excavation of another mass grave, showing only the first layer of bodies. The local Russian people did the work on both graves.

Next to the grave there was a temporary hut, where a team of pathologists under Dr Buhtz, [Gerhard Buhtz, *Heeresgruppenartz Mitte*, Head of Army Group Medical Services] Professor of Forensic Medicine from Wrocław [Breslau] was working. When in uniform, Prof Buhtz held the rank of a Colonel. It was evident that the excavation had only started. On a grass field nearby lay about 200 excavated bodies waiting for a post-mortem. The corpses were numbered and put in several rows. Around Buhtz's hut several of them lay, probably already inspected. Parts of uniforms were hanging on the branches of the trees. The whole scene gave the impression of an as yet unplanned start to the work. Prof. Buhtz asked us to choose a body and he would perform a post mortem in our presence, so we pointed to one in the middle of the grave. The post-mortem showed a shot through skull with the entry and exit points of the bullet. The pockets cut open by knife during the post-mortem revealed a postcard addressed to a Cavalry Captain, whose name I do not remember, it was written by his wife and came from the Grodno region, sent to the Kozelsk address.

Among the bodies laid out around the hut were those of General [Mieczysław] Smorawiński and General Bohatyrewicz [Bronisław Bohaterewicz]. At my request, Dr Buhtz cut off Smorawiński's rank insignia and the ribbon of the *Virtuti Militari* from the coat of Bohaterewicz. These items, together with some buttons from other overcoats and a handful of soil, I took with me to Warsaw.

These reliquaries I kept at home until the Warsaw Uprising, when they were destroyed by fire along with my house.

We toured round the whole terrain and soon learned how to identify unearthed graves; their edges were sunken in, the surface uneven; besides, they had young pine trees planted on them, without a doubt purposefully. These small, even-size trees stood out among the rest of the woods, which was wild looking and neglected, although not that old. The pines planted on the graves looked healthy and well rooted, and must have grown for more than a year. Dr Buhtz gave me a list of names of the dead that he had already identified; there were about thirty names. I managed to update the list later in Grushchenka [a village] on my return journey.

During our stay in Koze Gory, broadcasts of German propaganda were transmitting the progress of our visit. They tried several times to entice us to state that the Bolsheviks committed the massacre. We tried to avoid it, but eventually, after being persistently harangued, I said only one sentence, that in my understanding, inside those graves there were bodies of prisoners of war from Kozelsk, about whom there had been no information since April 1940. Someone named Wąsowicz gave a longer and rather pathetic speech.

Before departing from Koze Gory I asked the Germans to leave us alone for prayers. They moved away and Director Seyfried said the following words: 'I call the whole Polish delegation to hold a minute's silence, to pay homage to those Poles who died so that Poland might live.' I included these words when I wrote my report for the *PCK* and at my request, a copy was sent to the German Propaganda office.

Besides taking part in radio propaganda, we were not troubled by the Germans in any way. We had freedom of movement and the conversation we had with the local people were unrestricted and freely given. On our return journey to Smolensk, we stopped at Grushchenka, where at a roadside building, neatly arranged in glass show cases, were artefacts found on the bodies in Koze Gory.

I should mention that during our stay in Koze Gory, some delegates from our group talked with the local people, when I did not take part but listened. These people confirmed totally the German theory regarding Koze Gory as a place of longstanding scenes of crime, as well as of the shooting of Polish officers by the Bolsheviks. I did not take part in these talks, because lack of time and strained nerves did not allow us to ask more precise questions and receive answers.

That evening we returned to Warsaw. After that, I wrote a report for the *PCK*. Its copy, with my comments and the list of names of the first identified victims was sent via Buczkowski to 'Hubert', and through 'Koral' for Julian Piasecki. Presenting the report to the *PCK* I asked them also to send a copy to Dr Grundmann of *'Propagandaamt*.' The reason why I acted this way had nothing to do with the 'co-operation' with '*Propagandaamt*' on Katyn. By sending a report for Grundmann, I wanted to force the German authorities to put the investigation into the hands of the Polish Red Cross – as well as to overcome the reluctance seen in the Red Cross and equally in other institutions, to look into the Katyn affair. Wanting to present the question more dramatically, I made several copies of the report and gave them to people I trusted. It is difficult now to tell who read and remembers the report. I know for certain that people who read it in Poland are: Jerzy Zagórski, Marian Buczkowski [Wilhelm] Horzyca, Józef Targowski and Alfred Wysocki. People living in England: Wiesław Wohnout and Lt Wiktor Trościanko.

The report described our trip to Katyn, its first impressions and the conclusion – that the graves contain, according to every possible conjecture, all the officers from Kozelsk and maybe other victims. Also I gave an assurance that 'I would not give any other statements in this respect, now or in the future.' It also contained a recommendation that the International Committee of the Red Cross should be entrusted with the investigation of Koze Gory.

I am giving all these details about the report, because in 1945, when I was being issued with a warrant, I asked my daughter to contact the *PCK* and obtain a copy of my report, as mine had been burned with other documents in Warsaw. The reply was that they did not have the report; if this were true, it would be interesting to find out where it had gone. A few days after my arrival I got the news from 'Hubert' that my report was immediately delivered to General [Stefan] Rowecki [Leader of the *AK*], who asked for his appreciation to be passed on, that I had 'served Poland well by [my] conduct regarding Katyn'. The report was going to be sent forthwith to London. Marian Buczkowski who acted as a go-between 'Hubert' and myself, passed this information to me. Buczkowski co-operated with the Propaganda Department of the *AK* in Warsaw, where he was in charge of 'cell R'.

After the Bolsheviks entered Poland and had issued a search warrant for me; I was still in Poland for a time. The idea of attending court interested me, in the belief I could possibly raise the Katyn case. However, the authorities did not pursue me. The *PCK* has somewhere 'mislaid' my report on Katyn, and the news reached me that the majority of Poles who visited Katyn, whatever the mission, had signed a declaration presented to them by the [communist] procurator. The declaration read that they were forced by the Germans to visit Katyn and once they were there, they were convinced that the massacre was the deed of the Germans. I realised then, that under no circumstances would I be allowed to say a word about what I knew of Katyn. I left Poland in December 1945. In January 1946 I was in Italy and in October 1946 in England.

Ferdynand Goetel

London, 19 December 1946.

Ivan Krivozertsev's Deposition

On 31 May 1945, in the British Zone of occupied Germany at a Displaced Persons camp at Verden (Aller), a Belorussian by the name of Ivan Krivozertsev turned up looking for help. One of the camp's Liaison Officers was a Pole, Major Wiktor Grubert, one-time consular official of the Polish government in London, to whom Krivozertsev presented his *Arbeitskarta* No.6910/40/439014, issued by *Staat- sangeh-origkeit-ungeklart* in Berlin, dated 2 September 1944. It was a special card for Russians who collaborated with the Germans. According to Grubert's report, Krivozertsev, a peasant who was barely literate was of average intelligence but canny and knew what awaited him on the Russian side. Born on 20 July 1915 in Nove Batoki, he lived all his life in nearby village of Grushchenka, about 3 km from Gnezdovo, where he had a smallholding. He was trained as a metal turner in a repair shop, but at the outbreak of war worked on a kolkhoz – a state collective farm.

At the beginning of March 1940, Krivozertsev with other locals noticed a gang of prisoners from Smolensk arrive at Koze Gory to dig ditches in the woods. The work lasted a few days and everyone understood the sinister aspect of the preparations. During the Russian Revolution and the years of Stalin's purges, Katyn became a place of execution and burial. Krivozertsev, like other villagers knew about the arrival of the Polish officers who were brought into the woods from Gnezdovo railway station; they heard the shots and never saw them return where they came from. Trespassing in the woods was severely forbidden by the *NKVD*.

In mid-July 1941, the Germans had overrun Smolensk district including Gnezdovo and in the summer of 1942, the local people informed the Poles who were amongst the travelling workers of *Organisation Todt* that the Polish officers were buried in Katyn woods nearby. Krivozertsev did not notify the Germans until April 1943, which is quite late, but apparently he thought the Germans were not that bothered. He only came out with the information when the news of a large number of missing Polish officers was published in the newspapers and realised then, that the German propaganda machine was interested in publicising his statement. During the German retreat from Smolensk in September 1943, Krivozertsev fearing for his life, left with them and was given a job as a labourer on the railways in Berlin. When the Russian army captured the city, he escaped westwards looking for the Polish army units stationed in the northwest of occupied Germany.

Grubert, in his interrogation of Krivozertsev before the Field Court, was not interested in details, but short personal descriptions and what Krivozertsev knew of the Katyn massacre, who had done it and when. He informed his superiors about the arrival of Krivozertsev, General Klemens Rudnicki as well as Major G.F. Hunt, RA the British 102 MGD(R) – Military Government Detachment (Relief) – by sending them three copies of the interrogation report, signed by Krivozertsev, asking Major Hunt specifically to pass one copy to the Polish government in London. Having no reply by June 1945, Grubert once again sent two translated copies to Major Hunt and to the Polish Minister of Foreign Affairs, Adam Tarnowski. The report was called a 'rough copy' of what Krivozertsev had said. Apparently, none of the copies had reached London and no traces are found in the War Office files, except in the Polish Institute and Sikorski Museum. On 25 June 1945, Grubert was transferred to another post, while Major Hunt was still awaiting a decision from London as to what to do with Krivozertsev.

The next mention of a DP (Displaced Person), is in a secure signal from Washington on 28 May 1952, from Sir Oliver Franks, the British Ambassador. He enquired on behalf of the Congressional investigation into the Katyn massacre about the submission of relevant documents of which they had heard, such as: Colonel Hulls' second report, documents seized from the Germans by the British authorities, Captain Gilder's report, and the whereabouts of Ivan Krivozertsev and Ivan Andreev who once lived in England, or any information concerning the circumstances surrounding Krivozertsev's death. No doubt the question of German pressure on Russian witnesses to give the evidence they wanted must have been on their minds, but the FO would not oblige the Americans with frank replies, arguing that the British-held material was not to be disclosed on grounds of security. In April 1952, a reply came from Robert Cecil, Head of the American Department of the FO, that Krivozertsev (alias Mikhail Loboda) had committed suicide by hanging in 1947. According to the Home Office, no suggestion was offered at the inquest as to the possible motives behind Loboda taking his own life.[13]

As mentioned before, there are two typescript copies of Krivozertsev's deposition, one written in Germany on 22 May 1946, in the presence of a Judge Advocate General, Kazimierz Lewicki, and signed by both men; the other in Italy in October 1946 drafted in narrative form by Ferdynand Goetel in Ancona, where he was engaged in the Culture and Press Bureau of 2 Polish Corps. Although the latter is more revealing and easier to read, the initial interrogation in Germany is the most important of all the extant witness depositions ever written:

> At the beginning of March 1940 it was rumoured that the *NKVD* would be erecting some buildings in the forest in Koze Gory as the ground was being excavated for foundations. These were dug by the civilian prisoners, brought there from prison in Smolensk, in three or four lorries under *NKVD* guard. I saw with my own eyes the transport of these prisoners. This work was started at the beginning of March. I imagine that these prisoners came from Smolensk because the lorries arrived from that direction. When this work was completed, transports of officers began to arrive at Gnezdovo station. I recall that these transports first came when peace was concluded with Finland and it was even said at first that the *NKVD* were transporting Finnish officers. But already on the second day some of the neighbouring inhabitants had recognised Polish uniforms and it became known that these were trains containing Polish officer prisoners of war.

Special trains composed of the engine and 3-4 *'stolypinki'* [prison wagons] brought these transports. Sometimes there were small two-axle wagons and sometime larger four-axle wagons. The whole train was shunted to the siding near the storehouse, where there was a small yard. There, a *chorny voron* [14] [black crow – a 'black Maria, slange for a prison van] would back up to the wagon and the officers were then transferred into it. There were two *chorny vorons* and in addition a lorry on which the belongings of the officers were piled. There was also a car. The supervisor (*nachelnik*) travelled by passenger car, he was an *NKVD* officer. I was not able to see his rank insignia very clearly, but it seems to me that he was a Major General (in the Red Army). After the officers were loaded into the *chorny voron* the entire column composed of these four cars drove away in the direction of Koze Gory in order to execute them. In spite of the fact that no one actually saw the execution, it was known that no [PoW] camps existed in the forest in Koze Gory and moreover, this place was known to have been a place of execution for a number of years.

The escorts consisted of *NKVD* men from Smolensk and I knew personally the driver of one *chorny voron*; his name was Jakim Razuvayev, he was called Kim for short. I also knew a driver called Pietka (I do not remember his surname) who drove a lorry on which the belongings of the officers were conveyed to the forest of Koze Gory and who had been dismissed from *NKVD* services and was working in the *Soyuz-trans* in Smolensk. He stated even before the arrival of the Germans that the *NKVD* had shot these officers.

A relative of mine told me that when the wagons with the officers were shunted to the blind-siding; he had seen among the escort an *NKVD* man of his acquaintance. He started talking with him and asked him whether these officers were being transferred to camps. This man replied: 'And where are these camps here? Why do you talk such nonsense, don't you know where they take such people?'

The personnel of the *NKVD's dacha* (country house) was composed of three or four persons, they stayed there for a short time and did not live there. Not far from the *NKVD's dacha*, in the village of Borek, there was a large *NKVD* sanatorium. During the German occupation, a senior German officer lived there with his ADC; he was said to be a General. No military unit ever stayed there. Approximately ten persons including the General might have stayed there at the most.

After the 1939 campaign there were no camps for Polish prisoners of war in the vicinity of Gnezdovo and Katyn or further west. Neither was any road works carried out in the neighbourhood, apart from normal maintenance work by roadmen. German troops occupied the region of Gnezdovo on 27 July 1941 and Smolensk (the upper part of the city) on approx. 16 July. For 13 days, until the entry of German troops, no one was in authority and everyone was his own master. There were, it is true, a few defeated Soviet units in retreat, the last of which had withdrawn by 26 July after blowing up the rail-track and road bridges; but no order whatever prevailed.

In the spring of 1942, Polish workers employed by the *Organisation Todt* and who were collecting scrap iron learned from the local inhabitants that there were graves of executed Polish officers in the Koze Gory forest. I myself overheard such a conversation. I learned from [Parfeon] Kiselev that these workers went to see him and asked him to point out the graves and Kiselev led them to the spot; the Polish workers marked the graves with a small wooden cross. I myself saw this cross.

In January 1943, there appeared in the *Novy Put* [local newspaper] published in Russian by the Germans in Smolensk, an article describing the crimes committed by the Bolsheviks on territories occupied in 1939. There was a mention of the deportation to Siberia of hundreds of thousands of people of whom a large number had subsequently died there; and finally, it was remarked that General Sikorski had failed to trace in Russia the whereabouts of several thousand Polish officers, while he was organising the Polish Army in the USSR.

When I read this article, I began to talk it over with the German interpreter and I said to him, among other things, 'Why are they searching for these officers in Russia, they were shot in the Koze Gory forest and their bodies lie there.' This interpreter, who was working for the *Geheim Feldpolizei*, told me that I would be going somewhere the next day with the *Geheim Feldpolizei*. On the following day, two locals and myself set off by cart in the direction of Koze Gory. With us went two *feldwebels* (constables) [German senior NCOs as field police with power of arrest] on motorcycles. One of them called Arholz or Eicholz [Friedrich Ahrens] spoke Russian. I am practically certain that in March or April 1946, I came across this man in the camp in Fallingbostel, where he was a prisoner of war. This Arholz or Eiholz might possibly be able to supply information as to the fate of Ivan Vasilevich Andreev from Nove Batoki, who evacuated himself and his wife together with Arholz to Minsk, where a daughter was born to them. I do not know what happened to them afterwards.

When we arrived near the *NKVD dacha*, these two NCOs asked me where the graves of the Polish officers were. I replied that I did not know but that I would go to Kiselev, who was living nearby and who would certainly know something about it. Kiselev was at home, lying in an alcove over the heated stove, and when I told him what it was about, he replied that the Polish workers had already asked him the same question a year ago. So I said 'We are now going to dig up these graves.' Kiselev got dressed and walked out with me and took us to the graves.

We first broke up the frozen soil with pickaxes and then started digging with shovels. After we dug a fairly deep hole, there arose a smell of decay. As my two colleagues could not bear this smell and suffered from acute nausea, I, who suffered less, was left alone to dig to the end. We were digging up sand the whole time and at the bottom of the pit, there was a thin layer of darkened soil under which lay the corpses. I saw a military grey coat and short belt at the back, because the corpses lay face downwards. I then pulled off the button from the short belt and polished it and saw it was a button with an eagle on it. I gave this button to the German who looked at it and then wrapped it up in a bit of paper. They left off digging and returned to Koze Gory.

Shortly after reaching Gnezdovo, *Leutnant* [Ludvig] Voss of the *Geheim Feldpolitzei* arrived. I showed Voss the button and told him that we had dug a hole and mentioned that there was a strong odour of decay arising from it. Voss therefore took with him a bottle of alcohol in the event of one of us becoming sick. We all went back to Koze Gory by motorcar and motorcycle. When we arrived on the spot, Voss ordered us to widen the excavation and to cut off the head of one of the bodies and remove it. Voss looked at the head and ordered us to put it back and put some earth on it. Voss strolled about in the forest, on the other side of the clearin, beyond the bog and we then returned to Gnezdovo.

The same day, *Unteroffizier* Gustav Ponka, an Austrian, took down a statement from me, through an interpreter Arholz, as to what I knew about the execution of the Polish officers. They also interrogated Ivan Andreev, nicknamed Rumba, from Nove Batoki.

I wish to state here that while I was making the statement, I was simply questioned as to what I did actually know. There was no question of threats or bullying. They treated Andreev, who was making a statement, in the same manner. I was not present during the depositions made by other inhabitants, but had the Germans beaten or threatened anyone I would have heard of it later. Anyway, the best proof of their behaviour during the interrogations is provided by the fact that since Kiselev was very old, he was not summoned to report in Gnezdovo, but Ponka and the interpreter went to his house and there took down his statement. I saw Kiselev fairly often afterwards and although aged, he was perfectly well and on the last day as I was evacuated westwards, i.e. on 24 September 1943, I saw him walking along with his wife and pushing a barrow in front of him. Moreover, there was no reason to beat up or threaten any of the interrogated people, because Kiselev as well as the others made their statements quite of their own free will.

Some days later the Red Cross Commission arrived. A large Red Cross flag was run up and the interpreter told us that this area was now at the disposal of the Red Cross. The Red Cross Commission talked with us, we were questioned as to what we knew of the execution of the Polish officers, but only the interpreter was present during these interrogations. We talked freely and no one bullied us.

I also talked with the delegation of Polish prisoners of war. At first we talked through an interpreter but one of the delegates of the Polish prisoners of war, an officer with two or three rank pips, told the interpreter that he spoke Russian and began to talk to us without an interpreter. In the delegation there was a Polish Lt Col but he could not speak Russian.

I also talked with the delegation of British prisoners of war. The Englishmen looked at the graves and then approached us; they were with the German chief of Propaganda. The Germans began to call for a *'Dolmetcher'* and one man from the British group, a *Polkovnik* (Colonel) stepped forward and asked *'Skoro platit nam diengi Germancy?'*(How much are you paid by the Germans?) Kiselev answered that he was not paid by anybody. The British delegates still asked us through this officer, how the Bolsheviks had brought the Polish officers to Koze Gory. Then they went to look at the graves of the executed Poles.

I also talked with members of the Polish Red Cross. I remember that when one of the bodies was exposed, the Poles on seeing his papers began to talk excitedly among themselves and it seemed to me that I heard them saying something about 'Piłsudski' [Marshal Józef Piłsudski, First World War hero]. This interested me so I walked up to them and asked what they were talking about. Then they shown me the papers and said they had discovered the body of Piłsudski's personal doctor [Wiktor] Kaliciński.

At the end of May, the Germans finished digging up the seven graves on the near side of the bog and by that time all the bodies from these seven graves had been exhumed. From the small eighth grave on the other side of the bog, the Germans also exhumed some bodies but they laid them back in the grave and did not dig up any more. Among those who were making statements before the Germans was Ivan Andreev, nicknamed Shlopechka, aged 44, from the village of Zytko. This was not Ivan Andreev nicknamed 'Rumba', because of his bowed legs. In the summer of 1943, when rumours began to spread of the approaching Red Army, Shlopechka's wife threw him out of the house, refusing to live with him. Then I understood that she was afraid that when the Reds came, all those who had made statements for the Germans would be punished for it.

During 1941 and 1942, after the arrival of the Germans, no military units ever stayed in the *dacha*. Neither was the whole area guarded or surrounded with sentries; there was no fence as this was taken down for fuel. It was permitted to walk about and I myself looked for mushrooms. Walking in the forest surrounding the; *dacha* was permitted by the Germans. Neither did I see the arrival of any motorcar except that belonging to the officer who was actually living there.

The inhabitants nearby did not take much interest in the whole affair, because everybody knew that the *NKVD* was shooting people in Koze Gory and what was happening there. Semyon Andreev from Nove Batoki, who was employed in a workshop attached to Depot No. 95 in Krasny Bor (Red Forest) and who used to arrive there by train, had been told by railwaymen that the *NKVD* were bringing the Polish officers from Kozelsk. I never heard it said that officers were also brought from Ostashkov or Starobelsk. Andreev left Russia before the German advance.

When the Red Army approached, I decided to leave with the Germans. Ivan Andreev (*Rumba*) was uncertain whether to go or to stay but I advised him to go for fear of the *NKVD* shooting him. After due consideration, he left by car with the German interpreter Teodor, whose surname I do not know. I also wanted to go with them but they did not offer to take me. I did not go till a day or two later, on foot. I asked a German gendarme who was controlling the traffic on the highway to help me to get away. He stopped a car, which was going to Orsha and so I was able to leave. I have heard the name [Borys] Meshagin, who was head of the town in Smolensk during the German occupation, but I do not know what has happened to him. I imagine he also went with the Germans.

I wish to add that when I made my first statement before the Germans, the first person being interrogated was Vasilkov, who came with us as the third man undergoing interrogation, Vasilkov was very nervous and when asked what he had seen, said he knew nothing. Then the interpreter told him' If you know nothing and you won't talk, you can go home.'

The interrogation was conducted in Polish, on occasions less understandable words were asked in Russian with the help of Lieutenant Marian Heitzman of the Polish General Staff in London. The witness signed all four pages of the document.

For exact translation.
Major Stanisław Rodziewicz,
Chief Judge Advocate of the Polish Navy.
London 27 July 1946.

Polish Red Cross *PCK* Involvement

Certain extracts and conclusions of the Katyn report written by Kazimierz Skarżyński, Secretary General of the *PCK*, the Polish Red Cross in Warsaw, reached London by secure signals from the *AK* and these were incorporated into memoranda prepared by the Polish government for the use of Ambassador O'Malley and other departments of the Foreign Office. The report was never printed in its entirety, except in Polish books a few years after the war.[15] The first time the British were aware of it was in 1946, when a diplomatic bag arrived with a brief from Robin Hankey,[16] a Senior Counsellor of the FO who was posted to the Warsaw Embassy for the second time in his diplomatic career.

Hankey had contacts with prominent Poles in Warsaw, among them Skarżyński, Secretary General of the *PCK*, whom he regarded as 'an exceptionally trustworthy and honest man'. Because of its sensitivity, Hankey decided to despatch the lengthy report to London without translation from the Polish. It consisted of two parts; one, the official version, written in June 1943 while participating in the investigation at the insistence of the Germans and the second, more personal and confidential, written in the summer of 1945 just before his escape from Poland on 10 May 1946.

Skarżyński wrote the second part because he feared arrest by the Polish communist-led security police (UB) who in collaboration with the *NKVD* were looking for everyone involved with Katyn visits. He had already been interrogated three times by Judge Procurator Karol Szwarc on behalf of the Ministry of Justice in Warsaw. Szwarc informed him that the Polish communist authorities intended to carry out their own investigation of the Katyn affair, to prove that the Germans had committed the crime. Skarżyński realised that even after being dismissed from the Red Cross, he still felt morally bound to tell the truth and making a statement under duress was abhorrent to him.

As to the fate of the report, it was put away as a historical document, of not much relevance to post-war issues, until it was rediscovered in the East European and Soviet Department (EE&SD) of the FCO on 1 November 1972, more of which later.

Skarżyński escaped to the West with Hankey's assistance and on reaching Paris, he slightly edited the report to make it more readable and added a new introduction marked '*Norymberga, maj 1946*', presumably while temporarily stopping there. These narrative alterations do not interfere with the facts, which remain unaltered. While in Paris, Skarżyński made another deposition[17] before the military Judge Advocate, Captain Zygmunt Kindler, on 3 September 1946. This report is different, as it deals mainly with what had happened after June 1943, when nine boxes of documents from Katyn arrived in Kraków and their subsequent loss in Germany. Dr Werner Beck, Director of the Institute under German management and assistant to Dr Buhtz, revealed the ultimate fate of these documents much later, in 1951, at the Congressional hearings when he disclosed that the boxes had been destroyed on his orders, on a Dresden railway siding, just before the Red Army occupied the city.

Skarżyński's Paris deposition contains the information that during his visit to Katyn, he was surprised to see an Auxiliary Police unit of Polish NCOs, created by the Germans and brought from the region of Lwów to carry out guard duty over the graves. From his report, we learn that there must have been a serious disagreement between him and Dr Marian Wodziński, the forensic medicine specialist, whose report carried more weight than the two Red Cross envoys put 'in charge' by Skarżyński, namely Hugon Kassur and Jerzy Wodzinowski, quoted in some publications as doctors.

His personal reminiscences of his short stay (15–17 April) at Katyn complements Dr Wodziński's technical report, which was quoted freely but without attribution to him in the 'Facts and Documents' report of 1946. The two reports are to be considered as the most vital Polish evidence in establishing the truth about Katyn. The young pathologist Dr Wodziński had performed the exhumation work on seven mass graves for five long weeks. His report is informative and technical and encompasses all other events and visits to Katyn, including that made by a group of British and American PoWs.

News received via the BBC radio monitoring system[18] of enforced visits by the PoWs to Katyn alarmed the British, as the broadcast expressed the convictions of the Anglo-American group that the Soviets were the guilty party. The last part of the radio message is unclear due to bad reception. An extensive search for the reported conversation between 'Ivanov' and 'Crighton' has drawn a blank. Otherwise the message reads:

> On 12th May, delegates of English and American prisoners of war were admitted to Smolensk to inspect the graves of the 12,000 Polish officers who were shot by the Bolsheviks. The delegation consisted of an English Lieutenant [probably Lt Col F.P. Stevenson], an English Staff Doctor [Gilder], an American Colonel [Van Vliet], an American Captain [Stewart] and also four English N.C.Os. This delegation was given the possibility of becoming acquainted, immediately after their arrival, with Russian volunteers, who were spending their leave in Smolensk. The Anglo-American prisoners of war were convinced that the Russian volunteers were completely independent and were in no way under German pressure.
>
> After having inspected the Katyn graves, the English Lieutenant declared that he was facing the truth. The investigation of the Katyn crime should be the concern of (one sentence inaudible) … the Parliaments of all countries. The crime of Katyn is so base a Bolshevik action that the whole world should be told about it.
>
> After this, the English Lieutenant [Crighton?] with the help of the English staff Doctor, who knows Russian well, talked with the Lieutenant of the Russian army of Liberation, Ivanov. [Interview between Crighton(?) and Ivanov follows].

The visit became one of the most well known aspects of the story of Katyn, gaining notoriety during the US Congressional Committee hearings in 1952. Apparently there were two original reports, one written by Captain Stanley Stewart Browne Gilder (RAMC) Royal Army Medical Corps and another by Lieutenant Colonel John H. Van Vliet Jr, which could not be produced as evidence as it was 'lost' somewhere in the Pentagon. At the Congressional enquiry[19] Major General Clayton Bissell, the former Assistant Chief of Staff, Army Intelligence (G-2) mentioned in passing that a British officer, who likewise was taken to Katyn by the Nazis, wrote a report that 'substantiates in effect the statement of Van Vliet', which was forwarded to Julius Holmes, Assistant Secretary of State in London, on 25 May 1945, something he denied during the 1952 US Select Committee hearings.

The unknown British officer, Captain Stanley Gilder, was in fact a medical officer who after returning to the *Feld Lazarette* in *Oflag V B* at Rottenmunster informed the British authorities that he had been to Katyn under protest, afraid that German propaganda might portray him as a willing participant. He submitted a written report, probably at the instigation of a representative of the International Red Cross who visited the PoW camp on 27 July 1943. A copy dated 30 May 1944 was forwarded to the British Legation in Berne on 3 July 1944. In the British Archives, there are two versions of the report, the latter, which is reproduced here, is more detailed and comes from a file held by the American authorities.[20]

Various documents reveal that the FO was unwilling to disclose to the American Committee any documents on Katyn, giving the excuse that even British MPs had no access to them as of right.[21] After prolonged consultations, Sir William Strang, the Permanent Secretary of State of the FO, stuck to this line until after the departure of the Congressmen from London. It can only be assumed that the reason for secrecy was the wartime operational method of contact between PoWs and MI 9 (British Military Intelligence (branch 9 of the War Office), which needed to be safeguarded. Some PoWs were able to write in code hidden in the text of normal correspondence and were able to receive broadcast radio transmissions on clandestine makeshift radio receivers. Captain G. Gorrie, RAMC, in *Oflag V B*, was one such code writer known to Gilder. Whatever the reasons for hushing up the existence of the only British report on Katyn, there was surely enough evidence collated at the East European and Soviet Department of the FO, to confirm that the perpetrators were indeed the Soviets. Yet, the five Katyn photographs taken by the Germans, which were deposited with Gilder's report at the FO, were met with scepticism: 'They tell us nothing except that we may be pretty sure, they were used for propaganda purposes.' Regrettably, the photographs can no longer be traced among the WO files.

Gilder remembers the meeting he had with a Polish member of the Red Cross, who according to him was uncommunicative; while Wodziński clearly describes the conversation he had with Gilder. In the last sentence of his report, Gilder also downplays what he had seen at Katyn and the Germans seem to leave him alone.

In 1946, Skarżyński and Wodziński managed to escape the oppressive communist regime in Poland and reached the West. Wodziński made his deposition in Italy on 27 February 1946 and after his arrival in the UK, submitted testimony in September 1946, but his whereabouts were unknown until his death in 1986, registered in the UK by the Merseyside Borough of Sefton. Skarżyński settled comfortably in Canada and unlike Wodziński, took part in Congressional hearings of 1952. The whereabouts of Gilder were not followed up and we shall never know how he felt on reading van Vliet's accounts in the newspapers, or in later years, each time the Katyn massacre was mentioned in Parliament or the press.

To keep the chronological flow of the events, the three reports by Skarżyński (translated by the author) Wodzinski (translator unknown) and Gilder are interwoven.

Kazimierz Skarżyński's Report

On 9th April 1943, the President of the [*PCK*] Polish Red Cross, Wacław Lachert was summoned by telephone by Dr Heinrich, a delegate of the German *Generalgouvernment* to the Polish Red Cross, to present himself at a meeting in Brühl Palace, without indicating the purpose of the meeting. He refused to attend immediately offering to come in one hour; to which Heinrich replied that it would be too late and the substance of the meeting will be communicated to him later. The same day at 18.00 hours, Dr Heinrich telephoned the President, to tell him that it had been decided to send a delegation to Smolensk district to inspect the graves of Polish officers murdered by the Bolsheviks; he named the persons who would take part in the delegation: two literary writers [Ferdynand] Goetel and [Emil] Skiwski, a representative from the *RGO* (Council for Social Welfare) Dr [Edward] Grodzki, Dr [Konrad] Orzechowski from the Warsaw City Council and others, indicating that a place has been reserved also for the *PCK* President, in the aeroplane departing for Smolensk the next day at 8 o'clock. President Lachert himself and on behalf of the remaining members of the *PCK* Executive Committee, again refused to take part in the delegation due to its propagandist nature.

As it turned out, those mentioned above and a representative of the Roman Catholic Curia, who were at the meeting in Brühl Palace, heard the representative of the German *Propagandaamt* talk at length about a Polish-German understanding under the banner of the defence of Europe against the Bolsheviks, announcing to all present the discovery of the Katyn graves and the proposed departure to the place by a delegation. The representative of the Curia also declined to take part in the delegation. The previously unheard new tone of voice of the *Propagandaamt* delegate as well as the circumstances surrounding the sending of a delegation to Smolensk clearly indicated that the German authorities were aiming at drawing the Polish Red Cross into the orbit of the existing propaganda action. It was clear then, that the Katyn massacre as an object of propaganda for the Germans would grow on a grand scale to serve their political aims, which might create unexpected problems for the Polish Government. In the next few days, while waiting for the matter to unfold, these issues became a constant topic for discussions within the *PCK* Executive Committee. In the first instance, the Executive Committee reacted with great distrust to any news on Katyn that came from German sources. This was based on the daily occurrence of perverse and bestial treatment suffered under the German occupation of four years.

On 12 April [1943], a well-known writer, Ferdynand Goetel, a participant of the expedition staged by the German authorities with whom, up to now, the *PCK* had no close association, presented a report on his own initiative to the Executive Committee about his visit to Smolensk and Katyn. It was apparent from this first eyewitness report, which has not come from German sources, that he had seen a concealed mass grave of the Polish officers and that everything indicated that the murder took place in March–April 1940. The suspicion of a direct involvement by the Germans in the murders started to wane.

On the morning of 14 April, Dr Grundmann from the *Propagandaamt* in the Warsaw District turned up personally at the *PCK* office and gave a verbal summons to the President, urging him to send a delegation of five persons the same day at 13.00 hours to depart to Smolensk At the same time he stressed that the same plane was leaving Kraków with Mr [Stanisław] Plappert, a plenipotentiary of the Polish Red Cross Executive Committee of the Kraków District and his Deputy Dr [Adam] Schebesta,[22] as well as representatives of the clergy sent by His Excellency the Bishop. We immediately tried to get in touch with Dr Schebesta in Kraków by telephone but he had already left the office. The Executive Committee had to face the fact that representation from Kraków's *PCK* was already en route for Smolensk by order of the German authorities.

After a short discussion a decision was made, which became the basis of the *PCK's* attitude with regard to the Katyn case. It was based on these premises:

1. A demand to send a delegation of the *PCK* Executive Committee should be absolutely opposed, as it could be used for German propaganda purposes and would directly serve its political aims, in which the *PCK* should not take any part and should detach itself from completely.
2. The identification of the bodies of the officers in the mass graves, both for the Information Office of the *PCK* and for thousands of Polish families, is vital.
3. The *PCK* guarantees that it will undertake with due care and piety all exhumation works, identification and reburial of such a large number of bodies.
4. Accordingly, it is advisable that the *PCK* Information Office should send a propaganda-free Technical Commission to Smolensk, which would initially investigate the extent of exhumation work and under what conditions it can be undertaken by the *PCK*.
5. The exceptionally difficult task of the first committee, as well as the compulsory presence of two high ranking officials of the *PCK* from Kraków, requires unanimity of the entire committee, in their attitude towards the expected scheming of German propaganda and other unforeseen measures. This can be done by sending a member of the Executive Committee to take charge in setting up a Technical Commission on site, reporting back immediately to the Executive Committee.

From a tactical point of view, the actual decision of the Executive Committee was phrased thus:

'The Executive Committee decided to send to Smolensk a Technical Commission of five persons from Warsaw. One member of the Executive Committee, the Secretary Skarżyński and four others who could remain there, if need be. Because the *PCK* was deprived by the German authorities of its functions, including the care of the graves, Skarżynski is limited to the tasks of the Information Office and as such, is authorised only to act within its confines.'

I dictated this text on the telephone to Dr Grundmann, to pass the message to Kraków's authorities, adding that I would not pay lip service to any political or propaganda purposes.

At 13.00 hours, together with others from the Technical Commission: [Ludwik] Rojkiewicz, [Jerzy] Wodzinowski, [Stefan] Kołodziejski and Dr [Hieronim] Bartoszewski, met at Okęcie [Warsaw] airport and departed at 15.00 hours for Smolensk. During departure and throughout our stay, cameras surrounded us, a real pest, which we could not get rid of. During our journey I gave instructions to all the *PCK* representatives to keep close in one group, not to be drawn into unnecessary conversation with the Germans; not to sit with them at the table, and when being filmed, to close ranks.

Canon [Stanisław] Jasiński joined the group, representing Kraków's Metropolitan Bishop, as it turned out, just to take care of the prayers and execute the last rites. There was also Dr [Tadeusz Susz-] Pragłowski from Kraków, who as a criminologist was sent without precise instructions and after a general view of the graves declared that there was nothing for him to work on and promptly departed. Besides them, there were in the aircraft *Herrn* Zenzinger from the office of the German *Propagandaamt* in Kraków and three German policemen from Berlin's Criminology Department, apparently to work on deciphering difficult documents found on the corpses and three young, suspicious looking Poles on service with the Germans, one of whom was a camera operator.

On arriving in Smolensk on 15 April, I found out that the responsibility of overseeing the works on the graves lay in the hands of Lieutenant [*Oberleutnant* Gregor] Slovenzik, commander of the local company of the *Propaganda Abteilung (Aktivpropagandakompanie)*. This company was led by front line officers, the *Oberleutnant* and his second in command *Leutnant* von Arndt [Ahrens] had a military mentality, though, at the same time, the specific, national-socialist character of Goebbels' Department. It forced us to be on our guard.

In the evening of 15 April, after a meal in the company's mess, *OLt* Slovenzik spoke to us at some length about the work so far done on the graves. According to his first sentence of the introduction, the Polish officers fell into the Bolsheviks' hands as a result of the German Reich's subjugation of the whole of Poland in September 1939; part of the territory gained was handed over to the Russians. He adduced further that news had reached his company that 15 km from Smolensk and 4 km from Gnezdovo [railway] station, in a place called Koze Gory in Katyn woods, Polish workers had, in the spring of 1942, at the instigation of the local people, dug up a grave, and finding the bodies of the Polish soldiers, backfilled them and put up two crosses made of birch wood to mark the spot. This is where the Polish officers murdered by the *NKVD* were found. The work undertaken had revealed several mass graves, containing layers of bodies of the Polish officers.

It was evident, continued *OLt* Slovenzik that (among sparsely planted pine wood forest, 20 to 30 years old) the graves were cordoned off by barbed wire and people had ben forbidden to go there since 1934. On this wide terrain, there is a house, [*dacha*] which was used as a summer retreat by the Smolensk *NKVD* officials. Apparently it was here that execution of Russian civilians took place. The local people (railway workers at Gnezdovo station and peasants) who were questioned declared that from the beginning of March to the second half of April 1940, two or three caged wagons would arrive daily at Gnezdovo station with the Polish officers. They would be loaded into trucks, which then drove to the fenced-off area of the wood. One of the witnesses declared that the noise of the shootings and screams would reach his house daily.

Photograph copies of statements from the three or four Russian peasants were shown to us. Talks undertaken by our committee members with the local people over a number of weeks have confirmed these stories.

Furthermore, Slovenzik added that after reporting these facts to his authorities and by receiving an assignment to inspect the graves, his soldierly duty had been done. On being moved to the core by the tragedy of the Polish officers, he had tried to do this work with care and attention, knowing that the families of the dead were waiting for information and the return of artefacts that had been found on the bodies. He was proud of the fact that a telegram from the Führer with instructions that the families of the dead should be allowed to receive this information, proved that his efforts in this case were on the right track. He ended his speech with an appeal to the Polish nation to be vigilant against the dangers of the Bolsheviks with who the German Reich was now at war.

In response, I explained that as a representative of the *PCK* Executive Committee, we had arrived for one purpose only – to ascertain the situation of the graves and to leave behind a Technical Commission, which within two or three days would grasp the scope of work of identification of the corpses and their re-burial in the freshly dug up graves; and to safeguard the artefacts of a personal nature and return them to the families of the dead. I got the reply that the German authorities would give us all the help required and the committee on site would have access to all the gravesites for the exhumation and identification purposes as well as the collection of documents and papers and their deposit in an office some 4 kilometres away from the graves. The documents for the time being belong to the Army Command and before proper utilisation was made, they must remain with the Field Police [*Geheimfeldpolizei*]. After their use, they would be turned over to the *PCK* to be delivered to the families.

After certain formalities were completed, regarding provision for the Commission and all other costs that would have to be covered later by *PCK* expenses, it was agreed that in a few days time the committee would be strengthened by several other members according to a plan that would be presented to the authorities by Mr Rojkiewicz in Warsaw.

In conclusion concerning the *PCK*, I ended by saying that the discovery of the mass graves of the Polish officers would certainly have a devastating effect on the country. Familiar with a series of tragedies since the war started, every Pole could not but connect that today's enemy of the Reich, previously their ally, with whom they enjoyed cordial relations after the August pact, carried out the murder. On this occasion, I took the opportunity to correct inaccuracies in *OLt* Slovenzik's speech, that in fact Soviet troops invaded Poland on 17 September 1939 during the German-Polish campaign, as a result of the Russo-German Pact. I did not receive any reply to my two remarks. *OLt* Slovenzik blushed and was visibly embarrassed.

In private, avoiding politics, I brought up the news of the recent successes of the Russian Army. The German officer admitted their prowess, but claimed that the war wouldl end in the summer of 1943, following a decisive success in the East and later a victory over England.

The following day, 16 April, we arrived at our destination at nine in the morning. The Koze Gory woods are situated a few metres away from the road. In a clearing, amongst the graves, the corpses of the exhumed officers lay stretched out. Above them flew a large Red Cross flag. There was no doubt that we were dealing with a mass execution carried out by expert hands. All the corpses I saw had bullet entry holes at the nape of the neck and exit holes in the forehead. The uniformity of wounds by firearms and the course of the shots indicated that they were done with pistols at close range, fired at the victims in a standing position. Some corpses had their hands tied with a rope; presumably those who struggled in self-defence. The Polish uniforms, decorations, rare insignia, regimental badges, coats and boots were in good condition, in spite of contact with the earth and decomposition. Deep inside the graves, there were other layers of corpses showing parts of legs, arms and trunks sticking out of the sand. Of note was the proportion of senior officers, Majors, and Lt-Colonels. I inspected the corpses of two Generals identified as [Mieczysław Makary] Smorawiński and [Bronisław] Bohatyrewicz; their General's insignia and stripes on their trousers indicated their rank.

Amongst the older pine trees, grew younger ones, in my opinion self-propagated, which would indicate that the execution must have taken place in the spring of 1940. It was alleged that a competent forester recognised the same age of the pines based on root identifications. I did not see any of the pine trees over the graves, as the graves were already opened. As to the number of the dead in all the graves, I had a feeling that the number declared by the Germans to be 10 to12, 000, was largely overestimated. After a short prayer and blessings said by Canon Jasiński, we left by car for the office, some 6 kilometres away. Just before departing I categorically refused three times to speak in front of the microphone.

Inside the house there was an office for sorting and looking through the documents; the more interesting ones were displayed in glass cabinets. We studied some of the documents and diaries, all of which ended with early dates of April 1940. After a courtesy meeting with Dr [Gerhard] Buhtz, a criminologist from Wrocław (Breslau), University, we departed for Smolensk. At the last moment, I was asked again to say something into the microphone and I refused. However, asked to say a few words privately about my feelings, I replied that I am departing with a heavy heart, deeply moved by what I had seen. I took this opportunity to acknowledge the hard and methodical work at the site of the graves undertaken by the army.

In Smolensk, it was again agreed with *OLt* Slovenzik to leave behind Rojkiewicz, Wodzinowski and Kołodziejski, and that after two or three days, Rojkiewicz would return to Warsaw with a better action plan for the work of the Commission. In the meantime, it was hoped that some understanding would prevail between the German authorities in Kraków and the *PCK* Executive Committee, that a new head of the Commission would be despatched forthwith. The rest of the *PCK* team departed directly for Warsaw with me on 17 April.

On the morning of 18 April, I presented a verbal report to the Executive Committee. It was incorporated into the minutes of the No. 332 meeting, which stated that:

1. In a place called Katyn near Smolensk, there are partially dug up mass graves of Polish officers.
2. Based on a visual inspection of some 300 dug up corpses it can be stated that the officers were murdered by shots to the back of the head, furthermore, the same type of wounds undoubtedly indicated a mass execution.
3. Plunder was not the reason for the massacre, as the bodies were in full uniforms with boots and decorations and besides, a significant amount of paper money and coins was found.
4. According to documents found on the corpses, the murders took place in the months of March–April 1940.
5. To date, only a small number of names had been established (about 150).
6. To identify and register all the dead men, it is necessary to increase the present team in Smolensk by five to six persons.
7. The work of our Technical Commission can only be developed and moved forward with the co-operation of the competent German Army unit in the area.
8. Our committee on the ground has met with an exceedingly courteous manner and total co-operation from the German Army authorities.

The first six points do not require explanation. Regarding point 7: in the undertaking of exhumation work on this scale, outside Poland in a foreign country devastated by war and occupied by our enemy, and additionally on the front (Smolensk was only 30 to 40 kilometres away from it), the *PCK* could only contemplate the work with the assistance of the German Army.

Otherwise the problem could not be overcome technically or financially. It must be remembered that in the case of Katyn, or in any other matter, the aim of German politics and that of the *PCK* were completely divergent. The aims of the *PCK* were to exhume and identify the bodies and re-bury them in new graves as quickly as possible. The Germans however, were concerned entirely with propaganda. This divergence of aims led to frictions, of which I shall write later.

It was unrealistic to think that German propaganda would let go of its control, just to make a good impression on the Polish public, though there was an element of this, albeit of a secondary nature. The *PCK* had a choice, either to resign from further work, or to agree to a lesser role operating under the supervision of the German Army. Taking account of the above the *PCK* chose the second alternative.

Regarding point 8. By leaving behind a small Technical Commission in Smolensk, which was totally dependent on the Germans and having in mind its honourable aim, the *PCK* Executive Committee considered it appropriate to agree to the motion. Thus a good start was ensured.

At the same meeting, the Executive Committee decided to announce that on the basis of my report, it was ready to start work in Katyn, pending written consent from the German authorities. It came as a verbal declaration from a delegate of the *Generalgouvernment* at a meeting in Kraków on 22 April.

That same day, 18 April, I was summoned to the Bruhl Palace, where in the presence of Dr Grundmann, Dr Heinrich and two other Gestapo officers, I was asked to give a report of our visit to Katyn. During our conversation I had been asked to give interviews to the press, which I declined. They then demanded from me a written report of what I had seen, so that it could be published in the press, allegedly for the benefit of Poles living overseas in England and America. Again, I declined to write such a statement, indicating that to my mind it would not be effective, as exiled Poles would know that I had a choice of either signing the report or being sent to a concentration camp. Dr Grundmann, laughing, agreed with me. Then, Dr Heinrich in his role of overseeing the *PCK* angrily demanded a written official report by 5 o'clock in the afternoon. As a result, the *PCK* Executive Committee sent him a resumé of extracts of my minutes.

About noon the same day, in the Warsaw office of one of the bank managers, I gave a clandestine verbal account of my journey before the *AK* [Home Army] Civilian Warfare Commissioner, who acted as the Delegate of the Polish Government [in exile].

A. General organisation of works

Once the decision was made regarding exhumation work, the Executive Committee and Chief Director of the *PCK*, [Władyław] Gorczycki, took charge of the organisation. It depended on:

a. Completion of the Technical Commission and selection of a new leader in place of Mr Rojkiewicz.
b. Provision of suitable equipment, clothing and office materials for the Technical Commission.
c. Arrangement of communications between Warsaw and the Technical Commission on site.
d. Establishment of the means of contacts with the families of identified victims.
e. Arrangement of a suitable form of transportation and preservation of the deposits (documents and memorabilia).
f. Establishing the form of new graves.

I must point out here, that contact between Warsaw and Katyn was entirely dependent on the whims of the Germans and it was a failure. The work in Katyn was carried out far from the normal conditions of any organisation, which had to be improvised. Only the exceptional dedication and energy of the Commission members, especially those that stayed there to the end, had any serious influence on the results of the work.

Ad/a. As mentioned before, there was a plan to send a new supervisor of works and others, following Mr Rojkiewicz's return from Katyn, and now with a clear picture, the fear arose that the loss of each working day might be irreplaceable due to the expected approach of warmer weather, which would stop the exhumation work till autumn. Additionally, the possibility of military operations moving to the west of Smolensk increased our fears. It was decided not to waste any more time but to dispatch a new supervisor, as per my plan, during my stay in Katyn. The special requirements of physical resilience against the smell of decomposed bodies had made the choice of personnel difficult.

On 19 April, the following left Warsaw for Katyn: Hugon Kassur, head of the Office of the Plenipotentiary of the Executive Committee of the *PCK* for the Warsaw District was chosen to lead the committee, accompanied by Gracjan Jaworowski, a clerk and Adam Godzik, a labourer. Precise instructions were not given to Kassur but his task was to continue the work started by Rojkiewicz; if possible speed it up and send regular reports about the progress made and needs of the Commission and refer to them for advice on important issues. Kassur, who found himself in unexpected circumstances as regards communications, did not let us down with his organisational skills and initiative.

The German authorities in Kraków insisted on increasing the Technical Commission by three doctors specialising in forensic medicine (at first three were suggested), the choice depended on Dr Beck, the German Head of the Institute of Forensic Medicine in Kraków. Dr Schebesta had recommended to Dr Beck three candidates, one each from Warsaw, Kraków and Lwów, adding that Dr Marian Wodziński, could be sent straight away with three helpers [laboratory assistants] namely: Władysław Buczak, Franciszek Król and Ferdynand Płonka. This group departed for Katyn on 27 April 1943. Finally, Messers Stefan Cupryjak and Jan Mikołajczyk, both working [in administration] for the *PCK*, departed on 28 April 1943.

Dr Marian Wodzinski's Report

My name is Dr Marian Wodziński,[23] I was born on May 28th 1911 at Tarnów, my parents being Władysław and Rose nee Rusinek. I am a Roman Catholic. Higher education – Doctor of Medicine. Before 1939, I lived at Cracow [Kraków], at 16 Grzegorzecka [Street].

After having qualified at the Faculty of Medicine of the Jagiellonian University in Kraków in 1936, I held the post of Junior Assistant in pathological anatomy at the University under Professor Stanisław Ciechanowski until 31 August 1937. After that I became Senior Assistant in Forensic Medicine at the Jagiellonian University under Professor Jan Olbrycht. In 1939 I was nominated as medical expert in forensic medicine to the Court of Appeal in the Kraków District. After the outbreak of war, I continued to work as Assistant in the Institute at Kraków until December 1944. The Director of this Institute was Professor Olbrycht. In March 1940, Professor [Gerhard] Buhtz of Forensic Medicine in Wrocław (Breslau) [*Professor der gerichtlichen Medizin und Kriminalistik an der Universitat Breslau*], came to the Institute to announce that a German doctor would be assigned to the Institute to conduct all the legal expert work connected with the Germans. At that time I came in touch for the first time with Professor Buhtz, to whom I was introduced by Professor Olbrycht. In April 1940 the occupation authorities appointed a German doctor, Dr Werner Beck, an Assistant to Professor Buhtz, as a Director of the Institute. In spite of this, even during the period of German management, all the staff of the Institute was Polish, with the exception of the administration of the Department of Serology and Department of Weapon Identification.

Dr [Jan] Zygmunt Robel in particular, worked as Director and legal expert in the field of medical chemistry in another building but at the same Institute. In May or June 1942, Professor Olbrycht was arrested by the Germans and taken off to Oświęcim (Auschwitz). The work at the Institute was unpleasant and several times I asked Dr Beck to release me, giving the reason as bad health. To this request I received the answer that my choice was either continue working at the Institute or go to the concentration camp at Auschwitz.

Independently of my work at the Institute, I worked as a doctor for the *PCK* at Borek Fałęcki near Kraków and as a doctor for the Social Insurance administration in the same place. From March 1940 I belonged to the Underground Organisation *ZWZ* [*Związek Walki Zbrojnej* – Union of Armed Struggle] and from 1943, to the *AK* [*Armia Krajowa* – Home Army].

The Nation Confronts the Murder

I knew about the case of Polish officers lost in Russia at the end of 1939, when talking casually with my friends who lived in German occupied territory, but whose next of kin were in Russian captivity. From these conversations I realised that there was great anxiety as to their fate on account of sudden cessation of all correspondence from them in the spring of 1940. I got this impression, in particular, from conversations with the wife of Colonel [Adam] Maciąg, who was at Starobielsk and with other members of the families of Professor Stefan Pieńkowski and Major Dr [Wiktor] Kaliciński, who were at Kozelsk. The families of these people, good friends of mine, feared the worst as a result of cessation of the correspondence but they did not give up the hope that perhaps the Polish prisoners had been sent somewhere farther into Russia, from where communication would be very difficult. As a result of this, they lived under a great strain, continually expecting some news of their next of kin.

Because of the large number of members of families of the several thousand Polish prisoners lost in the USSR, a great number of whom came from the German-occupied territories, the German communiqués about the Katyn discovery came as a great shock to the whole Polish nation. In spite of having lived through several years of cruel German occupation at first one could hear on every side doubts expressed that a crime of such colossal magnitude could be committed, especially by the Soviet authorities. As a result, Polish opinion was divided into two camps, those who did not believe in the German communiqués and regarded them as propaganda tricks and the others who believed them to be true. The Katyn discovery aroused universal interest and commotion and became the subject of many discussions and conversations, everybody trying to get hold of the information so far as possible direct from independent sources.

On 14 April 1943, my colleague from the Institute of Forensic Medicine at Kraków, Dr Tadeusz [Susz] Pragłowski went to Katyn with the first Red Cross delegation. On his return, in private conversation I asked him his impressions and details of what he had noticed on the spot and who, in his opinion, had perpetrated the crime. Dr Pragłowski said that when he arrived at Katyn, the graves had not yet been completely uncovered and that young spruces three to four years old were growing on them. On the basis of this evidence, it had to be assumed that the graves were more than two years old, which indicated that they were made at the time when the Katyn territory was in Soviet hands. In connection with the possible doubt that the Katyn graves really contained the bodies of the missing Polish officers Dr Pragłowski told me that, among the few bodies uncovered during his stay at Katyn, he found and recognised the body of his University colleague Captain Dr [Zygmunt] Zbroja, which had removed every doubt as to the bodies having been really those of Polish officers.

Departure for Katyn Woods

On the Tuesday after Easter, 27 April 1943, the Director of the Kraków Branch of the *PCK*, Dr Szebesta [Adam Schebesta], summoned me to him and proposed that I should depart immediately to Katyn in the capacity of forensic medical expert. This proposition took me by surprise and at first I gave no reply, saying that I had to think it over and seek advice. Sharing the general attitude of the Polish people who attached tremendous importance to the classification of the whole Katyn question, and as a result of the insistence of Dr Schebesta and being firmly convinced that other Polish and foreign medico-legal experts would be working at Katyn (at that time everyone in Poland was convinced that the Katyn question would be the subject of an investigation by a neutral committee of experts from the International Red Cross), I decided on the same day to agree to Dr Schebesta's proposition. Late that evening, I set out by train to Warsaw from where we had to go on. Together with me went a group of laboratory assistants comprising: Ferdynand Płonka, Wacław Buczak and Franciszek Król, medical orderly of the 5th Military Hospital in Kraków.

On leaving Kraków, I took from the Institute of Forensic medicine everything necessary for the work at Katyn, things such as lancets, saws, metal callipers, overalls, rubber boots and gloves, phials for specimens etc. as well as for my personal use a Leica camera, together with the necessary number of films. This equipment made us subsequently independent of the Germans to a certain extent and throughout our work at Katyn we did not have to ask for assistance in this respect. Besides, we received from the Executive Committee of the *PCK* in Warsaw other equipment such as thick clothes, knives for slitting clothes, disinfectant spirit, rubber boots and gloves. On the other hand, the Polish authorities did not brief us or give indications or instructions as to the line of action we should take on the spot. We knew only that there was already at Katyn a so-called 'Technical Commission' of the Polish Red Cross, with which we had to co-operate.

On the 28th of April 1943, we flew direct from Warsaw to Smolensk, together with a delegation of the Executive Committee of the *PCK* in Warsaw Messrs [Stefan] Cupryjak and [Jan] Mikołajczyk, General Smorawiński's brother [in-law] and other people unknown to me. Only on my arrival there, did I realize with considerable dismay that I was the only medical expert in the party, as contrary to what Dr Schebesta had assured me, neither the medical expert from Warsaw, who was to have been Dr Manczarski, nor the expert from Lwów, who should have been Dr Popielski, had come with me. Consequently, I was the only Polish doctor there and as a result, too big a responsibility fell on me. After a short stay at Smolensk, the Germans took us direct by car to the place where the *PCK* Technical Commission were staying at the village of Borok, beyond the Katyn woods. There we met Messrs. Stefan Kassur, Jerzy Wodzinowski, Gracjan Jaworowski, Adam Godzik and Ludwik Rojkiewicz.

The Katyn Woods

On the following day at nine in the morning I found myself at the scene of the crime in the Katyn woods, which was about 3 km distant from our quarters. The terrain of the Katyn woods consisted of a number of small hills among which were marshes covered with marsh grass. Along the top of the hills, woodland paths branched off from the main road through the woods, running from the highway in the direction of the Dnieper River to the so called *NKVD* bungalow [*dacha*]. The trees in the woods were mixed, being both deciduous and coniferous. The older pine trees, measuring up to 20 metres in height and 25 centimetres in diameter at the foot, were found in the region of the biggest sandy mound. In the wetter parts, the trees were silver birch and alder. To the south of this mound, in the direction of the Dnieper, the trees were of one kind, being spruce less than twenty years old, planted deliberately. In the region of thes biggest mound, which was about 300 metres distant from the highway, were the mass graves of the Polish officers. A big flag of the Red Cross flew above the graves from an especially erected wooden structure. In spite of the fact that it was the end of April, it was chilly in the hollows of the ground and snow was still lying in the Katyn woods.

At the time of my arrival at Katyn a group of 310 Polish officers' bodies had been exhumed and reburied in the communal grave No.I. Besides this, there were two individual graves, which had been made for the bodies of two Generals, Bohaterewicz and Smorawiński. The graves, which were subsequently numbered I, II, III, and IV, were already completely uncovered so that the upper layer of earth was removed and the top layer of bodies completely exposed. The subsequent graves were numbered V, VI and VII, were at that time already partly opened as the upper layer of earth was being removed. In connection with this I had no possibility, personally, to see how the covering layer of an untouched Katyn grave looked and in particular, I was unable to examine the spruce planted on the graves.

The sight of such a great mass of bodies in Polish uniforms caused everyone a great nervous shock when coming for the first time to the Katyn graves. I myself was not able at the beginning to undertake any actual work, although *OLt* Slovenzik, who was representing the German authorities at Katyn, told me that I might organize the work of exhumation along my own lines and that I could count on being given every assistance by the German authorities necessary for the conduct of this work. In the afternoon the body of General Smorawiński was dug out once more and examined in the presence of his brother [in-law] Mr Smorawiński identified it by parts of the clothing, teeth etc known to him. The body was not dissected on account of the opposition of the brother.

The Arrival of the International Commission of Experts in Forensic Medicine

On the following day, 30th April 1943, I was still unable to start normal work on account of the arrival on that day, of so called 'European Commission of Medical Experts'. On its arrival by bus from Smolensk at about 9 am, the Germans ordered the complete cessation of all the work. After a general inspection of the woods and the graves, members of the committee spoke with witnesses who had been brought to Katyn woods from among the local inhabitants. Professor [Ferenc] Orsós in particular spoke with them without the mediation of an interpreter for, as I learned later, he had spent several years in Russian captivity in Siberia during the 1914–18 war and therefore spoke fluent Russian. Professor Buhtz acted as host to the Commission at Katyn and at his suggestion the members of the Commission chose at will individual bodies from different graves, which they subsequently dissected.

My role on this day was confined to that of a silent observer. I noticed then that the members of the Commission, after a detailed examination of the clothes, conducted a very detailed examination of the bodies and dissections of them and dictated reports immediately, on the spot, to the military typists. They also examined the general layout of the bodies in the graves and examined individual bodies in situ. The Commission finished its work at Katyn at about 1 pm and afterwards went to the *NKVD dacha* on the river. In the early hours of the afternoon, the Commission departed in the direction of Smolensk.

Professor Orsós of Budapest showed the greatest interest among the members of the Commission. For a long time, he conducted a detailed dissection and took away material (a skull) with a view to further examination to determine the length of time the body had lain in the ground. This he could fix by the number of layers of calcium on the inner side of the bones of the skull. Professor Orsós demonstrated on a sawn off skull the presence of two layers of calcium which, according to him, proved that the body had lain more than two years in the earth. Having closely watched the dissection conducted by him, I subsequently approached him personally and had a short conversation with him.

Professor [Francisek] Hajek of Prague was especially friendly towards Professor Buhtz and also showed particular interest in the diary he found on the body he was dissecting. I personally had the closest contact with Professor [Francisek] Subik, a Slovak, who in private conversation with me stressed his inimical feelings towards the Germans and sharply criticised the quisling government of Tito, declaring at the same time that he had no doubt that the crime of Katyn had been perpetrated by the Soviets. Dr [Marko] Markov, the Bulgarian of Sophia University Forensic Medicine also showed a considerable interest. He personally conducted the dissection of a body and dictated in German a report on the examination and dissection. The Rumanian dictated his report on the dissection that he made with the aid of an interpreter, because he did not know

German well. The Italian Professor [Vincensio] Palmieri also conducted a dissection personally and made a detailed examination of a body. The Finn [Dr Arno Saxen] did not dissect but watched closely Professor Orsós while he performed his dissection. The only genuinely neutral member of the Committee was a Swiss Professor [Francois] Naville from Geneva. He did not personally conduct a dissection but watched the other members of the Committee. But he examined the undergrowth in the vicinity of the graves, looking for cartridges and examined closely the trees near the graves, searching probably for traces of embedded bullets.

I noticed that the approach of the German Prof Buhtz, his assistant *OLt* [Gregor] Slovenzik, Dr Schmidt, and others, to the members of the Committee of Experts was extremely courteous. Dr Schmidt in particular offered drinks during their work. It should be said that it was a chilly day and the experts had removed their coats while working. I did not see the signing of the medico-legal statement by members of the Committee and only knew of its contents later from the German press, published in the Russian language.

Five Weeks of Work in Katyn Woods

I worked at Katyn from 1 May to 3 June 1943. To half way through May, I lived with the Technical Commission members in a wooden barrack assigned to us by the Germans in the grounds of an advance hospital unit of the Organisation *Todt* in the village of Borok, about 3 kilometres South-West of the Katyn woods. [Before the 1914–18 War the whole estate belonged to a Polish landowner – the Koźliński family – it was confiscated after the Revolution.] In the second half of May, we were transferred to a four-room house, about 1½ kilometres to the north of the Orsha-Smolensk main road, situated in the vicinity of the Katyn railway station. In the beginning, we were not satisfied with this transfer, because we had farther to go to work but afterwards we were glad to be thus separated from the Germans.

At first, we ate our meals, breakfast, lunch and dinner, in the hospital staff mess at Borok village, afterwards on our transfer to the house allocated to us for this purpose, a Russian woman who was working on the staff of the hospital brought our meals to our quarters. I assumed this change of living quarters and separate meals to mean that the Germans did not like us having the opportunity of getting in touch with members of the Organisation *Todt* (amongst whom there were Poles), who more than once did not conceal their dissatisfaction with the conditions under which they were working.

During the period of our stay, we continually felt that we were subjected to silent German observation, but with regard to this we were never restricted or hampered in our work. Every member of the Technical Commission was supplied with Red Cross armbands, with the result that according to general instructions given by the German authorities, we were able to use military lorries, which occasionally passed along the main road to take us from our living quarters to our place of work. Sometimes we had to wait an hour, which interfered with the regularity of our work. Sometimes we had to walk. In principle, work went on from 8 to 12 in the morning and from 2 to 5 or 6 in the afternoon; during the lunch interval we either drove or went on foot to our quarters.

On the Smolensk-Orsha main road, in the vicinity of the road leading to Katyn woods, were German Military Police posts, they were on duty during the whole of my stay at Katyn and were not only directing the traffic on the road but also preventing unauthorised persons, those who were not working there or were not members of visiting parties, entering the area. At the entrance of the road to the woods leading from the main road was a barrier and the visiting parties were assembled on the other side of the road from where they were conducted by the German guide. Near the barrier there were two notices signed by *Leutnant* Voss of the *Geheimfeldpolitzei* declaring: 'Entrance to Katyn woods is absolutely forbidden except to those working therein' and 'It is absolutely forbidden to take photographs of the scene of the crime.'

From the main road and along two sides of Katyn road, the woods were fenced off with barbed wire. Apart from the posts at the beginning of the main road, I did not see any other permanent German police posts. Local inhabitants were not recruited into the so-called 'Polish' or 'Russian' auxiliary police. However, I heard from the Poles in Organisation *Todt* that before my arrival at Katyn and the arrival of other delegations, some dozens of Poles were given caps with the eagle emblem on them and acted at that time as guards in the forest. They were called 'special Polish police'.

Being the only Polish doctor on the staff of the *PCK* Technical Commission, I was naturally interested in and took part in all the work being conducted. Despite some German obstruction, I tried as far as possible to develop a proper system of work. Of course my orders concerned only members of my committee. As for the Germans, they stopped the work several times for propaganda purposes, especially at reburial in new communal graves after examination. In general, the Germans were not obstructive, leaving the Technical Commission considerable freedom and limiting themselves to the supervision of our heavy and extremely unpleasant work.

The Germans

At the beginning, I did not see any German doctors undertaking examination or dissection. Only much later, in the second half of May, on the orders of Professor Buhtz, the German Doctors Schmidt, Müller and Hüber carried out several examinations of the bodies. I had the impression that they carried out their work thoroughly, without thinking of its propaganda nature. At any rate I did not notice any propaganda activity on their part. For several weeks towards the end, a lecturer in chemistry named Specht from a German university worked at Katyn. He made a detailed chemical analysis and in particular measured the acidity of samples of earth taken from different layers in the graves and in the vicinity. From this research, it was discovered that the upper layers showed a slight alkaline content but the earth gave a decidedly acid reaction on the deeper layers. Besides this, Dr Specht was interested in all the work at Katyn and took many photographs of the area of exhumation. As with the other German doctors, Dr Specht's attitude to us was courteous. He communicated to me personally the results of his research. Also working at Katyn was a German geologist, Dr Themlitz, who was especially interested in research on the consistency of the layers of earth in the individual graves.

During my stay at Katyn, Professor Buhtz lived at Smolensk and his trips to Katyn were irregular, one to three times a week. He usually appeared there when more important parties of visitors and delegations arrived at Katyn. In my opinion, Professor Buhtz approached the work as a man of science and because of his attitude he even had some disputes with the local chief of *Propagandaamst* section. Personally, I did not have close contact with Professor Buhtz and did not communicate with him about the material I collected.

The chief of German propaganda was an officer with a rank of Major. I do not remember his name. He lived at Smolensk and I saw him in Katyn at the most two or three times. His deputy *OLt* Slovenzik, who was a journalist by profession from Vienna, also lived at Smolensk and came to Katyn regularly, morning and afternoon. He devoted himself entirely to the exploitation of the Katyn woods as propaganda. Among other things, he expressed great indignation many times about the delegations of Polish officer PoWs from German camps, who, in spite of his great efforts, did not want to say anything during their stay in Katyn, declaring that, as prisoners, they had only duties and no rights.

OLt Slovenzik was also a local representative of the German authorities, with whom I had to be in touch rather often. There were disputes between us more than once, particularly on account of the fact that as the graves were being emptied in the course of our work, the number of exhumed corpses was still very far from the 12,000 as given out by the German propaganda. *Leutnant* Voss of the *Geheimfeldpolizei* represented the German Military authorities, besides *OLt* Sloventzyk. He was a typical German policeman, scrupulously executing orders, without reservation. It was his duty to find witnesses among the local population who would give information about the circumstances under which the Polish officers were brought to Katyn for liquidation. With regard to these witnesses, such as Kiselev and the man who worked in the station yard at Gnezdovo whose name I do not remember, I was not aware that the Germans subjected them to any compulsion or threats. *Leutnant* Voss' duties also included guarding the Katyn woods and supervising the work carried our there. He had at his disposal five or six NCOs of *Geheimfeldpolizei* who came regularly to Katyn. When any of them did not supervise the work undertaken by the Technical Committee, he was immediately summoned to Voss and threatened with punishment. Voss also made sure that no photographs were taken at the scene of the crime and ordered temporary confiscation of cameras or removal of films. This order, however, did not apply to our Technical Committee members or to the German experts. I personally took many pictures of the scene but despite Slovenzik's insistence I did not develop the films on the spot but took them back to Warsaw undeveloped and handed them over to the *PCK* Executive Committee.

Leutnant Voss also supervised the work connected with the documents found on the bodies and their removal to the laboratory for deciphering and conservation. He also had Russian civilian workers at his disposal who worked on the exhumations and Soviet prisoners who, at his or *OLt* Slovenzik's request, were sent to Katyn from Smolensk. More than once, *Leutnant* Voss gave orders to the Russian workers on his own account, without consulting with the Technical Commission, thus interfering with the organisation of the exhumation.

During my stay at Katyn, I was never at the *NKVD's* bungalow, which was situated about 800 to 1,000 metres from the scene of the crime, on the bank of the Dnieper River. However, I saw the bungalow, which was a one storey, roomy villa, situated about 15 metres from the bend of the river. Steps led to a small pier to which a small boat was moored. There were no German posts near the villa, but occasionally a *Wehrmacht* soldier would stroll around the grounds. There were a large number of telephone wires leading to the villa, which gave the impression it must have been some sort of headquarters. I was told that a Colonel stayed there. From time to time, I saw cars containing German officers driving in the direction of the villa. I did not recognise the colours of their uniforms, at any rate, they were neither officers of the *GFP* (*Geheimfeldpolitzei*) nor the Gestapo. They did not show any interest in the work we were doing and I never saw the Colonel who was supposed to be living in the villa. I did however see Germans saluting the passing car.

Local People

In the vicinity of the Katyn crime, about half a kilometre away, were the houses of local people. Nearest to the woods was the hut inhabited by the Kiselev family. Old [Parfeon] Kiselev was brought to the scene more than once to be a witness. The next, larger settlement was the village of Borok mentioned earlier. On the edge of the village, there was an advance hospital unit of the Organisation *Todt*, to which, as I mentioned above, the Technical Committee was attached for the purpose of room and board.

German orders not to trespass in the Katyn woods were strictly obeyed by the local Russian population. It should be stressed that during our time at Katyn the Germans were masters of the main lines of communication; the partisans held the woods and more distant localities. Their presence undoubtedly acted as a brake on gossip by the locals. As I myself do not speak Russian I had no conversation with the local people. Messrs Wodzinowski and Jaworowski could speak good Russian and talked to them on different occasions. This is how we learned from them that they did not know of any camps with PoWs, or of Poles particularly, when the Soviets were in Katyn. They had hoped that the Germans would free them from the Bolshevik tyranny, but the Germans were treating them no better, indeed worse, than the Soviet authorities. It was difficult to get more information about the crime out of the locals, because they feared the partisans and the reprisal of the Soviet authorities.

The Principal Work Undertaken at Katyn Woods

1. Lifting out the corpses from the original graves
2. Examining them and determining the cause of death
3. Searching bodies for documentation and labelling them with new numbers
4. Identifying the bodies by items found on them
5. Reburial of the corpses in new communal graves.

1. Lifting out Bodies from the Original Graves

The local Russian civilians, about ten, dug the graves and uncovered the bodies under the supervision of individual members of the *PCK* Technical Commission overseen by Mr [Hugon] Kassur. The Russians worked in teams of two, so three groups worked on the graves, the others were tasked with carrying away the examined bodies. For the work of lifting the bodies, they used iron hooks to detach individual bodies from the mass. In spite of repeated warnings from Technical members, the bodies and especially the uniforms were often damaged in the course of this work. Besides the hooks, shovels were used for lifting, sometimes picks, because the bodies were firmly stuck together. I was obliged to agree to the use of such methods, but always recommended the use of hands where possible to avoid the possibility of artificial mutilation (artefacts). The fact that the bodies were so firmly compressed together precluded any suspicion of the bodies exhumed by the Technical Commission having been previously disturbed. The equal degree of putrefaction in the individual graves depended on the quality of the layer of soil and on the pressure put on each layer of bodies, which proved that all bodies had lain in various graves for the same period of time, which also meant that after the original closing of the graves, they had not subsequently been opened with a view to later burial of other bodies in the same graves.

The presence of lumps of calcium and pressed spruce cones among the bodies in grave No.I led to the supposition that this grave had been open for a longer time and the layers of bodies had been sprinkled with some calcium compound, most probably calcium chloride, in order to prevent premature decomposition.

After separation of individual bodies from the mass, bodies were placed on wooden stretchers and lifted to the surface and laid out in rows on the ground.

Usually in the course of the day 70 to 120 bodies would be lifted in this way. The largest number we ever lifted was 160, on average 100 bodies were lifted from the graves. In principle we aimed at reburial of corpses the same day and in the same order. But because Russian prisoners from Smolensk were working in these graves, over whose arrival or failure to arrive at Katyn we had no control, sometimes the bodies after examination lay unburied for a while longer. I had the impression that was done deliberately by the Germans, because it happened most times before the arrival of a major party of visitors at Katyn, thus making a striking impression on anyone coming for the first time.

2. Examining the Bodies and Determining the Cause of Death

Originally, I personally conducted the examination of all the bodies dug up from the graves, in order to determine the cause of death and its circumstances; especially with a view to collecting material with which to answer the seven principal medico-legal questions:

a. Who was murdered
b. When the murder was committed
c. Where the murder was committed
d. With what instrument
e. In what manner
f. Why
g. Who committed the murder

On account of this, my work was considerably extended beyond that of the normal examination. I had to be present at the lifting up of the bodies, observing on the spot their position and the relationship between the degree of putrefaction and the layer of soil in the mass graves. I had also to be present at the searching of the bodies and to take special interest in the last noted date in the diaries, certificates of anti-typhoid inoculations, of the letters received or not yet sent by the prisoners, also the dates of the newspapers found in pockets and other circumstances which might be significant for the overall evaluation of the crime.

The most important part of the work was the examination of the bodies themselves. As a rule, Ferdynand Płonka assisted me. After having shaved off the hair on the back of the head, we found, generally, the width of two fingers below the occipital protuberance, most often in the mid axis of the body, an entry wound in the form of a round aperture, with a diameter of about 8 mm. After cutting the skin, a bullet channel could be seen, running forwards and upwards into the cranial cavity, through the base of the occipital bone. After the entry aperture had been cleared of soft tissue, its diameter was measured by means of a metal rule and was generally not quite 8 millimetres. The entry aperture was characterized by smooth outer edges, which expanded crater-like towards the interior of the cranium.

After the examination of the entry wound, we looked for the exit wound, which was almost always located on the forehead of the victim, more or less at the edge of the scalp, sometimes in the mid axis line of the body and sometimes a little to the right or left. Greater dimensions than those made by the bullet's entry characterized the exit wound. The diameter was sometimes 15 mm and the rough edges sometimes contained small bone splinters in them. After the measurement, the skin was cut open, the edges of the bone aperture cleansed of the soft tissue and measured. It generally had the form of a truncated cone, base facing upwards. The outer edges of the aperture were rough and the diameter varied from 1 to 1.5 cm. By means of a probe, the direction of the shot was determined and it was established that it had usually damaged the vital centres in the medulla causing the instantaneous death of the victim. In some cases the cranial cavity was opened up and the pre-agony reaction established, which took the form of large, rust coloured *haemochromogen* [sic] deposits at the base, on account of the haemorrhage into the cranial cavity. After the skin and soft tissue was cut, often bloody stains, *enchymosis,* were found in the vicinity of the entry wounds. In about 0.2 % [sic] of the bodies examined, revolver bullets of 0.75 mm calibre were stuck under the skin of the forehead or in the exit wound. The length of the body was then measured and examined for other lesions, which would testify to a struggle with an aggressor before death.

In order to determine the location of the crime we searched for cartridges in the graves, as well as close to them, and found a large number under the spruce needles in the vicinity and scattered among the bodies within the graves. This fact permitted us to assume that the crime was committed in that place, adjacent to the the graves. Also the large number of bullets stuck in pine trees, growing close to the edge of the longer arm of grave No.I and at a height of 1.5 to 2 metres from the ground, led us to suppose that a number of executions were carried out after the victims had been led to the aforementioned pine trees. The question of the cartridges was at the beginning passed over in silence by the Germans, on account of the fact that the ammunition used by the perpetrators of the crime had been of German make. The Germans evidently did not want a question raised about the origin of the weapon, which the layman normally associates with the perpetrator of the crime, in connection with their extensive propaganda.

From the medico-legal point of view, it is a well-known fact that in cases of premeditated crime the perpetrator as a rule uses a foreign weapon in order to divert inquiry into the wrong channels. Originally, I kept the cartridges and bullets found in the graves, but evidently the Germans noticed this. Once when I was searching for them, *OLt* Slovenzik approached me and asked what I thought about the ammunition with which the Polish officers had been shot. I said that it was of German origin, calibre 7.65 with a trademark 'Geco' series D; Slovenzik immediately replied that the Germans had supplied large quantities of this ammunition to the Baltic States. In any case that was the weakest point of the German propaganda and because of this they did not allow visitors to take any empty cartridges they found. The rule did not apply to the Technical Committee.

It was understandable that one doctor could not bear the weight of the work and I approached *OLt* Slovenzik and Professor Buhtz several times, asking them if it was possible for at least two more medico-legal experts to come to Katyn. I mentioned to them that before my departure to Katyn, I was assured by Dr Schebesta that those three doctors from Warsaw, Kraków and Lwów would be coming along. It was not only the amount of work but the great responsibility on those who were carrying it out. I took this opportunity to mention Professor Jan Olbrycht, a great authority on the subject, who was imprisoned in Auschwitz and who could be freed to help out in the work. Slovenzik accepted the suggestion but a week later informed me that the Ministry of Propaganda in Berlin had not agreed to my proposal to free Professor Olbrycht. As a result I remained alone until the end of the work; having examined about 800 bodies, I was not able personally to conduct further examination of exhumed bodies. I confined myself to a thorough examination of only those bodies on which no documents were found and which were listed as N.N. [*Nicht Namen* – without name]. In such cases I only measured the length of the corpse and recorded dental particulars, and the age based on the length of the narrow cavity within the head of the humerus. Clothes were described and special attention was paid to monograms and trademarks. In cases where the height could not be established because of decomposition, I measured the length of the two long bones in order to determine approximate height, an accepted formula in forensic medicine. Of the more interesting cases, those that differed from the norm, I took photographs, for instance signs of a shot having been fired from close range or bullets being stuck in the exit wound or the body lying in an unusual position, as in grave No. II.

In the course of my work I came across the bodies of two people well known to me personally. Dr [Wiktor] Kaliciński and Professor [Stefan] Pieńkowski of Jagiellonian University both held the rank of Major in the Polish army. Dr Kaliciński was an army medical doctor and was recognised by an identity card issued by the Ministry of War and other personal documents including a visiting card, on the reverse side written in pencil 'in case of my death inform my wife, Warsaw, 1 Matejko Square, dated 6 IX 1939.' I also recognised him by the shape of his skull, the height of the forehead and strongly developed forehead protuberances and the chestnut hair. On Pieńkowski's body we found an identity card issued by Kraków University and a notebook with personal notes. His body also was not difficult to recognise, as I knew his shape of head and his red hair, and both their different heights. Similarly, the body of Dr [Antoni] Stefanowski was recognised by Mr Kassur, who knew him well before the war.

3. Searching the Bodies and Listing Them

About the middle of May 1943, I ceased to examine personally all the bodies lifted from the graves without exception; the pace of work had greatly increased. From that time on, I examined only those bodies which were unidentifiable and these were examined immediately. The search was conducted under the control of the members of the Technical Commission and under the supervision of German NCOs of the Field Police. Messrs Buczak and Płonka assisted by two Russian civilian workers would slit open the pockets of the garments and pass them onto Messrs Godzik and Król. All the objects of value were put into numbered envelopes. Other objects not suitable to help identification were left on the spot, typical examples were bank notes, sometimes in large quantities, and other money. Newspapers, which were very often found on the bodies, were also thrown away after dating them. They were all dated from March and April 1940, they were Soviet papers mostly *Głos Radziecki* (Soviet Voice) which was printed in Polish in Kiev. Because there were so many of them, only a few were retained, the rest lay scattered about the graves.

When all the corpses were dug out, the newspapers were thrown in and the graves filled up with earth. Bodies on which no documents were found and no other evidence of rank had one epaulette taken and put into the envelope. Numbering of corpses and their documents was vital. They had to correspond. To identify the examined corpse a metal disk with corresponding number was pinned onto the uniform, or where decomposed, the metal disk was fixed to the bones with a wire. Leggings of boots were also slit as razors, penknives and other valuables were hidden there. The work described was under the strict supervision of German NCOs from the *Geheimfeldpoltzei*; this made it impossible to conceal objects and documents or avoid putting them into the envelopes. The Technical Commission did not conduct the inspection of documents, envelopes were laid on a table in rows and when work ceased at 5 o'clock in the afternoon, they were collected by a German dispatch rider on a motorcycle, often accompanied by Mr Cupryjak of our committee, who took the documents to a house about five to six kilometres in the direction of Smolensk beyond Gnezdovo station. There, a commission drew up a list of bodies and the documents found on them.

4. Reburial of the Exhumed Bodies

The bodies, having been searched and marked with metal discs, were then reburied in new communal graves, dug out by the Soviet prisoners brought from Smolensk by the Germans in a group of 30 to 40. Because the Germans, for propaganda purposes, wanted to exhibit a large number of bodies to their visitors, there was a long interval before they were filled up with earth. We had to intervene with the Germans to get some more manpower for digging work. These graves were situated in the clearing between the shorter arm of grave

No. I and the road, which run through the woods, reaching on the right side more or less to the middle of the passage between the longer arms of graves I and II. Originally the *PCK* Technical Commission wanted to bury the bodies in separate, individual graves, but the Germans categorically forbade this.

The attitude of the Germans towards the reburial of officers born in territories occupied by the Germans and whose names had a German sound was interesting. They intended at first to make a special cemetery for them, as they considered them to be citizens of German origin. But in the end, owing to the lack of space in the area and because they feared that such discrimination would not make a good impression they abandoned the idea.

Step by step the work progressed. The first communal grave I found on my arrival contained 310 bodies and was already covered over. It was situated on the left side facing Smolensk to the east. Close to it were the two individual graves of Generals Smorawiński and Bohaterewicz. To the right of the first grave, two communal graves were adjacent to each other, touching the edge of the path through the woods. At a distance of several metres from the first row of graves a second row of three graves was afterwards dug, in line with the graves of the first row. Each layer of bodies was sprinkled over with a thin layer of earth. Bodies were carried to the graves on wooden stretchers. The order of the numbers and the arrangement of the bodies in the graves were supervised by Mr Jerzy Wodzinowski. As it was hoped that in future the bodies would be re-exhumed to take them to their homeland, Mr Wodzinowski produced detailed plans, descriptions and noted the numbers of the graves.

The individual graves were trapeze shaped; being raised about 0.5 meters above the level of the ground. The sides were covered with turf and on the top of the graves were large crosses, made of earth, running the whole length of the grave, which was later covered with turf. In the centre of the first row stood a large wooden cross. On all the graves, members of the Technical Commission planted wild flowers nearby, choosing the colours white and red.

5. Examining the Documents and Preparing Identification Lists of Bodies and Objects

About five to six kilometres from the Katyn woods in the direction of Smolensk on the left side of the road a temporary laboratory was set up by the Germans in several rooms of a wooden hut, where the documents were brought for deciphering. I went to this hut several times, observing the work and finding out the results. On the veranda of the hut two members of our Commission were constantly working on deciphering documents, they were Messrs Cupryjak and Mikołajczyk (up to 1 V 1943, Messrs Rojkiewicz and Kołodziejski) under the supervision of one German NCO who was stationed there and lived in the hut. Another German assisted him when necessary. Also working on the veranda was a *Volksdeutsch* woman [Irina Erhard, see Congressional Hearings of Albert

Pfeiffer], possibly from Poznań district, who immediately translated into German the more important of the deciphered documents, especially the diaries found on the bodies. I do not remember the names of these Germans who worked in the temporary laboratory. *Leutnant* Voss of the local *Geheimfeldpolizei*, issued various orders connected to the work in the laboratory. Thus, for instance, it was on Voss' orders that all the foreign currency and valuables were to be retained in the hut. Other documents were put back into numbered envelopes and put in wooden cases in serial order. The routine was as follows. All the objects in the envelope were taken out and a detailed list of them was made on the envelope under the number. After this, the name, if any, military rank and other personal data were established on the basis of personal documents found on the body, or if not, on the basis of the uniform epaulette.

Deciphering presented a lot of difficulties as the documents from partly mummified bodies were desiccated and the paper disintegrated if not handled carefully. These were moistened with water, and with an ivory knife pages were separated and then read. Some were covered with a very thin layer of white wax. Writing in ink could not be deciphered with the naked eye on account of the ink having faded. Writing done with lead pencils presented no problems in reading. Diaries were given for translation to the German woman. In spite of this, the Polish members of the committee were able to copy some of these diaries in the course of their work. I also noticed that text that was anti-German in nature was not translated. For instance, in a poem quoted in a diary, the translator omitted a passage about the black eagle and the defiled cross, leaving only the passage about the unavoidable fall of the 'hammer and sickle'. Letters sent by the prisoners from Kozelsk and those which had been received by them there, were read by the Polish members. All dates of these letters were no later than April 1940. I have seen and read these letters myself and the Polish officers had serious misgivings as to their future and complained of the bad conditions in the camp. Documents that could not be deciphered by these primitive methods were sent by the Germans to the field laboratory at Smolensk, where without the participation of the Poles they underwent detailed examination by the German personnel working under Professor Buhtz.

Members of the *PCK* Technical Commission made the two copies of the lists, one for its exclusive use and one for the Germans, in the Polish language.

The Anglo-American Party of PoWs and Other Visits

After the visit of the European Commission of Medical Experts, the next important party to visit Katyn during my stay was a delegation consisting of British and colonial prisoners of war from German 'Oflags' [*Officierlager*]. In the middle of May, about ten persons, among them an English doctor with the rank of Captain, a South African Colonel, a New Zealander, a Canadian, an Australian and an American airman, arrived at Katyn. I do not know their names, but in that party was a Pole by the name of [Władysław] Kawecki, on his second visit to Katyn. The day before the arrival of this delegation, *OLt* Slovenzik was very excited, as were the other Germans, and he announced to me that a delegation of Anglo-Saxon PoWs was expected. We arrived for work about eight in the morning. I noticed that the entrance to Katyn woods was guarded by a larger group of German police. They did not allow us to start work, saying it would be possible after the delegation had gone. At a distance of 30 metres, I saw a car hidden in the woods, with recording apparatus. At 9 am the party of PoWs arrived by bus accompanied by a special interpreter and NCO from the camp guard. I do not know which camps these prisoners came from. *OLt* Slovenzik welcomed them, he indicated the topography of the graves and gave the general picture of the crime. The whole of his speech was translated into English. Members of our Commission, who were prevented from working, stood on one side, beyond the area of the graves, watching the 'ceremony'.

Not long after, Professor Buhtz arrived and also made a speech, saying among other things that all the work of exhumation at Katyn was being done by the *PCK* under the direction of a Polish medico-legal expert. Then I was called by Professor Buhtz to come over to the scene and was introduced to the delegation of Anglo-Saxon prisoners. As I do not know English, I was not able to speak directly to them, except with the English doctor [Captain Stanley S. B. Gilder R.A.M.C. Royal Army Medical Corps] who spoke some German and even a little Russian.

As was the case with the other major parties, two Russian witnesses, Kiselev and the railway worker from Gnezdovo station called I think Zakharov, appeared at Katyn woods. Asked by the English doctor if he had seen Polish prisoners brought by the Soviets to Gnezdovo station in the spring of 1940, Zakharov replied that he had and that they were brought in parties of two or three wagon-loads, sealed and strongly guarded by *NKVD* in the morning. After unloading in stages, all personal baggage of the prisoners was taken away and the prisoners were shoved into a *chorny voron* ['black crow'] and driven off in the direction of Katyn woods. The witness [Parfeon] Kiselev, when asked the same question by the same doctor, replied that he had also seen the arrival of the cars at Katyn woods in the spring of 1940 and had afterwards heard shouts and shots coming from there. This procedure had continued for some time. After these replies, the English doctor asked both Russians if the Germans paid them anything for such statements and they replied together that they were getting no pay from the Germans.

The Germans showed the whole delegation around the Katyn graves, explaining through the interpreter and Professor Buhtz. The South African Colonel [Stevenson] and the English Captain [Gilder] showed special interest in the graves and the bodies. After the inspection and demonstration by the Germans, they stopped at grave No. II, where Professor Buhtz emphasised the particular way the bodies lay in the grave. The English doctor then turned to me with a request to be shown some bodies and especially the place of the bullet wounds. I did so and then the English Captain asked me what my opinion was of the Katyn question, to which for a moment I did not reply, on account of the presence of the Germans. But from that moment I stuck by the English Captain, waiting for an occasion for a free conversation.

The Germans conducted the tour to the other side of the road, to old Russian graves, then along a path through the woods to the Dnieper in the vicinity of the *NKVD* bungalow. During this walk, the English Captain and I got a little apart from the rest of the party and he asked me again for my opinion about the Katyn crime. I replied that up to then, no proof had been found which could incriminate the Germans and indeed all revealed circumstances and discovered proofs pointed to the fact that the Soviets had committed the crime. Asked what would be the reaction of Polish public opinion to the disclosure of the Katyn crime, I replied that I was convinced that in view of the German death-toll such as at Auschwitz and other similar places, Katyn would not result in any active reaction by the Polish nation, and in no case would it lead the Poles to follow German wishes, namely military co-operation between Poles and Germans. Our conversation stopped there, because of the approach of several Germans.

After the halt at Dnieper and the inspection of the *NKVD* bungalow, the delegation of Anglo-Saxon prisoners was driven to the house where deciphering of documents was performed, and more interesting objects put on display. I stayed behind, but Messrs Cupryjak and Mikołajczyk had told me that the delegation left for Smolensk after about half an hour. Other members of my Commission have told me that they had noticed hidden microphones installed by the Germans in the trees to catch the conversation of the party. Many photographs were taken, official and non-official, a procedure that was unopposed. I also heard *OLt* Slovenzik propose that the South African Colonel should say a few words on the Katyn question to the microphone, to which the Colonel replied that he had not yet reached a final conclusion on this matter and therefore could not make any pronouncements.

OLt Slovenzik told me after the visit a week later that the South African Colonel intended to write down his impressions of the visit to Katyn and had therefore been transferred by the Germans to another PoW camp, in order to have more suitable conditions for the work. I do not know if Slovenzik's remarks were true.

Władysław Kawecki, the editor of *Goniec Krakowski,* a daily paper in Polish published in Kraków by the Germans, [known as *gadzinówka* – reviled press], who came with the Anglo-American prisoners, stayed at Katyn on this occasion for about a week and on *OLt* Slovenzik's orders was billeted in the barracks where we were living. We were very dissatisfied, because we regarded him with great suspicion as being a collaborator with the Germans, and living with him embarrassed us and we could not have an open conversation. Kawecki told us at length about his stay in Monteluppi prison [in Kraków] and his hostile attitude to the Germans, but he showed little interest in the real work at Katyn, and came to the woods for conversations with *OLt* Slovenzik. He collected some material for his newspaper and scrupulously noted our conversations, which disturbed us. He was interested in copies of letters dug up with the bodies and my typewriter with my notes. He stayed much longer than he or we wished, but there was no early plane to return to Kraków. As far as I remember, he left with the party of foreign journalists or with the Polish workers from the *Generalgouvernment.*

After his return to Kraków, Kawecki published an alleged interview with me on the subject of the work at Katyn, although in fact I had given him an interview but asked him not to mention my name in the press in connection with the work. After my return to Kraków I saw Kawecki and reproached him for not keeping his promise and for fabricating the interview. He excused himself on the grounds that he had been forced to do it by the Germans and that under the pressure from them he had written up the alleged interview on the basis of his notes he had made during his stay at Katyn from copies he had made of my notes. Furthermore, he told me that he had been to Vienna, where he had lectured on the subject of Katyn and he had published a pamphlet on Katyn in German. It was the last time I saw him.

After the Anglo-Saxon party had left, we continued our normal work, until one day we were told by *OLt* Slovenzik and Voss that all the work was to be stopped and we had to leave the site. Russian civilian helpers were also ordered to leave and to return when called. On leaving the site, we noticed an unusual number of German policemen and at a distance a limousine with a German general in it. On alighting, he limped and leaned on a stick while inspecting the graves. I learned afterwards that it was General von Kleist [*Generalfeldmarschall* Paul von Kleist, *Operationgebeit der Herresgruppe 'A'*], the Commander of the Smolensk sector of the Eastern front. In the second half of May (about the 20th) a party of Polish workers from different factories in the territory of the *Generalgouvernment* arrived in Katyn. With them came journalists from abroad, amongst them [Józef] Mackiewicz. *OLt* Slovenzik showed them around the graves. At this moment I was conducting an examination of a body recently dug up from the lower layers of a grave, which was watched by everyone. I showed them the documents found on the body, which they deciphered. Mackiewicz was very interested in a Soviet newspaper that came from grave No.I. Later, as with all other delegates, they were taken to the house to see the exhibits.

I remember also a planeload of European journalists who came to Katyn. I did not take much interest in them; on the contrary, wishing to avoid publicity, I tried not to draw their attention to me and continued the work. Besides the visitors already mentioned, there were hundreds of people who came to Katyn, escorted by the Germans, stressing the enormity of the crime and warning the visitors that the same would happen to them if they fell into Soviet captivity.

People from Smolensk district also came in hundreds, taken round by a Russian in civilian clothes who translated *OLt* Slovenzik's information into Russian. Amongst that lot, a Russian artist from Smolensk sketched the position of the bodies in the graves and made a sketch of a body taken from grave No.V, showing the characteristic method of knotting the rope to tie the hands, of throwing the greatcoat over the head and tying it round the neck.

Captain Stanley Gilder's Report

The statement entitled 'History of Visit to Katyn' in the files of the FO, Prisoner of War Department,[24] starts with a preamble:

By agreement with Colonel Stevenson[25] Senior British Officer with the party, I committed no account of the visit to paper at the time and therefore I am dependent on memory for details. The only other occasion on which I wrote a summary of the visit, and at that, a partial one, was this summer, at the request of the Protecting Power's representative, who on his visit to *Lazarett Rottenmuenster, Stalag V B,* stated that the British Government required a report from me. He suggested that I should give my opinion on what I had seen but I refused to do this, stating that I expected soon to be repatriated and could then communicate with the competent authorities.

I was employed at the Prisoner-of-War Hospital of Rottenmuenster at Rottweil-on-Necker in 1943 as Medical Officer to the British patients and also Senior Medical Officer to the Russian POW Hospital. On an afternoon early in May 1943, I was sent for by Dr Essig the German *Stabsartz.* On arriving in his office, I found him at the telephone and he informed me that he has just received an *OKW* [*Oberkommando der Wehrmacht*] order transmitted from the *Feldgendarmerie* Stuttgart, to send two British prisoners to Berlin, whence they would be flown to Russia to see the mass graves at Katyn. His orders were that one prisoner of war from the Dominions and one *'Inselbriten'* i.e. one from the British Isles should go. I protested that this was unwarranted involvement of prisoners in political affairs, and he repeated that it was an order. Two men would be sent, but we would be allowed to choose them. He required an answer as soon as possible. After discussion with my two colleagues, Captain W. Lumsden R.A.M.C. and Captain G. Gorrie, R.A.M.C., it was agreed that one of us should go, especially as Captain Gorrie was in a position to transmit short messages home. During the discussion, Dr Essig came in and asked our decision. On hearing that we had decided on a doctor, he told me that I would go. Sergeant Suttie of the N.Z.M.C. [New Zealand Medical Corps] was also detailed to go. My colleagues thought that it would be an advantage if I went since I speak German and Russian.

Nothing more was heard for over a week, when I was informed that I should leave on the morrow alone. The next day, Tuesday, 11 May (?), a guard arrived from *Stalag* V B and I was taken by the *D-Zug* to Berlin. I was taken next morning to a house in Schlieffen-Ufer, Berlin, which was used to house a *Kommando* of mixed French and Russian prisoners. The French officer to whom I spoke later told me that the French there formed a bona-fide *Kommando* plus some of the Commission Scapini [The Vichy French Government Paw aid organisation], but that the others were all suspect, e.g. Russians, who seemed willing to collaborate and occasionally British 'segregated prisoners'. At this house I met the other members of the Katyn party: Lt Col Stevenson of the South African Forces, Lt Col van Vliet [Lt Col John H van Vliet, Jr, Infantry] and Captain Stuart [Capt Donald R Stewart, Field Artillery] of the American Army, three British Other Ranks and a British civilian internee. The other three officers had come from *Oflag IX, A/Z* Rotenburg and had come on a German order, after protesting and addressing a communication to the 'Protecting Power'. It was decided to make a further protest and that Colonel Stevenson should be our spokesman. In the early afternoon several German officers arrived and we were interviewed in turn.

The interviews seem to have been substantially the same for all of us. My interview was conducted in English and Captain [*Hauptmann*] Bentmann; a German Staff Officer spoke to me. He said, 'you have shown interest in this affair.' I replied that I had no interest in this matter, and that they had no right to involve a prisoner of war in propaganda of this nature. I said that I was only there under duress. He said 'You will proceed to Katyn tomorrow.' I said that if I received an order backed by force, I should have to go. He said, 'You will receive such an order.' I asked what possible use such an expedition could have, and the only answer was 'It is so impressive that when you see it, you cannot help believing it.'

The interview of the other members of the party was similar except that it was made clear that any further negotiations should be done through our Senior Officer. The Germans asked if we would give parole [an officer's verbal promise not to attempt to escape] for the journey. This we naturally refused. The next morning, Wednesday, we were taken in an omnibus to Tempelhof aerodrome, a *Sonderfuehrer* von Johnson (half American) and unobtrusive guards accompanied us. At Templehof we were put on a Junker transport plane and taken to Smolensk, making two stops at Breslau [Wrocław] and Biała Podlaska (lunch here). We got to Smolensk at about 5pm and were taken by car to a tenement block used by German troops and installed in two rooms (officers in one and ORs [other ranks] in the other), fitted up with the usual double-decker beds. Shortly after, a group of troops in German uniform appeared in the courtyard under our window (as if by chance!) and began singing in Russian. After a few minutes, a German officer had asked us to come over to the officer's mess in the adjacent building. He took us past the singing soldiers and it was suggested that we might like to listen to them. They were Russians, who had changed sides and at Colonel Stevenson's request, I asked their officer, an alleged ex-Red Army officer, some questions. He started a long political harangue, which sounded like a lesson learnt by heart.

The rest of the evening was spent in the German officer's mess, where we were given supper, drinks and cigarettes. Everything had obviously been prearranged, e.g. a pianist and piano-accordionist were present, playing and singing Anglo-American songs, while an English speaking mess waiter (Brixton born) made himself agreeable to our Other Ranks, who however kept him at a distance.

The German officers were as charming as only Germans can be, when they have orders to be charming. Some preliminary spadework was done on us when the German Press correspondence officer [*Kreigsberichter*] in charge of the Katyn 'show' appeared and gave us the history of the find, illustrated with many photographs. He was told that it was all very interesting, but of course our view was our Government's view and we had no comment to make. I may here add that after our visit, as far as I know, no attempt was made to ask us our opinion by our escorts.

Next morning, we were taken in an omnibus to Katyn, which is a wood just to the south of the main road west of Smolensk, perhaps 12 miles out. The scene of the excavations is only 100 yards or so from the main road in a clearing of the wood. A number of soldiers wearing Polish steel hats and a modified German uniform were guarding the environs – alleged to be Polish ex-soldiers. When we arrived, the Press Officer was there to conduct us and introduced us to the Professor of Forensic Medicine at Breslau, a man called Butz or Buhtz. Colonel Stevenson suggested that as a doctor, I was more competent to converse with the Professor, and the latter addressed most of his conversation to me.

The story of the alleged finding of the graves by the Germans, after an old Russian peasant had informed them was first told us and we were then shown the excavations. There were three adjacent graves, partly dug up. In one, rows of bodies were still lying one upon another, for the most part neatly arranged face downwards and like sardines in a tin. It was said that the graves probably contained 11,000 bodies, of whom 3,500 had been already exhumed. I should think that it was a fair estimate. There were a number of odd bits of clothing and gear scattered around, including quantities of Polish bank notes.

The soil was very sandy, the graves fairly dry and the bodies in a good state of preservation, a certain amount of mummification having occurred. They were fully clad in uniforms, some of which I considered similar to that I had seen Polish Prisoners of War wearing. Some had their hands tied behind their backs with string. Those which we looked at closely, had a bullet hole in their occipital bone and often a bigger exit hole in the frontal region. Post mortem examinations were done by a German doctor on the tables near to the graves with another examining the contents of the pockets.

We were then shown a group of individuals standing a little distance away, who were alleged to be Russian witnesses. One was a very old man, who was alleged to have informed the Germans [about the killings]. At Colonel Stevenson's request, I spoke to him in Russian. He repeated the story, which the Germans had already told us. Asked how much the Germans paid him for telling his tale, he replied 'Nothing'. Asked how a peasant could afford to waste his time there for nothing, he said 'I do not understand.'

After conducting us round the wood and showing us smaller excavations with human remains in them and a small house overlooking the Dnieper alleged to be the seat of *GPU*[26] orgies, we were taken back to the omnibus. En route, I spoke alone with a man, who was said to be a Polish Red Cross doctor, and tried to find out his opinion, but he was very discreet. On the way back to Smolensk, we halted at the house by the roadside, which the Germans had fitted out as a Katyn museum. In glass cases, they had various papers, diaries, and letters in Polish, allegedly to have been found on bodies at Katyn. I cannot read Polish, so a lot of this was lost on me. We were given cocktails and a talk about the exhibits here by the Press Officer and then taken back to Smolensk to lunch in the mess. After lunch, an excursion had been arranged to a nearby village with the object of showing us (a) an alleged untouched *kolkhoz* [kolhoz] village; (b) a village 'improved' by the Germans; (c) a model farm run by a German Major.

The show was extremely well stage-managed, and a troupe of Russian actors and actresses (alleged to have been captured at Wjasna in 1941 and to have been an 'ENSA' [Entertainment National Service Association – the British organisation that provided entertainment for the armed forces] troupe with [Semyon] Timoshenko's army), were even produced as if by chance, to give us an entertainment. On our return in the evening to Smolensk, we declined an invitation to the mess.

Next morning (Friday), we returned to Berlin by plane by the same route and reached our *Kommando* by evening. We asked for Red X [Cross] parcels and were given them within an hour plus our cigarette ration.

Colonel Stevenson complained that the accommodation was not good enough for officers, a justifiable complaint, and the German *Sonderfuehrer* came back with the story that we would be moved to better quarters.

I suggested that in view of the delicate situation in which we were, it would be wise to accept no favours from the Germans, beyond the privileges due to our rank, and Colonel Stevenson told the Germans that we would prefer to remain at the *Kommando*. We were kept there a week, during which we were given a daily walk in the Tiergarten for which parole was given but nevertheless an armed *Sonderfuhrer* went with us 'to protect us from the populace'.

Colonel Stevenson had several interviews with the Germans, once with an official of the Foreign Office [*Auswartiges Amt*] but stated that he could not find out what the object of the visit had been. Once, Captain [*Hauptmann*] Bentmann made a vague suggestion about a broadcast but nothing came of it and no pressure was put on us. Colonel Stevenson stated that he had been assured that the photographs and newsreels made of our visit at Katyn would not be used for propaganda in Germany.

As far as I know, the promise was kept; neither did I see any reference in the Press to our visit. At the end of a week, we were sent back to our camps. (The Other Ranks were sent back as soon as they returned to Berlin, save for one New Zealand private kept as a batman).

Colonel Stevenson left first, then the two American officers and lastly myself. My guard who, although only a corporal and a Berlin businessman, told me that they had lied to Colonel Stevenson. He was not going back to camp, but was to be retained. (He subsequently arrived at a Prison Camp in Italy). On my return to my hospital, I made no statement about what I had seen, and after abortive attempts to pump me, the Germans also forgot all about the matter.

Stanley S.B. Gilder, Capt. R.A.M.C. 98570

Wodziński's report Part Two

7. The Location of the Graves and Dispute over the Number of the Dead
During the first two weeks of my stay in Katyn, only 1,700 bodies from grave No.I were exhumed and in spite of the fact that the grave was not yet emptied, the Germans wanted it that way, for propaganda effect to show the visitors that the largest grave was still full of corpses, particularly the sap which showed 12 layers of bodies. This resulted in further exhumation of bodies from the remaining six graves at random, also half emptied for some time, they did not contain as large a number of bodies as No.I, but in stages they were emptied: Grave No.III was first, followed by IV, VI and VII, so graves No.I, II and V were emptied later. The reason for doing so was that No.I was the largest, II because of its characteristic arrangement of the bodies and V, because it was flooded with water. In general I tried to direct the work as systematically as possible, so that one group of workers, having started work on one grave, would do so for one whole day. But because of different dimensions of the graves, sometimes two groups of workers would work at the same time. Thus an average three groups were working every day and bodies were exhumed from neighbouring graves at the same time, which made it impossible to establish exactly which body came from which grave.

Grave No.II was special as the bodies were laid carefully, face down, with arms crossed behind the back. At first glance it gave the impression that the victims were led onto the edge of the grave, then pushed over and shot in a prone position. For this reason the Germans drew it to the attention of visitors, stressing the cruelty of the crime. By the last days of May, graves No.I and II at last were completely empty. As far as I remember, the following number of bodies was exhumed from the Katyn graves:

No. I grave about 2,500
No. II grave about 700
No.III grave about 250
No.IV grave about 150
No.V grave about 5 plus 46
No.VI grave about 300
No.VII grave about 300

Total about 4,250

Not having my notes at my disposal at present the numbers are only estimates, nor do I remember exactly the dimensions of each grave, nor the layers of bodies in each grave. The measurements were done by the Germans in my presence and passed over to Professor Buhtz, and I have no reason to question the accuracy of the dimensions of the graves given in his report. I have read the report after its publication in the German book on Katyn and I have compared it with my notes and I could not find any discrepancy.

8. The Topography of Graves Nos. I, II, III, IV and VI

As already stated the largest grave No. I was an 'L' shape, its long arm running along the slope of the western side of the sandy mound. It was also the deepest and revealed different layers of soil. The upper layer consisted of airy, light sand, below that was a layer of sandy clay and below that a layer of compact, wet black peat of which the walls of the lower part of the grave consisted. The bottom of the short arm was level, but the bottom of the long arm was terraced. There were five of these terraces. The depth of the longer arm decreased gradually as it sloped downwards and westwards. On the terraces, the bodies were laid alternately in an orderly manner, but higher up, they were helter-skelter, put in headlong in haste. The bodies in the upper layers were light and fragile. The facial features had disintegrated, giving the appearance of a partial mummification. Proceeding downwards and coming to the clay layer, we found well preserved bodies, with distinct facial features, covered over with a whitish layer of sticky grease [adipocere – mortuary wax], which had an unpleasant, sharp, putrid smell. This layer of grease protected the bodies from external influence and was a sign of fatty degeneration. Bodies within the peat layer were relatively the best preserved. They showed a marked flattening, resulting from pressure upon them by the upper layers. Likewise, the clothes of bodies in the upper layers were faded and brittle to the touch, becoming progressively stronger the lower the layer.

The most interesting detail of grave No.I was that bodies were dressed in winter clothes, warm underwear, sweaters and so forth. Wooden soles, so-called *apelówki* (parade soles) attached to the shoes were found in great number. A certain number, not many, had their hands tied behind their backs with a cord or a rope.

Grave No.II had a sandy soil only in its upper layers, which quickly passed into clay. In graves Nos.III, IV, VI and VII, the sandy layer was perhaps a little thicker, but underneath it, there was clay, as in No.II. The bodies were carefully laid out face down with arms crossed behind the back. They were laid so that the faces of one layer were lying on the thighs of the one below. The bodies in graves Nos.II, III, IV, VI and VII were well preserved and exhibited a partial fatty degeneration. Where grave No.VI and VII differed was that all the bodies had their arms tied behind the back. In all these graves, bodies were dressed in winter overcoats and warm underwear and some had wooden *apelówki* attached to the shoes.

With regard to the sketches of Katyn graves shown to me, I do have some comments and corrections to make:

The short arm of grave No.I ran almost parallel to the path through the woods, at a distance of more or less 40 metres, curving from it (like a knee) into the long arm, which lay at right angles to the short arm, sloping towards the western side of the sandy mound. The lower edge of the longer arm of grave No.I was at the same height as the lower edge of grave No.IV.

At a distance of about 15 metres from grave No.I in the southeast direction at the same level as its outer curve, grave No.II was situated. It was rectangular in shape, the longer side running parallel to the long arm of grave No.I. The long axis of grave No.II ran from northeast to southwest. In spite of different data in Professor Buhtz's report, I stand by the description given above.

At a distance of three to four metres from the northeast side of grave No.II and about 30 metres from the woodland path, there was a one-room wooden shed with a table. In that shed the German doctors dissected the bodies and there, documents were kept on rainy days. The shed was already there when I arrived at Katyn, but I heard that it was at a different site across the main road.

Slightly below the lower, shorter edge of grave No.II grew a pine tree nearly twenty metres high. Underneath this pine, lay obliquely from northwest to southeast the rectangular grave No.III.

Grave No.IV was situated opposite the bottom edge of the long arm of grave No.I and was also rectangular in shape the long side was running slightly north-west to southeast.

The distance of the three graves described above from the long arm of the grave No.I was more or less the same. In my time, there was a footpath running between them, used for carrying exhumed bodies. As there was shortage of space, the outside examinations were done there and then, on tables provided.

Grave No.V was situated at a distance of about five metres from grave No.IV it was the lowest of all the graves, near the edge of the marshes. Its long axis ran northeast to southwest.

Grave No.VI was squeezed in between grave No.IV and the obliquely lying grave No. III. It was rectangular in shape, with the longer axis running east to west.

Grave No.VII was parallel to grave No.VI and about five metres away.

Opposite the main group of Polish graves, on the other side of the road, in the woods, in a triangle of footpaths running through the woods from the Dnieper to the main road in the direction of Kiselev's farm, old Russian graves were located. They were hidden among trees, some 20 years old, mostly deciduous on sandy soil. The Germans prior to my arrival uncovered them. I do not remember the exact number of these Russian graves, but they were rather shallow, 1.5 metres deep, they contained parts of human skeletons scattered at random. Judging by the number of skulls in different graves, one can reckon that they contained somewhere around 20 bodies each. On closer examination of the skulls, one could see the holes made by gunshots, which were found regularly at the back of the head and the exit holes were in the region of the forehead. In some cases it was impossible to determine exactly the place of entry. I fixed from the condition of the skeletons the time the bodies had lain in the graves at approximately 15 years. The bottom part of the soil in the graves was sandy clay, which favoured mummification and preservation of the skeletons.

As the work progressed and the initial graves were emptied and the bodies registered, it became more obvious that the total number of bodies exhumed at Katyn would not exceed 4,500. As this was a glaring contradiction to the German propaganda, which continually gave the figure of 12,000, the Germans started a vigorous search for further graves in the area. They used metal acoustic sounding rods on the ground, without success. But in the last days of May, near a small woodland path, running in the direction of the Dnieper River, at a distance of 100 to 150 metres from the sandy mound, in a spruce grove of 20 to 30 years old, they found two mass graves under a thick layer of pine needles. They contained less than twenty corpses each, in an extreme state of decomposition. On closer inspection, it was stated that they were bodies of Soviet citizens, some of whom were in Soviet uniforms with green and red braid. Among the corpses, clad in civilian clothing of Soviet type, were several women, wearing Russian type boots. Judging by the degree of decomposition, I fixed the time in one as 10 years, and in the other at about five to seven years. All these bodies had bullet wounds, with the entry apertures in the occipital bone and exit aperture somewhere in the frontal bone. The calibre of the bullets was calculated as being not more than 8 mm. No documentation was found on them.

Towards the end of May 1943, the activity at the Eastern Front increased as the front appeared to be moving westwards. At Katyn we heard the sound of guns and one night we had an air raid of several dozen Soviet planes in the vicinity of Katyn woods that destroyed the German supply stores located between Katyn and Gnezdovo station. After that all members of the Technical Commission felt uneasy, fearing our fate in the event of the Katyn area being reoccupied by the Soviet offensive. I saw *OLt* Slovenzik and told him that our work was practically done and in the next few days would be finished and it was our wish to return to our country. Slovenzik replied that the number of exhumed bodies so far was definitely too small and we must wait for the final result of the search which was going on. When I insisted, Slovenzik demanded that in my final report I should give the figure of 12,000 as being the probable number of bodies. I asked him on what basis I should give this deceitful figure. Slovenzik answered that if the German authorities announced this figure, no one was allowed to question it, and if he did he might have to pay with his head. That was the end of the conversation.

9. Graves No. V and VIII

As already mentioned, all the Katyn graves were empty, except No. V lying at the lowest level, on the edge of the marsh, which had for some time been two-thirds full of water. This created a considerable problem and only five bodies had been taken out, which had risen to the surface. I asked Slovenzik and Voss to provide us with a pump and I was promised that one would be brought from Smolensk fire station. Towards the end of May, the weather turned very warm and the ground water in grave No. V fell considerably, but it was still very muddy. The promised pump did not arrive and I distinctly felt a passive or even obstructive attitude on the part of Slovenzik and Voss. On 30 or 31 May, I saw the Russian civilians starting to fill in grave No. V. When asked why they were doing it they replied that the Germans had ordered it. I saw Slovenzik immediately and argued that he must recall his order as the members of the Technical Commission wished to exhume all the bodies of Polish officers at Katyn and to bury them in new communal graves and make a complete list of bodies. He argued that because of the increased smell of the corpses, he could not force the Russian workers to do this unpleasant work. He said that if we wanted to, we could do the job ourselves. Slovenzik wanted to know more and asked me for my estimate of how many bodies there were in grave V. I replied probably not exceeding fifty, he shrugged his shoulders and said that in his opinion, there were more than 200 bodies.

On 1 VI 1943, members of our *PCK* Technical Commission made a bridge across the grave and started to lift the corpses from the mud. It was the most arduous work ever undertaken because of the conditions of the corpses, which fell apart when lifted. It was a most revealing grave, the five corpses and the rest taken out of the bottom of the grave – all had their hands tied behind their backs with a white cord, tied in a typical double running knot. Greatcoats covered the heads and were tied with the same kind of knot at the neck level and sometimes a second knot had been made above the head of the victim. At the neck, there was a simple knot and the rest of the cord was passed down the back and wound round the tied hands and was again tied at the neck. In this way, the hands of the victims were pulled up to the height of the shoulder blades. Victims tied in this way were unable to resist, because every move of the hands tightened the noose round the neck, thus choking the victim. From the point of view of forensic medicine and criminology, such a way of tying up the victims before the execution should be regarded as a refined torture before death. In one case a small quantity of sawdust was found around the mouth. Sawdust would enter the bronchial tubes when the victim took a sharp breath or cried out, causing suffocation. In other cases I saw felt gags applied to the mouths of the victims.

The corpses examined from grave No.V were also shot in the back of the head, but they were not the same as those of the victims of the other graves. The coats were shot through, corresponding to the entry and exit wounds in the head. On closer examination, after the cords and coats were removed, it was found that the entry wounds were not regularly placed beneath the occipital bone as with other bodies, and the bullet channel ran more horizontally, exiting in the lower half of the frontal bone. From this, we can conclude that with the greatcoats being tied over the heads of the victims, precise shooting was difficult.

On 1 VI 1943, while we were at work on grave No.V we were alarmed to see the Germans running towards us with news of the location of a new grave of Polish officers. We stopped work and moved over to the newly discovered grave No.VIII, which was located 100 metres southwest of grave No.V, in a direct line with the long arm of grave No.I. It was on a small rise, on the other side of the marsh and behind the footpath in the woods, which branched from the main path leading to the *NKVD* house on Dnieper River running in a northwest direction. On arrival I saw a dug out hole four metres square and one metre deep already escavated by the Russian workers; and bodies in Polish uniforms. On top of the grave we could see a trough-like hollow of about 40 square metres, over which lush grass was growing. Close to the edge there were only four layers of bodies. Wooden piles were knocked into the ground and a woven fence erected, presumably to mark the boundary.

On 1 VI 1943, ten bodies were taken out of the grave and immediately it was evident that the bodies did not wear greatcoats, or warm underwear, sweaters, scarves or *apelówki*. The pockets contained newspapers in Polish, *Kijowski Głos Radziecki* (Kiev's Soviet Voice) from early May. The latest date of any newspaper found on the bodies in grave No.VIII, was 6th May 1940. All the documents found on the bodies were of the same kind as the other graves, marked 'Kozelsk'. In addition, wooden cigarette holders and cases bore the inscription 'Kozelsk'. On these bodies were found the typical gunshot wounds at the back of the head beneath the occipital bone, with the exit wound in the forehead, most often in the centre. Perhaps in two cases, there were characteristics of close range shooting, the singeing of the skin at the edge of the wound and grains of unburnt powder lying concentrically round it and stuck in the skin. Similarly, as far as I remember, I found in two cases the bullet stuck under the skin of the forehead. This bullet was 7.65 mm calibre, similar to those in the other graves already described.

Close to the edge of grave No.VIII at the southeast end, wooden pickets were knocked down into the bottom of the grave for a woven fence. I cannot explain the reason for this fence, except to mark the boundary of the grave. I did not see a similar structure in the other graves. In parts of the grave, close to the edge, there were only four layers of bodies laying one on top of the other.

On 2 June, a digging test was done in order to establish the dimensions of the new grave No.VIII. I do not remember exactly what they were, but remember that they were not any larger than grave VI or VII, which could have been eight by five by two metres deep, and according to my estimation, holding not more than 200 bodies. When I mentioned this figure to Slovenzik, I noticed that he became nervous and angry. He told me once more that the total number of 12,000 was not to be questioned.

I must stress that during one of the conversations with O*Lt* Slovenzik on the subject of the number of Katyn victims I stressed that no way could 12,000 bodies be found at Katyn, because judging by the documents found, all the victims had come from Kozelsk and there were never such a large number of Polish prisoners there. Slovenzik declared to me that in reality the Katyn woods were one big cemetery and that undoubtedly other groups of graves of Polish prisoners from other camps would be found, especially those from Starobelsk. Thus, when the new grave No VIII was found, located away from the others, the Germans assumed that they had found groups of graves of Starobelsk prisoners.

Meanwhile the dimensions of the grave, the documents and other objects (cigarette holders) found on the bodies indicated that these victims had also come from Kozelsk. Typical shot wounds to the back of the head were found beneath the occipital bone, with an exit wound in the central part of the forehead. In two cases, shots must have been fired closely as singeing of the skin and grains of unburnt powder lying concentrically around it was observed. In two cases, bullets stuck under the skin of the forehead. I measured one bullet and it was 7.65 mm, similar to those found in other graves. This shattered the Germans, as they hoped that in the new grave officers from Starobelsk and Ostashkov could be found, making up the total figure of 12,000.

Slovenzik disagreed, stating that all of Katyn woods were one big cemetery and undoubtedly other graves could be found and ordered the work to continue. I declared categorically that the Technical Committee had worked for over a month in terrible conditions and wanted to leave Katyn. I drew his attention to the increasing heat and stench and the danger of epidemic. Besides, there was the danger of the Soviet offensive approaching Katyn. I assured him that we still wanted to exhume all the bodies and rebury them properly, but that could be resumed in the autumn. Slovenzik agreed, and ordered grave No.VIII to be filled in with earth and the rest to be left undisturbed.

Departure from Katyn and its Aftermath

The whole Technical Commission wished to leave Katyn as soon as possible, in view of the approaching personal danger from the Soviet offensive as well as from the German tension over the number of Katyn bodies. I agreed to *OLt* Slovenzik's decision. I was influenced by the following facts:

1. As I have already said before, contrary to what I had originally expected, no more Polish doctors were sent to Katyn, I was the only one during the whole period of exhumation work. I hoped that in the autumn that might change, and more doctors would finish the work. It would undoubtedly carry more weight with the Polish nation to know that several people were examining the conditions, the circumstances and the date of the murder. I also thought that a larger delegation of Polish experts would be able to tackle the untouched grave No.VIII and examine the material in it.

2. In view of war developments (the expulsion of the Germans from North Africa) I did not think it impossible for the Katyn woods to be free of German occupation by the autumn. There was also the hope of seeing the International Red Cross or an Allied Medico-Legal Commission of some sort taking over. Thus, leaving the greater part of grave No.VIII untouched by the Germans would present them with very valuable evidence.

After coming to this agreement with Slovenzik, the next day, 3 June 1943, together with Messrs Cupryjak, Mikołajczyk and Jaworowski, I left Katyn. The remaining members of the Technical Commission were to complete the work on grave No.V, ie. to empty it and bury the rest of the unburied bodies, together with the ten dug up from grave No.VIII, in new communal graves. Before my departure, Buczek and Płonka gave me the figure of 46 bodies in grave No.V. It remains to say that during my stay in Katyn, I did not see Professor Buhtz examine the few bodies from grave No.VIII, this was done by a German Dr Müller, neither do I know if he visited Katyn woods after I left. When we arrived at Smolensk, there was no plane for us, and we had to wait a day there to travel by train. During that time, I was invited by Dr Schmidt to visit the forensic laboratory and inspect the preparations made from the exhumed bodies. In particular, I was shown a sample from the entry wounds with the characteristics of shots fired at close range, and those of skull wounds and material used for gags. Besides the histo-pathological laboratory there was a well equipped photographic darkroom.

We left Smolensk by train for Warsaw on 5 June 1943, passing through Minsk and [Brest] Brześć-on-Bug, arriving there on 7 June. I did not take any official documents from Katyn, other than my notes made during the course of my work there. I took rolls of film, which I had not developed at Smolensk, despite German pressure, and samples of cartridges, bullets and cord used to tie up the bodies; also some close-up slides of skin and sections of heart muscle, liver and kidney, taken by me when a dissection was unusual, for example in the absence of a bullet wound, when the cause of death was not established.

On my departure from Katyn, Slovenzik ordered me to report to the local office of German propaganda on my arrival at Kraków. I realised that they would use me for propaganda purposes. I decided to go on leave for a number of weeks to Zakopane. When I returned to Kraków, the Germans did not bother me on this account. I went back to my previous work at the Institute of Forensic Medicine and Criminology, keeping close contact with Dr Robel. It is from him that I learned that Dr Beck handed over the materials that had been sent by the Germans to Dr Beck, the German Director of the Institute in Kraków, for further investigation. Dr Robel examined the material with infrared rays and all the documents were photographed. He mentioned that many errors had been made in deciphering documents, which resulted in alterations to names of many Katyn victims on the official list. He particularly wanted me to preserve carefully the material I brought with me in order to compare the data collected by us both.

By the autumn of 1943, Katyn woods had been occupied by the Bolsheviks, *OLt* Slovenzik came to Kraków. A meeting at the Propaganda office was called, and my presence was demanded. Dr Schebesta and Dr Plappert were already there and after a short conversation, Slovenzik announced that the work in Katyn could not now be finished, on account of the Germans having been driven from the Smolensk region. He asked me to meet him in private in his hotel that afternoon, Dr Plappert was meant to be there as well, but I did not go, I did not see Slovenzik again.

At the beginning of August 1944, immediately after the outbreak of the Warsaw Uprising, all the cases with Katyn documents were taken from Dr Robel and conveyed from the Institute of Medical Chemistry of the Jagiellonian University to the Institute of Forensic Medicine and Criminology at 16 Grzegorzewska Street, where, on the orders of Dr Beck, they were specially guarded by the Gestapo. In the middle of August 1944, on account of the Eastern front approaching at an alarming rate, the cases of documents were transported from Kraków and deposited at the Institute of Forensic Medicine in Wrocław. I do not know what has happened to them, or the fate of Dr Beck after leaving Kraków.

The Conclusions of the Report

1. The exhumed bodies numbering 4,145 were buried in eight mass graves. Seven of the graves with different contents lay close together and were situated on a sandy mound at a distance of about 500 metres from the Orsha-Smolensk

main road. The largest 'L' shaped grave contained about 2,500 bodies, the others from 700 (No.II) down to 50 (No.V). On exhumation, the bodies were closely packed side by side in layers, mostly face down. The only haphazard burial was noted in the top layer of grave No.I. Grave No.VIII, situated at a distance of about 100 metres from the others, was only partially emptied and by comparing its dimensions with those of the other graves, it could have contained about 150–200 bodies.

2. Taking into account the fact that the bodies in the large majority of cases were dressed in Polish officers' uniforms and provided with inoculation certificates from Kozelsk camp, we must assume that they were the bodies of the Polish officer prisoners of war of 1939 from Kozelsk camp.

3. The post mortem examinations of the bodies established the cause of death to be a shot to the skull, damaging the brain (for the most part the medulla) causing instantaneous death. This shot, aimed as a rule from the back, slightly below the occipital protuberance and running upwards and forwards for the most part, terminated in an exit wound within the upper part of the forehead. Only in a few cases, a double or even treble shot in the back of the head was found.

4. This consistent bullet channel proved that the executioners were systematic and experienced.

5. All the shots were fired from pistols and ammunition bore the trade-mark 'Geco 7.65 D'. The fact that the edges of the wounds were singed and that the grains of unburned powder were stuck around them, proved that the shot had been fired from close range.

6. A relatively large quantity of cartridge cases and bullets in the vicinity of the graves, under the pine needles and even inside the graves, were a sufficient basis for the supposition that execution was carried out nearby the graves or even after the victims had been led into the dug-out graves.

7. The absence of any traces of a struggle having occurred before death led to the supposition that the victims were overpowered by assistants and only then shot by the actual executioners. In nearly 20% of the cases, the hands were tied behind the back with a cord tied in a double slip knot, suggesting that it was used as a preventative measure against self defence; this method was used with individuals who could offer resistance because they were physically fit. In addition, the throwing of the greatcoats over the heads of the victims (in grave No.V) and the tying of the cord around the neck and connecting this knot with that used to tie

the hands behind the back, suggested that this refined method of disabling the victim was intended to prevent any shouting before the execution.

8. The precision with which each victim was shot, the fact that each layer was spread with a calcium compound (grave No.I), the period covered by the dates of the Soviet newspapers and diaries found on the bodies and finally, the careful laying out of the bodies in each grave (with the exception of the upper layers of grave No.I) was sufficient proof that the crime was carried out over a long period of time.

9. It was impossible to fix exactly the length of time the bodies had lain underground by the degree of the putrefaction alone. It is true that the research of Prof. Orsós (from Budapest), is supposed to have established that an encrustation of calcium salts on the inner side of the skull does not occur before a body has lain in the earth for three years. This phenomenon was discovered on several occasions on Katyn bodies, but [the theory] has as yet to be accepted in the field of forensic medicine and cannot therefore be used as a basis for the calculation of the exact period of time the bodies had lain in the earth. The exhumed bodies showed a varying degree of putrefaction, depending on the layer of soil, its reaction, the accessibility of the air, humidity and the pressure under which they were lying. Thus, in the upper sandy layers the bodies were light and brittle and presented a picture practically of mummification, whereas in the lower layers of clay or peat (grave No.I), they exhibited so called fatty degeneration [adipocere], characterised by the preservation of the general features of the body. The skin of these bodies was covered with sticky, grey grease, which had an unpleasant, sharp smell, which had also permeated the clothes of the bodies. This above-mentioned layer of grease protected not only the bodies, but also the documents found on them. The clothes on the bodies in the upper layers were more faded and fragile than in the lower layers, which were strong and with the colours preserved.

10. The above-mentioned degree of putrefaction being dependent on external factors and the exact matching together of adjacent lying bodies proved that the original arrangement of the bodies had not been disturbed.

11. The presence of wooden soles (*apelówki*) attached to the boot legs by means of a string of leather straps on a considerable number of bodies in grave no.1 and the absence of them in the other graves, led to the supposition that grave No.I was filled with the victims of the first executions, carried out in the colder time of the year and that only later, step by step, the other mass graves were filled in. From the notes found in the diaries on the exhumed bodies, it could be calculated that the time when the first seven mass graves were made was the end of

March and April 1940. Grave No.VIII discovered on the first of June 1943, was the latest and must have been made in the first half of May 1940. The bodies in it were clad in summer uniforms and the Soviet newspapers found on them were dated the first days of May 1940.

12. The examination of the material evidence found on the bodies, such as anti-typhoid inoculation certificates from the Kozelsk camp, identity cards, *PKO* (Post Office Savings Bank) savings books, diaries, letters received at Kozelsk or not yet sent from Kozelsk, military aluminium identity discs, visiting cards, sketches, photographs etc made it possible to establish for the greater number of the victims their surname, Christian names, military rank, profession, age, place of residence, religion etc.

13. The above mentioned material evidence and more than anything else the diaries and notebooks, made it possible to establish more precisely the time of the crime. They all ceased in the second half of March and April 1940. These also made it possible to establish the route along which the Polish prisoners were brought to the scene of the crime, which was Kozelsk–Smolensk–Gnezdovo. The route continued in prison vans to the place of execution in the Katyn woods. So, for instance, the diary of Major Adam Solski [exhumed body] No.0490, finished on 9 April 1940, with the note: 'We have been brought to a wood, 6.30 hours – they take away watches, belts, pen knives, roubles.'

14. The data collected as a result of the examination on the scene of the crime and the examination of the bodies agreed with the depositions of the Russian witnesses (Zakharov and Kiselev), who saw the Polish prisoners being brought in parties, in prison wagons, in the spring of 1940 to Gnezdovo station and from there, being driven in prison vans in the direction of the Katyn woods. The witness Kiselev, who lived nearby, had even heard shots and shouts coming from the forest.

15. The finding of other graves in the area at Katyn woods, containing Russian bodies with typical bullet wounds in the skull, led to the supposition that the Katyn woods had already been used for some time as a place of execution. Judging by the degree of putrefaction of the bodies in the different Russian graves, the time they had laid in the earth should be calculated as being between five and 15 years.

16. The undersigned expert reserves the right of giving a supplementary forensic medical statement, after he has finished analysing further material.

Skarżyński's Report Part Two

On 1 May 1943, Messrs Rojkiewicz and Kołodziejski returned from Katyn. Kołodziejski, for family reasons, could only stay for two weeks. Rojkiewicz began his work on site and awaited Mr Kassur's arrival. For the next ten days he requested, to no avail, a place on a plane to deliver the awaited first report to the Executive Committee. His presence in Katyn during that time was beneficial, but the delay in his return proved how right the decision of the Executive Committee had been to increase the numbers without waiting for Rojkiewicz to return. Thus, Rojkiewicz had brought to Warsaw not a plan of work but the current report made by Kassur on the progress of the Commission. Through Rojkiewicz, Kassur informed the Executive Committee that the state of his health required a return to Warsaw. A search for a new manager for the Technical Commission began. By 8 May, the Director of the *PCK* had arranged a candidate in the person of Count Władysław Zamoyski, a former employee of the *PCK*, who agreed to take over and complete the work. Having read the available material about Katyn held by the *PCK* Executive Committee concerning the character of the work involved and the position taken by the *PCK* vis a vis the Germans, Count Zamoyski was ready to depart and replace Mr Kassur from 10 May [1943].

Quite unexpectedly, Mr Kassur arrived in Warsaw on 12 May and gave a full account of the situation. Kassur, to whom the *PCK* owes much for the efficient arrangement of the work of the Technical Commission, as well as providing initiative in a difficult situation whilst dealing with the Germans, should be reproached for leaving Katyn before his replacement arrived. Neither did he nominate a deputy from the members of the Commission. What is more, he unnecessarily agreed to Slovenzik's request to bring a box with hundreds of documents and items of the murdered officers and deliver it to the German authorities in Kraków. Because of his great merits, his exhausting and stressful work, as well as the fact that a few days after his return to Warsaw, Kassur fell ill – his faults cannot overshadow his achievements.

In his report illustrating the Technical Commission's approved procedures and its good results, in spite of the frequent difficulties, Kassur had some reservations regarding cooperation with Dr Wodziński – a forensic medicine representative and by necessity a member of the *PCK*, with other members of the committee, because of his submissiveness to the German authorities. In these circumstances, the decision to appoint Count Zamoyski was vital. The *PCK* Executive Committee believed that Count Zamoyski's initial work would be more difficult if no one was present to officially hand over the leadership of the Commission. Therefore the Committee decided to send Mr Rojkiewicz with him, who knew the conditions and the authorities there. At the same time Dr Schebesta was instructed to try and recall Dr Wodziński to Kraków. It was agreed that in his place Dr Starostka from

Tarnobrzeg, who had volunteered for the job, although he was not a member of the Institute of Forensic Medicine but had the required qualifications, would be dispatched. However, Messrs Zamoyski, Rojkiewicz and Starostka waited in vain for some time for their departure, which never materialised.

Meanwhile, after Kassur's departure without nominating his successor, the Technical Commission decided to choose from amongst themselves the oldest and most experienced person on the Red Cross team – Mr Jerzy Wodzinowski – to be the head of the Commission. With great energy and tact he brought the work to its conclusion on 9 June 1943, when the exhumation of seven graves was completed. After removing ten corpses from it, the eighth grave, discovered on 2 June, was filled in and work was postponed until September.

Between 8 and 11 June all members of the Technical Commission returned to Warsaw from Katyn. According to their last report it is clear that the initial difficulties between Dr Wodziński and the rest of the members were straightened out and Dr Wodziński, by submitting to the *PCK's* requests, contributed on a par with the rest of them to carry out the difficult task.

Ad. /b. All members of the Committee were in receipt of 50 *złoty* per day, plus expenses. The table shows the dates of their assignments:

Ludwik Rojkiewicz from 14 IV 43 to 1 V 43
Stefan Kołodziejski from 14 IV 43 to 1 V 43
Jerzy Wodzinowski from 14 IV 43 to 11 V 43
Hugon Kassur from 19 IV 43 to 12 V 43
Gracjan Jaworowski from 19 IV 43 to 9 VI 43
Adam Godzik from 19 IV 43 to 11 VI 43
Dr Marian Wodziński from 27 IV 43 to 8 VI 43
Władysław Buczak from 27 IV 43 to 12 VI 43
Franciszek Król from 27 IV 43 to 12 VI 43
Ferdynand Płonka from 27 IV 43 to 12 VI 43
Stefan Cupryjak from 28 IV 43 to 7 VI 43
Jan Mikołajczyk from 28 IV 43 to 10 VI 43

List of stores for the Technical Commission, taken to Katyn in April 1943:
One rubber coat; a pair of rubber boots; 10 pairs overalls; 10 pairs of underwear; 13 pairs rubber gloves; one rug; 12 pairs socks; one litre of toilet water [Eau de Cologne]; 8.5 litres of spirits; 7,000 cigarettes; one kg of soap; 6 toilet soap; 2 boxes of matches; three rolls of string; 10 kg of sugar; 9 kg of lard; 3 kg of bacon; 5 kg of dry bread; 5 rye bread; one hammer; a set of measuring instruments; one typewriter.
The greatest problem was getting hold of the required number of rubber gloves. The 13 pairs taken were not enough and they were soon used up, leaving the

men working with their bare hands. Lack of rubber boots was also catastrophic. The food our men received from the [Organisation] *Todt* canteen was sufficient. Spirits and cigarettes were in effect handed out to the local people as an incentive for their hard work in digging the graves.

Ad. /c. All efforts to keep in touch with Warsaw turned out to be a failure. It consisted practically, of a description of the members' journeys to Smolensk and back. The struggle of the Executive Committee for proper contacts can be divided into two phases. The first, when the German authorities in Warsaw and Kraków had shown a willingness to help the Red Cross, trying to accommodate us with scheduled airline communications between Berlin and Smolensk, which did not have the expected results. The second phase indicated to us that all the agencies of the occupation authorities had come to the same understanding, the further work of the Technical Commission had to be tolerated but they stopped short of assisting it – thus ignoring its demands for regular communications. Several factors were the reason for this change of policy.

First of all, they were truly disillusioned with the lack of change in the Polish attitude towards the Germans. In their characteristic misinterpretation of the psychology of a conquered nation – they somehow expected it [to change]. This disillusion was evident in *Herrn* [Frederich] Ohlenbusch, Propaganda Chief in Kraków, at a conference called on 10 June, where he reproached the representatives of the *PCK* with a whole stack of recriminations against the Poles regarding the Katyn massacre. Despite their expectations, the Polish nation would not embrace the Germans because of the bestial murders committed by their ally of 1939. German propaganda admitted that the presence of the *PCK* Technical Commission in Katyn was necessary and served their purpose; that hundreds of visitors could observe the Poles being unrestricted in the exhumation of their fellow countrymen. They understood that the tragic task undertaken could not be interrupted – but aimed to restrict their own responsibility to bare essentials. Lack of contact with Warsaw created difficulties. The flights were regulated by Berlin, and seat reservation could only be done by the intervention of the Kraków authorities. The number of available seats was small, while on the return journeys their military personnel going on leave took precedence.

To these German difficulties, at the beginning of May to mid June, a new and unforeseen difficulty was added – the murder of the remnants of the Jewish nation concentrated in the Warsaw ghetto led to a desperate self defence against the Germans. Armed operations in the northern district of Warsaw had caused fires, which for several weeks covered the whole of the city with smoke. German planes, carrying propaganda-inspired visitors to Katyn to show them Soviet bestiality, received orders to bypass Warsaw due to the large columns of smoke that clearly indicated a bestial act about which the German press kept silent.

In the beginning, the *PCK* Executive Committee kept receiving promises from the German authorities to improve our communications, which remained as promises; afterwards we received only excuses. At the conference in Kraków on 23 April, Deputy Propaganda Chief *Herrn* Steinmetz, declared that he would look into the problem of contacts with Katyn. A few days later, *Herrn* Heinrich informed the Executive Committee that one seat in the plane would be available for the Polish commission each week. The postal connection would be arranged within three days and the field post would arrange the delivery. Regrettably it never happened and the message from Kassur asking for electrical equipment necessary for drying the documents, never reached Warsaw. This was not good encouragement to use the field post.

After Kassur's return to Warsaw, the period of German excuses commenced. Messrs Zamoyski, Rojkiewicz and Starostka waited in vain for a plane to be taken to Katyn, and each day *Herrn* Heinrich informed us that the plane would depart any day. The aeroplane had in fact departed in the morning and two seats were free; perhaps the reason for this misunderstanding was the absence of the *PCK* President from Warsaw but again, Dr Heinrich knew other members of the Executive Committee and their telephone numbers. Finally on 20 May, Heinrich declared in confidence that the military authorities in Katyn had decided to stop the work before the month was out, and hence sending a new manager was unnecessary.

A few days later, I questioned Dr Grundmann about this and he replied that he was unaware of it and promised to find out from the Army in Smolensk, if such an order had been issued. He answered by letter that from 5 June 1943 all exhumation works have to be stopped temporarily and members of the Technical Commission would be sent back to Warsaw between 4 and 9 June. He confirmed that sending a new supervisor was unnecessary. One cannot but have the impression that the forceful agitation from Mr Kassur when he was first in charge of Katyn was not to *OLt* Slovenzik liking and the latter got rid of Mr Kassur. He relied on the fact that once the Commission was left without a supervisor someone would automatically come to the fore, perhaps a person who spoke fluent German like Dr Wodziński, on whose submissiveness he obviously counted. Otherwise it is difficult to explain the reason why Slovenzik managed to persuade Kassur to take personal charge of a case of 400 envelopes of important documents from the first exhumation of the bodies; on 12 May, he had shown great care in their despatch. It is also significant that nothing was said about sending the rest of the documents, some 4,000 envelopes, on 12 June, the date when the Commission members left Katyn all these deposits were still there.

Ad. /d. The hysterical German propaganda that surrounded Katyn did not shrink from the cruelty of informing the families of the victims as the exhumations progressed. The loudspeakers on the streets started to broadcast at certain times the names of those identified. The news electrified the people who started to gather around the speakers, to which until then, the Warsaw public paid little attention. There were instances of women fainting after hearing their husband's or son's names. At the same time the German press took the opportunity to increase their circulation by publishing in Polish the names of the victims in small daily doses, edited in such a manner that people believed it was done on behalf of the Polish Red Cross. Translated from the German language, the Polish names were frequently misspelled, causing much grief and uncertainty for the families. On the intervention of the *PCK*, the calling of names through loudspeakers was discontinued, probably the only success story of the *PCK*. The German authorities ignored our repeated pleas not to print the names in the newspapers, but leave it to the *PCK* to pass the information to the families. They were seemingly indignant about the publications, which pretended to be those of the *PCK* and promised to stop them, but did nothing ...

The Germans demanded from the *PCK* a list of names of those reliably identified, as well as another list of names, which were doubtful, and finally, the number of still unidentified persons to be published with a list of items found on their bodies. The *PCK* could not agree to this without some objections. Foremost, the Executive Committee declared that the list of names hastily produced in Katyn could not be announced as proof positive that these persons were dead. This could only be attested after a complete Katyn list had been received and examined, together with the documents, correspondence, diaries and other deposits of the deceased. Even then, this should be treated with caution, as the *PCK* could not definitely identify the corpses, but only declare that the insignia on the uniforms and the documents found led to the assumption that they belonged to the named officer. Only bodies which had identification discs, and as is known, only a minimal number had these discs in 1939, could be definitely identified. In several instances (in one case three), different corpses had documents that belonged to a single individual. One cannot exclude the possibility, however small, that the owner of the document still lives. They were not soldiers killed in battle but groups of men who before their death were taken to the camps, and for whom the thought of escape, disguising themselves or borrowing clothes, must have been a daily occurrence. In instances where identification is certain, the family is informed by the *PCK* in a manner that befits the tragic circumstances; special announcements are superfluous.

If there is uncertainty, the *PCK* checks its own list of missing persons, which has been compiled since the beginning of the war, based on information from families. If the information is inadequate, then we turn to the sender of the letter found on the body. Thus the *PCK* instructed all its agencies to gather full particulars about Poles who were kept in the Soviet camps and Russia generally, with full details and description of items that they might have had on them. The official *PCK* letter was published in the press and is the only real official document the Red Cross has ever published. This sort of system is more secure and effective than publishing a list of missing persons, which in instances of identical surnames and Christian names may cause great misery and mourning. As to the third category of unidentified persons, we agreed with the Germans that it made practical sense to publish a description of the items found.

Negotiations and meetings with the Germans concerning these matters lasted throughout the period of the Technical Commission work; and none of these issues were settled. The publication of names in the press continued and judging by the amount so far published, it is unlikely that it will end before August this year. The propaganda machine has its own agenda. Finally on 10 June 1943, two meetings were held, one in the German *Propagandaamt* office and one in the German Red Cross office, on the subject of death certificates. The German proposal was read thoroughly and considered to be inappropriate for Polish conditions. One side of the death certificate was to be filled out by the *PCK*, the other by the German Red Cross; the completed form was to be certified by the German military authorities in Smolensk. The *PCK* could not accept their text certifying death, for the reasons stated above and because it would be against Polish civil law. It was agreed that it would present its own version, once the International Red Cross approved it, which has not happened to date. The *PCK* planned to put the following text on the certificate:

'The Information Bureau of the Polish Red Cross declares that during the exhumation of the bodies at Katyn woods near Smolensk,
the following items of evidence were found on them:
These documents allow us to judge that the body belongs to _______
This person is on the list of those exhumed at Katyn in 1943 under the number _______
This certificate is issued at the request of Mr or Mrs: _______
who reside at the address:
Signature:

Ad. /e. The documentation and other deposits of the dead are, up to now, beyond the *PCK* sphere of responsibility. The military authorities in Smolensk have informed us that the documents would be returned after they have been looked over by a higher authority. German propaganda expected more from these documents, but the value of them proved to be problematical. For the Poles they represent a priceless treasure from the point of view of history and sentiment. The diaries and wry notes in the pocket diaries indicate the martyrdom of our officers, starting from the 1939 Campaign, to imprisonment in Kozelsk and eventually death in Katyn. In the words of *OLt* Slovenzik, the spirit of these men was never broken, they remained good Poles to the end, and that this may be the reason why they died together in the pits of Katyn.

To be precise, members of the Commission engaged in looking through the documents on the bodies had no permission to examine them in detail while they worked. Opening of the envelopes in the office of the Field Police was undertaken in the presence of the Commission members but the tempo of the work was such that there was only time for a superficial inspection. There will be more about this later.

As mentioned before, Kassur agreed to take one box of documents with him, to deliver it to the German authorities in Kraków. The plane had to bypass Warsaw and Kassur had to alight in Biała Podlaska. The box of documents had to be sent by rail to Kraków, where it arrived in bad shape. It was alleged that some of the envelopes were missing, the box was damaged, and some contents from the opened envelopes were accidentally mixed up. The German *Propagandaamst* office passed the documents to the Institute of Forensic Medicine in Kraków, under the guidance of a Pole, Professor Robel.

On 10 June, the Chairman of the *PCK* Executive Committee and another member, Mr Józef Wielowiejski had a chance to acquaint themselves with the work on the documents. The work was cautiously executed and with great scrupulousness as writing even under a magnifying glass looked blurred. This is how a large number of the documents will be deciphered. Reading these documents is slow, but bearing in mind the propaganda pressure, one should wish them to be kept under Dr Robel's care for as long as possible. One should not expect the Germans to hand over the complete collection of documents found by the *PCK*. ... Way back in Katyn, when the first segregation of documents was done, diaries and letters were taken out of the envelopes for translation into German. The Commission could not tell if they were returned censored. No doubt, derogatory references about the Germans, and probably there were many, would be cut out or destroyed. We have proof of this. For instance, Rojkiewicz, a Commission member, had read a paragraph in Colonel [Rudolf] Zieliński's diary of October 1939, which, while praising the fighting spirit of his regiment, expressed his mortification that the Germans were ill treated defenceless Polish civilians. This forced him to cease fighting and get in touch with the Soviet units. The German authorities in Katyn disapproved of a Pole reading such extracts, and stricter control on all members was applied. The German woman [Irina Erhardt] who was responsible for translations admitted that she chose only a section of the diary, which referred to Kozelsk camp. Nobody knows what happened to Zieliński's diary. These illegible notes identified by Prof. Robel might be of a similar nature ...

Amongst the diaries[27] read by members of the Technical Committee were the notes of Major [Adam] Solski, found on his body, with the date 9 April 1940, describing probably the last moments before he was shot dead. It stated: 'A group of Polish officers from Kozelsk camp has arrived in Smolensk at 3.30 in the morning. A few minutes before five, we were woken up and put into prison trucks with cells (dreadful), in each of them was a guard. We arrived in the woods, which looked like a resort/retreat, there, our wedding rings and watches were taken from us, the time was 6.30 (8.30), as well as penknives and belts. What will happen to us?'

A shot, probably minutes afterwards, ended the life of Major Solski. At a meeting on 10 June in Kraków, *Herrn* Ohlenbusch, Propaganda chief of the *Generalgouvernment*, accused the representatives of the PCK of delaying tactics at the Institute of Forensic Medicine and ordered that the work must be brought to a close quickly as a travelling exhibition of these documents and items is being planned.

Ad. / f. The question of the new graves for the murdered officers in Katyn was the first subject for discussion with the German officers in Smolensk. They assured me that everything we needed would be at our disposal, to improve the image of the new graves according to our wishes, even if the *PCK* chose individual burials. They were willing to give us more ground; on marked-out terrain there would be rows of graves making a geometric shape with temporary pegs, leaving spaces for footpaths and in the centre there was to be a mausoleum. Setting up of a cemetery for thousands of bodies in such a place required manpower and a vehicle column, which the Germans, being in a war zone, would not be able to supply. The second choice was a communal grave. The third alternative was to transport the corpses back to Poland, which was abandoned for technical and transport reasons. Future re-exhumation of the bodies from communal graves after the war was also considered as theoretically possible but in reality was not at all practical.

In our discussions within the Commission and after consideration of other people's opinions, the option of communal graves was the answer. Arguing against producing a large area of individual graves was the fact that when the Soviets took over the Smolensk district, they would definitely devastate such graves completely, so that there would be no sign of them whatsoever. Simple, inconspicuous communal graves had a better chance of survival. It was also appropriate that they should be buried together as they had died together. From the moral point of view, mass graves were preferred. It is better that they should all have eternal rest as comrades in arms. This is what we pondered, while waiting for Rojkiewicz's return. Instructions were being prepared for the new head of the Technical Committee.

The delay caused by lack of contact had forced Kassur into an independent decision regarding the graves. Having several hundreds exhumed bodies on hand, due to atmospheric conditions he could not wait any longer and decided to bury them forthwith. This is how six communal graves of Polish officers were created in accordance with the independent decision made in Warsaw.

It was possible that the Bolsheviks could destroy simple crosses from the pine trees and a modest metallic wreath with an eagle badge taken from an officer's cap, with an added crown of barbed wire. But there is an idea for a joint memorial for those who died on these far eastern, one-time Polish borders – a cross on a mound, symbol of martyrdom and the sacrifice of life for the freedom of the motherland. The *PCK* Executive Committee came up with the project; perhaps one day it will become a reality, during the peace conference or by other means.

One cannot end the story of the organisational work of the *PCK* without mentioning that in Kraków on 22 April 1943 an unfortunate initiative was undertaken by the Germans, namely to create a new 'Katyn Committee' from members of the Red Cross: Lachert, Skarżyński, Schebesta and the *RGO*: [Adam] Ronikier and [Edward] Seyfried. The Chief of the Social Services in Kraków, *Herrn* Weirauch stated that this was the *Generalgouvernment's* idea. All present accepted the idea, not wanting to create any waves in front of the Germans; however, we all thought it a nonsensical move. At Mr Lachert's suggestion, the Committee's function would be reduced to aiding widows and children of the Katyn dead.

Summoned suddenly to Kraków on 9th May 1943, the Warsaw members heard *Herrn* Weirauch's complaint that the committee was not functioning as they had not passed any information to him. He insisted that at least one of them should stay for two days in Kraków. When he was told about the communication difficulties between the Technical Commission and the Executive Committee of the *PCK*, Weirauch fell silent. Nothing more was heard of the new committee.

B. *PCK* Involvement in Talks with the Germans in Warsaw and Kraków

With regard to the Katyn affair, the German authorities were bent on involving the *PCK* in political and propaganda issues.[28] Although not directly involving Katyn, this illustrates the relationship between the *PCK* and the forces of occupation; therefore a short account of it is necessary.

As a member of an International Organisation, the *PCK* functioned under Polish law. According to the 1905 Hague Convention, national laws should have been upheld in an occupied country, changed or ignored only when the security of the occupying force was involved. Such interpretation of the foundations of the Convention, which does not envisage the occupation of the whole of a country by two invaders, but constantly refers to the division of territory between occupier and the other territory under national rule [the *Generalgouvernment*], enabled German interpretation at will, which meant an open violation of the law. The Red Cross had to take into account the Convention rules regarding occupying forces to be able to fight for their own law. Finding itself in great difficulties, the *PCK* wanted to remain in existence and at the same time maintain the trust of the people. Keeping in mind this joint objective, quite often, seemingly complicated issues were brought down to clear and simple decisions. Katyn was such an example; where the vile murder could not be pinned directly on the occupying forces, but could easily have misled Poles in their thinking. A clear separation from the propaganda machine was the only way out for us.

1. Polish prisoners of war, September 1939.

2. A *Stolypinka*, a Soviet prisoners freight car. (Riga Railway Museum)

3. *Stolypinka* interior cells.

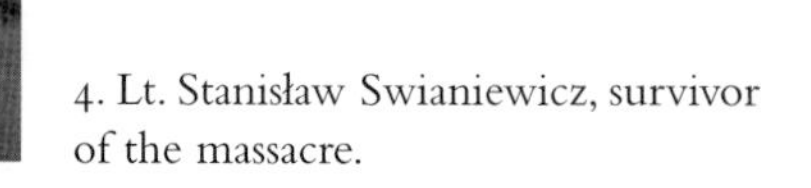

4. Lt. Stanisław Swianiewicz, survivor of the massacre.

5. General Władysław Sikorski, C-in-C on the podium, next to him Deputy Commissar for Foreign Affairs Andrei Vyshinsky and Ambassador Stanisław Kot. Standing below, Gen. W. Anders. Tockoye, USSR, December 1941. (Courtesy of The Polish Institute and Sikorski Museum, PISM)

6. Lt General Noel Mason MacFarlane, Head of British Military Mission in Moscow, with Captain Martin, visiting the Russian Front, October 1943. (IWM No.RUS 1904)

7. Colonel Leslie Hulls, Liaison Officer to General Anders and Brigadier General Dr Bolesław Szarecki, Inspector of military field hospitals and survivor of Kozielsk camp, Jangi-Jul, USSR, 1942. (PISM, No A II)

8. Aleksei Tolstoy (right), later a member of the Burdenko Committee, visiting the Polish camp at Jangi-Jul, USSR, 1942. Centre, Gen. Z. Szyszko-Bohusz, head of Military Mission; left, Capt. Józef Czapski. (PISM, No. A II 1)

9. Signing of the Soviet-British Treaty, May 1942, 10 Downing Street. Left to right: Vyacheslav Molotov, Ivan Maisky, behind him just visible Clement Attlee, Winston Churchill, Anthony Eden. Hidden behind or in the background are Arkady Sabolev, Dr Herbert Evatt, General Hastings Lionel Ismay, Oliver Lyttleton, 1st Visount Chandos and Sir Alexander Cadogan. (IWM, No. CH 570)

10. Ambassador Clark-Kerr and Sir Alexander Cadogan at the Hague Conference 1945. (Harry S. Truman Library, US Army Signal Corps)

11. Frank Kenyon Roberts, Head of Central Department of the Foreign Office. (National Portrait Gallery, London)

12. Denis Allen, Deputy Under Secretary of State of the FO (left) welcoming UN Secretary General Dag Hammerskjold with Mr Huan Hsiang, Chinese Chargé d'Affaires, London, 31.December1954. By kind permission of the family. (UN Photo Library, ID 386430)

13. Sir William Strang (right), Private Under-Secretary of State in his office 1948, with from left Mr Roger Allen, head of African Department, Mr Geoffrey Furlonge, Middle East Department and Mr Alan Campbell. By kind permission of the family. (Churchill Archives Centre, Churchill College, Cambridge STRN 6/9)

14. Sir Owen O'Malley (left) being presented with Letters of Accreditation by Władisław Raczkiewicz, President of the Polish Republic. London, February 1943. On the right is Ambassador Edward Raczynski. (PISM, No.12599)

15. Dacha with 15 rooms, a cinema, a rifle range, *bania* (steam baths) and outbuildings where the NKVD officers stayed till August 1941. (*PK-Aufin: Kriegsberichter Neubauer* 1943, *Amtliches Material zum Massenmord von Katyn,* AMMK publication)

16. *Above right* German officers in charge of the exhumation work at Katyn Wood, April 1943. Left to right: *OLt* Gregor Sloventzyk, Lt Ludvig Voss and Professor Gerhard Buhtz. (AMMK)

17. *Right* International Medical Commission, headed by Professor Orsos (left) presenting the protocol to Dr Leonardo Conti, *Reichsgesundheitsamt Führer,* in his office in Berlin, 4 May 1943. (Bundesarchiv, Federal Archives of Germany, Koblenz. Bild.183-314110)

18. The first delegation of Poles invited to Katyn by the German Propaganda Department, 10 April 1943. Left to right: Emil Skiwski, Dr Orzechowski, Ferdynand Goetel, Dr Grodzki, Dr K. Didur, Dr E. Seyfried, German officer; behind him, W. Kawecki, correspondent and S. Prochowiak, labourer. (AMMK)

19. Ferdynand Goetel who led the first group of Poles to see the mass graves at Katyn in May 1943. (Private collection)

20. Józef Mackiewicz, writer, one of the first to visit Katyn. (Private collection)

21. The Polish Red Cross delegation at Katyn, 15 April 1943. Local resident Parfeon Kiselev talking to Kazimierz Skarżyński (extreme right), General Secretary of the Polish Red Cross, and others. (AMMK)

22. Kazimierz Skarżyźski, Secretary General of the Polish Red Cross (*PCK*) 1943. (Reproduced by kind permission of the family)

23. Dr Marian Wodziński, a leading and longest-serving member of the Technical Commission of the Polish Red Cross that undertook the exhumation at Katyn woods. (Reproduced by kind permission of a private collector in Kraków)

24. A group of American and British PoW officers from Oflags visiting Katyn, May 1943. Left to right: (with back to camera) Col John Van Vliet (USA), Professor Buhtz, Captain Stanley Gilder (UK), Lt Col Frank Stevenson (Africa Corps), Captain Donald Stewart (USA), surrounded by NCOs. (AMMK)

25. Waffen-SS Lt Hans Walter Zech Nenntwich, alias Joachim Nansen, codename 'Columbine'. (TNA London)

27. Sir Bernard Spilsbury, leading pathologist. (National Portrait Gallery X 91932)

Opposite 26. Staff of the Institute of Forensic Medicine in Kraków 1943–4. Seated from left to right: Dr Józef Biborski, Dr Paszkowski, Dr Jan Robel, head of the Institute, Prof. Janusz Supniewski, Dr Maria Paszkowska. Standing left to right: unknown, probably Laboratory Asssistant Jan Patera, Dr Irma Fortner, Dr Gerard Pytasz, Dr Jan Cholewiński, Dr Jadwiga Askermann, Dr Jacek Głogoczowski. The institute staff absent from the photograph were Dr Ludwik Kamykowski, Maria Dembicka and Rozalia Plizowska. (Katyn Institute in Poland)

28. Nikolai Burdenko, President of the Academy of Medical Sciences of the USSR, head of the Soviet Committee. (*RIA Novosti*)

29. Professor Benedict Humphrey Sumner. (National Portrait Gallery X 132512)

30. Sir William Malkin, Legal Adviser to the Foreign Office at the San Francisco Conference 1945, with Chinese delegate. (Churchill College Archives MALK 12; UN Photo Library ID 178651)

31. Professor Douglas Savory at Crumlin, 1950. (Northern Ireland Archives, Belfast. Ref. D 3015/4/2)

32. Sir Reader Bullard, British Ambassador to Persia with Reza Pahlavi, Shah of Persia and an unidentified officer, Tehran, March 1946. (IWM No. E 31784)

33. *Opposite from top* Left to right: Robin M.A. Hankey, Mrs Sokolnicka, wife of the Polish Ambassador and Mr T. R. Shaw, Ankara 1943. (Private collection)

34. Members of the British War Crime Executive at Nuremberg 1946. Sitting left to right: Sir David Maxwell-Fyfe, Sir Hartley Shawcross, Attorney General, G.D. Roberts. Back row: Major J.H. Barrington, Major E. Elwyn-Jones, Mr E.G. Robey, Lt Col M. Griffith-Jones and Colonel Henry James Phillimore. (IWM No. SFX 9D)

37. Members of the US Select Committee visiting London, 1952. Left to right: Congressman Alvin O'Konski, General Marian Kukiel (wartime Minister of Defence), General S. Bor-Komorowski (wartime leader of the Home Army), Congressman Daniel Flood, Congressman Thaddeus Machrowicz, August Zaleski (President of Polish government-in-exile), Congressman Ray Madden, Maj. General Roman Odzierzyński, General Władysław Anders. (Columet, Regional Archives, Indiana University, Northwest; Ray Madden papers)

35. *Opposite from top* Pre-Nuremberg Trials meeting in Berlin, October 1945; Fedor G. Denissov (left) and Lt Gen R. Rudenko, Procurator General at the Nuremberg Trials. (IWM No. SFX 9)

36. American House of Representatives Select Committee to investigate the Katyn massacre with President Truman in the White House, 1952. Left to right: Congressmen Foster Furcolo, George Dondero, Thadeus Machrowicz, Ray Madden (Chairman), Alvin O'Konski, Daniel Flood, and advisers John Mitchell and Timothy Sheehan. (Corbis Images 646 1506)

38. Members of the Katyn Memorial Fund Committee. Left to right: Louis FitzGibbon, Lord Barnby (Chairman) President of Poland in exile Stanislaw Ostrowski, Lord St Oswald; standing to attention Major John Gouriet (left) and Tadeusz Kryska-Karski (right). (PISM, Bednarski collection)

39. The unveiling of the Katyn Monument, Gunnersbury Cemetery, London 1976, by Mrs Chełmecka, widow of Katyn victim. On the left is Major John Gouriet. (PISM)

KATYN
1940

40. Airey Neave MP, (left) wearing the cross of Commander of the Order of Polonia Restituta, with Major John Gourlet. (PISM)

41. There are some horrific images of the Katyn massacre; one will suffice as a visual reminder of what the lies, the legal wrangling and the diplomatic compromises concerned.

a. A planned propaganda visit to the Poles in PoW camps in Germany
On 20 April 1943, the Chairman of the *PCK* was again summoned by the German Propaganda Chief Dr Grundmann, for a *PCK* and the *RGO* delegation meeting in Kraków, with a view to taking part in a planned visit to the Polish Prisoners of War in the camps in the German Reich. The day before, he approached me about it and when I declined, he tried forcefully to persuade the Executive Committee to think it over, indicating that the German attitude towards the *PCK* might open up. Repeated telephone calls to the Chairman indicated how important the PoW camp visits were to the German authorities.

By visiting these camps in Germany, the *PCK* would be compelled to make a public statement that the prisoners are well treated, which on the whole was true. However, it would be difficult to emphasise more complicated matters than just the daily life in a prison camp, examples of the Germans violating the Convention.

After some discussion, the *PCK* Executive Committee stood by their decision that such visits as ordered by the Germans would simply show co-operation in an area covered by international conventions and as such were necessary, provided they were considered as a one-sided submission of the *PCK* in a single aspect, while other convention rights of the PoWs and those of the *PCK*, were ignored or violated. ... Accordingly, on behalf of the Executive Committee I handed a note to Dr Grundmann, which stated:

'With regard to the proposition of sending a delegation of the *PCK* to visit the PoW camps in Germany, the Executive Committee is willing to co-operate with the German authorities, within the set rules of the International Conventions, with the logical assumption that the *PCK's* privileges would be reinstated, according to the Convention; therefore we ask you to review the following issues:

1. The *PCK* Information Bureau's rights to be returned in accordance with the laws of the Convention, and that all prohibitions and limitations, not involving the security of the Army, also be revoked as follows:
b. The activities of the *PCK* Information Bureau should also cover the territory the prisoners come from, or where their families reside, i.e. the region where the recruitment for the Poles took place (irrespective of the present day administrative boundaries).
c. The *PCK* Information Bureau should have free correspondence with the prisoners and their families and vice versa (which up to now is controlled by the German authorities), also there should be permission to send parcels, according to the camp rules and with regard to the welfare of their families.

2. To allow those prisoners who are ill to be released and be given written permission to return to the *Generalgouvernment* region (vide: the question of the refusal to return the PoWs from Ostashkov camp in 1941).

3. Released PoWs should not be handed over to the civilian authorities or the police or to the examining magistrates for alleged crimes committed before the war but according to the Convention they should be judged by court martial with full legal assistance. Those already convicted should be returned to the camps, presented to the military courts and their verdicts annulled.

4. The cases of the reservists who were being held in concentration camps should be examined immediately and if no specific allegations proven, they should be released forthwith.'

The *PCK* Executive Committee also asked for intervention on behalf of Mrs Maria Bortnowska, in charge of the *PCK* Information Bureau, who, six months earlier, was arrested and sent to Berlin. If her release was not possible immediately, the Committee hoped that the authorities would acquaint themselves with appeal No.1474, written to the German Red Cross on 1 April 1943 and release her under the personal assurances of the members of the *PCK* Executive Committee.

In point 1, we demanded assurances that the *PCK* would receive full recognition, according to the Geneva Convention. In point 2, we raised the question of soldiers assessed by the camp authorities as invalids. They were not allowed to return home to their families, and as a result many of them died. In point 3, we wanted to tackle the problem of executions of PoWs. According to our information, 18 executions had taken place after convictions by a 'special court', and some more were being processed. Point 4 refers to the occupying authorities' power to send registered reservists to PoW camps, but not concentration camps. In the last paragraph, not in the same form as the preceding points as it was a private matter for the *PCK*, we raised the case of Mrs Bortnowska,.

All these points bar the 4th were previously tackled in correspondence between the *PCK* and the German Red Cross. The case of the reservists sent to Auschwitz was not raised before because we would have received a stock answer from the Germans that all inmates faced some sort of individual indictment. Such intervention could only have created a wave of arrests. These requests were only made possible after the Katyn revelations.

Our notes were thoroughly discussed at a meeting of the *PCK* Executive Committee, with our Chairman present, on 22 April. *Herrn* Weirauch instructed that each point should be articulated more succinctly. These motions were later presented, but no results came of them.

Neither he nor *Herrn* Ohlenbusch, who was present at the meeting, could see the connection between the requests in our note and the proposed PoW camp visits. They understood only after the Chairman of the *PCK* had explained to them that the propaganda-motivated visits to the PoW camps in Germany, where humane conditions were being maintained, would lose them the trust of the Polish people, because thousands of Poles were still perishing in the concentration camps. This trust was of paramount importance to the *PCK* and as such, should be acknowledged by the German authorities. As a result, the visits to the German Oflags [*Oficierlager*] by members of the *PCK* never materialised.

At the meeting, the Chairman raised the question of the prohibition of sending parcels to prisoners, as well as transferring the care and maintenance of the graves of those who were killed in 1939 from the *PCK* to the Council. Some were coping well, whilst others were not. The Chairman insisted that he did not see any reason why the *PCK* could not take over the care of the remaining graves. We received some promises, which remained only promises. The meeting ended with a typical German move by the Chairman, he was pleased to announce that the Chief of Security in the *Generalgouvernment* was going to order the release of those prisoners who had little reason for being in Majdanek concentration camp. He told the *PCK* representatives to take the news with them to Warsaw and pass it around. In reality, towards the end of April the Germans released several women from Majdanek and in June, several hundred men and women. Yet, thousands arrested without reason were still deprived of freedom or sent away as forced labour.

b. The Polish Red Cross Telegram Dispatched to Geneva

Wacław Lachert, Chairman of the Polish Red Cross, informed the Executive Committee on 20 April, (a week after the formal announcement of the discovery of the Polish graves in Katyn woods), that the previous day a demand from Dr Heinrich had arrived that they write an official telegram to the International Red Cross in Geneva, requesting an investigative committee to examine the graves of the Polish officers near Smolensk.

The Executive Committee knew that it could turn to the International Red Cross with all sorts of reports and requests, however, it was not entitled to request the setting up of a committee to investigate matters of an international nature, which was the prerogative of Governments, not the Red Cross. The reply to Dr Heinrich was negative, knowing full well that the Polish Government-in-exile in London had already put such a request to Geneva. However, the Executive Committee decided to send the President of the International Red Cross in Geneva the report following my visit to Katyn (with the eight points as mentioned earlier) as one of the elements that might serve for guidance.

The Germans, not recognising the Polish Government-in-exile probably had the intention of wooing the Polish side via the *PCK* into sending a commission. That is why; against all logic, the Germans requested the same via the German Red Cross, not the Government. The Executive Committee received the following telegraphic acknowledgment of the report from the President of the International Red Cross:

'Vous remerçions votre dépêche reçue 22 Avril concernant identifications effectuées a Smolensk qui a retenue toute notre attention stop Comité Internationel Croix Rouge saisi cette question par deux requêtes anterieures et sensible a confiance qui lui est temoignée a répondu en substance comme suit stop Sommes disposés a proceder designation experts neutres a condition toutes parties en cause nous le demandent l'accord entre toutes les parties et le Comité devant également se faire quand aux modalités du mandat eventual stop Ces conditions sont conformés a memorandum adresse par nous septembre 1939 aux Etats belligerents et publiée dans Revue Internationale Croix Rouge même mois par lequel Comité a fixé dès debut guerre principes selon lesquels il pourrait eventuellement participer a des enquêtes stop Pour cas ou accord entre toutes parties en cause se réaliserait nous efforçons des maintenant trouver personalités neutres qualifiées.'

['We acknowledge your telegram received on 22 April, concerning the identifications undertaken at Smolensk, which has drawn our attention stop The Committee of the International Red Cross is interested in this matter after the two earlier requests and appreciate the trust you have bestowed upon us and replies as follows stop We are ready to assign experts on condition that all the parties concerned are agreeable, this stipulation between them and the Committee must take into account the conditions of a possible mandate stop These conditions conform with a memorandum presented by us in September 1939 to all the countries at war and published in the same month in the Review of the International Red Cross, which states that the principles established at the beginning of the war would allow [the IRC] to take part in investigations stop On assumption that the agreement between the parties is realised, we shall look for the right persons of authority and neutrality.']

Max Huber, President Intercroixrouge.

[Skarżyński added the following explanatory paragraph in 1946:]

Because Russia was the other interested party regarding Katyn, her acceptance of a request by Geneva was essential, as according to international agreement, neutral experts could then be allowed to inspect the scene. With no such acceptance by the Russians, the International Commission did not survey the massacre in Katyn. Thus the *PCK* was left on its own to attend Katyn, without assuming an official international character. The enormity of the massacre of the Polish officers as well as reciprocal accusations of the Germans and the Russians as to the perpetrators, forced the *PCK* to assume strict neutrality, faced with a responsibility towards the nation and history.

c. The Propaganda Pamphlet

On 2 June 1943, the *PCK* Chairman was informed that the German Propaganda Department was thinking of writing a pamphlet about Katyn; the proposition came with a request for a contribution in the form of a foreword. The pamphlet was to have a high print run and the distribution would be given over to the *PCK* along with half of the profit from sales. They also proposed the inclusion in the foreword of an appeal to the nation, similar to that already issued by the *PCK*, requesting detailed information of missing persons in Russia. In the rest of the pamphlet, there was to be the *PCK*'s report and the answer from the International Red Cross in Geneva in French with a Polish translation; and also the report written by the International Commission of Medical experts at Katyn in April, at the beginning of the exhumation work and handed to the German authorities. Needless to say, the *PCK* Executive Committee declined to take part in this publicity project of the German propaganda office.

d. Meetings with Prominent Poles

Deprived of any formal means of contact with the Polish people, the *PCK* established a habit of organising regular meetings with prominent Poles to inform them of the *PCK's* operational difficulties ... On 14 May 1943, a special meeting was called concerning Katyn, and after the Chairman's introduction, I, as the *PCK* General Secretary, gave a full account of the issues involved, while Mr J. Wielowiejski, a member of the committee, provided arguments for the decisions made by the *PCK*.

e. Meetings with Members of the German Red Cross Executive Committee

Mention has been made several times of the meetings held in Kraków on 10 June 1943 in the German Propaganda and the German Red Cross offices. At these meetings the delegates of the *PCK* Executive Committee and of the German Red Cross were represented by *Herrn* Grunneisen and Countess Waldersee. I have also mentioned the attack made by *Herrn* Ohlenbusch, Chief of Propaganda in *Generalgouvernment* on the Polish nation and the *PCK's* discussion regarding the text of the questionnaire. One should also mention that during the meeting at the offices of the German Red Cross, a Polish member of the Executive Committee, Mr Wielowiejski, with prior approval of his Chairman, had a chance to speak. After a courteous introduction thanking them for their cooperation, within the constraints of wartime, in easing the work of the *PCK*, he referred to the previous presentations made by *Herrn* Ohlenbusch, the *Generalgouvernment* Propaganda chief. According to him, the methods of the German propaganda regarding Katyn, together with the appeal to the Poles to fight against Bolshevism, had a negative effect. The Poles were already prepared to fight against the ideology of Bolshevism and forcing the *PCK* to take part in propaganda action, constantly using its name, was unacceptable. The propaganda, which did not convince but only orders – would not bare fruit. Therefore the *PCK* advertised the fact that, concerning the projected report on Katyn to the International Red Cross in Geneva and the list of names of those already exhumed, it wanted to be clearly disassociated from the German propaganda. If this was done, the report mmight even gain some credibility.

During further discussions between the *PCK* and the German Red Cross, it was clear to us that decisions in such matters lay beyond the remit of the German Red Cross. The impression on those present at the meeting was that the delegates of the German Red Cross Executive Committee were tired by the work and were trying whenever possible to detach themselves from the official government line and trying hard to maintain the humanitarian aspect of the Red Cross work.

C. Technical Commission Report of the Work Undertaken in Katyn [by Jerzy Wodzinowski]

On 17th April 1943, work had started with three members of the Commission, whose assignment were as follows:

1. Mr Ludwik Rojkiewicz – examination of documents in the office of the Field Police.

2. Mr Stefan Kołodziejski and Jerzy Wodzinowski – searching bodies for documents and preserving them.

However, on that day the work was interrupted by the arrival of a delegation consisting of Polish officers, PoWs from Oflags in Germany:

1. Lt Col Stefan Mossor Cavalry Oflag II E/K No. 1449
2. Capt Stanisław Cylkowski Oflag II E/K No. 1272
3. 2 Lt Stanisław Gostkowski Oflag II D No. 776/II/B
4. Capt Eugeniusz Kleban Oflag II D
5. 2 Lt Zbigniew Rowiński Aviation Oflag II C No. 1205/II/B
6. Capt. Konstanty Adamski Artillery Oflag II C No. 902/XI/A

Members of the *PCK* Commission, together with the officers, had the opportunity of viewing the graves as well as the documents.

The attitude of the officers towards the Germans was reserved and dignified. During a short conversation to one side, they were visibly pleased to learn that the *PCK* was taking care of the technical side of the exhumation, thus eliminating any political issues.

On 19 April, members of the Commission tried to contact *OLt* Slovenzik to agree on details concerning the work, but lack of transport that day put an end to this. After waiting till 2pm on 20 April, Ludwik Rojkiewicz decided to walk to the office of the Field Police, some 10 km away, with a view to contacting

OLt Slovenzik. He turned back on meeting a vehicle carrying other members of the *PCK* Commission, Hugon Kassur, Gracjan Jaworowski and Adam Godzik. They had left Warsaw on 19 April at 12.15, together with the foreign press delegation, among them a Swede, a Finn, a Spaniard, a Belgian, a Dutchman, an Italian, a Czech as well as a Russian émigré from Berlin, together with Professor Leon Kozłowski,[29] a former Polish Premier who arrived from Berlin together with three officials from the *Propagandaamt* Office in Berlin.

Hugon Kassur took over the chairmanship of the Technical Commission. Talks were undertaken with *OLt* Slovenzik on the following topics:

1. Living quarters for the *PCK* members of the Technical Commission
2. Place of work
3. Transportation for members of the committee
4. Work Organisation
5. The safe keeping of documents
6. Choice of site for the new burials.

Due to the 14 km distance between Katyn and Smolensk as well as the lack of transport, members were lodged in a separate hut in a village called Borek, once owned by a Polish family,[30] the Lednickis, before the First World War. It was situated some three km from Koze Gory, where a field hospital belonging to *Organisation Todt* was stationed. The Technical Commission stayed in this place from 15 April to 20 May 1943. From 20th May to 7th June 1943, they were lodging in a schoolhouse by Katyn station. The question of provisions was sorted out with *OLt* Slovenzik and food was brought up from *Organisation Todt* officers' mess at the same time as rations were distributed to the units at the front. It must be said that the food was adequate.

Lack of proper working facilities in the woods, necessitated a division of the work in such a way that the gathering of the documents and reburial had to be done on the spot, in Katyn woods, while the initial examination of the documents was done in the office of the German Field Police, some 6 km away in the direction of Smolensk.

OLt Slovenzik thought that the *PCK* should send their transport to Katyn. It was explained to him that the Red Cross vehicles had been requisitioned from them a long time ago. The problem of transport was solved in the following way:

1. We were allowed to keep a vehicle on the road when travelling to Katyn and back, a distance of about 4 km

2. For the 10 km journey to the office of the Field Police, a motorbike was sent.

The work was divided thus:

a. One member doing the exhumation work

b. Two members searching for documents on the bodies
c. One member controlling the numbering of the bodies before removal for reburial.
d. One member for reburial of the bodies
e. Two or three members to read or decipher the documents
f. From 28 April, after the arrival of more members of the Technical Commission – namely Stefan Cupryjak and Dr of Forensic Medicine Marian Wodziński – Wodziński together with laboratory assistants Mikołajczyk Jan, Król Franciszek, Buczak Władysław and Płonka Ferdynand undertook a thorough investigation of those bodies that could not be identified from documents.

The following works were undertaken:
a. Digging and extracting bodies from the earth
b. Searching and extracting the documents
c. Medical inspection of the unidentified bodies
d. Reburial of the bodies

The work lasted from 8 am to 6 pm with a 90-minute break for lunch. The Commission declares that the extraction of the bodies was difficult, because they were stuck together, haphazardly thrown into the ditches, some with tied hands, some had coats thrown over the heads and tied round the neck with a rope, the hands also tied at the back in such a way that movement of the rope tying the coat tightened the rope around the neck. These corpses were found in a special grave, which was flooded with water. In view of these difficulties, the German military authorities wanted to refill the grave completely. Only one grave was found to contain 46 corpses, evenly layered in the face down position.

Substantial difficulties were caused by not having enough rubber gloves. The local people, driven in by the Germans, lifted out of the corpses. The bodies were carried out from the grave on stretchers, and laid side by side. The search for documents would begin on each body by two workers, watched by a member of the *PCK*. The workers would cut up the pockets and all the contents would be passed on to the *PCK* member. These documents and other items would be put in envelopes, marked with the same number as a metal identification tag that was attached to the corpse. In a comprehensive search for documents, the underwear and boots were cut open. If nothing was found; maker's labels on clothing were cut out and kept as evidence.

Members of the Commission engaged on the search were forbidden to examine or sort out any item. Their duty was to pack everything in separate envelopes. The most common items were:

a. Wallets with all their contents
b. Loose papers

c. Insignia and memorabilia
d. Crosses and medallions
e. One epaulette
f. Purses
g. All valuable possessions

Items such as: money, newspapers, receipts, sachets of tobacco and paper, wooden or metal cigarette cases the Germans allowed to be removed, so as not to overload the contents of the envelopes. If there were many items, they were put in another envelope marked with the same number.

The packed envelopes were tied with string or wire, sorted according to number and put on a conveyer table specially made for the purpose. They were then checked by the Germans and taken by despatch rider to the office of the Field Police, twice a day.

There, a German team and one member of the *PCK* would examine the documents. Envelopes would be opened, documents removed and prised apart with a wooden baton, cleared from dirt, grease [adipocere] and decaying matter. First they would look for any indication of name or surname, which would come from identity cards or inoculation cards done while in Kozelsk camp. If the information was missing, there were others, such as letters, postcards, notebooks, pieces of paper with writing etc. Wallets, purses with banknotes of the Polish Bank or coins were burned, however, foreign money, excluding Russian, was put in the envelope with other gold objects. Envelopes marked with a known surname and number, were registered in German on a separate sheet of paper. Apparently the reason why these first lists were prepared only in German was that the German authorities said the list would be sent directly to the *PCK* together with documents, after having they had made use of them. The Polish committee had no reason to make a second list, especially as it was short of manpower. Barely visible writing, which could not be identified, was sent to a special chemical laboratory for treatment. If positively identified under the same number, the name would be registered on another, separate list. It must be said that there were many corpses that had no identification whatsoever and these items were also given a number with the annotation 'unidentified' [NN – *Nicht Namen*].

After registering the contents of an envelope on a separate list, the documents were put in a fresh envelope marked with the same number as the listed items; all this work was done entirely by the Germans. Thus re-inspected, segregated and numbered, the envelopes were put in boxes. They remained exclusively for the use of the German authorities. The lists typed in German could not be checked with the rough notes of the Technical Commission, as they had no access to them. This method of registration from Nos. 0421–0794 was done in the presence of Ludwik Rojkiewicz. Identification from Nos. 0795–03900 was carried out in the presence of Stefan Cupryjak Gracjan Jaworowski and Jan Mikołajczyk. The method was identical, with one difference that the list was prepared in Polish and when possible sent to the Executive Committee of the *PCK*. Jerzy Wodzinowski witnessed the last numbers from 03900 to 04243, keeping to the same format. Before the arrival of the Polish Technical Commission, the Germans attempted identifications of bodies from Nos.1 to 112 and from 01 to 0420 alone. The committee stresses the fact that during the inspection of the documents, the Germans took diaries and some letters out of the envelopes for translation. The Commission is unable to say if everything came back, or was put in the right envelopes.

The *PCK* Technical Commission worked in Katyn woods from 15 April to 7 June 1943, and exhumed 4243 bodies, of which 4233 came from seven graves located a short distance from one another, which were dug up by the German military authorities in March 1943. Corpses were dug up from all seven graves.

The eighth grave, which was about 200 m to the south of the first group of graves, was located on 2 June 1943, from which only ten bodies were excavated. They were reburied in a new sixth grave, which was still uncovered. Due to the approaching summer, the Germans ordered a break in exhumation untilSeptember 1943. That is why grave VIII, after partial excavation, was filled in with earth.

The Germans, to make sure that the number of 10 to 12,000 bodies as declared by the *Propagandaamst*, should not be far out from those excavated, carried out a very thorough search of the terrain. It is unlikely that grave No. VIII holds more than a few hundred and no more graves are to be expected. The search, however, has disclosed several mass graves of Russians, in various stages of decomposition.

The total number of exhumed bodies of 4241 [4243] was reburied in six new mass graves nearby. The bodies of the two Generals were buried in separate graves. The terrain from either side of the mass graves lies low and is wet, however, the graves are on a higher ground of dry and sandy soil. The size and depth of the graves are not equal, due to the conditions of the site and technical problems that came up during the work. The bottoms of the graves are dry and each grave, according to its size and depth, holds several lines of corpses, and each line has a few layers. The top layers were at least one metre lower than the terrain, so that after refilling with earth one metre higher than the terrain, the top layer of bodies had two metres of topsoil. All the graves are levelled and at the same height, with the sides clad with turf. Each grave has a wooden cross two and a half metres high and some field flowers have been planted. The graves are numbered as they were constructed, according to the numbered bodies, which are placed facing the East, one on top of another with heads slightly higher and hands crossed on the chests. Each layer has 20–39 cm of soil. In the graves Nos.I, II, III, and IV, the corpses were laid from the right side, as they were carried from the left. Their number was noted in the process. The number of bodies in each grave is enclosed with this report as well as the plan of the cemetery covering 60 x 36 m i.e. 2160 square metres. On the day of departure from Katyn by the last members of the Technical Commission, on 9 June 1943, they hung a large metallic wreath made by one of the members from scrap metal and wire and placed it on the highest cross of the fourth grave, to which a solid metal eagle, taken from the badge of an officer's cap was nailed. The wreath, although crudely made, has an aesthetic appearance, painted black with a crown of thorns made from barbed wire. After laying the wreath, members of the Commission paid tribute to the memory of the dead, paid homage with a minute's silence and prayers; last farewells were said in the name of the country, their families and themselves. On leaving the cemetery, the committee members thanked *OLt* Slovenzik, *Leutnant* Voss of the *Geheimfeldpolizai* and other ranks as well as the Russian workers for their cooperation and two months of hard work on the exhumations.

To sum up - the Commission states that:

1. The exhumed bodies were in various stages of decomposition and identification of them was difficult. The uniforms were in a good state, especially all metal parts such as decorations, insignia, buttons, etc.

2. The cause of death was a shot to the back of the skull

3. Documents reveal that death occurred between March and the beginning of May 1940.

4. The work was carried out under the constant control of the Germans who detailed a sentry at each Polish work - station.

5. All of the work was undertaken by the Polish Technical Commission of the *PCK*, the German authorities and local people from neighbouring villages, a daily number of 20-30 persons. Some 50 Russian PoWs helped each day in digging the graves and tidying the terrain.

6. Generally, working conditions were hard, exhausting and stressful. Apart from the tragic circumstances, the smell of decomposition was unbearable.

7. Frequent arrivals of delegations, daily visits by military men, the post mortem executed by the Germans and the presence of the international delegations complicated the already difficult working conditions.

The Chief of the Technical Commission Hugon Kassur, had to leave Katyn on 12 May 1943, and could not come back; Jerzy Wodzinowski took his place.

A few words of explanation about the above report:

The Commission declares that the pressure of expectations from the German *Propagandaamst* has made the task difficult. Two days before the arrival of an important delegation, work was halted, as a result, only 7 to 10 workers turned up on the site. It was said that the workers from the local villages did not arrive in spite of being ordered to.

When the international delegation of Professors of medicine arrived in Katyn from Germany and other Axis countries, the bodies of high-ranking officers were reserved for them for inspection; as well as those who, besides having fatal shots, received bayonet wounds or were tied up. Interventions by the head of the committee went unheeded and ignored, resulting in losing the reburial sequence of bodies in the second grave. The post mortems done by the Professors from abroad were performed without consultation with the Commission, which on occasion led to difficulties in the identification of the body and to minimise the problem, members of the committee often collected and buried the corpses left by the Germans themselves.

German Army units stationed on the central war front were given orders to visit Katyn. Each day hundreds of persons looked at the place of mass murder. After an intervention by the Commission the visits were limited to certain hours and gendarmes were assigned to keep order.

I have already mentioned the documents were under the control of the Germans. At one point, they asked Mr Cupryjak to show his notebook, in which he made some notes while inspecting the documents.

Likewise, one cannot disregard an incident between Mr Kassur and *OLt* Slovenzik. The latter turned up one day at the beginning of exhumation work with information they had learned that some Polish officers were of German nationality, i.e. *Volksdeutche* and requested a separate grave for them, or at least a prominent place among the mass graves. He was told that all the murdered were Polish officers of the Polish Army, whose nationality is impossible to ascertain, hence Kassur suggested a communal grave for all, without exception. *OLt* Slovenzik agreed with the argument.

The bullets from corpses and from the spent cases found in the sand can be declared as fired from a 7.65 mm calibre pistol, allegedly of German make. Afraid that the Bolsheviks might use this fact, the Germans were very strict in watching over the Poles, so that none of the spent cases or bullets were hidden or taken by members of the committee. This order was naïve and could not have been implemented; besides, trustworthy *NKVD* officials executing the murders could have had small arms of all makes.

So far, the *PCK* Executive Committee has not received a full report from Dr Wodziński. From his initial report after the exhumation of 1,700 bodies, it looks that in spite of decomposition in the uppermost layers of bodies, thanks to the sandy and clay soil, partial mummification has taken place, whilst in the deeper parts of the grave there is the so called inversion of fatty to waxy substances [adipocere]. In 98% of the cases shots were identified, with entry to the back of the skull and exit at the forehead or face; 0.5 % were of double shots to the back of the skull and 1.5 % shots were found to the neck. It is quite likely that the final figures will not be far off from the ones above. It would be worthwhile to find out how many corpses had their hands and neck tied with a rope and those that died by bayoneting.

The report of the Technical Commission only superficially mentions that they exhumed 46 bodies from the waterlogged grave, which I saw myself while in Katyn; it was part of the lower kerb of one of the seven large graves, which appeared like terraces going down to the lower ground. It was filled with dark water in which parts of skeletons were visible. The Germans promised to deliver water pumps but it stayed waterlogged to the last day of work. One day Wodziński noticed that the Russians were filling up the grave, he stopped them, but found out from *OLt* Slovenzik that the Fire Brigade would not deliver the water pumps due to constant Russian air raids as well as other demands. Only then, did five members of the committee led by Wodzinowski descend into the grave and lift out 46 bodies in a space of 17 hours.

Whilst bringing attention to this moving gesture of the Technical Commission, I should like to quote a sentence from the address made by the President of the Polish Red Cross at a meeting of the delegates of the Polish community in Warsaw:

'Polish history is marked with graves – no other one like this.'

Kazimierz Skarżyński
Warsaw, June 1943

Notes

1 PISM KOL 12/16/d L.dz. 518/43 secure signals from the *AK* (Home Army) dated 19 IV 1943 give a list of names of people who were taken to Katyn to visit the graves: Goetel, Skiwski, Seyfried, Orzechowski, Grodzki, Prochownik, Kawecki, Didur. Second group: Rev. Jasiński, Schebesta, Pragłowski, Plappert, Martens, Skarżynski, Rojkiewicz, Wodzinowski, Bartoszewski, Kołodziejski, Dmochowski, Banach; TNA FO 371/34552 C4842, L.dz. 1960/43 original and translated *AK* signal signed by Lt Col Michał Protasewicz, Chief of *Oddział VI*, dated 26 IV 1943, annotated by WS (William Strang) 'given to S of S by General Sikorski 28/4/43'; *SPP Studium Polski Podziemnej* (The Polish Underground Movement Study Trust) A 7.1.1. Ref L.dz. 2290 dated 15 May 1943, a signal in Polish from 'Kalina' [Gen. Rowecki] for Gen. Sikorski, information among other things about the 7.65 mm bullets made by GECO and twisted ropes; PISM KOL 12/16d L.dz. 2475/tjn.43, dated 27 V 1943 gives comprehensive information about the graves as seen by the first group of the *PCK* committee including Skarżyński's report in French to the International Red Cross Committee in Geneva.

2 IWM (Imperial War Museum) FO 645/289 German archives captured by US in 1945 No.A084591, USSR-507/PS-402 held at Duxford, Teletype nr. 6 of 3 May 1943 17 20 Warsaw, from Heinrich to Weirauch in Kraków.

3 TNA HS 4/137 and FO 371/34582 C 7677/258/55G ref SK/AK/912 carbon copy of a letter 30 June 1943, from cryptic designation SD [Pay Lt Commander Ralph C. Hollingsworth RNVR] to MPX [Richard Truszkowski] SOE Polish Section, enclosing translated report by Dr Tramsen, Danish forensic expert, who visited the graves at Katyn.

4 TNA FO 371/56476 N5269G typed copies of the report in Polish, translation by EM: also at PISM KOL 12/4/9; official statement by Kazimierz Skarżyński (1887–1962) a successful industrialist, educated in Vienna, Paris and Trade Institute in Antwerp, spoke seven languages. Worked for a French firm, mining copper in the Caucasus. With political unrest, acted as a liaison between the Tartars and the Kurds. In 1919 on the intervention of the British Army (note Colonel Hulls' presence), decided to return to Poland and join the newly formed Polish army. Fought the Bolsheviks in 1920 War of Independence. In between the wars worked for a French paper firm. In 1939 finding himself without work, offered his services to the Polish Red Cross, which was duly accepted and was given the post of General Secretary. Visited Katyn burial site, wrote two reports. Fearing for his life left Poland with wife and two children in May 1946. Stopped in Nuremberg during the trials on his way to Paris. After a short stay in England, immigrated to Canada. Employed in real estate and the old Credit Froncier, this time in Calgary. Took part in Congressional Hearings in Washington in 1952. A mainstay of Polish community in Calgary.

5 PISM KOL 12/4/37 Marian Wodziński (1911–1986) studied medicine at the Jagiellonian University in Kraków, specialised in pathology. Worked for the Court of Appeal and the Institute of Forensic Medicine in Kraków. Part of a team of Poles from the Red Cross, at the invitation of Dr Adam Schebesta of the *PCK* in Kraków, took part in Katyn exhumations (29 IV 1943 to 3 III 1943). In October 1943 under threat of death left Kraków for a while for Kielce district under assumed name of Cioch. In April 1944 returned to Kraków and with the Soviet front approaching, left again, this time hiding in Poznań district until September 1945, when he decided to escape from Poland for good. Settled in Liverpool, married Dr Wanda Wójcik in 1948 and continued his medical profession in Liverpool. Avoiding publicity and contacts with émigré Poles, died in 1986, his ashes were returned to Tarnów, his birthplace in Poland in August that year.

6 TNA FO 371/56475 N 4406/108/55G 'Facts and Documents', 454-page book, Roneo-machine duplicated in foolscap for 'private circulation only' February 1946, PISM KOL 12/12A the original typescript in Polish, 489 pages. Includes reports and depositions by Polish PoWs, documents and correspondence, gathered from Poles inside and out of Russia compiled and edited by a special team of experts, military and civilian, called upon in December 1944 by the Council of Ministers of the Polish Government in London, among them: Colonel Jerzy Łunkiewicz, Lt Marian Heitzmann, Captain Alfred Hergesell, Roman Pucinski (translator), Wiktor Sukiennicki and many others.

7 Józef Mackiewicz (1902–1985), eminent writer and popular journalist, known for his anti-communist views. From 1922 to 1939, together with his editor brother Stanisław published a popular Wilno newspaper *Słowo* (The Word). In 1939 Stanisław managed to escape to the West, while Józef stayed under the Soviet–Lithuanian occupation in Wilno, He began to publish for a short while the *Gazeta Codzienna* (The Daily Newspaper) as both publisher and editor-in-chief but had to shut down. With German occupation of Wilno in June 1941, he was offered editorship of a new newspaper in Polish but categorically refused. In May 1943, he accepted an invitation from the German Press Bureau *Gebietskommisaria Wilna- Stadt,* to visit the graves at Katyn. He considered the task of national importance and was approved by the *AK*. On his return, he gave an interview to the infamous German-controlled *Goniec Codzienny* (The Daily Herald). After the war, while in exile he was castigated for doing so by the émigré Poles.

8 Ferdynand Goetel (1890–1960), born in Poland and educated Kraków, writer and editor, as a student belonged to the Socialist Youth organisation. Keen mountaineer, wrote

many articles on the subject of sport and travel. Studied architecture in Vienna, moved to Warsaw in 1912, continued his literary career, was a keen follower of Piłsudski's ideology but did not join the Legion. Caught while crossing the border, exiled by the Russians to Uzbekistan 1915–20. Returned to independent Poland via Iran, India and England. From 1925, lived and worked in Warsaw. Published books and numerous articles, edited a periodical, *Nurt* (The Current). Was Chairman of the Polish Literary Association 1926–1933, his book *Z dnia na dzien* (From day to day) was admired by the English writer John Galsworthy, who wrote a foreword to its translation in 1930. Chairman of the Polish PEN Club till 1939, published work on political matters *Pod znakiem faszyzmu* (Under the Banner of Fascism) citing Mussolini's Italy as an example. Under the German occupation controversially appealed to his members to register with *Propagandaamt* (the German Propaganda Office). He was accused of being a fascist. After his escape to the West, he tried hard to clear his name. Lived in poverty and died an exile in London. In 2003 his ashes were returned to Poland. Biographical notes by Marek Gałęzowski: *Wierni Polsce 1939–1947* (Faithful to Poland 1939-1947), Warszawa, 2005.

9 TNA WO 208/3732 MI 19 (RPS) 21995 (S), interrogation of Polish civilian Stanisław Wójcik, reporting on his visit to Katyn Woods, at the Royal Patriotic School, 29 May 1944.

10 Polish Institute and Sikorski Museum (PISM) KOL 12/16d L.dz. 2575/t.jn.43. Typescript reports on the first visit of the Polish delegation to Katyn, among them Ferdynand Goetel, sent from Warsaw and translated by *Oddział VI* Special Operations Bureau, headed by Lt Col Michał Protasewicz for the Polish Ministry of Defence and Ministry of Internal Affairs, dated 27 May 1943. The report also covers the news of Skarżyński's report of 16 April 1943 to the International Committee of the Red Cross in Geneva.

11 PISM KOL 12/3 5 page typescript report in Polish by Ferdynand Goetel dated London 19 December 1946. Translation by EM.

12 *Organisation Todt* derived its name from Herr Fritz Todt, an engineer and Minister of Armaments in 1940, an instigator of the German plan of building *autobahn,* motorways, by engaging unemployed workers in 1933. In wartime, this operation under the German Ministry of Labour used PoWs and civilians of the occupied countries as labour force, *Arbeitsbeschaffung.*

13 PISM KOL 12/3 typescript copy translation Bo.5/S, Court Martial Section No. 8, 22 May 1946, witness interrogation record of Ivan Krivozertsev, son of Gregory, a metal turner, born 20 VII 1915 Nowe Batoki, Katyn District, Russian Orthodox and had spoken Polish.

14 *Chorny voron*, a Russian nickname meaning 'black crow' for a square shaped windowless prison truck, similar to a 'Black Maria', with seats for two guards low down by the door, accommodating six persons with three separate solid cells with doors on either side of a narrow middle passage. In such vans, prisoners were unaware who travelled with them.

15 TNA FO 371/56476 N 5269/G, a 60-page report in Polish (translation by EM) in two parts by Kazimierz Skarżynski, Secretary General of the Polish Red Cross. Part 1 '*Sprawozdanie poufne*' (Confidential report) dated Warsaw, June 1943; Part 2, dated September 1945, *Nowa Wieś* near Warsaw. Duplicate report with slight variations kept at PISM, KOL 12/4/19.

16 Robert [Robin] Maurice Alers Hankey (1905–1996) joined the Diplomatic Service in 1927 as Third Secretary in Berlin, then Paris, Secretary to the League of Nations in 1935, transferred to Warsaw in 1936 as First Secretary. Created Second Baron in 1939; moved to Bucharest in 1939–40 as Chargé d' Affaires, moved to Cairo, then in 1942 to Tehran and Budapest. The rest of war years spent in FO, London. In 1945 moved to Warsaw, again in the FO as Head of the Northern Department. In 1949, Chargé d'Affaires in Madrid and in 1951 Minister Plenipotentiary in Budapest. KCMG in 1955, Ambassador to Sweden 1954–1960. Retired in 1965, much respected and liked by the Poles.

17 PISM KOL 12 /4 /19 SOW17/46 a typed protocol of events by Kazimierz Skarżyński (signed by Judge Zygmunt Kindler) Paris, 3 September 1946.
18 TNA HS 4/137 typescript copy of a message received 'by most secret means' from a British PoW in Germany on 2 May 1943, followed by a BBC monitoring report of 26th May 1943,of a German propaganda (*Weichsel*) broadcast in Russian for the Russians.
19 TNA FO 371/100719,The Katyn Forest Massacre Hearings, Select Committee to conduct an investigation of the facts, evidence and circumstances of the Katyn Forest Massacre, second session Washington D.C., 4 February 1952, pp. 31–59
20 TNA FO 916/827 and 828 British Legation in Berne despatch 6605, 20 August 1943 for the FO, under ref KW 2/4 Information concerning journey to Katyn of Captain Stanley B. Gilder, includes a two-page typed copy of Gilder's report dated 30 May 1944 of the British and American PoW visit to Katyn, together with five photographs, which was delivered to the British Legation in Berne on 3 July 1944; FO 916/828 ref MI9/BM/973, another account of the same visit sent by Director of Prisoners of War, War Office dated 22 November 1944 to FO Political Intelligence Department as well as the South African Union Defence Force representative Lt Col C.H.S. Runge at South Africa House in London.
21 TNA FO 371/97632 ref U1661/22, minutes of the meeting between Mr Penfield and Mr R.C. Courtney both from the US Embassy and Mr Roderick Barclay of the FO 18 April 1952; PREM 11/311 record of conversation with the US Ambassador of Sir William Strang and Sir Roger Makins, 3 April 1952.
22 Adam Edward Schebesta (1893–NN) studied medicine in Lwów and Vienna, chief Medical Officer, Lieutenant Colonel during 1920 War of Independence. In 1930 became a member of the Executive Committee of the Polish Red Cross in Kraków.
23 PISM KOL 12/4/37, a full report was compiled and written in September 1947 in London.
24 TNA FO 916/828, MI 9/BM/973, 'Top Secret' under cover at WO BM 3420 (P.W 2) 22 November 1944, an account of the visit of Col Stevenson and Capt. Gilder to Katyn.
25 TNA HW 40/88, PWM/G/712, Lt Col Frank P Stevenson C.S.O. Senior British Officer of South Africa Division, captured at Tobruk in 1942 and taken to Oflag VI B, Dossel, near Warburg. Stevenson communicated with MI 9 in code through a correspondence officer (Captain, name kept secret) in the same camp location. Similar arrangements were made in other Oflags, for example Captain Gorrie was one such officer who used a secret radio transmitter for communication with London.
26 *GPU Gluvnoye Politicheskoye Upravlenye*, (State Political Administration between 1924–1934) afterwards a Security Service of the Comissariat of Internal Affairs, which became a precursor to *NKVD – Narrodny Komissariat Vnutriennyh Diel* – the Secret Police.
27 *SPP* (*Studium Polski Podziemnej*) The Polish Underground Movement Study Trust, Ref A.1.3. Typescript copies of diaries and notebooks found on bodies of officers were despatched to London by courier Roman Rudkowski on Wildhorn II operation 29/30 May 1944. Some pages were illegible and the person who typed them in Kraków's Institute of Forensic Medicine, has parentheses to indicate a probable reading.
28 On the invasion of Poland in September 1939, the Germans abrogated the sovereignty of the Republic of Poland, and the Red Cross was not allowed to exercise its normal functions. Connected to the International Organisation, the Germans could not entirely liquidate it but confined its activities territorially to the area of the *Generalgouvernment* and only to the care of surviving soldiers of the September Campaign. An Information Bureau was set up, headed by Kazimierz Skarżyński to deal with PoW affairs.
29 Leon Kozłowski (1892–1944) archaeologist, politician of extreme right-wing convictions, Member of *Sejm*, Polish Parliament between 1928–1935; in charge of agricultural reforms and in the last two years Prime Minister. Not a popular figure. Imprisoned by the NKVD

in 1939, exiled to Siberia, released in August 1941 with intensions of joining the Polish Army – decided to cross the war zones, heading for Berlin. His motives are still a mystery to many historians. The Germans used him for propaganda purposes by publishing his experience in Russian prison and labour camp. They also took him to Katyn. Sir Stafford Cripps, the British Ambassador in Kuibyshev informed the FO about Kozłowski's death in Berlin during Allied bombing; see FO 371/26780 C 14255/7068/55 and FO 371/39451 C 6537/131/55. Left a diary *Moje przeżycia* (My experiences) edited by Bolesław Gogol and Jacek Tebinka, Warsaw 2001.

30 F. Goetel in his book *Czasy wojny* (Wartime) refers to the Koźliński family. In 1997 Vocatio published a biographical work *Czas Wernyhory* by Zbigniew Koźliński, grandson of Piotr Koźliński, who up to the Russian Revolution in 1917 owned Katyn wood.

chapter four

THE FOREIGN OFFICE ATTITUDE

The German news release and the reaction of the Russians made the FO all the more determined that the press should be strictly controlled, especially the official Polish press in London – *Dziennik Polski* (Polish Daily) and the independent literary weekly *Wiadomości* (News). There was also a daily *Dziennik Żołnierza* (Soldier's Daily) printed for the Army, stationed in the Middle East and Scotland. *Dziennik Żołnierza* published an exceedingly emotional article *'Kula w kark'* (A bullet in the neck), advising the Allies to accept the German accusation of the Russians as a fact, which ought to shake them into reality. Their motto of justice and freedom should weigh on their conscience, each time they praised the struggle against the aggression of the German murderers. The Soviet press *Pravda* (The Truth) published an article on 19 April 1943 accusing the Polish Minister of Defence, General Marian Kukiel, who had turned for help to the International Red Cross, of 'an act of direct and open co-operation between the Poles and the Germans in fabricating vile lies'. In answer to *Pravda*'s article, *Dziennik Polski* replied that any sort of political agitation would not stop the pursuit by the Polish Government of establishing the truth and punishing the guilty.

On 25 April, Vyacheslav Molotov, the Soviet Foreign Minister delivered a note to the Polish Ambassador Tadeusz Romer severing diplomatic relations with the Polish government-in-exile. Repercussions were to follow; first a shameful letter arrived at the Polish government's HQ, Stratton House, from the Executive Committee of the 'National Council for British-Soviet Unity'. Its President the Bishop of Chelmsford and Vice-Presidents David Lloyd-George MP, the Dean of Canterbury, Sir Granville Bantock the composer, Sir William Bradshaw J.P., H. G. Wells and others had passed a resolution:[1]

> That this National Council for British-Soviet Unity views with alarm the events that have led to the break in diplomatic relations between Poland and the USSR. That we call upon the Allied Governments to do all that lies in

> their power to restore Allied Unity. We believe this can only be done by the withdrawal by the Polish Government of accusations of crime against Polish officers and men at Smolensk. Further, that an undertaking should be given by the Polish Government, that immediate steps will be taken to eliminate all anti-Soviet propaganda by Polish Societies in this country. Failing this undertaking being given, we demand the withdrawal of supplies of paper for their publications.

Churchill's order on censorship of the Polish press was imminent. Fearful of the consequences, Foreign Minister Romer was advised to seek Ambassador O'Malley's opinion as to what the official Polish daily *Dziennik Polski and Dziennik Żołnierza* could say about the Katyn murders. After discussions with Frank Roberts and Sir Orme Sargent, the Deputy Under Secretary of State, Ambassador O'Malley composed a conciliatory statement on behalf of the Poles, which eventually appeared in the Polish press:[2]

> About our attitude towards various public reports and statements we wish to say only this: that we never accepted the German report and that we never accused the Russians and that we do not now accuse the Russians of anything. Our attitude last April, as today, is that we were and are anxious to ascertain the fate of Poles for whom, as a Government, we have a responsibility. When our appeal to the Red Cross to assist in this was misunderstood we withdrew it. We can only welcome the circumstances which have enabled the Russians to hold their own investigation into the matter and publish their own report. The dead cannot be brought to life and we now wish to say nothing more about the Katyn affair.

German reaction to the Soviet report

Soviet War News as well as *The Daily Worker* in London announced that the Soviet Commission's report on Katyn, led by academician Nikolai Burdenko,[3] would vindicate the Soviet Government in the eyes of the Allies and discredit the stubborn Polish government. On hearing the news, *Auswartiges Amt*, the Ministry of Foreign Affairs in Berlin sent a secure signal to all its diplomatic posts on 19 January 1944. Intercepted by the British and deciphered on 25 January with the title 'propaganda', it reads:

> A *Tass* report dated 17 January, states that a Soviet special commission for investigation and determination of the circumstances in which captured Polish officers were shot at Katyn by German-Fascist intruders has been formed in the guise of a commission, the establishment of which can be traced back to the resolution of an Extraordinary State Commission for the Investigation of Crimes Committed by German-fascist intruders. Chairman Burdenko, members: Tolstoy, Gundorov, Kolesnikov, Potemkin, Smirnov, Melnikov. According to the above-mentioned

report, the commission will shortly conclude its task and publish a communiqué concerning the results of its findings.

In view of the present difficulties existing between the Soviets and the Poles, it does not appear desirable to forestall this forthcoming Soviet communiqué, by taking action ourselves, as the latest commentaries, even in the English press, express doubt as to the truth of Soviet assertions regarding Katyn. On the other hand, it does appear necessary to prepare a statement of the findings of the forensic medical men who have already visited Katyn, in order that we may be able to furnish a prompt reply to the expected Russian publication. Please therefore, get in touch with the forensic medical men known to you, who took part in the investigation and arrange for their agreement to the preparation of any necessary report following a Soviet statement. We intend to make use of such a reply only if this proclaimed Soviet statement does receive publication and if a review of the position at the time of publication appears to render it necessary for our Foreign Information Service to concern itself with the matter. It is intended further to publish this counter-manifesto of the forensic medicine experts in the form of a supplement to our Katyn White Book.[4] This latter step will be taken in conjunction with publication of the counter-declaration, which we have already prepared, of the former Polish Prime Minister [Leon] Kozłowski:

You gave me the opportunity to examine the facts of the Katyn affair on the spot, which permitted no doubt of the murder of the Polish officers by the *NKVD*. You sent me the report of the Soviet Extraordinary Government Commission of Enquiry in which was set out the Soviet attitude to the Katyn murderers. This exposition, after careful examination, could not alter the conclusion reached by me at Katyn. The whole thing gave me the impression of a scene in a very bad film and it cannot shake the facts established by me. In light of these facts I remain convinced that in the Katyn affair we are confronted with murders committed by the *NKVD*.

On 3 February 1944 another deciphered German diplomatic secure signal[5] was circulated from Berlin, this time indicating that for the first time the Soviet report admitted that when the area was in Soviet hands (1939–1940), three camps for Polish PoWs were established, something that had never been said before.

Auswartiges Amt Kult Pol L VI.
The Soviet Government claims that the shooting had taken place in autumn 1941. Prudently, the Soviets did not allow this statement to be checked by examination of the bodies found, either by international experts or by their Allies, but employed only their own Commission and arranged for the enquiry to proceed in the spectacular way devised. The statement by the Soviets that the bodies found originate from the year 1941 is clearly refuted by the results of the International Katyn Commission of experts in forensic medicine on 30 April

> 1943 (see White Book page 118 and report on the post-mortem by German doctors pages 92/94). For the rest, any medical expert can easily demonstrate that bodies buried in the spring of 1940, would appear different from those buried in autumn 1941 … (particularly so) if exhumation took place, as was the case on the German side, exactly three years after burial …

An example of how badly the Germans were prepared for the International Military Tribunal at Nuremberg is exemplified by a different deciphered secure signal of 18 February 1944,[6] soon after the release of the Soviet report. Von Haeften, Foreign Affairs in Berlin, informed all stations about remarks made by Professor Georg von Wendt, Doctor of Medicine and Philosophy at Helsinki. On hearing that the Soviets had examined the mass graves at Katyn he quoted the proverb 'the work reveals the master.' Wendt had studied the mass graves at Vinnitza in the Ukraine, which preceded Katyn by almost ten years, a crime perpetrated by the Bolsheviks, which confirmed that accurate shooting through the base of the skull demands considerable practice, hence most shots were fired with true mastery. The Bolsheviks routinely used this type of execution, and it was, he asserted, 'completely unknown in other countries'. It was clear to von Wendt that the same 'master hand' was engaged at Katyn as at Vinnitza.[7] Not to be outdone by the Vinnitza revelations, academician Burdenko claimed that he examined a similar incident at Orle, where the Germans shot hundreds of Russians in the back of the neck. Burdenko was apparently convinced that the Germans used the same method on the Katyn officers.

Foreign Correspondents and J. Balfour's Report

In January 1944, after the discovery of the graves by the Germans and their ultimate retreat in September 1943, the Soviets invited foreign correspondents to inspect the site. They came of their own free will, probably out of curiosity. They had the chance to meet some technical members of the Soviet Commission, who still lingered at the site. It is important to state at this juncture that the investigation of the Katyn graves by the Soviet Commission lasted only a week. Mr John Balfour, Minister Plenipotentiary of the British Embassy in Moscow, despatched an immediate secure signal (January 25, 1944, 10.55 GMT), saying that the correspondents' stories had yet to be released by the Russian censor, but he had seen Reuter's account and thought it was fair. He also talked to several correspondents who were not that reluctant to accept the Soviet version, but were not altogether satisfied with what they saw and heard. The Americans, according to Balfour, were not impressed, and Miss Kathleen Harriman, daughter of the American Ambassador, Averill Harriman, 'was quite satisfied that the Germans had done the deed'. Balfour was anxious that if anti-Soviet criticism were reflected in British or American editorial comments, there would be an explosion in the Soviet press. In his report Balfour gave the following reasons why the correspondents were so hesitant; he is not clear about the Polish Division, or the identity of the Pole in question, however, the rest of his report is plausible:

> a) Credibility of Soviet version of the affair hinges almost entirely on the medical evidence. Some correspondents consider that the evidence adduced to prove the victims were killed after July 1941 is inadequate. To complicate matters Soviet authorities now allege graves also contained the remains of men who were killed before that date but that these are bodies of Poles killed by the Germans in Western Poland and shifted to Katyn to incriminate the Soviet Government. In strictest confidence, one Soviet official informed an International Tribunal Correspondent that in the Second Polish Division [*Tadeusz Kościuszko*], there was a Pole who could testify that the victims were alive in the autumn of 1941. This testimony will presumably not be called for unless findings of the Commission are challenged.
> b) Witnesses produced by the authorities are suspect. The correspondents attended a hearing on Saturday afternoon and heard witnesses confess to having helped or co-operated with the Germans in one way or another. The correspondents were irritated to discover that witnesses did not produce any evidence that was new to the Commission. It was clearly not a *bona fide* hearing. The witnesses had evidently told their tale before, to the same people and repeated it parrot-wise.
> c) Unexpected questions flung at the Commission by some of the American correspondents were received with noticeable irritation.
> d) No press excursion to any part of Russia has been arranged with greater luxury than the Katyn party. The correspondents travelled in electric train, comfortable sleeping compartments and large saloon car. They were given very good food and supplies of vodka, wine and cigarettes were plentiful. No doubt some of these amenities were provided for the benefit of Miss Harriman (now described here as the poor man's Mrs Roosevelt).

A telegram summarising all these points was despatched on 1 February 1944 by the Under Secretary of State for the Dominions, Sir Orme Sargent, to the Governments of Canada, Australia, New Zealand and South Africa. No noticeable reaction was forthcoming from these quarters; no doubt they all followed the official British policy line – 'suspension of judgement'. However, unknown to Anthony Eden, Churchill and others had already received the news, and he suggested that 'the passage in brackets about Miss Harriman might well be left out for War Cabinet.'[8]

Interrogation of 'Columbine'

At the height of the Russian counter-accusations, B.1.B branch of the Security Service (MI5), was dealing with a German Waffen SS officer named Hans Walter Zech

Nenntwich, *alias* Joachim Nansen, British codename 'Columbine'. At the outbreak of war, he, like his father, was in the police and later joined the *Waffen-SS*. He served on the Russian front as a PoW interrogator and received a decoration for gallantry. It was alleged but not proven that at some time he was Himmler's ADC. Known to be in opposition to the Nazi regime, he was also alleged to be involved in selling arms to *AK*. He was caught red handed by the German security police and imprisoned but with the help of his German friends in a clandestine organisation managed to escape to Sweden. He stayed with a Swedish aristocrat Folke Bernedotte as a guest, and was interviewed by Lt Colonel R. Sutton Pratt, the Military Attaché at the British Legation. He was transferred to Britain in August 1943, having offered his services to the British. He was interrogated on several occasions, starting with Major Brian Melland of MI 14d, later a Cabinet Office historian and University lecturer and subsequently by B.1. (Branch of 'B' Division) of the Security Service (MI5) headed by Guy Liddell.[9] These interviews indicated to the British that Zech Nenntwich was anti-Nazi but they were not completely convinced and asked *Oddział VI* of the Polish General Staff through SOE for a Polish confirmation from Warsaw.

Documents reveal that as far back as 1 October 1943, MI5 offered the Poles the opportunity to interrogate Zech Nenntwich – 'in a reasonable manner' – about his dealings with the Polish Resistance. Apparently, the Polish security services in London did not take up the offer, prior to investigations by *AK* to identify Nenntwich. On looking through the Polish archives at SPP (Polish Underground Movement Study Trust) in London, only one of several Zech Nenntwich's interrogations was translated from English, dealing mainly with his exploits in Warsaw. The subject of Katyn is not mentioned in these papers, which is puzzling. On reading the MI5 document, the truth is revealed, that at the request of 'D.B.' (Director of B Division, Captain G. M. Liddell), Major Valdemar B. Caroe questioned Zech Nenntwich about the Katyn affair whilst collecting information on German atrocities. On finding his deposition so revealing, MI5 had decided not to pass this information to the London Poles, for fear that 'if it gets to the Poles, there may be political trouble with the Russians.' This is what Caroe recorded.[10]

> You asked me to see 'Columbine' and find out his opinion about these murders. I saw him yesterday and he is quite convinced that the Russians are solely responsible. He gives the following as his reasons: he was with the German Army when they marched into the part of Poland, which the Russians had occupied. He says there is absolutely no doubt that when they (the German Army) arrived the population welcomed them as liberators in spite of the fact that the Poles have no love for the Germans. Their hatred of the Russians is considerably greater and the latter had treated them during the months of occupation with very great cruelty. He gives as examples the large number of all classes of Poles who were deported to European Russia (chiefly Archangelsk) and Siberia for slave labour. In Lemberg [Lwów] the population was made to parade in front of the Russians

and show their hands. Anyone whose hands showed they were unused to manual labour was deported; no one was shown any consideration. He says this is a fact and not just a rumour. The Russians also treated all P.O.W.s and especially Polish officers shamefully.

At the time when Smolensk fell and when, according to 'Columbine', the officers were probably murdered, Sikorski was in Moscow and the Russian-Polish treaty was being signed. Had the Russians taken these P.O.W.s with them when they retreated, they would have supplied Sikorski with plenty of evidence of Russian cruelty and ill treatment and been against a Russian-Polish alliance. On the other hand, had the Russians let these officers fall alive into German hands, they would fear that the Germans would promptly make use of them on the wireless to show up the treatment the Russians had dealt out to them and prevent the treaty being signed.

'Columbine' is convinced that had these men, in anything like such numbers, fallen into German hands, he would have heard of them, they would have been shown to the Red Cross as evidence of Russian cruelty and would have been made use of for propaganda purposes amongst their own troops. The Germans were extremely keen to impress on their soldiers the sort of treatment they could expect if they fell into Russian hands so as to make them fight to the bitter end and the evidence of these officers would have been useful. When the Russian-Polish treaty had been signed the Russians flooded Poland with leaflets dropped from 'planes informing the population of the treaty. The Germans were anxiously looking round for counter-propaganda and these officers would have been useful had they been available.

When the Germans captured Smolensk, they were not hard-pressed. There was in those days no talk of a possible German retreat but merely of an advance to the Ural line, so there seems no reason why the Germans should have murdered these officers at that time.

He thinks it unlikely that the Germans would have kept these officers alive and murdered them at some later date and then blamed the Russians for the murders so as to make difficulties for the Allies because he is convinced that they would have been made use of in the meantime and that their being alive, after the Russian retreat, would have become known.

He says consideration should be given to the fact that Eastern Poland had not yet in those days experienced the cruelty of the *Gestapo* but only occupation by the Russians and the population, when the Germans marched in, was anti-Bolshevik and almost pro-German and not a liability that they wanted to get rid of.

I think when considering 'Columbine's' point of view one must remember that he was friendly with the Poles and is very anti-Bolshevik. He is quite willing to admit that both the *Gestapo* and *Allgemeine S.S.* would have been capable of these murders; in fact he knows they are guilty of worse crimes against the civilian population. He relies on the fact that these officers were cruelly treated by the Russians and as such, if captured alive by the Germans, would have been made available for propaganda purposes.

After 'Columbine' had given me his point of view I put forward your suggestion that probably both the Russians and the Germans were responsible and that the Germans murdered the bodies from the top of the graves. He acknowledges that the *Gestapo* will have shot a number of Polish officers during the last four years and these may, of course, have been added by the Germans to the large graves containing the ones shot by the Russians but he will not admit that the ones in P.O.W. camp near Smolensk can have been shot by the Germans.
B.1.H/VBC 3.2.44 V. B. Caroe

There is no indication in the Foreign Office files that Zech Nenntwich's revelations were taken into account, although O'Malley uses similar arguments. In hindsight one would have expected a more rigorous interrogation from Major Caroe, especially on the German-Soviet Pact of 1939 as well as close cooperation regarding PoWs later that year, prior to Germany's attack on Russia. Perhaps his simple statement that he would have heard, had these officers fallen into German hands earlier – is the most convincing statement of all.

The Soviet Commission of Experts

The *Tass* statement published in *Pravda* on 17 January 1944, advised that the Soviet Special State Commission investigating the Katyn wood murders was to publish its report shortly. A signal came from the British Embassy in Moscow to this effect on the same day, promising to send a translated version later. The Central Department of the FO made immediate observations: 'To avoid any new outburst of recrimination, it would be useful if the British press could be induced to give the report, when it appears, the minimum of publicity.' A revival of the Katyn controversy was obviously not in anybody's interest. Sir Owen was informed about it on 28 January.[11] Full translation of the complete report was still to come, but for his purposes he had enough information in the report of the Soviet forensic experts, the description of recovered documents as well as the general conclusion signed by all the members of the 'Extraordinary State Commission for establishment and investigation of the crimes committed by the German Fascist invaders and their accomplices'. At this stage, neither O'Malley nor the Russians were aware that in point 3 of the conclusions of their report, there were hidden blunders, which became a pivot and the downfall of the Katyn case at the Nuremberg Trials of 1946. The most striking were the names of the German officers and their Battalion, accused of murder by the Soviets, wrongly attributed. The State Commission, better known as the Burdenko report, was in fact not prepared by Burdenko but by the two trusted *NKVD* 'experts', Vsevolod Merkulov and Sergei Kruglov, who, with a team of workers, were despatched by Beria to

Smolensk in October 1943. Their task was to 'prepare an initial investigation' involving forging of documents and placing them with corpses. Witnesses were rounded up and at least seventeen were made to swear false statements. Sergei Kruglov was in charge of the operation and presented the purged report to distinguished members of the Special Commission for signing on 10 January 1944.[12]

Russian Scientific Sub-commission's Conclusion

Enclosure 2

The Commission of experts in forensic medicine, taking into consideration the results of the examination of the corpses from the point of view of forensic medicine, has reached the following conclusion:

When the graves were opened and the corpses taken from them it was established that –

a. Amongst the mass of corpses of Polish prisoners of war there are corpses in civilian dress; their number is only an insignificant proportion of the total number of corpses examined (only two out of 925 corpses taken out of the grave); these corpses were wearing shoes of military pattern;

b. The clothing on the corpses of the prisoners of war showed that they belonged to the officer class and partly to the rank and file of the Polish army;

c. Cuts in the pockets and the boots, pockets turned inside out and tears in the pockets, discovered when the clothing was being examined, show that the whole of the clothing of each corpse (the overcoat, the trousers, etc.) as a rule showed signs of a search conducted on the corpses;

d. In certain instances when the clothing was examined the pockets were found to be intact. In these pockets, and also in pockets which had been cut and torn, under the lining of the uniform, in the trouser belts, in the clothes in which they wound their feet, in their handkerchiefs, were found pieces torn from newspapers, brochures, prayer books, postage stamps, sealed and open letters, receipts, notes and other documents and also valuables (a bar of gold, gold dollars), pipes, penknives, cigarette papers, handkerchiefs and so on;

e. On part of the documents (even without special investigation) we found dates going back to the period from 12 November 1940 to the 20 June 1941;

f. The fabric of the clothing, especially the overcoats, uniforms, trousers and shirts, has been well preserved and could only be torn with one's hands with great difficulty;

g. A few of the corpses (20 out of 925) have their arms bound behind their backs with white plaited bonds.

The conditions of the clothes on the corpses and particularly the facts that the uniforms, shirts, belts, trousers and underpants were fastened, that they were wearing boots and shirts, that their scarves and ties were fastened round their necks, that their braces were fastened and their shirts were inside their trousers, bear witness to the fact that there had been no previous examination of the trunks or extremities of the corpses.

The good state of preservation of the skin on the head and the absence either here or on the skin of the chest or belly (except in three cases out of 925) of any cuts, gashes, or other signs of expert examination indicate that, to judge by the corpses examined by the Commission of experts in forensic medicine, there had been no previous examination of the corpses from the point of view of forensic medicine.

The superficial and internal examination of 925 corpses give ground for asserting the existence of bullet wounds in the head and neck, in four instances in conjunction with injuries to the bones of the vault of the skull inflicted by a dull, hard, heavy object. Moreover in an insignificant number of cases we found abdominal injuries as well as head injuries. The cavities where the bullets entered were, as a rule, single, more seldom double. They were situated in the nape of the neck near the occipital protuberance, or near the great occipital cavity or at its edge. In a few instances, the cavity where the bullets entered was found at the back of the neck opposite the first, second or third vertebrae of the neck.

The cavities through which the bullets left the head were usually found in the region of the forehead, occasionally in the region of the temples and parietal bones. In 27 cases the bullet wounds were blind (i.e. there was no exit cavity) and at the end of the canal made by the bullet under the soft cover of the skull, in the bones of the skull, in the covering membrane of the brain and in the substance of the brain were found deformed, slightly deformed or completely un-deformed … (Russian: *obolochechnye*) bullets, used for firing from automatic pistols, chiefly of 7.65 mm calibre. The size of the entrance cavities in the bones round the nape allows one to conclude that the shooting was done by firearms of two calibres: in the vast majority of the cases less than 8 mm., i.e. 7.65 mm. and less; in a smaller number of cases above 8 mm., i.e. 9 mm. The character of the fissures in the bones of the skull and the discovery in certain instances of traces of powder in the entrance cavity proved that the shots were fired either point-blank or almost point-blank.

The relations to each other of the entrance and exit cavities show that the shots were fired from behind with the head bowed forward. The canal made by the bullets went through vitally important parts of the brain or near them and the destruction of the tissues of the brain was the cause of death.

The injuries to the bones of the vault of the skull caused by a dull, hard, heavy object should be taken in conjunction with the bullet wounds of the head; they themselves did not cause death.

The examination of the corpses from the point of view of forensic medicine which took place in the period from 16 to 23 January 1944 is evidence that there are no corpses in a state of putrid dismemberment or decomposition and that all 925 corpses are in a good state of preservation – at the first stage in the loss of moisture by the corpse (which was observed most frequently and clearly in the area of the chest and abdomen, sometimes in the extremities; that is in the earliest stage of adipocere or in the high proportion of adipocere in the corpses exhumed from the bottom of the grave) or in conjunction of the loss of wax by the tissues of the corpses and the creation of adipocere.

Special attention should be paid to the fact that the muscles of trunk and of the extremities have preserved intact their macroscopic structure and almost their ordinary colour.

The internal organs of the chest and the abdomen have preserved their form and in a large number of instances the muscles of the heart when seen in section had retained their clearly individualised structure and the colour peculiar to them, while the brain revealed its characteristic structural peculiarities with a sharply expressed boundary between the grey and white matter. In addition to microscopic examination of the tissues and organs of the bodies, the experts in forensic medicine obtained corresponding material for subsequent microscopic and chemical investigation in laboratory conditions.

The peculiarities of the soil in the place where the bodies were found had a certain influence on the state of preservation of the tissue and the organs of the corpses.

When the graves were opened and the corpses were taken out and exposed to the air, they were subjected to the influence of the warmth and damp of the spring and summer of 1943. This might also have affected the quick development of the process of the decomposition of the corpses.

However, the degree of loss of wax in the corpses and the formation of adipocere in them specially good state of preservation of the muscles and internal organs, as well of the clothing, give grounds for maintaining that the corpses had been in the ground for a short time only.

If the condition of the corpses in the graves on the territory of Goat Hills is compared with the condition of the corpses in other cemeteries in the town of Smolensk and its immediate environment, e.g. Gedeonovka, Magalenshchina, Readovka, Camp No.126, Krasny Bor, etc. (see the report of the experts in forensic medicine dated 22 October 1943), it must be admitted that the burial of the corpses of the Polish prisoners on the territory of Goat Hills took place about two years ago. This is fully confirmed by the discovery in the clothing on the corpses of documents excluding the possibility of earlier burial (see point D in article 36 and the description of the documents).

On the basis of these data and the results of the investigations, the Commission of medico-legal experts: –

Considers as established the fact that prisoners of war, officers and partly privates of the Polish Army, were done to death by shooting.

Maintains that this shooting occurred some two years ago, i.e., in the period between September and December 1941.

Regards the discovery by the medico-legal commission of experts of valuables and documents in the clothing of the corpses bearing the date 1941 as proof that the search of the bodies carried out by the German-Fascist authorities in the spring and summer of 1943 was not thorough and that the documents discovered are evidence that the shooting occurred after June 1941.

Observes that in 1943 the Germans conducted autopsies on an extremely insignificant number of corpses of Polish prisoners of war.

Notes that the method of shooting the Polish prisoners of war is identical with the method of shooting peaceful Soviet citizens and Soviet prisoners of war so widely practised by the German-Fascist authorities on the temporary occupied territory of the U.S.S.R., including the towns of Smolensk, Oryol, Kharkov, Krasnodar and Voronezh.

V. I. Prozorovsky,
V. M. Smolianinov,
D. N. Vyropaev,
Dr P. S. Semenovsky,
M. D. Shvaikova.

Smolensk, 24 January 1944

Documents found on the Bodies

Besides the facts recorded in the deposition of the medico-legal commission, the time of the shooting by the Germans of the captive Polish officers (autumn 1941 and not spring 1940 as the Germans claim) is established also by documents found on the opening of the graves dating not only to the second half of 1940 but also to the spring and summer (March–June) 1941.

Of the documents discovered by the experts in forensic medicine, the following deserve special attention:

1. On corpse No. 92:

A letter from Warsaw addressed to the Red Cross, c/o The Central Bureau for Prisoners of War – Moscow, Ulitsa Kuibysheva 12. Letter written in Russian. In this letter Sofia Zigon [Zofia Żygoń] asked to be informed of the whereabouts of her husband Tomash Zigon [Tomasz Żygoń]. Letter dated 12.1.40. On the envelope there is a German postal stamp 'Warsaw IX. 4C' and stamp 'Moskva Pochtamt 9 Expeditsya, 28.IX.40 Goda' and note in red ink in the Russian language: 'Find the Camp and forward for transmission to addressee, 15.XI.40.' (Signature illegible).

2. On corpse No: 4:

A postcard, registered No: 0112 from Tarnopol with a postal stamp 'Tarnopol 12.XI.40'. The manuscript text and the address have lost their colour.

3. On corpse No: 101:

Receipt No: 10293 of 19.XI.1939 given by the camp at Kozelsk in respect of the receipt from Edward Adamowich Lewandowsky [Edward Lewandowski] of a gold watch. On the back of the receipt there is a note dated 14 March 1941 regarding the sale of this watch to *Yuvelirtorg*. [*Glaviuvelirtorg* – Jewellery Trading Commission]

4. On corpse No: 46:

Receipt (number illegible) given on the 16.XII.1939 by the camp at Starobelsk in respect of the receipt of a gold watch from Vladislav Rudolfovich Arashkevich [Władysław Araszkiewicz]. On the back of the receipt there is a note dated 25 March 1941 to the effect that the watch had been sold to Yuvelirtorg.

5. On corpse No: 71

A paper Ikon with a picture of Christ, found between page 144 and 145 of a Catholic prayer book. On the reverse of the Ikon there is an inscription of which the signature is legible – 'Jadwinja [Jadwiga] 4 April 1941'.

6. **On corpse No: 46**:

A receipt of 6 April 1941 issued by Camp No: 1-ON regarding the receipt from Arashkevich [Araszkiewicz] of money to the amount of 225 roubles.

7. On the same corpse No: 46:

A receipt dated 5 May 1941, given by Camp No: 1-ON regarding the receipt from Arashkevich of money to the amount of 102 roubles.

8. On corpse No: 101:

A receipt dated 18 May 1941, issued by Camp No: 1-ON regarding the receipt from E. Levandowski [Lewandowski] of money to the amount of 175 roubles.

9. On corpse No: 53:

A postcard in Polish, not sent off, addressed to Warsaw, Bagatelja [Bagatela] 15, Kv. 47 Irene Kuczinskaya [Irena Kuczyńska], dated 20 June 1941. Sender Stanislaw Kuczinsky [Stanisław Kuczyński].

General Conclusions

The data in the possession of the Special Commission, namely, the testimony of more than 100 witnesses questioned, the material submitted by the medico-legal experts, documents and material evidence removed from the graves in the Katyn Woods, point with undeniable clarity to the following conclusions.

1. The Polish prisoners of war located in three camps west of Smolensk and engaged in road building work up to the outbreak of the war remained there also after the German forces of occupation overran Smolensk up to September 1941 inclusive.

2. In the autumn of 1941, the German occupation authorities affected the mass shooting of the Polish prisoners held in the above-mentioned camps in the Katyn Woods.

3. The mass shooting of Polish prisoners of war in the Katyn Woods was carried out by a German military institution camouflaged under the name of 'Headquarters of the 537 Construction Battalion', at the head of which were Lt Col Arnes [Friedrich Ahrens] and his assistants *Oberleutnant* Rekst [Rex] and *Leutnant* Hodt.

4. In the beginning of 1943, when the general military and political situation deteriorated for Germany, the German occupation authorities undertook a series of provocative measures aimed at charging the Soviet authorities with crimes they themselves had committed for the purpose of stirring up antagonism between the Russians and the Poles.

5. To this end: –
a. The German Fascist invaders, by means of persuasion, attempted bribery, threats and barbarous torture, attempted to find 'witnesses' among the Soviet citizens from whom they tried to obtain false testimony to the effect that Polish prisoners of war had been shot by Soviet authorities in the spring of 1940.
b. In the spring of 1943, the German occupation authorities brought bodies of Polish prisoners of war they had shot elsewhere and laid them in graves dug up in Katyn Woods with the aim of covering up the trace of their own crimes and increasing the number of 'victims of Bolshevik atrocities' in the Katyn Woods.
c. When preparing for their act of provocation, the German occupation authorities used some 500 Russian prisoners of war to dig up the graves in the Katyn Woods, to remove the incriminating documents and the material evidence. Upon completion of this work the Germans shot the prisoners.

6. The Data submitted by the medico-legal experts established beyond all doubt the following:
a. The shooting took place in the autumn of 1941.
b. The German executioners who shot the Polish prisoners of war used exactly the same method of firing a pistol in the back of the dead as had been used by them in the wholesale slaughter of Soviet citizens in other towns, in particular Oryol [Orel], Voronezh, Krasnodar and Smolensk.

7. The conclusion drawn from the testimony of witnesses and the findings of the medico-legal experts regarding the shooting by the Germans of the Polish prisoners of war in the autumn of 1941 are fully confirmed by the material evidence and documents found in the Katyn graves.

8. In shooting the Polish prisoners of war in the Katyn Woods, the German fascist invaders were consistently carrying out their policy of physically exterminating the Slavic people.

N [Nikolai] N. BURDENKO
Member of the Academy of Sciences of the U.S.S.R.
and the Extraordinary State Commission. (Chairman of the Commission)
ALEXEI [Aleksei] TOLSTOY
Member of the Academy of Science and the Extraordinary State Commission
METROPOLITAN NIKOLAI [Jaruszewicz]
Member of the Extraordinary Commission
Lieut. General A [Aleksandr] S. GUNDOROV
Chairman of the All Slav Committee
S [Sergei] A. KOLESHNIKOV
Chairman of the Executive Committee of the Union of the Red Cross and Red Crescent Societies
W.P. POTIOMKIN [Vladimir Potemkin]
Member of the Academy of Sciences and People's Commissar of Education of the R.F.S.R.R.
Col General E [Efim] I. SMIRNOV
Chief of the Central Medical Service Administration of the Red Army
R.E. MELNIKOV
Chairman of the Smolensk Regional Executive Committee.

Smolensk, 24 January 1944

Ambassador O' Malley on the Soviet Report

Sir Owen wrote an emotional despatch to the Secretary of State Sir Anthony Eden, in which he challenges the Soviet statements on every point.[13]

No. 25
British Embassy to Poland
45 Lowndes Square, SW 1
11 February 1944

Sir,

1. On January 24 the Soviet Government issued the report of a special Commission appointed for 'Ascertaining and investigating the circumstances of the shooting of Polish officer prisoners by the German-fascist invaders in the

Katyn Forest'. This report appears in full in the *Soviet War News* of January 27th, 28th and 31st, and February 1st runs to some 20,000 words and finishes with the conclusions, which are enclosed herein. Having dealt with the German account of this affair at some length in my despatch No. 51 of 24 May 1943, I ought perhaps now to deal with the question of what new light, if any, is thrown upon it by our Allies who, having regained possession of Smolensk, have been able to revisit the scene of the massacre and make an enquiry on the spot.

2. There was a difference between the methods employed by the German Government on the one hand and the Soviet Government on the other for convincing the world of the truth of the accusation, which each has levelled against each. The Germans relied primarily upon the findings of an international commission of fourteen pathologists and criminologists of whom two came from Germany, eleven from satellite or occupied states and one from Switzerland. Basing itself on the findings of this body, the German Government told its story to the world through every available publicity agency and they reinforced their case by bringing to Katyn a purely Polish delegation, composed of well known Poles from many different professions and classes of society, a delegation from the Polish Red Cross Society and delegations from Lodz [Łódz] and Poznan [Poznań]. The Russian Government on the other hand, relied mainly upon the report of a purely Russian commission, composed of eight Government officials, who had the assistance of a medico-legal sub-commission, composed of five Russian scientists. The Russian Government and German Government, however acted alike in this, that they both invited foreign journalists to visit the scene of the crime and both did their best to make the visit a pleasant one. The most up-to-date sleeping cars were provided by the Russians and aeroplanes by the Germans, for their guests: and in both cases, after a busy day among the corpses, these were served with smoked salmon, caviar, champagne and other delicacies. In both cases a religious ceremony terminated the proceedings.

3. No definite conclusions can, I think, be drawn from the differences between the German and Russian procedure, except perhaps that we shall be slightly more inclined to credit the opinion of the international experts brought to the spot by the Germans, than the opinion of a scientific sub-commission composed exclusively of Russians; for since it would clearly have strengthened their case, if the Soviet Government had invited British and American scientists to participate in the investigation; one can only suppose that a guilty concience prevented them from doing so. This inclination is strengthened by the facts, first, that Polish visitors to the graves (including members of the Underground Movement) who hate Germans and Russians equally were in no doubt that the latter had carried out the massacre; and secondly, that the journalists who accompanied

the Russian investigators from Moscow were, with the exception of Miss Kate Harriman, not favourably impressed by the Russian evidence or the means by which it was elicited.

4. Both Germans and Russians relied, among other things, upon two classes of testimony: first, verbal testimony given at first or second hand by individuals, who might be supposed to have personal knowledge of what occurred in Katyn in April and May 1940 (according to the German story), or in the last four months of 1941 (according to the Russian story) and secondly, the findings of experts who examined the corpses. It would, I think, be futile to try to appraise the trustworthiness of the testimony of witnesses examined by either the German Government or the Russian Government. Both were in a position to intimidate the soldiers, servants, peasants and other local residents who were called upon to give evidence and both are notoriously prone to use intimidation. Both allege that the other side had murdered material witnesses. The Germans, for instance, say that the Soviet Government itself gave orders for the destruction of the executioners employed by them; while the Russians affirm that the Gestapo liquidated no less than 500 Russian prisoners who had been ordered to open the graves at Katyn and assist with the examination of the corpses. It was for this reason that my despatch No 51 made no reference to any part of the verbal evidence given to the German investigators; for the same reason I do not propose to discuss similar evidence given to the Russian investigators although it occupies not less than nine-tenths of their report.

5. Since I enclose in my despatch No.51 the findings of the German (International) Scientific Sub-commission, [see annex III] it is only fair that I should annexe to the present despatch the findings of the Russian Scientific Sub-commission (see enclosure 2). The following are the most important discrepancies between the two. The German Sub-commission claims to have exhumed 982 bodies: the Russians 925. The Germans say that 'a considerable number of bodies were dissected': the Russians say 'no external examination of the bodies.... and no medico-legal examination of the bodies ... had been effected "previously".' The Germans say that 'there were varying degrees of decomposition of the bodies; that a large number of skulls were examined' for certain changes which only occur three years after death, and that this change was observed to 'a marked degree on skull no. 526': the Russians say that 'there are absolutely no bodies in a condition of decay or 'disintegration', that 'the bodies had not remained in the earth for long' and that the 'shooting dates back to... between September and December 1941'. The Germans say the latest document found on any corpse was dated April 22, 1940: the Russians say that numerous documents were found with dates between September 12 1940, and June 20 1941. It would be rash to draw any conclusion from these discrepancies;

but it would be very interesting if His Majesty's Minister in Berne could get an opinion on the whole matter from Dr Naville, Professor of Forensic Medicine at Geneva, who was a member of the German Sub-commission and is apparently the only neutral and accessible expert from either side.[14]

6. Dismissing as more or less unreliable the verbal accounts of supposed eye witnesses and findings of the scientific commissions on both sides, let us summarise the Russian story and see whether it affords reason for doubting the conclusion tentatively reached in my former despatch on the subject, namely that it was by order of the Soviet Government that the Polish officers were massacred.

7. The Russian report may be summarised as follows: before the capture of Smolensk by the Germans, Polish prisoners were quartered in three camps 25 to 45 kilometres west of Smolensk. After the outbreak of hostilities, the camps could not be evacuated in time and all the Polish war prisoners as well as some members of the guard, were taken prisoner by the Germans. Polish prisoners were seen working on the roads round Smolensk in August and September 1941 but not later. German soldiers frequently combed the neighbouring villages for escaped Polish prisoners. Access to the localities where the executions took place was strictly barred, but lorry loads of Polish prisoners were often seen being driven thither and many shots were heard. The report then passes on to the spring of 1943, when the Germans were alleged to have been preparing the ground for the announcements made on their broadcast system on April 12 of that year, and states that witnesses were tortured by the Germans into giving false evidence of Russian culpability; that 500 Russian prisoners, subsequently murdered, had been employed in March 1943 by the Germans to dig up the corpses and introduce forged documents into their pockets and that lorry loads of corpses were brought to Katyn in March 1943. In short, the Russian case amounts to this: that the occupants of the camps at Kozelsk, Starobelsk and Ostashkov were moved in April and May 1940 to three Russian labour camps near Smolensk, captured by advancing German armies in July 1941 and shot at various dates during the subsequent four months.

8. If the evidence of the Soviet Government's witnesses and experts could be trusted, it would be just possible to believe in the truth of the Russian story; but it would nevertheless be very difficult to do so, because it makes at lest one essential assumption, which is incredible and because it leaves altogether unexplained at least one indisputable set of facts, which urgently requires explanation before we can accept the Soviet Government's account of events.

9. The Russian story assumes that about 10,000 Polish officers and men, employed on forced labour, lived in the district of Smolensk from April 1940

till July 1941 and passed into German captivity when the Germans captured it in July 1941, without a single one of them having escaped and fallen again into Russian hands or reported to a Polish consul in Russia or to the Polish Underground Movement in Poland. This is quite incredible; not only to those who knows anything about prisoner-of-war labour camps in Russia, or who pictures to himself the disorganisation and confusion which must have attended the Russian exit and German entry into Smolensk, but the assumption which I have described as essential to the Russian case is actually destroyed by the words of the Russian investigating commission itself. The commission asserts that many Polish prisoners did in fact escape after the district of Smolensk had been overrun by the Germans, and describes the frequent 'round-ups' of escaped prisoners, which the Germans organized. The Russian story gives no explanation, why in these circumstances not a single one of the Poles who were allegedly transferred from Kozelsk, Starobelsk and Ostashkov to the labour camps Nos. 1 O.N, 2 O.N, and 3 O.N [*Osobovego Naznachenya* – special-purpose prison for designated persons] has ever been seen or heard of alive again.

10. So much for the assumption essential to the credibility of the Russian story. The unexpected set of facts is the same set of facts which has dominated this controversy throughout, namely that from April 1940 onwards, no single letter or message was ever received by anybody from the Poles, who were until then at Kozelsk, Starobelsk and Ostashkov (excepting the 400 to 500 sent to Griazovets); that no single enquiry about these men out of some 500 actually addressed by the Polish Red Cross Society to the Soviet authorities was ever answered and that no enquiries by representatives of the Polish Government elicited any definite or consistent information about them from the Soviet Government. If they had, as the Soviet Government now allege, been transferred from Kozelsk, Starobelsk and Ostashkov to camps Nos. 1, 2 and 3 O.N, why did not the Soviet Government say so long ago?

11. To all this, I am afraid I can only reply as I did in my previous despatch on the same subject, that while '... we do not know for certain who murdered the Polish officers buried at Katyn', the cumulative effect of the evidence is to throw serious doubt on Russian disclaimers of responsibility'. The defective nature of the report now issued by the Russian commission of enquiry makes these doubts even stronger than they were before. Stronger anyhow in the view of well informed persons in the United Kingdom, for having made enquiries through appropriate channels, I am satisfied that the great majority of responsible British journalists have during the last nine months come round to the same opinions as I have had myself throughout. Consistently with this, the British press coldly received the Russian report.

12. Let us think of these things always and speak of them never. To speak of them never is the advice, which I have been giving to the Polish Government, but it has been unnecessary. They have received the Russian report in silence. Affliction and residence in this country seem to be teaching them how much better it is in political life to leave unsaid those things about which one feels most passionately.

I have the honour to be, with the highest respect, Sir
Your most obedient, humble Servant
Owen O'Malley

The Foreign Office Response

After sending this despatch with its enclosures to Anthony Eden, O'Malley did not hear anything for some time. Churchill along with Eden found the arguments too close for comfort, and the decision not to give any circulation to O'Malley's second despatch was endorsed by Eden. Cadogan thought the fewer papers in circulation on Katyn, the better. He added that lies and propaganda came out of both the Russian and German side and reacted strongly to the FORD (Foreign Office Research Department) statement that the Soviet Commission was a strong one, 'this is an absolute nonsense as they were capable of manufacturing a case – or could find themselves in another mass grave'.[15] O'Malley was immensely angry and in a letter to Cadogan eloquently asserted his responsibility as Ambassador to Poland to report on current events and maintained that both of his despatches should have been printed and read in conjunction with the FORD memorandum. No answer was forthcoming from Eden, but typescript copies of the despatch were sent to the King and members of the War Cabinet in their official despatch boxes. The senior FO officals were concerned not to give the impression that Sir Owen's views on Katyn were of the same standing as that of the FO. There was a desire to distance the FO from the moral burden of Katyn.[16]

Sir Reader W. Bullard, the British Ambassador in Tehran, who witnessed the evacuation of a depleted Polish army and civilians to Persia in 1942, offered his support for O'Malley in his dispute with the FO. He wrote a personal letter to O'Malley, sharing his recollections of the attitude of the Soviet officials to the disappearance of thousands of Polish officers.[17] 'How can the Soviet authorities, who keep minute records of individuals, have lost trace of so large a body of men?' Bullard quotes Minister Kot's account of his last interview on 8 July 1942 with Minister Vyshinsky, who lowered his eyes to the ground and replied *'eh nyet'* (they are no more). While accepting that it was indirect evidence, Bullard wrote:

> My bit of evidence is convincing to me and I am sure that the Soviet Government would not have left within reach of the German advance 6,000 or 8,000 potential enemy officers. I have met two Englishmen who were in Lubyanka when Germany attacked Russia, and they reported that all the political prisoners in Moscow were immediately sent to camps further east. ... If ever an enquiry about the Katyn murders is held, I should be prepared to repeat my evidence for what it is worth.

Churchill was moved by the report and wrote one of his 'Personal Minutes' to Eden.[18]

> I think Sir Owen O'Malley should be asked very secretly to express his opinion on the Katyn Wood inquiry. How does the argument about the length of time the birch tree had grown over the grave fit in with this new tale? Did anybody look at the birch trees? All this is merely to ascertain the facts, because we should none of us ever speak a word about it.
> WSC
> 30.1.44

Sir Owen subsequently explained that, according to information from a Pole who lived in the Katyn region, the young trees were *Pinus Silvestris*, Scots pine, which propagates itself freely. A German broadcast on 28 January 1944 backed up this information. Fritz von Herff, a German forester who was present at Katyn woods, declared that they were planted as two- to three-year-old trees in 1940. However, spurred by Churchill's interest in this subject, O'Malley sought independent, scientific advice from Sir Roy Robinson, the Secretary of the Forestry Commission.

Sir Owen's despatch was read by Eden and Churchill on 3 March, and commented on with a handwritten note strongly objecting to O'Malley, a senior British diplomat, writing to Professor Naville, the Swiss pathologist and the only neutral member of the German International Commission of Forensic Medicine, who had visited Katyn in April 1943.

Sir Owen continued his investigation by seeking further opinions from other British authorities such as Professor Edgar D. Adrian of Trinity College, Cambridge, asking for a comparison of the two reports, German and Russian. The other report was to come from yet another renowned pathologist, Sir Bernard Spilsbury[19] of the Home Office. Sir Owen wanted to find out the status and character of the international experts appointed by the German authorities. He particularly wanted to find out more about Professor Orsós, a Hungarian, who was the only one who had made observations of the brain, stating that with rapid decomposition the evidence was completely destroyed by putrefaction. Perhaps it was on his instigation that *Oddział II,* the Polish General Staff Intelligence branch, contacted Professor Orsós for his opinion. Spilsbury, an authority on forensic medicine, replied on 18 April 1944 and was inconclusive, owing to the discursive language of the Soviet report he had read.[20]

From the medical descriptions in the reports, Spilsbury was unable to settle the controversy. He was 'impressed by the microscopic evidence of preservation given by the Russians as in favour of the shorter, rather than the longer period of burial'. He knew Dr Palmieri and Dr Miloslavich's status but had no knowledge of their work; as for the other members of the Commission, he did not know them at all. Sir Bernard's forensic observations make gruesome reading, but since this document, and Professor Orsos's Polish interview, are not generally known and have never been quoted by any historian to date both are included here.

Sir Bernard Spilsbury's Forensic Observations

I have read the papers on this subject, which were sent to me in February 1944, including the reports of the German and the Russian commissions respectively. The data furnished in these documents are inadequate to enable any accurate estimates to be made of the time of death. This is of less consequence since it is clear that the bodies did not undergo the ordinary processes of putrefaction by which the time of death may be fixed fairly accurately when the circumstances of the burial are known.

The Russian report, which is the more informative, states explicitly that no single case of putrefaction was seen in the remains and the same is applied in the German report, in which the condition described by Prof. Orsós would not be found on a brain which had undergone putrefaction.

The Russian report states that the organs of the body were intact and showed details of structure even microscopically and that the brain, which decomposes rapidly, shewed details of structure; these would all have been destroyed completely by putrefaction in much less a time than two years.

The known circumstances of the cause of death and the burial of these bodies explain why putrefaction was unlikely to occur:

1. All the deaths were sudden and in persons presumably healthy.

2. The passage of a bullet through the tissues of the neck and face – extensive smashing of the base of the skull where the bones are very thin, with an entrance and generally an exit wound, would ensure a fairly considerable drainage of blood from the victim before death.

3. The burials shortly after death, without coffins and large numbers of bodies packed together, which would help to exclude air from all but the topmost layers, and even from those if there was a thick covering of soil over the graves.

4. The burial of the bodies fully clothed which would also help to exclude air.

5. The low temperature presumably present at the time of the massacres, which would delay putrefaction indefinitely so long as it continued. When putrefaction does not occur and when carnivorous animals have not had access, two series of changes are found, mummification and adipocere formation, the second of these supervening, in certain circumstances, when mummification has already commenced. Mummification implies the general shrinking and drying of the body as fluid evaporates slowly from the surface; the rate is dependent upon the facilities for drying; even in favourable conditions several years are required for mummification to be completed.

Adipocere forming in the fat beneath the skin appears about three months after burial, and is completed in twelve months or more; it develops when the dead body remains immersed in water or in very wet soil; when it is complete no further change occurs and mummification is arrested.

Both of these conditions are referred to in the Russian report. The excavations for the graves were in sand which when dry assists in mummification.

The German report also states that the deeper graves extended down to the ground water.

The lowest layers of bodies would in these conditions show marked adipocere formation; this would be less at higher level and mummification alone would probably be found in the uppermost layers.

The presence of water in the graves would slow down the process of mummification, and although warm summer weather coming some time after the burial might speed up the drying process for a time, it would, in such conditions, be very difficult to estimate the period of burial from the degree of mummification so as to be able to distinguish between two and three years.

When adipocere formation had occurred there would be no further change after 12 to 18 months burial. Professor Orsós refers to the presence of calcareous incrustations on the surface of the brain, in one body to a marked degree, and he states that incrustations are not found in less than 3 years interment.

I am familiar with the presence of incrustations on the surface, especially of the liver, but I have seen them on the brain. They form when the drying process has reached a certain stage and so vary as to time of appearance with the rate of desiccation.

The brain has little chance of shewing this change when the skull is intact.

It may well be that its being found at all is due in these cases to the cause of death which would allow blood and other fluid to drain from the brain before death and by breaking the floor of the skull and providing openings, would allow of slow mummification of the brain.

It would therefore be impossible to draw any inference as to time from this process unless a large number of bodies had been exhumed at different but known periods after burial, and in which death had been caused by injuries similar to these cases, and in which the bodies had been buried in similar conditions.

I very much doubt whether there is any medico-legal expert who has had the necessary specialised experience to enable him to give a reliable opinion on the period of burial from incrustations.

My final conclusion therefore is that I do not regard it as possible from the medical data to give any reliable opinion as to whether in these cases death occurred two or three years before exhumation of the bodies.

No comments are necessary on the accounts given of the injuries produced by the bullets and the cause of death, these being well within the competence of any medico-legal specialist.

Bernard H. Spilsbury
April 18th 1944

On learning that Sir Owen had gone to such extensive trouble to seek expert assistance and being unaware that Churchill had encouraged him to make these enquiries, the Head of the Northern Department was scornful about the waste of a public official's time, commenting that Sir Owen would do well to leave matters alone. Nevertheless, Spilsbury's report was taken seriously by many at the FO, especially by Sir William Malkin,[21] the FO Legal Adviser, who commented with one sentence: 'This seems, if anything, to strengthen the case for suspension of judgement' on Katyn.

Professor Orsós' Confirmation of his Initial Report

Oddział II, of the Polish General Staff, Intelligence branch must have been involved in the search for the missing officers as far back as 1941. With the loss or destruction of its archives after the war, it is difficult to reconstruct the operations, which undoubtedly existed. Furthermore, *Oddział II* co-operated very closely with the British SIS (Secret Intelligence Service). Small fragments of Intelligence documents can be found among the archives of the Polish Government in exile at the Polish Institute and Sikorski Museum (PISM) in London. The most important in this case is a single transcript copy of a report from a meeting between Professor Orsós and a Polish Intelligence officer stationed in Budapest in June 1943. An *en clair* telegram arrived in London addressed to Colonel Stanisław Gano, Chief of *Oddział II* of the Polish General Staff in London, for the attention of General Kukiel, the Minister for Defence.[22]

On 16 June 1943 I had a meeting with Professor Orsós, who took part in the International Commission of medico-legal experts investigating the circumstances of the massacre of Polish officers in Katyn, and as the most senior, has led the work as *primus inter pares*. I wanted to know his opinion, strictly between the two of us, and perhaps receive some details, which did not appear in the press.

Professor Orsós does not want to talk about it or give interviews. I have tried to contact him through an official of the Council of Ministers, who with a polite pretext of readiness to help, in fact quite clearly wanted to get out of it. In the meantime, Prof. Orsós was about to present a photographic collection from Katyn to the Arch-Princess Magdalena, it is through her patronage that I managed to see Prof. Orsós privately in his house.

Personal notes about Professor Orsós: Professor at the Institute of Judicial [Forensic] Medicine, University of Budapest, 93 Ulloi. During the I World War spent four years in Russian captivity in Siberia; where he learned the language quite well, in speech and writing. He worked in Krasnoyarsk hospital in his expert field. The Bolsheviks wanted to keep him, by offering a Chair in Judicial [Forensic] Medicine in Tomsk.

Hidden mass murders during the Russian Revolution in Siberia enabled Professor Orsós to do research. His stay at the University of Debrecyna 1925–1936, during the complex increase of deaths by arsenic in that district, brought him some authority in the medico-legal field of medicine in Hungary and abroad.

According to the opinion of the mentioned Council of Ministers, Professor Orsós keeps to himself, away from the present politics, he is a typical scholar. However, at the Ministry of Education, it was said in confidence that Prof. Orsós reveals some right wing sympathies, the like of Imredy [Premier of Quisling Government of Hungary]

As regards the Katyn material in possession of Professor Orsós, it consists of:

a. The final protocol of the International Commission of experts signed by the 12 members. Fifteen copies of the protocol were prepared and sent to all the members and *Reichsarzteführer*, *Aalsenamt* [sic] and the German Ministry of Propaganda.

b. A description of a find of the graves, written by a German officer of the local formation.

c. Photographs taken by himself or sent to him by the German authorities *Reichsarzteführer.*

d. Papers written by Prof Orsós for German publication.

e. Text of an interview given to Hungarian newspaper *Eggidul.* (After Orsós' return from Katyn he was inundated with questions by the Hungarian press, but he refused to answer, referring them to the official statement. Some liberal press criticised him for it.)

f. A skull of an officer, and a doctor (as was evident by the insignia on the uniform and documents) showing the same marked injury as in victims of Hungarian *Cheka* [*Commissariat* for combating counterrevolution and sabotage, security police, a precursor of the *NKVD*] occupying Parliamentary building in 1919.

Decisive Hungarian Factors and Katyn Affair

I asked Professor Orsós if he is writing technical papers about Katyn or gives lectures on the subject; he replied that he has some difficulty and cannot publish anything or even inform individuals. Soon after returning from Katyn, he realised there was no disposition to work in public. Thinking that the Ministry of Education and Propaganda would be forthcoming in using his knowledge he found them uninterested, as if in expectation of a different outcome, in line their political vision. In reply, Professor Orsós informed them that he was objective in his description of facts, whether approved or disapproved of by people and nothing else should be expected of him. The authorities did not want to take care of the publication of Katyn materials, adding that even some of the Poles would not approve. Professor Orsós thought that behind all this façade lay the calculation of risks (antagonising the Soviets and relying on their favours).

Visual Inspection (post mortem) of Bodies at Katyn

The murdered Polish officers are buried in seven mass graves. The work of exhumation is slow. The majority are not even touched and the largest grave is not yet opened. The German Army employs some units capable of this work. Young lads of 14–16 years old are being used to unearth the graves. Among the exhumed corpses of Polish officers, a few Finnish officers have been found. The Katyn woods, not far from the Polish graves, hold layers of bodies from the time of the Russian Revolution 1917–1922. They are civilians, anti-revolutionaries, expected to be in the region of hundreds of thousands. This discovery is linked to the previous one on Poles. The Russian graves are not as yet examined, only a few inspection digs have been done; it was ascertained that they were people from the Russian intelligentsia.

This sad tradition in Katyn woods is linked to the fact that nearby, besides the Dnieper River is a summer retreat for the *G.P.U.* [*Glovnoye Politicheskoye Uprawlenye* – Main Political Security Office 1924–1938, forerunner to *NKVD*]. This facilitated rest after the 'heavy work' of executions for the *G.P.U.* The terrain looks quite normal; to hide the burials, some turf has been laid down and young pines transplanted.

Time of Death

1. The study of pine trees has shown five rings; in between the second and third ring is a gap of one month in further growth of the tree in new soil. This indicates that the pines were two years old when planted; in the new soil they have three years growth.

2. Notes found on the bodies (postcards, diaries etc) indicate the tragic moment came in the Spring of 1940, March–April.

3. The Russian newspapers found on bodies are dated not later than 22–23 April 1940. Several papers were from 22 April and only one dated 23 April 1940. It may be deduced that about this time the executions stopped.

4. A local peasant, who was employed at the local railway station in spring 1940, was interrogated. His task was to unhook the railway wagons full of Polish army men and redirect them into sidings. He declared that five or six wagons, crammed with 50–60 men, arrived each day. From the sidings, they were transported by lorries and driven towards the Katyn woods; they returned empty in readiness for the next lot of men.

5. On entering the woods, the men had to give up their possessions (suitcases, watches and other valuables).

6. The post mortem has shown that the men were quite adequately nourished. The inner contents of the stomach revealed black cereals; and the content of fat in the flesh was quite normal.

7. The corpses were laid down in 12 layers, two metres beneath the topsoil. The bodies are jam packed, joined together and as Professor Orsós said – one could not find a centimetre of space; separation was very difficult, due to a chemical process which excretes a sticky substance, while mummification takes place.

8. The first two layers of bodies in sandy soil are more decomposed; those further inwards are better preserved; the body and face can be recognised. The corpses were lying face down and all indicated the same cause of death, that of a shot in the back of the skull. The exit of bullets is either through the temple or forehead. The exception was bodies whose hands have been tied with a rope and had bayonets wounds, no doubt, from resisting. (In the adjoining Russian Revolution graves, bodies had their hands tied and sacks placed on the heads.)

Professor Orsós has brought with him one skull of an army medical doctor, showing the characteristic breaking of the jaw into three parts; the Professor explained that the *G.P.U.* and quite likely the *Cheka* broke the jaws of their victims who shouted protests before the execution. Bela Kuna[23] agents caused the same breakages during the executions of the 'white' Hungarians in Parliament in 1919. The similarity prompted him to take this particular skull with him as a sample to show other experts of Judicial [Forensic] Medicine.

On close examination of the clothes on the dead bodies, one could see sewn into the clothes all sorts of personal valuables and mementoes. Nearly all had their military identity cards, well preserved, sometimes enrolment cards, notelets where they wrote their daily experiences. All are interesting items and one can deduce where the persons came from, when, and which route they took. Besides, there were prayer books, rosaries, postcards written by families from Poland and abroad, with Russian postmarks and Russian newspapers; all these objects are collected, marked with the number of the body where found and put into a provisional museum set up in a peasant's hut.

The state of the corpses made a strong impression on Professor Orsós, especially the faces; he declared that even the faces of the dead by suicide, with whom he was familiar, were not as chilling. The dead of Katyn had a frightful look mixed with despair and failure.

While in Katyn, Professor Orsós met with two Polish doctors from the Polish Red Cross delegation. Together with the other staff, they stayed in a nearby location. He thought it was a very small team for the amount of work to be done. They gave him the impression that they were not used to this kind of work, and were 'deluded [sic] by the smell, almost half conscious'. The post mortems were done in haste and were not very thorough. Professor Orsós pointed out to them the importance of searching the clothing for the effects, which might be of historic value, at least as mementoes for the families.

On behalf of the International Commission, of which Professor Orsós was a member, he suggested to the Germans that they bury the examined and numbered bodies in separate new graves, and put the documents in a 'museum' labelled separately with the number of the body. It was very important to Professor Orsós that this was done in a proper manner, so that they would understand the meaning of a western civilisation and compare it with that of Bolsheviks.

Among the Polish officers, they unearthed some Germans of Polish nationality, who were in the Polish army and came from western regions of Poland. They were recognised by their German names and family letters written in the German language; the German authorities were going to take care of these corpses separately.

According to Professor Orsós, Katyn was a rare opportunity for the doctors to do research because the shooting method was the same on thousands of victims. This persuaded Budapest University to send an assistant for 2–3 months experience to Katyn. Already, there was somebody from the German side doing research, a professor from Wrocław.

Finally, towards the end of our conversation, Professor Orsós asked me not to let the Hungarians know about our meeting on Katyn, but he had no objection to my talking to the Poles about it; he even felt obliged to share his knowledge gathered in Katyn. Professor Orsós is an amateur painter and known in this field. The last picture he painted, that of Katyn woods, he presented to me.

Translation authenticated by
Captain [Rudolf Józef] Plocek [O II], 4 IX 1944

Orsós does not mention the *GECO* rounds found in the graves. It can be assumed that O'Malley was aware of Orsós' confidential interview, as the Poles had in the past shared all their information on Katyn with him. If he knew about it, he does not declare it, although as mentioned earlier, he followed up this crucial forensic aspect further, with Churchill's approval.

Notes

1 PISM KOL 68/42, letter of 6 May 1943 signed by Honorary Secretary C. E. Fearn, to the Prime Minister, Government of Poland, Stratton House, W1. Chairman Rev. W. A. Oyler-Waterhouse.
2 TNA FO 371/39437 C1357, dated 31 January 1944; also newspaper cuttings.
3 Nikolai Burdenko (1876–1946) Academician, Head of the first surgical clinic at the Moscow Medical Institute in 1930. Appointed a Senior Surgeon of the Red Army 1937-1946. Chairman of the Extraordinary State Commission of the Katyn massacre 1943–1944. President of the Academy of Medical Science of the USSR 1944–1946.
4 *Amtliches Material zum Massenmord von Katyn, Weiss Buche* (White Book) published by the *Deutschen Informationsstelle* German Information Bureau, Berlin, September 1943. Reproduced collection of documents and photographs relating to the mass murder of Polish PoWs. It contains an incomplete list of names of the victims. A final list was to be published by the *PCK,* after completion of the exhumation. In June 1943, a Polish list of only 2916 names was published without giving the particulars of the publisher, author, or place of publication.
5 TNA HW 12/297 127832, decrypt of a signal 3 February 1944, No.103, dated 29.1.1944.
6 TNA HW 12/297 128672, decrypt of a signal 26 February 1944, No.199, dated 18.2.1944.
7 TNA GFM 33/2525 E 24331-2, photostat prints of captured archives of the German Foreign Ministry in Berlin in 1945–6, held jointly by the American and British Governments, amongst them correspondence relating to the Vinnitza and Katyn murders. Documents were kept at Whaddon Hall near Bletchley Park and copied for the British, American and French governments. According to the head of the American team at Whaddon Hall, Dr Paul Sweet, they were to be published as part of the German War Documents Project. The Katyn prints contain reports and correspondence between the Foreign Office in Berlin and the German Legation in Berne 1943. The head of the FO Library, Mr E.J. Passant, objected on security grounds to Paul Sweet's appearance before the Madden Committee of the American Congress and to disclosure of the material held in joint custody, see FO 371/100719 N.P 1661/10, 17 4. 1952.
8 TNA FO 898/227, Political Warfare Executive view on Katyn and visit of USA party, 22 January 1944; FO 371/39388 C 1097/8/55, British and USA correspondents account on 25 January 1944 and C 1160 on 1 February 1944.
9 *Guy Liddell's Diaries 1942-1945* edited by Nigel West, Routledge, London-New York, 2005, Vol. II p.170.
10 TNA KV 2/397 PF 65879, (personal file) MI5. Interrogation of 'Columbine' by Major V.B. Caroe of B.1.D branch MI5 dated 3.2.1944.
11 TNA FO 371/ 39387 C939/8/55 secure signal from Moscow, Mr Balfour informs the FO of an impending public release of the Russian report on Katyn massacre. It includes statement from 'The Special Commission to Establish and Investigate the Circumstances of the Shooting by German Fascists Invaders of Captive Polish Officers in the Katyn Woods'. Signed Smolensk 24 January 1944.
12 *Katyn Dokumenty Zbrodni, Echa Katynia*, Vol. IV (Katyn Documents of the Crime), NKVD documents: No. 42 dated 10/11 January 1944, and No.46 dated 13 January 1944.
13 TNA FO 371/39390 C2099/8/55G, despatch 25 from Sir Owen O'Malley, 11 February

1944 to the Secretary of State, Sir Anthony Eden. This file contains 'enclosures': *Soviet War News*, published by the Press Department at the Soviet Embassy in London, extracts from the Burdenko report and forensic conclusions of the Commission.

14 Disapproval about contacting Dr Naville is expressed in a hand-written note by Eden, 'Certainly we should not do this'; 'I agree' signed 'WC' (Winston Churchill)

15 TNA FO 371/39393 C 2957/8/55G, hand-written notes by Sir Alexander Cadogan, dated 21.3.1944.

16 Ibid.

17 TNA FO 371/39419 C 17152, letter from Sir Reader Bullard, British Embassy Tehran to Sir Owen O'Malley, British Ambassador to Poland, 26 November 1944.

18 TNA FO 371/39390 C 2096/8/55G, Prime Minister Churchill's Personal Minute, serial No M 51/4 to Sir Anthony Eden dated 30.1.1944. Also C 2099/8/55G, Sir Owen's despatch 11 February 1944.

19 Bernard H. Spilsbury (1877–1947). Renowned pathologist who made forensic medical evidence acceptable to the British courts. He became known as the first great British crime scene investigator. Knighted 1923.

20 TNA FO 371/39398 C 5093/8/55G, typescript copy of a report by Sir Bernard Spilsbury dated April 18 1944.

21 William Malkin (1883–1945), barrister, diplomat, joined the Foreign Office in 1911, Senior Legal Adviser, 1929–1945. Knighted in 1930. Took part in Paris Peace Conference of 1919–20, Lausanne Conference in 1922–23, the United Nations Conference on International Organisation in San Francisco 1945.

22 PISM KOL 12/16 b ref 1168/ W Pol/43, typescript copy of a covering letter by Col S. Gano to General Kukiel, dated 3 VII 1943, enclosing a report by an unnamed Polish Intelligence officer working in Budapest, possibly Colonel Franciszek Matuszczak, 'Dod', who was in charge of Polish Intelligence Station 'Romek' from 1943 to 1945; or his Deputy Col Jan Korkozowicz 'Barski', describing a meeting with Professor Orsós on 16 June 1943. Translation by EM.

23 Bela Kun (1885–1939), leader of the Hungarian proletariat movement of 1919, member of the Comintern, imprisoned during Stalin's purges (1936–8) was kept until 1940 in a special prison with better conditions. Nikolai Yezhov, chief of GPU (NKVD) before Beria, had the same treatment.

chapter five

FORD ANALYSIS OF THE BURDENKO REPORT

The Foreign Office Research Department (FORD) entrusted the analysis of the Soviet Commission, otherwise known as the Burdenko report, to Professor Benedict Humphrey Sumner,[1] Fellow and Tutor in Modern History specialising in Russian history and language at Balliol College, Oxford. There, the Royal Institute of International Affairs had set up their Foreign Research and Press Department. Throughout the war he was engaged in the Russian Section and he was often consulted on Russian issues, especially in interpretation of intricate political manoeuvres and provided useful insights into the motives of Soviet policy.

Sumner's report or memorandum[2] was delivered at the beginning of March 1944. It contained many discrepancies, most glaring being the assertion by the WO that the Russians were not known to use the 7.65 mm pistol, but German Police and officers were using it widely! Sumner was not privy to reports that the FO kept, such as the *AK* concise report of 15 May 1943, or Capt. Gilder's deposition delivered by the International Red Cross, or the intercepted German diplomatic secure signals deciphered by GC&HQ, in April and May 1943.

On receiving the report, the Secretary of State directed distribution to the King and the War Cabinet only. This procedure was slightly delayed as Churchill decided that it should be circulated in a sealed box, which could only be opened by the named addressee. The memorandum was scrutinised by senior FO officials, amongst them Frank Roberts, who stressed that unlike O'Malley's despatches based on Polish material, Sumner's views were based entirely on the published Burdenko report of 24 January 1944 and was thus considered to be more objective, which is debatable.

According to Roberts' brief, Sumner's paper had shown the weaknesses in the German account, which he thought were always apparent – but neither did it dispose of weaknesses in the Russian; nevertheless, it presented them in a better light than earlier reports had suggested. Others thought that Sumner's paper had proved that there was no hard and fast conclusion to be drawn as in O'Malley's report, and it was important to them to distance the FO from O'Malley's point of view, of which nevertheless some approved and sympathised with.

On the whole, Allen approved FORD's analysis, although he had some reservations, as Sumner tended to lean more in favour of the Russian case than O'Malley, which according to Allen, 'called for a qualifying conclusion'.

Professor Sumner's Analysis

1. This paper attempts an analysis of the full version, as given in the *Soviet Monitor,* of the report of the Soviet 'Special Commission for Ascertaining and Investigating the Circumstances of the Shooting of Polish Officer Prisoners by the German-Fascist Invaders in the Katyn Forest'.

2. The conclusions of the paper are:

(i). Whether the Soviet or the German account is accepted, an appalling tragedy occurred in Katyn forest near Smolensk. Both accounts agree that 10-12,000 Polish prisoners of war, almost all officers who had originally been captured by the Russians in September 1939, were shot there by single pistol shots in the back of the head.

(ii). The Soviet account states that the Polish prisoners of war fell into the hands of the Germans in July 1941, when they captured Smolensk, and were shot by them between September and December 1941. The German account states that the Russians, between March and May 1940, shot them. The Germans gave the first announcement of the massacre to the world in April 1943.

(iii). Neither account suggests any definite reason why the shootings should have been carried out at the precise time when they were, but the date of the German revelation, April 1943, is significant. It promptly followed the first public manifestation of extreme tension between the Soviet and Polish Governments and it had the desired effect of causing the rupture of official relations and intensifying mutual hostility.

(iv). The only formal German document which appears to have been issued on the investigations held in April 1943, is the text of the protocol signed by the German International Forensic Medical Commission published in the German press on 5 May 1943. The Information Department of the German Foreign Office published in September a booklet on Katyn [The White Book] containing this protocol and other material, but no copy of it seems to be available. Whereas the German enquiries, which included one International Forensic Medical Commission and two Polish Commissions, were conducted with extreme rapidity in about a fortnight, the Soviet enquiry, except in its final stages, was apparently protracted and lasted several months. Allied press correspondents were brought down to Katyn during the last few days of the enquiry.

(v). The Soviet evidence is not conclusive in certain important respects. This fact tells against the accusation that the evidence was simply manufactured by the *GPU*.
(vi). The Soviet medical evidence, which is not yet available in full, requires expert judgement. So far only about one tenth of the bodies have been examined. The Germans similarly appear to have examined only about one tenth of the bodies. According to the Soviet account, some of the Poles have been shot at a different date elsewhere and their corpses have been brought to Katyn. To this further complication must be added the fact that the Russians were investigating graves, which have already been investigated by the Germans.
(vii). Making full allowance for what has just been stated in (v) and (vi), the report of the Special Commission may be said to make out a good, though not a conclusive, case for the perpetration of the massacres by the Germans.
(viii). The Soviet report does not throw any light on the question why the Soviet Government never told the Polish Government, despite its repeated requests for information, that these Polish prisoners of war had been captured by the Germans. The first Soviet statement that this has happened was made in reply to the German accusations in April 1943.
(ix). Nor does the report furnish any answer to the Polish contention that no letters or information from the prisoners were received after their removal in April–May 1940 to Katyn from three other camps, whereas before their removal news had been received from them.

3. An analysis of the Soviet enquiry is attempted in the following paragraphs:

4. There is as yet no information as to when the Special Commission was set up. The first reference to its existence was made in a public Soviet statement on 17 January (the same date as the Soviet Government's rejoinder to the Polish Government's reply on the Curzon Line proposal). At the same time Mr Balfour reported that the commission had been instructed to work at great pressure and produce its report rapidly. It did so: the report was signed on 24 January and published on the 26th. It is clear, however, from the commission's report that the initial enquiries were made, not by it, but by the Extraordinary Commission for Investigating German Atrocities, which got to work in the Smolensk region immediately after the Russians had recaptured Smolensk, 25th September last.

5. The Special Commission was a strong one. It consisted of eight members, three of whom are members of the Extraordinary Commission for Investigating the German atrocities. One of these three, Burdenko, Chief Surgeon to the Red Army, was the chairman of the Special Commission: he had certainly had much experience of this sort of investigation. One of the other members was a medical expert, Colonel-General [Efim] Smirnov.

6. A special committee of eleven medico-legal experts was set up by the Special Commission to conduct the medical investigations. Several of them have been mentioned previously as conducting similar investigations on the corpses of Russian victims of German atrocities in the Smolensk region. They exhumed and examined 925 bodies between 16th and 23rd January; quick work; but not so quick as that of the handpicked German International Commission of Forensic Medical Experts who, according to the German press, 'thoroughly and scientifically investigated the mass graves' in three days (28th–30th April 1943). The Germans exhumed 982 bodies. Though not all in those three days. Seventy per cent of them were reported as having been identified through documents or other material evidence on them. Thus, in each case the number of bodies exhumed was only about one tenth of the estimated number of corpses. Neither the Germans nor the Russians seem to have stated how many post-mortems were held, but they were apparently very few.

7. Allied press correspondents sent down to Katyn regarded the medical evidence as the most important. So far only the conclusions of the medico-legal experts have been published, but not the protocols of their examination of the bodies. Subsequent microscopic and chemical analyses were to be made.

8. Only an expert could express an opinion on the technical side of the medical conclusions, which testify 'that there are absolutely no bodies in a condition of decay or disintegration and that all the 925 bodies were in a state of preservation – in the initial phase of desiccation of the body', and which date the shootings 'back to about two years old, i.e. between September and December 1941'.

There is nothing in the report to show whether the medico-legal experts knew, before reaching their conclusion as to the date, that the evidence of the witnesses examined by the Special Commission (not by them) had given the autumn of 1941 as the date.

The German International Forensic Medical Committee certainly knew that the Germans had dated the shootings in the spring of 1940. This committee reported (not on the medical evidence) that the shootings took place in March and April 1940, and that 'various degrees and forms of decomposition are to be found … caused by the way the corpses were piled up within a pit, the position of the pit. In addition to mummification on the surface and along the sides of the mass of corpses, humid maceration [i.e., softening] is found in the centre parts of the mass of corpses.' Other data 'clearly point to primary stratification'.

According to a Danish pathologist [Tramsen], who was deputed by the Germans to visit the graves, there was among the experts 'considerable disagreement about how to form an opinion as to the time of death' owing to the condition of the corpses; 'on the borders of the graves the corpses were mainly skeletons and dry, whereas in the middle of the mass of corpses they were moist and well preserved ... most of the corpses were so surprisingly well preserved that the structure of the organs, and especially the contents of the stomach and the intestines were definable' even after three years.

9.The condition of the bodies was comparable with that of the bodies of Russian civilians and prisoners of war murdered by the Germans in other burial places in and near Smolensk towards the end of 1941 and early in 1942 and examined this autumn after the recapture of Smolensk by medico-legal experts, some of whom were the same as those conducting the Katyn investigation.

10.The description of the clothing and manner of shooting was closely similar to, and in certain points identical with, that given by the Germans; e.g. the victims were shot in the back of the head with a pistol; in exactly the same manner as many of the Soviet victims shot by the Germans in occupied U.S.S.R. This would involve a long drawn out massacre and a repeated succession of single shots – both of which points were testified to by a number of witnesses.

11.The Germans said that all shots were from a pistol with a calibre of less than 8mm. The Soviet medical experts reported that pistols of two calibres were used: 'in the bulk of cases, those of less than 8mm., i.e. 7.65mm or less and in a lesser number of cases, those of more than 8mm., i.e. 9mm'. The War Office confirm that the Russians are not known to use a 7.65 mm pistol, but that German officers and police widely use such a pistol, though it is not a regular army weapon.

12. On the bodies were found nine documents, with dates on them ranging between the 12th September 1940, and 20th June 1941 (i.e. the day before the German attack on the U.S.S.R.). Six of the documents were dated receipts; two were letters received from German-occupied Poland and Eastern Galicia; one was an un-mailed postcard to Warsaw. If the documents were genuine and genuinely belonged to the persons on whom they were found, they would conclusively prove that those persons were alive after the date (March–May 1940), given by the Germans for the alleged Soviet shootings. According to the German enquiry, the latest dated document was the 22nd of April 1940.

13.A strong point in favour of the genuineness of these nine documents is that no document was found after 20 June 1941. If the Soviet authorities were forging or substituting documents, why not completely clear them selves and incriminate the Germans by providing documentary evidence that the Poles were alive after, or at any rate up to, the 16th of July 1941, when the Germans captured Smolensk and according to the Soviet account the Poles fell into German hands? As it is, there is a gap of some weeks, the 20th of June–16th July 1941, during which (as far as the documentary evidence goes) it is theoretically possible for the Poles to have been shot by the Russians; though, it is true, the Germans could not use this argument because they have committed themselves to March–May 1940 as the time of the massacre.

14. Over a hundred Russian witnesses from the locality, were examined by the Soviet authorities. It is not surprising that the foreign correspondents were unfavourably impressed by the few witnesses that they heard giving evidence, since they were apparently giving it for the second time.

The evidence of some of the witnesses was given at great length in the report of the Special Commission, though not apparently *in extenso.*

It is notoriously difficult to gauge the credibility of witnesses when one has not seen and heard them. Further, it has to be remembered that, apart from the possible role of the *GPU*, most of the witnesses were giving evidence as to what happened, on their account, two years ago.

The same consideration applies with still greater force to the witnesses in the German enquiry last April, since they had to give chapter and verse for what was alleged to have happened not two but three years earlier.

Some of the most important evidence given by the Soviet witnesses was hearsay, i.e. inadmissible (in an English court of law) as establishing that the statement is true, though it may prove that the statement was made.

Allowing for the above considerations, the following observations may be made on the evidence given by some of the witnesses.

15. The Soviet chief of one of the three camps of the Polish prisoners stated that in July 1941 orders for the evacuation of the camp did not reach him, but that on his own responsibility he had attempted to secure railway cars from Smolensk for the evacuation of the Poles in the face of the rapid German advance, the responsible railway official in Smolensk had been unable to supply him. This official also gave corroborating evidence.

16. The non-receipt of evacuation orders and the failure to secure transport at the last moment sound extremely probable, given the conditions in Smolensk in July 1941.

This does not, however, in any way account for the fact that, according to official Polish statements, the Soviet authorities never told the Polish authorities what had happened, although from October 1941 onwards they repeatedly pressed the Soviet authorities for information as to what happened to the Katyn prisoners, no definite information was forthcoming. It was only in April 1943 when the Germans launched their version of the Katyn atrocities that the Russians definitely stated that they have failed to evacuate the Polish prisoners in July 1941, with the result that they had fallen into the hands of the Germans.

If this is so, the only possible explanation seems to be that there had been terrible confusion and that the *GPU* or other officials had blundered badly or disobeyed orders and had taken refuge in evasion and extreme procrastination in order to save their faces and perhaps their skins.

17. Numerous local witnesses testified to the presence of the Polish prisoners in German hands mid-July and September 1941. The evidence of three Russian peasant women was especially important, and was reproduced in great detail. They had been employed at this time in 'the Headquarters of the 537th Construction Battalion' in the Katyn forest. They gave the names of its commanding officer and others at this headquarters and a full account of what went on in and near the headquarters. It was these officers and this battalion, which, according to this evidence, carried out the massacre in the autumn of 1941. This, of course, is totally denied by the Germans, but as far as is known, they have not denied the existence of that battalion in the Katyn forest or the names of the officers and others given in the Russian evidence.

18. The evidence of a Professor of Astronomy in Smolensk, who was forcibly appointed by the Germans as assistant-mayor of Smolensk, showed that the mayor, another Russian (who was hand-in-glove with the Germans and subsequently decamped with them when they were driven out of Smolensk), had been told by the Germans that the Polish prisoners had been shot by them. Two entries in a notebook of the Mayor's supported this, though they did not conclusively prove the truth of the evidence given by the assistant-mayor.

19. A number of local witnesses gave evidence of having been tortured by the Gestapo and compelled to testify in February and March 1943 (i.e. before the first public German announcement of the Katyn graves on 11th April), that the Polish prisoners had been shot by the Russians in the late spring of 1940. One of these witnesses, aged 72, described how he had been specially trained in advance to give evidence before one of the two Polish commissions which the Germans sent to Katyn. The Germans in their account of the shootings had given the names of this and one other witness. These two were later searched for by the Germans, but succeeded in escaping their clutches. Five other witnesses, who had been similarly named in the German account, had died or remained in German hands.

20. Evidence was given that, besides the Poles shot in Katyn Forest, other Poles killed by the Germans elsewhere were transported by lorry to Katyn in March 1943, and thrown into the common graves. If these Poles were killed at a different date from the Katyn Poles, this fact might help to explain some of the confusion and discrepancies in the different accounts of the state of the bodies.

21. Five hundred Russian prisoners of war from camp No. 126 in Smolensk were employed at the end of February and beginning of March 1943 in transporting the corpses mentioned in the previous paragraph and in the 'preparation of the graves in the Katyn Forest', i.e., in removing everything from the pockets of the dead Poles: after examination by the Germans, these objects and documents except those dated after April 1940, were put back into the pockets, while the remainder were burnt. Nevertheless, as has been seen above in paragraph 12, some documents dated after April 1940 were inadvertently overlooked. The evidence of this 'preparation' rests solely on the testimony of a Russian local woman who harboured one of the prisoners of war who had escaped, but was subsequently caught and shot by the Germans: he told her the work he had been engaged upon, that it was now finished, and that his fellow prisoners were now being shot. The fact that about 500 prisoners of war were moved from Camp No. 126 at this time was, however, vouched for by two Russian doctors working in the camp, who were later rescued by the advancing Red Army. One of the German-sponsored versions issued in April 1943 mentioned that Russian bodies had been discovered on the site, and that they were believed to be political criminals executed by the *GPU.*

22. No reference was made at this point (or elsewhere) in the Soviet report to the young fir [sic] trees planted on the graves, which figured prominently in the German account and have been made much of by the Poles. The German 'coroner' and the head of one of the two Polish commissions sent to Katyn by the Germans described them in April 1943 as 'about three years old'. The International Commission sent to Katyn by the Germans at the same time, after calling in one expert, a German forester, found that they 'are at least five years old, small trees which have developed poorly in the shade of large trees, and were transplanted to the spot three years ago'.

The trees have been removed at the time of the German enquiry, so that the Soviet commission could not report on them direct; but the trees would have been there at the time the Russian prisoners of war were at work on the graves, unless they were planted immediately after they had finished their work.

The omission in the Soviet report of any reference to the fir trees might be regarded as a point damaging to their case, but it can, on the other hand, be regarded as a point in favour of the Soviet evidence being genuine, since the Soviet authorities can hardly have overlooked the use made by the Germans of the fir trees and, if they had been cooking the evidence, they ought to have provided something to counter the German account.

23. Very justifiably much has been made of the Polish contention that no letters or information of any kind were received from the Polish prisoners at Katyn, after they had been removed there in April–May 1940 from three other camps,

whereas previous to the move, letters had been received from them. This confirms Poles in their belief that the prisoners were shot by the Russians in the spring of 1940.

It might have been expected that the Russians, in proving that the Poles were in fact alive until they fell into the hands of the Germans, would have produced evidence to this effect, from Poles in Russia and disproved the above Polish contention. The Special Commission did not do so. One piece of evidence on this matter from a different quarter has, however, appeared in *Pravda*. A few days after the issue of the commission's report a delegation from the First Polish Corps in the U.S.S.R. [within the Soviet Army], headed by its commander General [Zygmunt] Berling, visited the Katyn graves and held a Requiem Mass. One of the delegation, according to the *Pravda* correspondent, told him that he had been in one of the Katyn camps until June 1940, had then been transferred elsewhere, and in February 1941, had received a letter from a Polish officer friend (name and regiment given) from that Katyn camp dated January 1941.

24. During the final week of the Soviet investigation a party of Allied (but not neutral) correspondents were taken down to Katyn. Though inclined to believe the Soviet account, some of the correspondents, according to Mr Balfour were not favourably impressed by what they saw and heard. Up to the present, at any rate, only two accounts from the British correspondents have appeared in the British press, and it looks as if the Soviet censorship was being particularly cautious in what it was prepared to pass.

25. The Germans immediately after their announcement of the discovery of the graves sent two Polish commissions and the International Forensic Medical Commission (picked by themselves) to Katyn. Much publicity was given to their accounts, which were of course in every respect favourable to the Germans. The Allied journalists were not sent to Katyn until nearly four months after the recapture of Smolensk, but (unlike the situation in April 1943) military operations have been in full swing near Smolensk ever since its recapture.

Foreign Office Research Department (Soviet Union Section) 17th February 1944.

Sir William Malkin's Judgement

A brief was drafted by Frank Roberts and approved by Sir Orme Sargent. It consisted almost exclusively of the judgement made earlier by Sir William Malkin, Legal Adviser to the FO, who had read all the papers on the subject and who as previously mentioned considered that 'the Soviet case is stronger than was first thought and calls, at any rate for suspension of judgement.'

Eden agreed not to prolong the issue by comparing O'Malley's despatch with the Russians – apparently unchallenged 'in fairness, for their account'. Sir William Malkin's advice became a conclusion as well as an official stance of the Foreign Office towards the Katyn issue for decades to come. Eden and Cadogan approved the following FO draft brief on 26 March 1944.[3]

> The essential point seems to be the genuineness or otherwise of the nine documents alleged in the Soviet Government's report to have been found on the bodies and referred to in paragraphs 12 and 13 of the annexed paper by F.O.R.D. If both the documents and their connexion with the bodies are genuine, they are practically conclusive in favour of the Soviet case; if they are faked, the inference the other way is almost irresistible. The truth may never come to light. But meanwhile the evidence at present available would seem to require a suspension of judgement on our part.

The Permanent Secretary of State for Foreign Affairs, Sir Alexander Cadogan added:[4]

> We shall not, for a long time, know the truth. Lies and propaganda will be poured out by both sides. I would like to draw attention to one sentence in the F.O.R.D. analysis (pt. 5. p.3) 'The Special [Soviet] Commission was a strong one'. This is absolute nonsense. However 'strong' the Commission on either side may be, they are simply instructed to manufacture a case – or find themselves in another mass grave. <u>All</u> evidence from <u>both</u> sides is faked. But, as I say, it may be as well, as we have given an estimate from one angle, to correct it from the other.
> AC [Alexander Cadogan]
> March 21,1944.

'I agree' AE [Anthony Eden – initialled in red pen].

Skarżyński's Conclusions

FORD's interpretation of the Soviet report became the bedrock of Sir William Malkin's judgement on Katyn. Had Sumner studied Skarżyński's confidential report[5] amended in September 1945, he would have found all the controversial information the Soviet report was lacking. Skarżyński by then had been dismissed from his post of Secretary General of the *PCK*, and afraid of being arrested by the NKVD, rewrote his report and delivered it secretly to Robin Hankey at the British Embassy in Warsaw. Fearing for his life, he sought Hankey's help in escaping to the West. The report was considered by Hankey too sensitive and too long to be translated by the 'confidential' translator of the Embassy, so it was despatched in its original format by diplomatic bag to London. It was the intention of the London Poles to use it as supplementary material for the forthcoming International Military Tribunal at Nuremberg, but was deemed inadmissible, following British policy to refrain from actively supporting the Polish cause. It was not until 1952 that the US Select Committee managed to confirm Skarżyński's story regarding the lost boxes of Katyn documents by calling witnesses such as Dr Beck and Herrman.

In June 1945, Skarżyński managed to reach Paris and awaited permission to enter Great Britain. While there, he overhauled the second part of the report, which had already gone to London. He added further explanatory notes to some paragraphs, making them more coherent and grammatically correct, but did not alter the facts or the meaning of the original text. These additions to his text are asterisked.

Although as from 1 May 1945 I am no longer a member of the Executive Committee of the Polish Red Cross, but still closely connected with the Katyn affair since the time I was leading the case, I feel it is my duty to illustrate further the course of events from June 1943.

Shortly after the exhumation of the bodies, German propaganda finally realised that their use of Katyn in the hope of turning Polish opinion to their advantage had failed and that the great commotion around it had ceased, leaving only sporadic mentions in the press. However, in the international arena the Germans had a partial success, chiefly brought about by the break-up of relations between the Soviet Union and the Polish Government in London. Katyn became a turning point in the attitudes of the two countries. Because of this, the English-speaking democracies, mindful of maintaining good relations with Russia in wartime, had met serious diplomatic difficulties inflamed by the Polish-Soviet situation, which, following the defeat of Germany, were partly solved at the Crimea Conference and by creation of the so called Government of National Unity in Poland.

From June 1943, the *PCK* concentrated on two problems:

1. How to continue studies of the documents placed at the Institute of Judicial [Forensic] Medicine in Kraków.

2. How to continue negotiations with the German authorities regarding the issuing of death certificates to the families of the dead in Katyn.

1. The German military authorities had sent to the Institute of Judicial Medicine in Kraków nine numbered boxes [similar to Ordnance stores] containing the envelopes of items from Katyn for the disposal of the Propaganda Department of the *Generalgouvernment* [*Propagandaamst*]. One smaller box, containing diaries, was not numbered. Dr [Jan Zygmunt] Robel began to work on these immediately and simultaneously undertook an undercover investigation of the circumstances of the murder on his own.

The official work was to establish a final list of names of those found at Katyn, as mentioned before, the initial list, could only be used for orientation purposes.

Many times the names had to be changed or crossed out. Eventually a card index of biographical data was made, containing all instances of descriptions of colleagues, their names and their life in Kozelsk camp. Some notes were contradictory while others confirmed the facts and slowly the whole monstrous truth began to appear. Professor Robel managed to deduce from them an accurate number of officers who were at Kozelsk camp in March 1940 (about 5,000). It appeared that several officers had been brought from Starobelsk camp to Kozelsk. The following facts became clearer. The total number of Kozelsk camp inmates lay at Katyn, which was confirmed by the number of exhumed bodies, with the addition of several hundred of those left in grave No. 8. The incidental names taken from the notes could easily be used to fill in the missing identities of unknowns on the list, which represented about 30% of the total. Slowly the dates of leaving Kozelsk camp could be established. The diaries revealed that from the beginning of April 1940, a hundred or more officers would occasionally leave Kozelsk to an unknown destination.

There were three reasons why the work at the Institute was slow moving:
1. The confidential arrangement between Professor Robel and the *PCK* to retain the documents for as long as possible in Kraków (The intention and motives have already been explained in part 1 of the report).
2. Numerous additional tasks, which absorbed Professor Robel's time and that of his assistants.
3. Lack of special optical and technical equipment, which was in short supply due to the bombardment of the factories in the Reich in 1944.

I know that up to the middle of 1944, the Institute had officially completed the examination of only 300-odd envelopes. The identification work was organised in such a manner that all names about which there was no doubt were placed directly on the new list of Katyn victims. All controversial material was submitted to an 'advisory commission', composed of Professor Robel, Dr Schebesta and a representative from the *PCK* Information Bureau in Kraków. As the amount of prepared material grew, the same persons under my chairmanship and with the representative of the *PCK* Information Bureau, acting then as an adjudicating commission, would make the final decision. The committee would prepare a special protocol for each named case with a list of contents found in each individual envelope with explicit information.

The investigative work on the cause of death was undertaken in secrecy, even though the results confirmed the German thesis. Besides, it was important that the Germans did not find out the Polish evidence of Russian guilt, while the Allies were still at war with the Reich. It was a peculiar situation: on the one hand, the Germans allowed the Poles to examine and investigate the legacy of the Katyn case, without laying down conditions or exercising much control over them; on the other, by truly believing the German thesis, the Poles who were directly involved tried to slow down the work, while also being interested in a prompt outcome.

Two motives could be detected in the Germans:

1. The claim that it was a Soviet Russian crime, a view based on the investigation of the Polish criminologists, would certainly assist German propaganda.
2. The Germans thus expected the Poles to speed up the work, in the interests of the families of the victims.

The slow tempo of work by the staff of the Institute angered the Germans and was the cause of their repeated efforts to hurry up, but Professor Robel continued to put forward sound, expert reasons in defence of the delay. Towards the end of 1944, Dr Schebesta brought to Warsaw typescript copies of 22 Katyn diaries, with assurances that several copies were kept in secure places in Kraków. I took them home overnight to read them. All entries ceased in the first months of 1940. Most of the space in the diaries was taken up by daily observations of camp existence and complaints about the food. Many expressed a firm belief in their prompt release, as well as news of a possible intervention as a result of letters sent by some officers to their acquaintances such as the military attachés or diplomats of neutral countries like Finland or Italy. Often there was news of alleged successes by the Allies on the Western front, reminiscences of family life (in one instance tragic) as well as letters despatched to but very rarely received from their families.

The diaries show an indomitable national spirit as well as contempt for the Bolsheviks. They are not particularly well written and have no literary content, but they clearly show the ghastly nightmare haunting thses perfectly normal people. Towards the end of the entries, there was frequent mention of the beginning of preparation for the departure of organised groups from the camp. The most thoroughly detailed is a diary of Major [Adam] Solski, ending with a note written in Katyn woods. The closest to it in proximity to death is the diary of a Colonel (whose name I cannot recall), who wrote his last words while leaving Smolensk in a railway prisoners' freight car [*stolypinka*]. After writing about difficulties in identifying the direction of the travel 'which is very important for us', the diary ends with the words: 'We are standing at Gneazdovo station where we shall probably alight as there are many soldiers milling about on the platform.' The rest of the diary entries end in Kozelsk.

With the Germans retreating from the Red Army and the forcing of the Dnieper River, the threat of the Bolsheviks invading Polish territory became a reality. In Poland, the stubborn belief that the Germans would not capitulate whilst they were far from their borders, had faded. The *PCK* Executive Committee was in great fear that the boxes of documents from Katyn might be evacuated to the bombed areas in the West, where they would irretrievably perish. A plan was devised to seize them by force from the Germans.

Dr Schebesta prepared the boxes, lined with tin plate, and an *AK* [resistance unit was going to take them away. Hermetically sealed and weighed down with stones, they were to rest at the bottom of a chosen pond. The plan, however, failed. In July 1944, Dr Schebesta sent a messenger with the news that during the liquidation of a communist cell in Kraków, the German security police had found out about the plan, closed down the Institute and set up an *SS* guard. This was the last information about the legacy of Katyn that has reached Warsaw.

1. * The boxes were taken to Breslau [Wrocław] by truck escorted by Dr Beck the German director of the Institute. The car he was travelling in, met with an accident and had to turn back to hospital in Kraków. After the German exodus from Breslau, Dr Schebesta went there in order to search for the boxes. He succeeded in establishing that the boxes had been kept for a time on the first floor veranda in the Department of Anatomy, in one of the buildings of the University of Breslau. They remained there for several weeks, until the city was surrounded on three sides by Soviet troops. A special military escort heading west with Dr Beck moved the boxes again. His parents can confirm this. Further search undertaken by Dr Schebesta through the intermediary of the Doctor's Association, established that Dr Beck was not in the Soviet Zone of Occupation in Germany. Considering the circumstances of transport from Breslau, whilst the Soviet army was reaching the Oder River and moving victoriously westwards, it is possible that the escorting unit took the documents even farther away, possibly reaching the British or American zones.*

2. Talks undertaken with the German authorities by the *PCK* on the subject of death certificates.

The question of death certificates was the subject of correspondence for over a year up to July 1944. It took so long, because letters from the *PCK* Executive Committee went via the official channels of the Bureau of the Governor of Warsaw, then to the offices of the *Generalgouvernment* in Kraków and still farther to the Central Offices of the Ministry of Propaganda in Berlin and eventually to the German Red Cross. The replies travelled the same route, so communication was once every several months. During the Warsaw Uprising in August 1944, the *PCK* correspondence perished in a fire; however, because I prepared the most important letters, I can recall them clearly.

At the demand of the Germans, the certificates were to carry the date of death as April–May 1940. The *PCK* retorted that they couldn't sign such certificates, which were beyond their official expertise. (To understand the situation of the *PCK* one must remember that one of the arguments presented to the Germans was that the *PCK* could only attest to the date of the murder after all possible issues had been examined, including the documents. For obvious reasons, as previously mentioned, we did not want to admit that the investigation of the documents from a legal point of view had reached a conclusion.)

Berlin by now demanded that the *PCK* should quote the findings of the International Commission of Criminologists, and declare the date of the murder. In reply, it was pointed out that the International Commission met without *PCK* co-operation, and by calling themselves 'A Committee of Professors from several European Universities', their findings were therefore not binding. We recommended the Germans to accept the wording 'The Polish Red Cross does not hold the data to indicate the date of death, but the International Commission of Professors from the European Universities, without the assistance of the Polish Red Cross, has declared that …' At the beginning of 1944 came an ultimatum that the death certificates must contain the formula: 'death has occurred at least four years prior to the issue of the certificate', additionally, not a single word could be changed. The German letter ended with a threat that in case of a refusal the work on the documents in Krakow would be halted and allowances for the widows temporarily stopped. The whole blame would therefore fall on the *PCK* Executive Committee.

The German proposition had a logical fault, which helped the *PCK* to ignore the ultimatum. It was pointed out to them that certificate issue could last several years; therefore the dates would also move. We advised a certain flexibility in the text to allow a lesser or greater probability of identification of the time of death as shown in some documents. Once again the *PCK* refused to declare the dates of the murder, taking full responsibility for doing so. The documents could only have hard facts, even if the *PCK* held different convictions.

The reply arrived at the beginning of July 1944, stating simply that the Executive Committee must reply by 1 August whether they agreed to include the date of death on the certificates, by using 'yes' or 'no' in answer. The future of the *PCK* depended on the reply.

By 1 August, postal communication in the *Generalgouvernment* did not function as the majority of its territory did not by now belong to the Reich. The German authorities were facing more serious problems than the Katyn affair.

3. Changes in the *PCK* after 1 August 1944.

From the moment the front reached the Vistula River, Poland was divided into two zones of occupation, and the *PCK* Executive Committee was fragmented. The *PCK* Vice Chairman, Countess Maria Tarnowska and another member of the Committee Józef Wielowiejski, as well as the Plenipotentiary for the Warsaw District Adolf Lewandowski, remained in Warsaw. During and after the Uprising, they played a crucial role in the history of the *PCK*. President Wacław Lachert and myself, who lived on the right bank of the Vistula, were cut off from *PCK* activities. Chairman Lachert moved to the Lublin branch where much charity work was done. I remained in the frontal zone and beside two short stays in Lublin, for consultation with the chairman, I found myself to be against the plan of transforming the district *PCK* into the Executive Committee; for several months I did not take part in *PCK* work.

When the Germans were chased out of Poland by the Red Army, the *PCK* Executive Committee, which was temporarily in Piotrków, moved back to Warsaw and once more took over responsibility for the whole of Poland. Regrettably, the political actions of the post-war authorities were such that it debilitated the normal work. Due to the close contacts of the *PCK* with the *AK* and loyalty shown towards the Polish Government in London throughout the German occupation, the Lublin Committee [the Soviet-backed Polish authorities] decided to nominate a new *PCK* committee with only two members from the old set-up. The representatives, Maria Tarnowska and Wielowiejski, accepted the nominations after a plea from deposed colleagues not to break with the past and to maintain some continuity of Red Cross work in Poland. Presently, even the new committee under the chairmanship of General [Andrzej] Szeptycki, proved to be inadequate in the eyes of the newly formed Provisional Government of National Unity, which set up a fresh committee without any of the old members. Additionally, against all logic, a supervising state agency was going to be formed, similar to the *PCK* National Council, which in 1939, according to its own rules suspended its activities during the war. It is this Council which should have been called upon to resume the work. The Katyn case was revived albeit with new slants.

In the middle of May 1945, I was summoned by Judge [Advocate] Szwarc, who informed me that the Polish authorities intended to carry out their own investigations of the Katyn affair and that in this connection, owing to my own praiseworthy part, the authorities were inclined to consider my report as the main core of the inquest. My deposition should illustrate in detail the whole course of events and in my own interest I should stress all those factors that proved it was the Germans who committed the Katyn crime. I replied that I was willing to highlight all the details that would show the German authorities in a true light, but nobody was going to find in my statement that the Germans committed the massacre.

Judge [Procurator Karol] Szwarc himself took down my statements during the three visits, each lasting from four to six hours on his insistence. I concentrated on the beginning of the affair, on the journey to Smolensk and our stay at Katyn. The case of the inspection of the documents in Kraków I treated superficially, realising that the *NKVD* had arrested Professor Robel, and I did not want to say more in case he wanted my silence. At my last meeting with the Judge, I have learned that my last two statements had been read by the Minister of Education and the Chief Prosecutor for the investigation of German crimes [Dr Jerzy Sawicki]. They declared that my statements were good, but stressed that they lacked the most important thing – proof of German guilt. Judge Szwarc therefore, had received an order to 'squeeze' out of me some sort of synthesis that would justify such a judgement. I replied that as a witness I did not feel that by law, it was possible for me to draw these conclusions from my statements, as I left that to the judiciary. Having managed to find out some useful information about Judge Szwarc I risked saying that I was personally and morally convinced of Russian guilt, I could not possibly go against my concience. A discussion took place in which Judge Szwarc sincerely admitted that I had convinced him of the perpetrators of the massacre and assured me that he would conduct my case in such a manner that I should not be called again for questioning, which, up to now, is true. I know that both Lachert and Wielowiejski with others were investigated and it was not the end. At the trials in Moscow of the 16 members of the Polish Government, Józef Stemler, who actively worked for the *PCK,* was also interrogated about Katyn and had to give a full dossier on all members of the Executive Committee and what motivated them to take care of the Katyn graves.

Finally, I should mention that some people who took part in the Katyn affair are dead: Ludwik Rojkiewicz was executed in the street in Warsaw by the Germans in 1944, Hugon Kassur and Count Władysław Zamoyski were killed in the Warsaw Uprising, serving as *AK* officers, while Władysław Gorczycki, Director General of the *PCK* died in September 1945. May their souls rest in peace.

4. Concluding comments

I have tried to recount the Katyn affair from the perspective of the work done by the *PCK*. As a person who during the war was involved in this tragedy, I can freely declare in conclusion, the irrefutable proofs pointing to the guilty party.

In the beginning, one must declare that the German conscience, if such a word can be used of a nation that has murdered so many millions of people, is not that clear as regards Katyn. The Soviet-German demarcation line on the River Bug in 1939 left many Poles under Soviet occupation, who were residents under German occupation. Many returned to the West through the so called 'green border'; the officers and men of the Polish army who were caught by the Soviets were held in camps, and were to all intents and purposes classed as interned. According to the neutrality rules, release of internees to a warring partner is disallowed. Russia however, was not strictly neutral, because on the basis of the pact with Germany, it had overrun the eastern territory of Poland. Facing this act of lawlessness, Russia and Germany therefore had to solve the repatriation problem between the two zones of occupation. In November or December of 1939, a Soviet-German commission was formed and met in Kraków to discuss this. I remember how it shocked the nation that 60,000 were going to be repatriated from the east. Among them were Polish soldiers who were intended for the German camps in the west. The Germans used them for labour. It is unthinkable that the Germans, who kept 16,000 Polish officers in Oflags, could not be interested in 10,000 officers in Russia. The relations between the Third Reich and Soviet Russia, after the recent pact, were not that close or sincere for the German High Command or government to tolerate such a large number of officers who could have been used in a war against them. In spite of their crushing victory, the Germans, according to their expressed feelings, seemed to have a high esteem for the fighting spirit of the Poles. If these officers remained in Russia, then the Germans must have been satisfied that they would not find them amongst their adversaries. It cannot be ruled out that a dishonourable, unwritten agreement to murder them was concluded between the Germans and the Soviets. The statesmen of the civilised West may frown upon this with indignation, but if it is seen as evolving from the mentality of Hitler and the Bolsheviks, for whom murder is like a daily bread, they may become more realistic in their reaction.

However, the irrefutable proof of direct Soviet guilt for the murder at Katyn is as follows:
1. When General Sikorski, during the time of the formation in the Soviet Union of the Polish Army, demanded an explanation from Russia about the fate of the missing 8,300 Polish officers, Russia did not inform him that the whole camp at Kozelsk, i.e. 5,000 of them, hence the majority of the missing, had fallen into German hands near Smolensk in 1941.
⋆ After longwinded and evasive replies, the Russians only remembered it when the Germans discovered the graves. A group of 5,000 persons cannot possibly be lost without trace, even during a rapid withdrawal of an army. ⋆

2. ⋆ Clothes, which were found on the bodies, indicate that the officers were murdered in early spring as they were wearing warm underwear and many wore winter coats. Warm clothing was also noticed by one of the foreign correspondents visiting Katyn after the liberation of Smolensk. His comments created a noticeable disturbance among the escorting Russians and remarks about the cold climate in Poland were not convincing. The officers would not wear winter clothes in September. Smolensk lies in the Continental climatic region of Russia with long winters and long summers. April can have freezing conditions while September can be scorching. Travelling by plane towards the east of Minsk, I have noticed patches of snow. The winter clothes were noticed by one of the foreign correspondents that were taken to Katyn by the Russians, after Smolensk was liberated. ⋆

3. Members of the *PCK* Technical Committee during the whole of their two months stay in Katyn, were not controlled by the German military authorities. They were able to move about and talk freely with the local people. [If the

Germans were the perpetrators of the massacre, they would not be so naïve as to maintain close contacts with the Committee, who otherwise would have been under strict German control, having the nearness of the Eastern Front as an excuse for this.]

Their first thought and duty was to verify the truth of the statements made by the local people. Their free interactions with the peasants in the Katyn region completely confirmed the accuracy and truth of the German reports. If the Germans, according to the Russian theory, had considerable means of transport and manpower in March 1943, and managed to prepare a false mass grave in Katyn, then during the course of the following months, this incredible fabrication would have clearly come up in conversations between members of the *PCK* and the local inhabitants.

4. * In dealing with the exhumation work, it is not difficult to recognise an untouched grave with compressed soil, contrary to fresh, recently dug ground. Members of the exhumation team did not anticipate the Russian theory that the graves were partially dug up in spring 1943, but other people could testify that all the ground was compressed and it was difficult to lift the corpses from it. *

5. The German decision to hand over the documents rescued from Katyn for scientific study by the Poles is evidence enough that they had nothing to fear with regard to the results of the examination. There can be no question of falsifying these documents before their arrival at Krakow, quite apart from the fact that the quantity was such that it would be technically impossible and secondly, the members of the *PCK* Technical Commission, during their work at Katyn, became acquainted with many of the documents so that there can be no doubt as to there authenticity. * Criminologists who inspected these documents in Kraków can verify this, provided they are allowed to express their opinion. *

6. The impression of the personal diaries and notes requires no commentary. All the entries broke off during the first months of 1940 at precisely the same time as the group transports began from Kozelsk. The last entry by Major Solski and another Colonel written at the railway station at Gnezdovo are shattering evidence of Russian guilt.

7. Why did the Soviet Union, in announcing that the Katyn massacre had been carried out by the Germans not invite an international commission to Katyn after Smolensk had been liberated in September 1943? The reason was precisely the same as when they could not agree to the visit by the Commission designated by the International Red Cross in April 1943. The Russians sent their own unilateral commission, which in January 1944, without any outside control, published an official brochure called 'Communiqué of the Special Commission

to investigate and determine the circumstances of shooting of the Polish officer prisoners of war by the German fascist invaders in Katyn woods'. The quality of this publication is so low that one is astounded that it ever saw the light of day, which it would surely have not, had it not been for the fact that the previously disclosed circumstances of the murder made it impossible for the murderers themselves to secure a better defence. The whole examination is based exclusively on the statements of Russian witnesses and on the nine documents, allegedly found with the corpses, bearing dates from the end of 1940 and the beginning of 1941.

What are the arguments of proof as presented by the Russians, the statements of the witnesses? We know the value of evidence extracted from citizens by the authorities of totalitarian states. Falsifying dates on nine documents does not require much skill. There were no more documents to be found on the already exhumed bodies, so one should assume that the Russians continued to dig grave No. 8 and chose a few documents with dates easily forged, while destroying the rest.

★ The dates given by the Soviets [The Burdenko report] do not stipulate any month in the second half of 1941, the reason being that documents with dates of the first six months of 1940 simply stopped. It is easy to forge the last number of the year, but not so the months written in Roman numerals.[6] As far as I know, nobody except Burdenko examined the documents. In these circumstances it is hardly important whether the documents were forged or not, as they might just as well come from individual graves of persons, who were buried there after the date of the massacre, as such graves were common. ★

★ The Special Committee was set up in January 1944, but Smolensk was liberated in September 1943. In their report, they have tried to explain the reason for this delay: 'The Committee had at its disposal a large quantity of material which was gathered by a member of the Academy of Science Nikolai Burdenko and his collaborators in forensic science, who arrived in Smolensk on 26 September straight after its liberation and began to study and investigate the circumstances of the murder perpetrated by the Germans.' It is a naive and revealing weakness that the Russians did not send the whole committee, but sent one person to investigate Katyn, with the help of a group of anonymous colleagues, to prepare the initial work for the committee. After four months the committee turned up in Katyn and acquainted themselves with the material, and as things are done in Russia – signed the report, as ordered. ★

★ In such circumstances, it is not that important whether the nine documents were forged, as they may have come from the individual graves of Poles who died in Russia and were buried in Katyn after the officers; there were numerous graves in Russia of this kind. ★

Finally, as mentioned by some supporters of the Russians, but never mentioned by the Special Soviet Committee, there are the empty bullet cases that were found on and inside the graves. Their origin, alleged to be of German make, is not a state secret as the Germans supplied the Russians with such ordnance.

★ It is not a difficult matter to settle. German ordnance can kill, not necessarily by German hands. It is well known that after the First World War, the Germans delivered ordnance to Russia. Special units of the *NKVD*, who undertook secret assignments, had the best weapons at their disposal. Experts agree that German arms and ammunition were one of the best. ★

Due to the unknown fate of the documents unearthed from the graves, it is difficult to predict if some time in the future the verdict on the Katyn massacre will be supported with this hard evidence. One thing is certain, that of all the institutions that visited Katyn, the *PCK* cannot be accused of being biased, whilst two enemies of Poland accused one another of the murder. All the time the main aim of the *PCK,* which was kept secret from them both – was to point at the murderers. The raising of voices by this authority today, as yet, is not in the interests of the Polish nation.

★ The committee of criminologists, who were invited by the Germans, in spite of prominent names and the presence of one representative of a neutral country, could be considered as sympathetic towards the Germans. The Soviet commission must be regarded as a worthless, one-sided showcase. Only the *PCK,* together with Dr Robel and his team in Kraków, have studied thoroughly and diligently for a year the documentation unearthed from the graves over a period of two months. Only for them, the aim of the Red Cross was transparent – to ignore the enemies and only serve the truth. Their main duty was to point authoritatively at the murderers. ★

★ According to the proverbial Second World War proclamations – the time will come, when murders of international notoriety will be punished and render such things impossible in the future. However, words expressed during war, differ in their practical realisation when the war is won. ★

★ Poland was first to enter the war, trusting and relying on her allies, and in return, was a staunch ally to Britain. For over six years now, her stature should not be overshadowed. At the end of the war Poland was among the victors – yet lost its independence and sovereignty. ★

★ In Nuremberg murderers are being judged. Yet it is not a judgement of civilisation over atrocities or an epochal awakening of the world's conscience. It is a judgement of the victorious over the vanquished – a very dangerous historical precedent. It would not be amiss to quote a Russian saying: 'Victors are not judged.' In the avalanche of crime and murder of the innocents that swept Europe since 1939, the Katyn crime is only one incident. From the Polish perspective, Katyn takes on a far greater meaning because it was an execution of prisoners of war organised in peacetime. ★

I have tried to present this statement mindful that none of the details should go amiss. It is not intended for the Poland of the present, where the slogans about strength, freedom and democracy are blatant lies, but for the future, in the name of a truly democratic, sovereign and strong Poland belonging to the united and civilised nations of the world.

Kazimierz Skarżyński
Józefów, near Warsaw, December 1945

Notes

1 Benedict Humphrey Sumner (1893–1951) Historian, scholar of modern diplomacy and international relations, took part in the Paris Peace Conference as Assistant Secretary. Appointed to the International Labour Office, toured Poland and the Baltic States in 1921. Drawn to Russian history and literature, became an authority on the subject. Fellow and Tutor in Modern History, Balliol College, Oxford 1925–44, engaged in the Foreign Research and Press Department (Russian Section) of the Royal Institute of International Affairs, Warden of All Souls College, Oxford 1945–51. Published: *Russia and the Balkans 1870-1880* in 1937; *War and History* in 1945; *Peter the Great and the Ottoman Empire* in 1949.

2 TNA FO 371/39393 C 2957/8/G, FO 'Green Print', copy 8, 'The Soviet Version of the Katyn Atrocities', Foreign Office Research Department (Soviet Union Section) 17 February 1944. Contains copy of the *Soviet Monitor,* English language radio bulletin, of Burdenko report, published by *TASS* in London January 26 and 27, 1944.

3 Ibid.

4 TNA FO 371/39393 C 2957/8/55G, comments on FORD report by Sir Alexander Cadogan, 21 March 1944.

5 TNA FO 371/56476 N 5269/G, Skarżyński's second part of his confidential report, with conclusions dated September 1945, cover note by Robin Hankey 23 April 1946. Skarżyński, who was removed from his *PCK* post on 1 May 1945, felt it was his duty to inform the British about the aftermath of Katyn, before his expected arrest by the *NKVD.* (Translation by EM)

6 It has always been accepted Polish practice to write monthly dates with Roman numerals. The Russians rarely if ever do this. As a forensic clue it was ignored by the British until Julian Bullard spoted it while analysing Katyn papers in 1972.

chapter six

PREPARATION FOR THE NUREMBERG TRIALS

In July 1945, the Three Powers in accordance with the Yalta Agreement withdrew recognition of the Polish government-in-exile and accepted the communist-led Provisional Government set up by the Soviets in Lublin. Deprived of any power, the London Poles had to seek representation at the Trials via intermediaries and seek to influence the decisions taken by their erstwhile Allies.

On 31 August 1945, the four Chief Prosecutors, Sir Hartley Shawcross (GB), Justice Robert Jackson (USA), Colonel Yona Nikitchenko (USSR) and R. Malezieux (France) met to discuss indictment rules, presentation of documents as evidence and other procedures, such as how many defendants and witnesses to call before the Tribunal. The minutes of that meeting indicate that Justice Jackson brought up the subject of possible evidence generated by the *Armia Krajowa (AK)*, which was to be investigated further by Nikitchenko. Nobody was clear about its content or where to look for it. Nikitchenko tried to explain that he had spoken with the Polish Chargé d'Affaires in London to procure documentary evidence from the FO, bypassing the Polish government-in-exile. He assured all present that he had already submitted some information on Poland's behalf to the United War Crimes Commission.[1] During the Sub-Commission meeting of 4 September 1945, Colonel Telford Taylor of the US Prosecution team revealed that the *AK* had indeed during the war produced a 'quite manageable report running to 126 pages', which had been sent to London. Was his observation prompted by the existence of Savory's intended report of truly manageable size of 31 pages, dated 13 February 1946, which *Oddział VI* had prepared for him, but which did not reach Nuremberg? There is a corollary to this much later, on 17 May 1946. During the Trials, General Anders received a letter from Otto Stahmer, the Defending Counsel for Hermann Goering, accused of mass murder, including those at Katyn, asking for any documents the London Poles might have in support of the defence. According to his book, Anders did not reply but turned to his British contact, Col J.L. Tappin of AFHQ suggesting that he should supply the documents only on formal request from the British War Crimes Executive (BWCE). Anders did not receive any answer either from AFHQ or BWCE.[2]

The responsibility for the accumulation of documents and records was in the hands of the US Delegation. They were assisted by the British team under Major Elwyn Jones, whose duty was to keep an eye on interesting documents for the purpose of the Committees dealing with East-West divide. The sheer volume of documents gathered exercised Shawcross to such an extent that in his memorandum of 5 December 1945, he opposed the ruling that all documents must be read in full. He argued that the Counsel, while submitting the documents, could summarise them and the Defence Counsel could challenge such a summary. He also considered it to be of the utmost importance to persuade the Russians to abandon the calling of oral testimony concerning 'general charges' such as Katyn; undesirable both because of the delay (hopefully they did not want go beyond spring or summer of 1946) and also because of the opportunities it would give the German defendants to raise the embarrassing matter of the Secret Protocol of the Soviet-German Treaty of 1939 regarding the partition of Poland and spheres of influence over the Baltic States. According to Lt Col Harry Phillimore of the BWCE, Dr Braun had procured a copy of this document from the German Defence Counsel, which he duly despatched to London.

This particular document and many others, once the property of the German Foreign Office, were in the possession of the Americans and were handed over to Dr Collins of the US archives by von Loesch, deputy to Dr Schmidt, Associate of the Defence Counsel and interpreter at many meetings between Hitler and foreign statesmen. Originally, the most secret archives were buried by the Germans at a lonely spot in what became the Soviet occupied zone, about 20 miles from Mulhaus, and were removed to Marburg within the US occupied zone. Apparently, these documents were so important that on the advice of Mr Thomson of the FO archives, they were taken to London and photostats were made in the Air Ministry.[3]

Before the Trials, there was initial consternation when the London Poles made a tentative request to be represented at the Bergen-Belsen trials, so say to observe 'the British judicial methods and legal procedures of Western Democracies'. Two officers were proposed: Colonel F. Arciszewski, head of the Inspectorate for the post-war Polish Military Administration in occupied German territory and Major Kwiatkowski, the Provost Marshal. Denis Allen of the FO was not keen on the idea; he did not want the London Poles meddling in war crimes matters. The FO was trying to encourage the communist-led Provisional Government to take an interest in the war crimes by producing more evidence, thus discouraging the Polish émigrés from further 'interference'. In any case the application was considered to be too late in arrival and only Lublin could speak for Poland on such matters. He was adamant that any available information on atrocities against Poles in concentration camps should go to them, rather than to the representatives of the now defunct Polish Government in London. The War Office Military Intelligence Directorate was instructed to refuse the exiled Poles 'politely'.[4]

In October 1945, Sir Hartley Shawcross, the Attorney General, informed Colonel Jackson, American Chief Prosecutor at Nuremberg of the requests from the Allies for representatives at the Trials as official observers. They agreed to allocate 250 places for the Press and 80 for spectators, with only two seats reserved for each country that had suffered at the hands of the Germans.

At a meeting of the Chief Prosecutors on 9 November 1945, chaired by Justice Jackson, it was anticipated that the German defence might attack the policies of the Allies, especially the Soviet aggression against Poland and the Baltic States as well as illtreatment of prisoners of war. Mindful of this possibility, each of the Prosecutors were asked to prepare a memorandum indicating the position they intended to take with reference to possible attacks by the German defence during the trials. Sir David Maxwell Fyfe, the British Deputy Chief Prosecutor, prepared such a paper, pointing to the potentially embarrassing consequences if the Four Powers were not in accord. Both Maxwell and Jackson stressed that such attacks should be treated as' irrelevant and inadmissible'. In reply Lt General Roman Rudenko, acting for the Soviet Chief Prosecutor, was in full agreement with the proposals. Furthermore, he asked for a firm commitment to abort German efforts at questioning the Allies; he considered they were 'irrelevant to the case and misinterpreted the meaning of individual acts of the Governments of the Allied nations'. No doubt it would have prolonged the trials – a paramount worry to the Prosecutors.

Rudenko had the audacity to suggest the following list of questions that should be eliminated from the consideration of the Court; questions connected with the social and political order of the USSR, its foreign policy, the German-Soviet non-aggression Pact of 1939 and questions connected with frontiers. Other suggested out-of-bounds issues were Ribbentrop's visit to Moscow and the negotiations of November 1940 in Berlin, the Balkan question, the Soviet Baltic Republics – but above, all Soviet-Polish relations.[5] Needless to say, his proposals were agreed to in their entirety by the British and the Americans.

In November 1945, an 'Immediate' and 'Top Secret' signal was received from the BWCE indicating that at the Chief Prosecutors' meeting in Nuremberg, Rudenko had put forward a motion that, according to his interpretation of Article 15 (E), representatives from Poland, Czechoslovakia and Yugoslavia should be appointed to the Soviet team during the trials.[6] Jackson was against this, as it would have created practical difficulties of translation and besides, he thought this was contrary to the intention of the Charter of the International Military Tribunal. Sir David Maxwell Fyfe, awaiting the decision of the British government, was also against lengthening the procedures and indicated that satisfaction could be given to these lesser allies by allowing them to prepare 'particular portions of evidence', which might be put by one of the four chief prosecutors on their behalf. He thought that Rudenko had gone back on a previous agreement of 7 November and that the present Soviet proposal had political motives, probably caused by Vyshinsky's unexpected presence at Nuremberg.

On 3 December 1945, Sir Hartley Shawcross presented the British case, which according to Lt Col Harry Phillimore's signal to the FO had a very good reception and was highly thought of, particularly its passages on the lead-up to the attack on Poland:[7]

> The part dealing with the attack on the USSR was not spoken in court as reported in the Press. Last night the Soviet delegation came round and pressed very strongly for the deletion of a number of passages in the published text, which gave the impression that the Soviet Government had in any way been misled by the Molotov–Ribbentrop Pact and subsequent protestations of German friendship. They maintained stoutly that the Soviet Government was fully aware of German intentions from the first and that they were prepared at any time to go to war with Germany. They also objected to the statement that after the collapse of France and the Low Countries, Great Britain was left alone to face Germany. The motive of these rather naïve arguments is difficult to see and to omit the passages to which the Soviet delegation object gives a false impression of the true position. The fact that they are all retained in the published version means that an accurate statement of the situation has been given to the world.

Akcja Kostar

Unaware of these legal wranglings among the Four Powers, the London Poles mobilised themselves for action. A typed copy of an official note, written on 20 March 1946, originally intended as briefing material for Adam Tarnowski, former Foreign Minister of the Polish government-in-exile,[8] became a plan of action for the Polish General Staff (*Oddział II*) in Britain, under the cryptonym *Akcja Kostar*. The proposed action would deal with the moral and humanitarian aspects of Katyn, and was not to be framed as a political issue. It was hoped that *Kostar* would be a briefing tool to be used by the British and the Americans at the Nuremberg trials and after, when strong arguments might be needed for the policy of appeasement towards the Russians to be abandoned. Although this could not be interpreted as a cause of military conflict, everything indicated that the Cold War was inevitable.

The Poles realised that at that particular moment, the proposed action might not succeed and furthermore, might lose them the most valuable argument they held, without any guarantee that the attempt would bring about results. Therefore *Kostar* was to have two phases; the first would be for the two Polish Ministries of Information & Documentation and Ministry of Defence under General Kukiel to prepare for the Nuremberg trials relevant investigative material for an inquest and updated documentation in the form of a 'small report', also for diplomatic use. Amongst the British politicians who took up the challenge to expose the Katyn case, were Major Guy Lloyd, MP[9] and Professor Douglas Savory, MP (N Ireland).[10]

This gathering of material was done by the Political Section of the Polish Ministry of Defence, headed by Lt Marian Heitzman, a lawyer, assisted by Major Alfred Hergesell, Captain Zdzisław Stahl and many others. The venues were the Middle East and later London, where a Special Commission for documentation was set up, led by an academic Dr Wiktor Sukiennicki. Pre-war and after 1945, he lectured in law at Oxford.[11] At 433 pages, it was considered indigestible for the FO desk officers and a shorter version entitled *Supplementary Report of Facts and Documents* was re-edited in haste. It was hoped that Savory would submit it to the BWCE, via the FO.

An attempt was to be made to reach the Attorney General and to work through British Members of Parliament and prominent people who might be sympathetic to the exiled Polish cause. Everything was to be done very carefully so that the approach would not be labelled as 'anti-Soviet'. A special effort was to be made to seek Labour and Liberal sympathisers, as access to Catholics and Conservatives was not considered too difficult a problem. Various names probably unknown to the London Poles were mentioned, such as Professor Bertrand Russell, K. Fairfax, chief editor of *BBC European News*, as well as Lord Robert Cecil (former Secret Intelligence Service officer), Professor D. Brogan, Darsie. R. Gillie of the *Manchester Guardian,* who translated Piłsudski's *Memoirs of a Polish revolutionary and soldier,* Professors Harold Laski and Gordon Murray. On the list also were writers and journalists like George Orwell, the author of *Animal Farm,* P. Winterton, Arthur Koestler of *Yogi and the Commissar* and Professor B. Humphrey Sumner. The latter is a surprise; whoever compiled the list was evidently unaware of his involvement with Burdenko's falsified report.

Early evidence of mobilisation for action can be traced in the FO files, in the typescript copy of a proposed letter, translated into English by Józef Godlewski, formerly of the BBC, written on behalf of the 'Parliamentary Group 74' in London to Jan Kwapiński, former Minister of Industry in the exiled Socialist-led government. The FO did not know how this paper had reached Whitehall but it was to be an open letter to 'Members of the Parliaments of Free Nations of the World', by the undersigned members of the exiled Polish National Council, about Katyn.[12] The signatories felt it was their duty to draw the attention of the Free World to the danger of investigating the Katyn affair through the Nuremberg trials. They stressed that the case should be investigated by a judicial body of international stature, which would include truly neutral bodies, not engaged on either side in the war.

MP Guy Lloyd

Guy Lloyd was one of the Parliamentarians who as early as October 1945 had given notice to the House of his intention of raising the question of the murders at Katyn. It was up to Denis Allen of the Northern Department at the FO to prepare an answer. Allen had expressed anxiety that Lloyd would politicise the question by indicating that the murderers should be sought in Soviet Russia rather than Germany. In view of references to Katyn expected to be included in the indictment of major German war criminals at the request of the Russians, Allen reminded everyone that:

> The principal item of evidence consists of nine documents alleged to have been found on the bodies, all of them dating from between 12 September 1940 and 20 June 1941. If these documents were genuine they seem conclusive in favour of the Russian case. On the other hand it is impossible to state that they may not have been forged. Moreover, the Russian report made no reference to the three-year-old fir trees of which much had been made by the Germans and it also contained nothing to explain the absence of letters from the men after March 1940, and the subsequent failure of the Soviet Government to provide the Polish Government with any information concerning their whereabouts.

Another high-ranking official, Thomas Brimelow, agreed with Allen's comments, adding that the behaviour of the Germans during the war made it impossible to attach credence to German evidence, which might be designed to mask their crimes. However, he thought the *prima facie* could be used against the Russians as well – 'but we cannot say so'. Allen argued that justifiably the Russians had produced *prima facie* evidence in support of their case, but that the whole matter was still *sub judice* and the FO was not sure if further evidence might be produced. He was of the opinion that since Katyn was to be included in an indictment at the request of the Russians, it was not up to Britain to take the initiative. He also claimed that the FO had no direct evidence, which was untrue, as the FO had in their possession Capt Gilder's report of his visit to Katyn in 1943. Finally Allen recommended that the best legal advice, including that of the late Sir William Malkin, was to suspend judgement on Katyn.

Denis Allen's Brief

The final brief[13] by Allen did contain a ray of hope that an opportunity might be given for relevant Polish evidence to be submitted at the Trials. Mr Patrick Dean, the FO War Crime Section Legal Adviser, read the text and disapproved of it by striking out the offending sentence and adding a handwritten note: 'I don't think we want a lot of evidence by both sides on this matter at Nuremberg, if it can be avoided, and we should not suggest that we do. Draft amended accordingly.' As it happened, Allen's amended brief, prepared for answers in Parliament, was not required and nobody outside the FO was made aware of its portent until the BWCE sought advice and instructions, more of which later.

> H.M.G. [His Majesty's Government] naturally hope to see justice done for the abominable crime, which undoubtedly was perpetrated at Katyn. They have no direct evidence on the subject in their own possession and so far as they know,

none of those responsible for the actual perpetration of the crime have yet been discovered and arrested. In the view of H.M.G. the facts that the victims of the massacre were of Polish nationality and that it took place on Soviet soil, would make it, under the terms of the Three Power declaration issued at Moscow on the 15th November 1943, difficult and inappropriate for H.M.G. to take any initiative in the matter. Under that declaration all German officers and men and members of the Nazi Party who have been responsible for atrocities, massacres and executions, will be sent back to the countries in which their abominable deeds were done, in order that they may be judged and punished according to the laws of the liberated countries. The actual perpetrators of the murders at Katyn would, unless they could be classed as major criminals, fall to be dealt with by the Government of the USSR.

As the House is aware however, the massacre has been placed at the insistence of the Soviet authorities, upon the indictment drawn up by the Prosecutors of the four major Allies, against the major German war criminals. H.M.G. consider this entirely appropriate. The onus of providing any further evidence that may be required in support of this item of the incident will in the circumstances, inevitably fall primarily upon the Soviet Government. It is hoped that an opportunity will be given for any relevant Polish evidence to be submitted and for any appropriate witnesses to be called either by the Prosecution or by the Defence.[14] Until this evidence has been assembled and the case has not been heard, the matter remains *sub judice* and H.M.G. would not be justified in attempting to express any final opinion on the matter. They have of course studied the reports published by the German and Soviet Commissions, which investigated the scene of the massacre in 1943. In their opinion the Soviet report, which was drawn up after the lengthy period of investigation by very distinguished and highly qualified Russian experts, provides sufficient *prima facie* evidence of German guilt to justify the inclusion of this charge in the indictment against the major war criminals.

Professor Savory's Engagement

Professor Douglas Savory MP was a well-known and respected figure amongst the London Poles. He was in Warsaw in 1934 and knew about their struggles against Russian oppression and was sympathetic to their cause, especially as regards Katyn. He took the case further by asking to see Ernest Bevin, the Secretary of State, privately on 28 November 1945. With him went Vice Admiral Ernest Taylor, who had the fruitless task of persuading Field Marshal Bernard Montgomery the C-in-C, BAOR to take on, besides the Polish armoured division and parachute brigade under his command in Germany, another Polish division trained in Scotland. There was a plan to leave the Polish Army on the Continent, as near to their country borders as possible, so that repatriation would be made easier and more palatable. The Poles were against the idea as the majority of them came from the Eastern part of Poland, already annexed by the Soviets.

Professor Savory's 'Report on the massacre at Katyn' written on 14 February 1944 was based on documents placed at his disposal by the Polish government-in-exile. It concluded that the Polish government was fully justified in demanding an impartial inquiry by an independent body, such as the International Red Cross. The then Foreign Secretary Anthony Eden had read it but not acted upon it. By November 1945, Ernest Bevin had taken over the Foreign Office and Savory took it upon himself to present the same 1944 report to him. The Northern, German and Russian Departments of the FO did not think there was anything new in Savory's report, which came to the same conclusion as O'Malley in his despatch. Bevin had sent the report to the Attorney General, Sir Hartley Shawcross, without reading it. In the meantime, the Poles had gathered fresh material with the intention of passing it onto the British War Crime Executive at Nuremberg. This time it was to be a supplementary report, referred to as a memorandum, a 31-page typed brochure entitled 'The Mass Murder of Polish Prisoners of War in Katyn', intended for internal circulation only. It was printed in March 1946 by the Polish Military authorities.[15]

The memorandum contained maps, statistics and questions of fundamental significance; primarily why, in 1944, the Russians did not call an independent international commission of enquiry. Secondly, if one was to accept the Soviet theory that approximately 15,000 officers were detained in the three 'special' camps, said to have fallen into German hands on 12 July 1941, why the Soviet authorities failed to notify the Polish military or diplomatic representatives at the proper time. Ambassador Maisky declared in London on 4 July 1941, (eight days before the Germans were supposed to have captured the camps), that the number of Polish PoWs in the USSR did not exceed 20,000. It was incomprehensible to the Poles that Maisky did not include those prisoners in his calculations. In fact, 28,000 were released in August 1941 and handed over to General Anders to enlist into the Polish army.

The Foreign Office Comments

Denis Allen, who wrote the brief for Lord Aberdare's Parliamentary session, was the first to read Savory's Supplementary Report and dismissed it brusquely as it did not contain any new material, because the FO knew about the Polish Government's enquiries of the Soviet Government between July 1941 and April 1943. Therefore no action was required from the FO. Others commented[16] that Britain was to stand strictly aside and leave the case to the Russians. Typical comments were that the key thing was not to undermine confidence in the Tribunal – that opinions were hopelessly divided – that the sooner the question was disposed of, the better, even if there was doubt whether the verdict met the highest requirements of justice. Some suggested that Savory's misgivings were irrelevant as nobody would be convinced at Nuremberg on the basis of Katyn alone.

Others were cautious, assuming quite rightly that the Supplementary Report would eventually be published by the émigré Poles and would lead to further investigations regarding the inmates of the other two camps of Starobelsk and Ostashkov who disappeared at the same time and who might in the future be discovered in similar graves elsewhere. Others from the Research Department ended the arguments stating that the Russians having brought Katyn to Nuremberg was sufficient evidence of their innocence and suggested it was not worth replying to Professor Savory. Robin Hankey's note[17] summed it all up: 'I wish the Russians would drop it, the whole thing stinks, but we can't butt in.'

Minister Bevin, on receiving his copy of the report, forwarded it to the Attorney General Sir Hartley Shawcross, who somehow managed to mislay it, but eventually managed to reply to Savory using Allen's arguments. In his reply to Bevin, Shawcross was more forthcoming and indicated what the British policy really was. A Parliamentary question by the Earl of Mansfield also cleared the air. A draft reply, approved by Shawcross stated:

> This crime was not overlooked when the Indictment of the major German war criminals was drawn up. So far as I am aware, the actual perpetrators have not yet been discovered and arrested. Since the victims were of Polish nationality and the offence took place on Soviet soil, it would under the terms of the Three Power Declaration issued at Moscow on 1 November 1943, be inappropriate for His Majesty's Government to take the initiative in this matter.

Shawcross decided not to take any action beyond passing the report to Sir David Maxwel Fyfe KC, MP, who in turn passed it to the barrister Lt Col H. J. Phillimore and Secretary of the BWCE, European Section, at Nuremberg, for the British side of the prosecution.[18]

Mindful of this strategy, Phillimore, after receiving Savory's paper, wrote to David Scott Fox at the FO for advice on how far the BWCE should go in supporting the Soviet Prosecutor. He presented to Scott Fox three arguments, which he thought would answer Savory's case:

> 1. It is very strange, if those murdered at Katyn were in Russian hands, that although 4,000 of them have been identified by letters, etc. found in the graves, in no case is it stated that any of those so identified were known to have been prisoners in Russian hands.
>
> 2. It is also strange that there is no statement that bodies so identified are known not to have been made prisoners of the Germans and that in no single case out of 4,000 is any information apparently available as to their place or date of capture.

3. The fixing of the date of death with such certainty after so long an interval is also obviously open to question. Is it certain that none of the written material found in the graves was dated after Soviet troops had retired from Smolensk?

There is no follow-up from the recipient or the FO officials. The advice came later.

Lord Shawcross' Statement

Lord Shawcross' reply to Ernest Bevin was more realistic and let the cat out of the bag.[19]

.... We did our best to persuade the Russians not to include a charge about Katyn in the indictment, but they insisted on doing so, although I believe they are now a little doubtful of the wisdom of their decision. In the circumstances there is nothing that we can do except to try and steer the Russians as carefully as we can over this exceedingly delicate and difficult ground. This we are doing as best as we can, but I must confess I am not at all happy about the situation, which may eventually arise if evidence is called in regard to Katyn.

Ambassador Bullard

In Major General Nikitchenko's opening indictment speech in Berlin on 18 October 1945, Katyn was cautiously mentioned for the first time: 'In September 1941, 11,000 Polish officers who were prisoners of war were killed in the Katyn Forest near Smolensk.' Katyn was raised again at Nuremberg on 14 February, 26 June and finally on 1–2 July 1946. The first documentary evidence of disagreement with the British stance on Katyn came by a secure signal from Tehran,[20] from the British Ambassador Sir Reader Bullard:

1. Nuremberg trial is not my business but as Soviet Prosecutor has accused the Germans of Katyn murders and my evidence suggests that the charge is at least 'not proven' I venture to send this telegram.

2. For over a year before the discovery of mass grave in Katyn forest many Polish officers and officials concerned with concentration of Polish troops in Russia passed though Tehran. Some like Anders and Kot were important, some unimportant. There was always talk about the number of troops collecting and always daily speculation as to the fate of thousands of Polish officers who had been held as prisoners of the Russians in one place. Several times Poles talked of this in front of me, wondering whether there could be any truth in a tale that a shipload of prisoners had been lost in the White Sea or whether the missing

officers had perhaps been sent to a remote place and the Russians either wished to hide them or (an improbable hypothesis) had lost the records. They said to all enquiries about the officers on that list Russians always said 'they are no more' or 'they must be about somewhere' etc. Kot informed me that in reply to a last earnest appeal, Vyshinsky lowered his eye and said 'Ikh nyet' i.e., 'They are not there.' I repeat that all this happened during the period before the discovery of the bodies in Katyn forest. Never, according to the Poles I saw, did the Russians give the reply 'In the hurry of retreat from the Germans we left these officers behind and we do not know what happened afterwards.' It was only when the bodies were discovered that the Russians (after I believe an interval for thought) made that statement.

3. One small piece of evidence. Two British subjects who later became R.A.F. officers were in *GPU* prison in Moscow when the Germans attacked Russia. They informed me that all political prisoners in Moscow, including them, were immediately moved far to the East. It seems unlikely that the Russians would leave behind thousands of Polish officers who might conceivably be employed against them.

If (as I personally believe) Katyn murders were committed by the Russians (possibly without authority as in the case of the execution of the Tsar and his family by [Yakov] Sverdlov), it would be unfortunate if the Russians managed to fob it off on the Germans before a court in which the British share is so important.

Frank Roberts' Comments from Moscow

Frank Roberts of the Northern Department, who was then in Moscow as an Acting Counsellor at the British Embassy, sent a telegram on 18 February 1946 to Sir Reader Bullard on the subject. His fluctuating opinions on Polish questions did not endear him to the London Poles.[21]

Having also heard a great deal about the Katyn affair from all sorts and conditions of Poles and having seen the available evidence in London, I share Sir R. Bullard's feeling that the Soviet case is as yet 'not proven'. But I also recollect that Sir William Malkin, after reviewing all documentary and other evidence in London, regarded the Polish case against the Soviet Union as far from proven.

But whatever the facts, I feel that I should emphasise that the effect on Anglo-Soviet relations of any apparent tendency on our part to accept the German case about Katyn, would be calamitous. You will recall that it was the Katyn affair, which finally ruined any hope of collaboration between the Soviet Union and General Sikorski's Government. It would surely be best for the future of Polish-Soviet and indeed of Anglo-Soviet relations, if the matter could be definitely decided once and for all at the Nuremberg trials. I hope, therefore, that the Soviet Government will be able to present a full and convincing case. Even if they do not succeed in doing so, it would I think, be wise for us to refrain so far as possible from showing any scepticism, and to guide public opinion accordingly.

Possible Charges against the *AK*

On 26 January 1946, General Stanisław Kopański, the former Chief of the General Staff of the Polish Army under British command, informed Lord Selborne, sometime Minister responsible for SOE, that information had reached him that the Soviet prosecution at Nuremberg was planning to bring charges against the *AK* in Poland; that the Nazis were not only aware of the existence of the Polish Underground Army but promoted it as a potential weapon against Soviet Russia.[22]

A number of prominent people were used as intermediaries, amongst them Major General Colin Gubbins the former head of SOE and Sir Alexander Cadogan, who in turn discussed it with Under Secretary of State at the Political Intelligence Department of the FO, Christopher Warner. The latter, wishing to avoid answering at Nuremberg, was concerned that H.M.G. should not be implicated in any Soviet charges. Sir David Maxwell Fyfe asked Dean to check the allegation, which proved to be unfounded, and Dean assured the FO that there was an arrangement for the British staff to check over some positions in the voluminous Russian documents just before presentation to the Court and that they sometimes received copies of Russian speeches.

Documents reveal that not only Katyn papers were available to the BWCE, but other documents – even a copy of the original secret additional protocol of the German-Soviet Treaty, signed on 28 September 1939, by Ribbentrop and Molotov.[23] Clandestine help could have come from the British, had they the moral will to counteract false Russian statements at the trials.

Notes

1 TNA WO 162 /265, notes of a meeting 31 August 1945, present: Sir Hartley Shawcross (UK); Justice Jackson, S. Alderman and Jackson Junior, all from USA; General Nikitchenko, Ivanov, Troyanovsky from USSR; and R. Malezieux from France.

2 Władysław Anders, *Bez Ostatniego Rozdziału* – literally translates as 'without the last chapter', English title *An Army in Exile*, Gryf Publication, London 1959 third edition. On Army List for 1945-6, there is a J.L. Tapping (W.S/Lt) of Emergency Commission, Queens Royal Regiment.

3 TNA FO 1019/ 95 and 96 L 3359/3043/G, Top Secret, P. Dean to Sir Hartley Shawcross, 3 November 1945; Shawcross to Sir David Maxwell Fyfe, 5 December 1945.

4 TNA FO 371/47734 N 13818/664/55, Foreign Office minutes 8 October 1945.

5 TNA FO 1019/ 95 and 96, correspondence between Colonel Robert Jackson Chief Prosecutor USA and Lt Gen. R. Rudenko, Chief Prosecutor of the USSR, 8–11 March

1946, with copies to Auguste Champetier de Ribes and Sir David Maxwell Fyfe, Chief Prosecutors for France and the UK.

6 TNA FO 1019 / 95 and 96, BWCN/N/30, Immediate Top Secret signal, Nov 29 1700 hours 1945 from BWCE [Patrick] Dean for [David] Scott Fox.

7 TNA WO 311/ 717, BWCE (ES) / N/ SIG/1-189 Nuremberg cipher 'following for Scott Fox from Dean'. The folder also contains a folio No. 246, sent by Col Phillimore from Nuremberg to R. A. Beaumont at the FO, indicating inclusion of a copy of the second part of the Soviet case, in particular pages 97–100, which deal with Katyn. This copy and further folios 247–250 are missing from the folder.

8 PISM KOL 12/16/G and H, *Oddział Kultury i Prasy 2 Korpusu, Biuro Studiów, Notatki służbowe w sprawie Akcji Koster* (official notes regarding Action *Koster* from Department of Press and Culture of 2 Corps) signed by Capt. Zdzisław Stahl chief of the Analytical Office, to be used as briefing material for Minister Tarnowski, dated London 20 March and 15 April 1946.

9 Guy Lloyd (1890–1987) MP, served in 1914–18 war (mentioned in despatches, DSO), Major in WW II; MP for Renfrewshire, Scotland. Knighted 1953.

10 Douglas L. Savory, MP (1878–1969) son of Rev Lloyd Savory from Suffolk, educated at Malborough College and St John's College Oxford, read French and English, became Professor at Queens University Belfast in 1909. Worked in Intelligence during the First World War as Secretary to the British Minister in Sweden 1918–1919. Left academia in 1940, elected as a Unionist MP. 1950–1955 an MP for South Antrim. Knighted in 1952.

11 TNA FCO 28/1475, copy of a letter written in Polish to Ambassador Raczyński by Maria Elżbieta Lach [Lachówna], former civilian employee of IV Dept. of *Oddział II*, who had worked in the general section (interpreters subsection) of the Polish General Staff Intelligence Service. Dated 26 April 1971, it refers to the fact that she typed the manuscript *Zbrodnia Katyńska w świetle dokumentów* (The Katyn massacre in the light of documents), edited by Professor Wiktor Sukiennicki. Documents were brought from Mr Heitzman's office in London to Oxford for typing. Later, some chapters were typed in London under supervision of Professor Swianiewicz, prisoner at Kozelsk, who contributed much to the work.

12 TNA FO 371 /56474 N 1386/108/55, an open letter by the Polish Parliamentary Group 74 signed by Józef Godlewski, requesting a signature from Minister Kwapiński, dated 31 January 1946. Also PISM, KOL 9/7, Professor Savory's correspondence file, includes a printed open letter dated 7 December 1945, printed by the Polish Parliamentary Group, 74 Cornwall Gardens, London SW1, entitled 'An Appeal to members of the Parliaments of all the Nations from the former Deputies and Senators of the Polish Parliament'; signed by following Senators: Ignacy Baliński, Józef Godlewski, Aleksander Heiman Jarecki, Wojciech Jastrzębowski, Jerzy Iwanowski, Tadeusz Katelbach, Adam Koc, Wanda Norwid-Neugebauer, Karol Niezabytowski, Konstanty Rdultowski,(sic) Stefan Rosada; Deputies: Konstanty Dzieduszycki, Stanisław Jóźwiak, Kornel Krzeczunowicz, Jerzy Paciorkowski, Tadeusz Schaetzel, Antoni Zalewski, Bronisław Wanke, Marian Zyndram-Kościałkowski, Władysław Wielhorski, Witold Zyborski.

13 TNA FO 371/47734 N 16482/664/55 and N 17514/664/G, minute from Denis Allen FO, with comments by Thomas Brimelow and Patrick Dean, Leading Prosecution Counsel, BWCE, indicating that Allen's draft was 'amended accordingly', 26.10.1945.

14 Ibid. The underlined sentence was crossed out by Patrick Dean, the British Leading Prosecution Council, BWCE and he substituted: 'So long as this evidence is still being assembled and the case has not been heard, the matter remains *sub judice.*'

15 TNA FO 371/71610 N 2599/2599/55, ' Most Secret' Memorandum dated October 1947, entitled 'The Mass Murder of Polish Prisoners of War in Katyn', 31-page, stapled brochure, typed in March 1946, marked 'not for publication'.

16 TNA FO 371/56475 N 4406/108/55G, second copy of a report on the Katyn massacre dated 25 March 1946; together with the documents and comments of the FO officials from 4 April to 10 May 1946.

17 TNA FO 371/56475 N4406/664/55G, 10 April 1946.

18 TNA FO 371/56474 N 569/108/55, draft reply by Sir Hartley Shawcross in answer to the Earl of Mansfield, whether any arrests were made in connection with the murders of the prisoners at Katyn, 23 January 1946; also N 568, letter from Lt Col Harry Phillimore, BWCE at Nuremberg to David Scott Fox, dated 3 January 1946.

19 TNA FO 371/56474 N 108/108/55, letter of reply from the Attorney-General Sir Hartley Shawcross to the Foreign Secretary Ernest Bevin, dated 28 December 1945 on the subject of memorandum prepared by Professor Savory.

20 TNA FO 371/56474 N 2111/108/55, cipher No. 210, sent to the FO and copied to Moscow, 1946 February 15, 15.42 hours.

21 TNA FO 371/56474 N 2228, cipher from Moscow sent by Frank Roberts, 18 February 1946 to FO.

22 TNA FO 371/56465 N 2248/86/55G, N 2825/86/55G, correspondence by General Kopański, Lord Selborne, Maj. Gen. Colin Gubbins and Patrick Dean to Christopher Warner PID, FO, 13 February 1946.

23 TNA FO 1019 / 95, copy of a secret additional protocol in Russian and translation into English, signed by Ribbentrop and Molotov, Moscow, 28 September 1939. Documents sent by H. J. Phillimore BWCE (ES) from Nuremberg to R.A. Beaumont, War Crimes Section, FO London.

chapter seven

BWCE AND MACHINATIONS AT NUREMBERG

The Katyn case, presented by Lt Gen. Roman A. Rudenko, Chief Prosecutor of the USSR at the International Military Tribunal at Nuremberg, was lamentable and inconclusive. It was evident that while the Soviets failed to impress the Tribunal with their accusation of German guilt, the German defence team was more concerned with neutralising their assailants rather than accusing the Russians in return.

Much can be learned from documents generated by the BWCE and their correspondence with the FO. Patrick Dean, legal adviser to the FO, was the primary recipient of all signals coming from Lt Col Harry Phillimore, Secretary of the BWCE at Nuremberg. At the beginning of July, a telephone call was received at the FO from Phillimore, informing them briefly that 'the Russians had much the best of the argument' and in the BWCE view 'rightly so'.

It was a farcical and unethical trial within a trial. A Tribunal summoned in the name of international justice permitted the Soviet state, which was under grave suspicion of guilt, to act both as judge and jury. Characteristic of the Soviet aproach was the Soviet Prosecutor's objection to the calling of witnesses and submission of the Burdenko report as the only necessary and unchallengeable evidence. The Court however, refused their claim and allowed three witnesses – but only three – on either side to be called.[1]

The defence was heard first, which in itself was a breach of the Charter of the Tribunal and only then witnesses for the prosecution followed; no rebuttal was allowed. All three Soviet witnesses lied or were silent on vital points. Dr Markov was not asked why he had changed his deposition or why was he imprisoned by the *NKVD* after signing the International Committee of experts report in 1943. The other witness statements were based on hearsay evidence, along the lines of 'he had not seen, but had been told by his Russian mate, who in turn heard it from …'etc.

Phillimore's passive summary of Katyn procedures[2] was in accordance with the FO instructions to desist from analysing the validity of the court, stating only what transpired. He expressed his satisfaction with the way it had gone for the Soviets, but what caught his attention particularly were the *GECO* fired cartridges found in the graves, which for him, tilted the balance of guilt onto the Germans. One can deduce that the BWCE team were ignorant of the Rapallo Treaty of 1920, signed by Russia and Germany in violation of the Versailles agreement, which prohibited Germany to rearm or allow her to deal in arms. The War Office should have briefed the BWCE about this matter and confirmed that in between the wars Germany had sold *GECO* ammunition to Russia and other countries of Eastern Europe. *The White Book on Katyn,* which includes the ballistic experts report, states that 'all bullets found in Katyn graves were of German make'. So the Germans were not covering up the fact, which could have been taken as proof of guilt.

NUREMBERG TELEGRAM FROM
BRITISH WAR CRIMES EXECUTIVE
DATED 6 JULY 1946. [Originated on 3 July]

After hearing 3 witnesses for the defence and a similar number for the prosecution, Soviet case has undoubtedly emerged very much enhanced and they are very pleased with the way it has gone.

The defence first called the Officer Commanding the Signals Regiment, whose H.Q. was situated close to the mass graves, from September 1941 onwards; his evidence with regard to the discovery of the mass graves was not very impressive. After hearing rumours of the shooting, his men discovered a cross in the winter of 1942-1943 round, which a wolf had been scratching. Shortly after human bones were brought to him and he spoke about the matter to other officers but admitted that he did not report the matter in writing. In the spring of 1943 a Professor Buhtz arrived and proceeded to excavate the graves. Although they were not more than 30 metres from the road to the Regimental H.Q., the Colonel had never noticed anything during the long time the unit had been stationed there, until the incident of the cross and wolf occurred.

An officer followed this witness from the Army Group Signals, who handled all secret messages and who said that he never handled any order to kill Polish prisoners and any order to this effect must have gone through his hands. He was confronted with a captured document annexed to the Soviet report, showing that in September 1941, *Einsatz Kommando B* and also *Einsatz Kommando Moscow* were situated at Smolensk and admitted that he did not handle secret orders between the *Einsatz Kommandos* and their superior authorities in the SS.

The third witness was the General in charge of the whole Signals of the Army Group, who's H.Q., was also nearby. He had constantly been along the track from September 1941 onwards and had never noticed anything unusual nor had he any knowledge of Polish prisoners being in the neighbourhood. He made virtually the only good point on behalf of the defence that no German Signals

Regiment would knowingly have pitched its H.Q. practically on top of these mass graves.

The prosecution called first a Professor of Astronomy whom the Germans had compelled to be Deputy Mayor of Smolensk during the occupation. This Professor reported being informed by the Mayor, who was a collaborator, of the Germans' decision to kill Poles in September 1941. He was subsequently told that they had been killed and it was clear that the Mayor had been so informed by the German Commandant. This second-hand evidence was greatly improved by defence counsel in cross-examination as he elicited that the witness had personally known the place in the [forest] so extremely well, it being a resort of the residents of Smolensk and had been there off and on until the German occupation, after which it became a forbidden area. He also elicited that in August [1940], namely some months after the Germans alleged that the murders took place; the Deputy Mayor had spent his holiday with his wife at Kozelsh [Kozelsk] and seen the Poles in the camp in which it is common ground that they were formerly detained. The witness further stated that although he had not seen the Poles after the Germans moved in, his students told him that they were walking along the road through the forest [where subsequently the graves were found]. He had never been told the precise location of the graves by anyone.

This witness was followed by a Bulgarian [Markov] member of the German [Medical] commission, who gave evidence at length of the very perfunctory nature of Commission's examination. They only spent some 7 or 8 hours at the site altogether and emphasised that everything they were shown, had previously been discovered or exhumed. He was less convincing in his explanation of why he had signed the joint report, finding that the murders had been committed in April or May 1940 but his explanation that they were all put under pressure to sign at a military airfield in Russia was not possible and the effect of his evidence was generally to discredit the German report.

The third witness was the principal member of the Soviet investigation [Prozorovsky]. He was undoubtedly a most effective witness and testified to having personally exhumed some 5,000 bodies at Kiev, Kharkov, Smolensk and other places. He spoke in great detail of the condition of the bodies and of the very careful investigation made. His commission had made a most careful autopsy of 925 bodies, only 3 of which had apparently been perfunctorily examined previously. He explained the condition of the clothing, which had been searched and gave details of a few documents found. They included receipts dated April and May 1941 and a letter from a wife to the Soviet Red Cross, bearing a Warsaw and Moscow postmark in September 1940 as well as postmark with the stamp of the Tarnopol Post Office dated 13 November 1940. He has personally discovered a letter dated 20 June. His mastery of the details of these documents was complete and his evidence delivered confidently and quickly, but obviously not parrot wise. He went on to deal with the bullet cases, which were found in the graves, which were those of a calibre which the German witnesses had admitted applied to the German pistols and which, he stated, bore the initials of a German firm GECO. This evidence was greatly fortified by a captured document produced by the Americans being a telegram dated May 1943 from an official of the Government General to the defendant Frank's office in Poland stating that members of the Polish Red Cross who had been visiting Katyn at the invitation of the Germans had been very much disturbed at finding bullet cases marked GECO, a well known German firm. The conjunction between this document showing German bullet cases found in the graves in May 1943 by the Poles and by the Soviet commission a year later in January 1944, was most convincing. He went on to give reasons why the bodies could not have been buried as early as 1940 and concluded by comparing the method of killing with that in the many other cases which he had personally investigated where German action was not disputed. Altogether, although not of course conclusive the evidence emerged strongly in favour of the Soviet case and the German report was largely discredited and their evidence unimpressive.

The Germandt Affair

Herrn Germandt was a German medical orderly in a military field hospital at Borok village near Smolensk from July 1942 until September 1943, when the Soviets took over the district. Janusz Laskowski, a Polish war correspondent who during the war worked on the Polish clandestine radio *Świt*, went to Germany during the Nuremberg trials to visit Germandt at his home in Underliederbach, near Frankfurt-am-Main.[3] He wanted to know more about the role of a local peasant Kiselev and the alleged German Army '537 Battalion' stationed at Katyn. Germandt must have followed the Nuremberg trials and was keen to talk about some of the things he heard on the radio. He told Laskowski that it was not a Battalion, but a Divisional *Nachrichten Abteilung*, a Divisional Signals unit under *Oberst* Ahrens, which had its HQ in the nearby Red Wood. The soldiers had found a short cut through the woods to reach the building in Katyn woods and it was then that the crosses were spotted.

Germandt said that the mystery of the crosses was soon connected to the German Organisation *Todt* that organised foreign PoWs, amongst them Poles, on construction work on the railway lines in the early spring of 1942. Hearing their language the local villagers, amongst them old Parfeon Kiselev, 'babbled' that in early 1940, the *NKVD* shot Polish officers and buried them in mass graves on Koze Gory. They were taken to the spot and finding the evidence, marked the place with one or two birch crosses. The following day the *Todt* workers departed towards the Eastern front. The crosses would eventually lead to the German *Geheime Feldpolitzei* investigation in October 1942.

Germandt's story involves another person, who does not figure in any other documents and is not mentioned in any depositions. He is Vasily Kiselev, the 32-year-old son of Parfeon Kiselev, who, according to Germandt, was recruited into the Russian army and later taken prisoner by the Germans. The story goes that while being transported west to a *Stalag* camp, young Kiselev, realising that the train had stopped on his home ground, started to call out to the local passers-by. He was recognised by his sister-in-law Olga who begged Germandt to help release Vasily and engage him to work for the Germans on rail transport. This he managed to do after haggling with his superiors. Kiselev was very grateful and cannily bargained with Germandt, promising that if he were allowed to see his wife on Sundays, he would show him the place where Poles had been shot and buried in early 1940. Germandt immediately informed *Leutnant* Voss commanding the local *Geheime Feldpolizei*.[4] True enough, bodies were found in the areas Kiselev pointed out. Germandt explained to Laskowski that while he was in the Russian army and later taken prisoner by the Germans, Vasily could not possibly have known that his father had been allegedly forced by the Germans to confess in front of the foreign visitors and again forced by the Russians to deny his original statement as in Burdenko's report.

Germandt was convinced that it was a Russian put-up job; for him, the most striking evidence was the presence of officers' belts on some of the bodies, which is not that unusual, although it differs from Major Adam Solski's diary note that on arrival, officer's belts were confiscated by the Soviets together with watches, penknives and other valuables. Germandt explained that the first German action when arresting an officer was to take off his belt. It had a dispiriting psychological effect on the prisoner. It remains a puzzle to this day why Germandt, who witnessed so much, was not called upon to testify in any enquiry on Katyn in later years, nor interrogated by the Allies, as was the case with other witnesses.

The Timing of *Akcja Kostar*

On 9 July 1946 a meeting was held in London. Present were General Marian Kukiel, the former Polish Minister of Defence in exile, Lt Marian Heitzman, legal adviser and head of the Political Section of that Ministry and Guy Lloyd MP. On the agenda was the last hearing on Katyn at Nuremberg.[5] Kukiel described the weaknesses of the German defence, which could have easily been transformed into attack, but was not. Their only success was cancelling one charge, for lack of evidence. Lloyd asked for the reason. Heitzman pointed out (Kukiel's English was limited), that the Soviet prosecution, unsure of its position, was also weak and was unwilling to unleash a counter-charge, or to present its case too forcefully. As to the German defence, Kukiel had the impression that they did not want to irritate the Soviets, an attitude which might have been influenced by discussions in camera. The last defence presentation was a document, allegedly 'from Polish sources', which gave the impression that the German defence did not want to be aggressive, almost as if to provoke the Polish delegation from Warsaw to come out with something more revealing instead.

Lloyd, who may have had some clue passed onto him by the BWCE, agreed with their assumptions and when asked by Kukiel his opinion on what to do next replied that he was deeply convinced the Tribunal would not give a judgement on Katyn and that this might be overlooked in the final verdict. With these prophetic words, he advised the Poles not to start a press campaign then, but wait until after the verdict. In the event of non-judgement at Nuremberg, he would once more personally bring the subject before Parliament and the press. Lloyd added that in any event, the future campaign (and he probably meant *Akcja Kostar*) should not start in Great Britain but America. He stressed that intensive preparations should start immediately, so that when the decision was made, the plan could be put into action within 24 hours.

The Nuremberg trials had raised many legal reservations among the Poles and even the British about allowing the accused Russians to sit in judgement on a crime for which they themselves were under suspicion. But the British government wanted to appease the Russians by denying a voice at the trials to a delegation of exiled Poles from London, who had damning evidence in their possession. This was an unforgivable decision, especially as they knew that the provisional government in Poland under Soviet domination had produced ample material on German atrocities, but none on Katyn.

The Second Phase of *Akcja Kostar*

After Nuremberg, it was time to start the second phase of *Akcja Kostar*, to prepare and publish in book format the accumulated confidential documents and papers compiled in London by Lieutenant Marian Heitzman and Professor Wiktor Sukiennicki.[6] They were to be complemented by articles under the general editorship of Captain Zdzisław Stahl, chief of the *Biuro Studiów* (Research Bureau) of the Department of Culture and Press of 2 Polish Corps in Italy. In June 1945 Stahl commissioned Józef Mackiewicz, the well-known writer, who witnessed the exhumation of bodies at Katyn in May 1943, to write a book about the crime. Mackiewicz managed to escape to Italy prior to Goetel's arrival. It was agreed the volume would be published as a 'White Book', that is, an official publication of the Polish government-in-exile. Mackiewicz put into narrative form all the relevant information gathered from documents and depositions given by witnesses amassed by the *Biuro Studiów*, including his own report of the 1943 visit.[7]

Stahl took the manuscript to London for consultation. The official note written by Stahl in Rome dated 15 April 1946 reveals that the decision had been made to accept the London version of *Facts and Documents* for *Akcja Kostar*, while the Rome edition written by Mackiewicz was to be 'eliminated', or rather, simply published as a book for general readership under the editorship of Stahl. Mackiewicz objected but had no written agreement with the *Biuro Studiów*. Mackiewicz's manuscript was re-edited and new material was inserted, such as Dr Wodzinski's report, events at

Nuremberg, the activities of the *NKVD* and the *UB* (*Urząd Bezpieczeństwa* – Polish Secret Service). Publication in Britain was difficult as firms were apprehensive about the British Government's reaction. Gollancz, who at first agreed, refused to publish in spite of intercession by Goronwy Roberts MP. It was finally printed in France in 1948 under the title *Zbrodnia katyńska w świetle dokumentów* (The Katyn massacre in the light of documents) with a foreword by General Anders but without any indication of the authorship. Over the years the book was reprinted several times but Mackiewicz was never acknowledged as the first editor and his personal report was removed from subsequent editions.

Undaunted, Mackiewicz survived this humiliation and wrote a very successful book, which was never published in Polish, *Katyn – Ungesuhntes Verbrechen,* published in Zurich in 1949 with a foreword by Ambassador Arthur Bliss Lane. In English it was called *The Katyn Wood Murders* and published in 1951; a French edition followed in 1952, Italian in 1954 and Spanish in 1957. It is important to stress that these publications on Katyn were the first to reach a wide readership.

The Polish Appeal for an International Tribunal

In November 1949, the second phase of *Akcja Kostar* came to fruition, this time not on British soil but in the US. The baton of advocacy for the truth about the Katyn massacre passed from one Ambassador to Poland, Sir Owen O'Malley, to another brave supporter, Arthur Bliss Lane, former American Ambassador to Poland. Taking advantage of the United Nations General Assembly in New York, Bliss Lane wrote to Andrei Vyshinsky, Foreign Minister of the USSR, reminding him of the correspondence he had had with Minister Kot (in autumn 1941 again in July 1942), regarding the missing Polish officers and requesting his help to establish the truth about the massacre of more than 4,000 officers at Katyn. Bliss Lane, as chairman of the newly constituted 'American Committee for investigation of the Katyn Massacre Inc.' referred to the vitally important document signed by the three wartime leaders Roosevelt, Churchill and Stalin at the Moscow conference in October 1943. He reminded Vyshinsky of the text of the joint declaration:

> Let those who have hitherto not imbued their hands with innocent blood, beware lest they join the ranks of the guilty, for most assuredly the three Allied powers will pursue them to the uttermost ends of the earth and will deliver them to their accusers in order that justice may be done.

These were powerful and compelling words; needless to say, he did not receive the reply he sought. At least one of the signatories – and possibly all three knew for certain that the blood of those Polish officers was not on German hands. Undeterred, he called a press conference and delivered a widely reported speech.[8] One of the earliest representations to arrive at the FO asking for intervention and support for the American efforts over Katyn, came from the Glasgow Branch of the Scottish-Polish Society, but it was to no avail.

General Anders' Plea

To mark the 10th anniversary of the Katyn massacre, on 28 April 1950 Lieutenant General Anders, commander of the Polish Army in Russia in 1941 and unchallenged leader of the free Poles, continued the quest for the truth by trying almost exactly the same approach in London. Anders released a statement to the press through the 'Polish Association of Former Soviet Political Prisoners'.[9]

> We Poles will never forget Katyn. Having lost the right to raise our voice on the international forum, after most of the countries had withdrawn their recognition of our Government, deprived of the possibility of appealing directly to governments and to the institutions of international justice, we have nevertheless persevered with preparing our indictment. For years we have collected every scrap of documentary evidence, we have scrutinised every detail and we informed both the governments of democratic countries and public opinion of the free countries about the results of our work. In our endeavours to make known the truth about Katyn, we were by no means alone. Time and again, we have found understanding amongst generous people, not least here in Great Britain. They have never hesitated to stand up for a righteous cause and have claimed justice for us in the face of the materialistic considerations and the short-sighted attitude which seems to force too many of the free governments into a policy of silence on the matter of Katyn for fear of irritating the Kremlin.

Anders called for the appointment of a new International Tribunal, which, unlike at Nuremberg, where Katyn was included in the indictment but not the judgement, would allow Polish evidence to be presented not by the puppet government in Warsaw, but by free Poles who wanted to speak in the name of the victims.

Anders also wrote to Foreign Secretary Ernest Bevin requesting he take an interest in condemning Katyn, not necessarily from the Polish viewpoint but as universal morality demanded. Anders' statement contained a strong indictment of the Soviet Union, which was disapproved of by Geoffrey W. Harrison the FO desk officer: 'HMG should not associate itself at the present time with the idea of appointing an international tribunal.'

The Foreign Office Reply

General Anders also approached several MPs for support, among them Sir Alfred Waldron Smithers and Michael L. Astor, once an MI5 officer. The file[10] is full of comments by various officials. Geoffrey W. Harrison, who had changed his tune, commented that playing down the Katyn murders during the war could not be a good reason for playing them down in the present circumstances and besides, the American tribunal might bring new developments. No reply was sent to the London Poles for some time, because of the source of the request, the 'National Council of the Polish émigré body'. However, mindful of General Anders' stature, a reply from Kenneth G. Younger MP, Minister of State FO, eventually arrived on 6 July 1950:

> In the Foreign Secretary's absence I write to thank you for your letter of 16 June with which you enclosed a copy of your statement on the Katyn massacre. I need hardly assure you that the tragedy of Katyn in which so many gallant Polish officers lost their lives, will always be remembered with horror by the British people and the whole civilised world. The motives, which lead you to seek further elucidation and redress for this terrible crime are readily understandable. I must, however, inform you that His Majesty's Government do not feel able to associate themselves with the idea of setting up, in existing circumstances and after this lapse of time, an international tribune of the kind you suggest.

Sir Waldron Smithers, who at Anders' request had again tried to raise the matter in the House of Commons, found the Speaker rejecting his submission on the grounds of it being a badly formed question and hence out of order. Smithers apologised to Anders for being unable to assist the Poles any further. Arthur F. Maddocks head of the Northern Department of the FO, advised Bevin not to approve or appoint an International Tribunal because an investigation could be successful only with the co-operation of the Soviet government, which of course, 'would not be obtainable'. Maddocks also thought that the matter was still too closely linked to Nazi propaganda, in spite of the time lapse. In his opinion the purpose of setting up a 'tribunal' was to spread anti-Soviet propaganda disguised as legal inquiry. Besides, it would bring the British too close to the exiled Poles. The reasons given were meretricious and disingenuous and indicate that the FO still did not know how to come to terms with their ally. Additional confusion was created by a more astute note, which came from the same department:

> We have laid off for these perhaps over-simple reasons – that we played down the Katyn murders at the time of their discovery, and therefore could scarcely rouse anything but deadly recrimination against ourselves if we now tried to make use of them; at least among Poles. We have assumed that it is impossible for us to claim that we genuinely believed them to be a Goebbels stunt. If we were to decide that the Poles and world public opinion generally, are realistic enough

to appreciate our reason for playing down Katyn at the time, then we ought to make a really big thing of it (only we have just missed the 10th anniversary); but I suggest this were best done by non-official action e.g. independent tribunals, memorial services, newspaper action etc. Any official action would involve us in high-level official contact with post war Poles here, and so in Polish politics, it seems to me. It may be worth it for the effect on public opinion generally, but it would merely revive unhappiness and bitterness among Poles. Moreover, once a propaganda stunt, always one: I think we should get a bad reception at the hands of the free world's press at such transparent manoeuvres if we acted officially; an unofficial action would be treated with some suspicion.

Notes

1 *Charter of the Tribunal*, Article 24 (e) 'Witnesses for the prosecution shall be examined and after that the witnesses for the Defence. Thereafter, such rebutting evidence as may be held by the Tribunal to be admissible, shall be called by either the Prosecution or the Defence.'
2 TNA FO 371/56476 N 8817/108/55, secure signal July 3 1946, 2035, from BWCE at Nuremberg for Patrick Dean and Scott Fox at the FO. Subject: Katyn Forest murder of 11,000 Polish Officers. Printed signal format marked 'confidential' can be found in FCO 28/ 2309 and WO 311/717 gives the date as 6 July 1946.
3 PISM KOL 12/15/2, 3, 4, three typescript articles written in Polish by Janusz Laskowski, *Krzyże z Brzeziny* (Birch Crosses), *Tajemnica Koziej Góry* (The Secrets of Koze Gory), *Katyn jest najważniejszą sprawą świata* (Katyn, the most important issue in the world). Written at Nuremberg 25/26/27 June 1946.
4 TNA GFM 33/2525 E424394, photostat of the original German secure signal 570 dated 4 March 1943, from Berlin to German Legation in Berne, about finding graves of the Poles shot by the *NKVD*, suggesting 10,000 probably were brought in; no eye witnesses as yet, only some local people having heard shots coming from the woods. Document signed by Field Police Secretary (*Geheime Feldpolizei Gruppe 570)* Lt Voss.
5 PISM KOL 12/16/G, minutes of a meeting held by General Marian Kukiel, Lt Marian Heitzman with Maj. Guy Lloyd MP on 9 July 1946.
6 TNA FCO 28/1475, copy of a letter in Polish to Ambassador Raczyński by Maria Elżbieta Lach (or Lachówna, indicating she was a spinster) former civilian employee of IV Dept of *Oddział II*. The letter of 26 April 1971 refers to the fact that she typed the first 80 pages of manuscript dictated by Professor Wiktor Sukiennicki in Oxford. Ms Lach states that documents were brought to London from the Continent by Prof. Marian Heitzman and Maj Alfred A. Hergesell and delivered to Sukiennicki in Oxford. Later, some chapters were typed in London under the supervision of Professor Swianiewicz. It can be assumed that the manuscript was the short 'Supplementary Report of Facts and Documents', re-edited in haste, in expectation of passing it to the BWCE at Nuremberg through Professor Savory.
7 Lewandowski Wacław, *Józef Mackiewicz Artyzm Biografia Recepcja*, Kontra, London 2000. Also Kazimierz Zamorski *Dwa Tajne Biura 2 Korpusu* (Two Secret Bureaux of 2 Corps) published by Poets and Painters, London 1990.
8 TNA FO 371/ 86679 NP1661/6, Ambassador Arthur Bliss Lane's letter to Mr Andrei Vyshinsky dated 17 November, statement to the press on 21 November 1949.
9 TNA FO 371/86679 NP 1661/3.
10 TNA FO 371/86679 NP 1661/1 to 14. Quotation is from NP 1661/3.

chapter eight

THE AMERICAN COMMITTEE

A confidential letter arrived by air courier at the Foreign Office Northern Department from the British Embassy in Washington, informing them that an American Committee had been formed to investigate the Katyn massacre. It was established largely through the efforts of Julius Epstein, a journalist who had served in the Office of War Information. Epstein's involvement with Katyn started with publication of two articles on Katyn in the *New York Herald Tribune* on 3 and 4 July 1949.[1] He became known later, in February 1952, when he put a question on Katyn to Churchill, who was giving a press conference in New York. Epstein put it in writing and awaited a reply, which came after Churchill had left for England. An acknowledgement came from the British Embassy in Washington, indicating that 'Mr Churchill did not wish to reply.'[2]

Epstein's efforts earned him the post of executive secretary to the newly formed American Committee for the Investigation of the Katyn Massacre, Inc., chaired by Arthur Bliss Lane. The Executive Committee included Max Eastman and Dorothy Thomson as Deputies, Montgomery M. Green as Treasurer. Other members included William Donovan and Allen Dulles, who had wartime connections with the Polish Intelligence Service, George Creel, James A. Farley, Constantine Brown, Mrs Clare Booth Luce, George Sokolsky, Samuel Levitas, Charles Rozmarek, President of the Polish-American Congress, Virginia Starr Freedom, Blair Gunther, James Walsh and the Rev John Cronin.

The British Embassy in Washington could not assess the degree of official support for the Committee. In conversation, Bliss Lane was not perturbed by the State Department's apparent 'hands off' attitude, but was disappointed at the lack of support from the American Bar Association, who had originally intended to conduct the investigation, but probably under government pressure decided not to participate. He had hoped that a group of independent jurors would undertake a semi-judicial investigation. He was also unable to persuade the State Department to release the important report of Colonel Van Vliet's visit to Katyn in 1943.

On receiving Washington's despatch on 29 June 1950, FORD, the FO Research Department, commented that as early as 1949 they had advised the Americans to 'lay off Katyn as it was hopelessly identified with Dr Goebbels' propaganda'. But not all of the staff at FORD was of the same opinion. Geoffrey Shaw of the Northern Department of the FO was forthright on the British report on Katyn, quoted in a later chapter, but his cryptic and fairly astonishing remark at this juncture is given here.[3]

> I have little doubt that we shall hear a good deal more of Katyn, despite official reluctance to air the matter. As far as 'occupied' Europe is concerned, Poland and Czechoslovakia have surely long since forgotten to be worried about Goebbel's connection with the original discovery of the atrocity. It has now been reported that shortly before the dismissal of Louis Johnson, the U.S. report was discovered to be missing from the Defence Department files. It is interesting to recall that several attempts have been made to steal the Katyn records held by the London Polish Government.

USA, House of Representatives Select Committee

The committee under Bliss Lane continued its work for almost three years, keeping the interest of the general public alive; but its primary aim was to bring Katyn to the attention of Congress. Success came in September 1951, when finally Congress authorised the House of Representatives to set up a Select Committee, under the chairmanship of Senator Ray J. Madden (known as the 'Madden Committee'). The aim of the Select Committee was 'to record evidence, data and facts that will eventually and officially establish the guilt of the nation that perpetrated the greatest crime of genocide in all recorded history'.[4] Despatches sent by Edward E. Tomkins of the British Embassy in Washington informed the FO that the State Department did not take this development very seriously as its Committee members were of Polish origin who had large numbers of Poles in their constituencies. He listed their names according to the political parties, amongst whom were five Attorneys; Democrats Ray J. Madden of Indiana as Chairman, Daniel J. Flood of Pennsylvania, Thaddeus M. Machrowicz of Michigan, Foster Furcolo of Massachusetts; and Republican George A. Dondero of Michigan. Republican Alvin E. O'Konski of Wisconsin was a teacher by profession and owner of a radio station, and the other Republicans were a businessman from Illinois, Timothy P. Sheehan, John J. Mitchell, Chief Counsel, Roman Pucinski, Chief Investigator and Barbara R. Brooke, Secretary.

The Committee began its hearings in October 1951 with Lt Col Donald R. Stewart, Field Artillery, testifying that he was one of the American prisoners of war who, together with Colonel John Van Vliet Jr of the US Infantry, were taken by the Germans to view the Katyn exhumations in May 1943. Van Vliet's original report written in 1945 was conveniently 'lost' in the Pentagon and in 1950 he had been asked to re-write it from memory. The State Department inspected his report and was satisfied that it could be regarded as evidence and passed several copies to the Committee as an act of goodwill.[5]

In March 1952, Sir Oliver Franks, the British Ambassador in Washington, sent a note by diplomatic bag to Sir Anthony Eden informing him that Madden had persuaded the House of Representatives to pass a resolution authorising the Committee to continue its investigations in Europe and that members of the Committee – Madden, Machrowicz, Dondero, Flood and O'Konski – were en route for London, Paris and Frankfurt. Sir Oliver thought the investigation raised constitutional issues and political and propaganda difficulties might arise.[6] He wanted to know if consent was required from the Government for O'Konski to begin interviewing Poles and other British subjects who might be willing to contribute.

Sir Oliver regarded the Congressional Committee as something akin to a British Royal Commission visiting another country to gather evidence. He hoped that if this was all O'Konski wanted to do, then for the sake of good Anglo-American relations, obstacles should not be put in their way. But Eden was fuming: 'I don't much like this, is there any precedent for such proceedings on British soil?' He was uncertain of the situation and clearly envisaged political and legal repercussions, which his Department would have to resolve.

On 1 April, a meeting was arranged between the FO officials Robert Cecil, Alastair G. Maitland and Henry Hohler, all from the American Department of the FO, and members of the Select Committee A. O'Konski and R. Pucinski assisted by R.C. Courtney of the US Embassy. On the agenda was access to the British documents and practical arrangements during their stay in London. They were advised to go through the proper channels, which meant US Ambassador Gifford. A formal request for records on Katyn made by the Russian, German or British authorities held by the FO reached Parliamentary Under Secretary Sir William Strang. Information was requested as to the present whereabouts of possible witnesses – Lt Colonel F.P. Stevenson and Captain Stanley Gilder; newspaper correspondents Egon Gallinger, Max Schneitzer, Adolph Benz and Stoffels; and Frank Stroobant, a British businessman who as a civilian had been taken to Katyn in 1943. Above all, the Committee wanted to know what had happened to Ivan Krivozertsev, Ivan Andreev and Yevgeni Samenenko, all resident in Britain, known to the British authorities in 1945, as well as the names of the British officials who had interrogated them. The British authorities met none of these requests and none of the persons named appeared before the Congressional enquiry.[7]

Convolutions of the Foreign Office

After consultations with Legal Advisers Sir Roger Makins, Gerald G. Fitzmaurice and Sir William Murrie of the Home Office, Strang had spun a perfect diplomatic story to confound the Americans.[8] He stated that the Government did not see any difficulty in voluntary attendance at the hearings in the Federal German Republic of private residents from the UK. As to taking depositions from witnesses privately in the UK, that was a different matter. The Committee would have no power in the UK to compel witnesses to testify on oath, in the absence of specific authority from Parliament. It would not be 'proper' of the Committee to do so, presumably on the grounds that one sovereign power does not tolerate the questioning of its own citizens by the political representative of another power. Besides, continued Strang, no privilege would be attached to the proceedings of the Committee, whether written or spoken, in respect of the English law of defamation. They would have to operate under the jurisdiction of English law. As a further objection, Strang was advised by Fitzmaurice and Murrie that the proposed enquiry was unwelcome on political grounds and that the proceedings could be forbidden altogether if it appeared that a breach of the peace was likely to occur. Armed with this latter argument, Strang concluded his brief:

> If we tell the United States Government that we do not wish a Congressional enquiry on this explosive subject to be conducted in this country, we shall get across not only the United States Administration (which we understand is embarrassed by this Congressional initiative) but across Congress as well. If the enquiry is conducted here in the manner apparently proposed, we may expect Communist demonstrations and possible breaches of the peace, in which case the police would have to interfere and if the disturbances were sufficiently widespread, we might have to ask for the enquiry to be suspended. There will also certainly be parliamentary questions. We must get the record straight from the start.

On 3 April Anthony Eden wrote:

> I dislike all this very much. The effect on Anglo-American relations may be bad. Can't I agree as a start we must find out from the US Ambassador what is required. Will Sir William Strang do this? Then we will have to consider our actions. Cabinet should be warned of the issue at an early date. Probably I had best do this by circulating record of Ambassador's interview and drawing attention to it.

As a result, Ambassador Franks informed the FO that because of the Foreign Secretary's strong objection to the idea of O'Konski conducting an open hearing in London, the US State Department would apply pressure on the Committee to drop the idea and instead, to collect individual statements in a hotel with no press or public present, with no publicity. The whole idea was to reduce the hearings to 'legitimate private enquiries'.[9] The Press did manage to get hold of the story and Warsaw radio reacted immediately – and outrageously:

> When, in 1943, Goebbels made the slanderous accusation that the Soviet government was responsible for the death of several thousand Polish officers at Katyn, Churchill and Eden, supported by the government and press, denounced this

> hideous lie. Today, Churchill and Eden are trampling upon their own words and on the orders of Washington, are allowing a US Congressional Committee to conduct in Britain a so- called 'investigation' of the Katyn crime. Both Churchill and Eden knew well that the Nazi criminals were responsible for the murders; all the same, they are helping the US Congressional Committee in spreading Goebbels' lie.

The FO took notice of the message and was on alert. On Easter Monday, five members of the Select Committee established their headquarters in two rooms at the Kensington Palace Hotel in London. They proceeded to take statements in private from some 32 witnesses, amongst them General Anders, General Kukiel, Edward Raczyński, Professor Kot, Ferdynand Goetel, Józef Mackiewicz, Stanisław Swianiewicz, and Lt Zbigniew Rowiński from Oflag II. Their statements were transcribed and afterwards notarised by a US consular officer.[10]

A separate meeting was held between US Embassy officials Penfield and R. C. Courtney and Roderick Barclay of the FO on 18 April 1952, on the question of access to documents the US Embassy had asked to be made available to the members of Congress.[11] Penfield feared that if the request were turned down, the atmosphere would be horribly soured. He almost pleaded for Madden to be allowed to read Hulls' reports only; but Robert Cecil for the Secretary of State informed Sir Oliver Franks in Washington that access to documents was to be denied as the policy was not to release confidential documents of the war period 1939–1945 and he regretted that no departure from this policy was envisaged. As to Hulls' three reports, all written in 1942, he pointed out, quite correctly, that they were produced months before the discovery of the Katyn graves and could hardly be used as evidence. He did not think other documents in FO possession were likely to be of any more help, since none of them could be considered to provide any direct evidence. Accordingly, he did not think that the strict observance of FO rules was hampering the Committee's investigations. In addition he produced what he thought was a slightly stronger argument, that the Committee could not be provided the requested access, since this was not available even to British MPs.[12]

The confidential minutes of that meeting are absolutely vital in pinpointing the collusion between the US and British diplomats in frustrating the Madden Committee. Penfield in desperation decided that if the documents were not available, he would like the FO's negative reply to be held back until the Congressmen had left, while he himself would send an interim message to the Committee that the British were still examining the request.

Barclay had already produced a draft for Penfield, which he duly agreed to hold up for a few days, with Eden's approval. But this is not the end of the story. Cecil, who redrafted Eden's letter to the American Ambassador, received a telephone message to say that the Ambassador thought it might be better if the FO did not reply at all and that an official reply was not necessary. Ray Madden, who was by then departing from

England for Germany, found it in his heart to say that he understood the difficulties and did not want to press the FO further. The Embassy request to facilitate the Committee access to the FO papers was duly withdrawn. Strang commented: 'This is a good solution. The US Embassy had been most helpful throughout. They have had some very anxious moments.'

No one was more pleased than Eden – to his signature, he added 'Splendid'. A telegram from the State Department in Washington duly arrived expressing relief that the Committee had left London without having caused any serious trouble and appreciation for the help and co-operation of the FO.[13]

There is an aftermath to this unsavoury affair. Unaware that these decisions would be made, diligent search was undertaken by Norman Statham, Northern Department of the FO, to look for Colonel Stevenson. He was contacted in Durban, Pretoria and a letter dated May 1952 duly arrived from him, stating that he was 'in possession of photographs, documents and personal evidence' of the massacre. He refused to give a statement but was willing to give evidence before the Commission.[14] This news was not passed on to the Madden Committee, in spite of a high-level decision by Alastair Maitland, Head of the American Department, to send a reply to Stevenson enclosing O'Konski's letter so that he might get in touch with the Committee himself.

Statham was trying to help the Americans again when he found out from a press attaché that a German film on Katyn had been shown in the British Consulate in Barcelona some time in 1948; it was offered to the FO but the film was of no interest to them. When it was searched for in June 1952, there was no sign of the film; but an eager *Daily Telegraph* correspondent, Alan Walker, had been invited to a private show in Madrid. He described it as a sober and moving film with a Spanish soundtrack, 15 minutes long, (probably a copy of the original). The person who held it offered it for sale for £200, but the FO did not follow up on the transaction, even after checking if 'friends' – meaning the SIS – had a copy, which they did not.[15]

FORD's Reaction to the Madden Report

The Interim Report which reached the FO on 2 July 1952 was debriefed by George S. Littlejohn-Cook, and commented upon by others from the IRD (Information Research Department), US and UN Departments of the FO and finally by Sir William Strang. It was observed that the Committee recommended that the US Delegate take the case to the United Nations Assembly, and action be sought before the International Court of Justice, against the Soviet Union. These clearly defined statements from the FO records show that there were two phases to the investigation carried out by the Select Committee of Congress. First, the gathering of evidence to determine who were the perpetrators of the massacre, ending in the declaration that the guilt lay fairly and squarely with the Soviet Union, and secondly, to establish why the Katyn massacre was never adequately revealed to the American people and to the rest of the world, and why the crime was not properly adjudicated at the Nuremberg trials. This of course touched a raw nerve for the American as well as the British FO.

When a copy of the second part of the Congressional Hearings arrived from Washington, the Research Department was first to examine it. Statham considered it to be a waste of time Littlejohn-Cook thought that Tadeusz Romer gave the most valuable evidence while Thomas S. Tull of IRD took a more thoughtful view. On reading the report, Tull agreed that it was increasingly clear that the Russians carried out the massacre, yet he disagreed with publicising the story as the Americans had done or intervening in any way at the international level. Katyn was not of prime importance; moreover, he was sure that the verdict of the Select Committee of Congress would not be accepted outside the US.[16]

Geoffrey Shaw's Opinion

Geoffrey Shaw at FORD had a totally different reaction. No doubt remembering his earlier association with Professor George F. Hudson, Professor Savory and Sir Owen O'Malley's ethical stand, Shaw shared their vision of Communist rule. He wrote an elegant and moving parliamentary brief, which was completely ignored by his superiors. Shaw's opinion is quoted here for the first time:

> The Poles in emigration and of course those at home – hope to gain several things from this enquiry. The first is naturally an answer to the question as to what really did happen to the Polish officers and soldiers, who were interned in the three camps, the majority having never been found at all; there are probably over 100,000 close relatives still alive, who have no definite answer to what has become of a father, a son, or a husband. This is a question which has practical implications and which any Polish authority worthy of the name is under pressure to solve.
>
> Secondly, it is their natural desire to establish responsibility for the murders of the men found in Katyn Wood. The Poles are unanimously of the opinion that it was a Soviet responsibility, and they believe that the West has still much to learn concerning the nature of Soviet communism. They are aware that the matter became of topical interest to the US Congress only when the massacre of American soldiers in Korea was made known, and they have followed, with very great concern, the parallel development of events – the counter-accusations (this time against the West), the refusal to accept International Red Cross investigations, the official embarrassment and the silences.
>
> From the communist point of view, there has been a great success scored in delaying a hearing, not being able to use it as a weapon against the London Poles during the war, but also in poisoning the fount of justice wherever it may be. They succeeded in suppressing it at Nuremberg (by making it their concern, and then

calling it off when it became apparent that it could not be pinned on the Germans). They use it now to test the strength of international justice and the attitude of western governments towards the exercise of justice between nations. This is not merely in theory, but as a practical guide to the operation of Soviet foreign policy in this particular field – i.e. through the International Association of Democratic Lawyers. Their activities are not so much concerned at this stage in codification of what might be termed Soviet international law – that would come later – but by bedevilling international relations by the manufacture of pseudo-legal arguments; it is an activity, which shows an alarming increase in the last few months.

However inexpedient the Katyn investigation may appear, it cannot be denied that it has strengthened the Americans in their conduct of the cold war. The need to defend our concepts of justice on any and every occasion in the face of a totalitarian power has been conclusively demonstrated in Korea, if only because, in the case of Soviet totalitarianism, that power is seeking to prepare a legal net for us. One feels, for example, that if Quintin Hogg [MP and Lord Chancellor] had investigated Katyn (not from the detective's point of view but from the point of view of the development of justice in our times) he would not have made such a poor showing in his [BBC Home Service] radio debate with D.N. Pritt some months ago. That very able Democratic Lawyer had, as usual, all the arguments.

From the point of view of recent European history, it is of considerable importance to be able to trace the great changes, which have taken place in the last decade or so. One of the most fundamental is the reduction of the civilised community to a herd by the systematic removal of its cultural leaders and the exposure of the mass to the arbitrary justice of the communist dictatorship. The European communities first to suffer this fate were the Baltic States and Poland. The Katyn victims and their more numerous missing fellow prisoners were selected by the Russians from amongst the elite of Poland – they were reservists drawn from every walk of life, professors, teachers, engineers, doctors, scientists, artists, priests, businessmen. Katyn belongs to the story of the struggle of independent men against Totalitaria.

Geoffrey W. Shaw 17 /V [17 May 1952]

The second phase of the Congressional Hearings was an effort to discover whether the massacre had been reported to the free world as it should have been. This phase can be seen as an attempted exposure of the missing dimension in British and American diplomacy. The Congressional Select Committee particularly wanted to determine whether the State Department or government officials including President Roosevelt had suppressed reports of Russian guilt. The British kept silent. Was there collusion in the higher echelons of both Powers to absolve the Soviets? The question is still open to debate. No relevant material was put into the hands of Colonel Robert Jackson, the American prosecutor at Nuremberg – and he called for none. Later, when interviewed by the *New York Herald Tribune*, Jackson regretted it, explaining he had been under pressure to speed up the trials, but agreed that 'it would have been helpful to have had the reports'. Patrick Dean (later Sir Patrick) of the British War Crimes Executive was unwilling to prosecute on material gathered by the exiled Poles. Averell Harriman, former American Ambassador in Moscow, emphasised at the hearings that they were predominantly, if not exclusively, concerned with keeping Russia in the war. The final statement of the Interim Report of the Select Congressional Committee, (despite its title) was accepted by the Foreign Office as a final judgment and this American statement became the requiem for the Poles:

> This Committee unanimously finds beyond any question of reasonable doubt, that the Soviet *N.K.V.D.* committed the mass murders of the Polish officers and intellectual leaders in the Katyn Forest.

The final report was despatched to London by Sir Oliver Franks, the British Ambassador in Washington on 20 November 1952. Norman Statham of the Northern Department summed it up in non-diplomatic language:

> Whereas the first part of its investigations resulted in a condemnation of Russian guilt, the second seems more likely to wash the Roosevelt administration's linen in public. Whether this linen is dirty or not, must be a matter of opinion; there were very good grounds for not publicising suspicions of Russia. Indeed, we have ourselves concluded that even now no purpose would be served by appearing to blackguard the Russians.

Ambassador Sir Oliver Franks' Words of Wisdom

Sir Oliver wrote to Sir Anthony Eden in a different tone.[17]

> ... This phase of the investigation could naturally have considerable domestic and political repercussions, in that should evidence be brought to light that the administration concealed, or failed to give adequate publicity to evidence detrimental to Russia which came into their possession, effective weapons would be placed in the hands of their critics. The question of possible suppression of evidence has been discussed publicly but sporadically for some time; it did not, however, figure to any extent in the recent Presidential campaign. The investigation is in fact being conducted by Congressmen representing heavily Polish districts in response to the general and vocal desire of Polish-Americans to get to the bottom of the story, the feeling among most of them being that the Russians were really the guilty party; The Democrats on the Committee, including the Chairman, have been at pains to show that they were as eager to get the truth as anyone; while the

Republicans have seemed especially anxious to prick the bubble of Roosevelt's reputation on a matter conveniently unconnected with his domestic New Deal programme, which is, of course, popular with their constituents.

4. A considerable volume of testimony is to be expected on this aspect of the Katyn massacre. Perhaps the most important witness so far is a former Governor Earle of Pennsylvania, who served during the war as Minister to Bulgaria, Minister to Austria and later as President Roosevelt's special representative in Turkey. Governor Earle testified that while in Turkey, he gained information allegedly proving Soviet responsibility for the massacre, but that President Roosevelt declined, in May 1944, to accept this evidence. In March 1945, Governor George H. Earle continued, that President Roosevelt wrote expressly forbidding him to publish an anti-Soviet article, saying that to do so, would be 'betrayal'.

5. Similarly, Major-General Bissell, former Chief of Army Intelligence, testified that a report pointing to Soviet guilt in the massacre was received in May 1945, but that it was marked 'Top Secret' and shelved because at that time the Soviet Union had just agreed at Yalta to join in the war against Japan and it therefore contained 'great possibilities of embarrassment'.

6. The State Department have informed us that in welcome contrast to the attitude of hostility so often shown by some members of such Congressional Committees, the Select Committee in this case accepted their testimony virtually without comment.

A further report will be submitted when the course of the hearings of the Committee in this second phase of the investigation is more clearly defined …

The British Government's Last Stand

There were many people who were keenly waiting for a clearer conclusion from the investigation. On 13 August 1952, a letter from Professor Douglas Savory appeared in the *Daily Telegraph*. He said that the Leader of the House had felt obliged to reject his appeal and that time should be found in Parliament to debate the motion, signed by 120 members, urging the British delegation at the United Nations to support the American delegation in bringing the Report of the Select Committee of the House of Representatives before the General Assembly; and eventually, that the matter be referred to the International Court of Justice.

An American representative approached Sir Gladwyn Jebb,[18] British Permanent Representative of the UK to the United Nations, who reacted immediately. He said the debate would not be allowed at the General Assembly, for the simple reason that the resolution was political and anti-Soviet, and gave the impression that the US and

UK were blackguarding the Russians. It would serve no purpose but inflame hostility between East and West. On receiving Jebb's brief, Statham of the FO agreed that it would be embarrassing to have a debate on the subject because it would publicise the UK's shoddy ambivalence. His colleague G. Littlejohn-Cook retorted:

> It is not that we wish to avoid all publicity on Katyn, but that we wish to avoid having to admit in Parliament or in New York, that in spite of much circumstantial evidence, the case against the Russians is not proven. An official publicity is all to the good, but we do not wish to have to comment on the evidence in the Select Committee's report, some of which was simply fantastic.

Nevertheless, Eden's telegram despatched to New York strongly objected to raising the question in the United Nations.[19]

The FO attitude towards the Katyn affair did not shift an inch. Sir William Strang reiterated that Britain was not associated with and did not subscribe to the conclusions of the Select Committee of the United States House of Representatives. The investigation did not shed any new light on the crime because it was not carried out with the full co-operation of the governments concerned.

From the FO files, it is clear that the Foreign Office did not pressurise the Russians in 1943, 1953 or 1956, when an unofficial brief of 13 April by the IRD (Information Research Department) of the FO was freely circulated:

> This view has been arrived at after careful research. Western opinion has for some years been in no doubt that the massacre in 1940 of more than 4,000 Polish officers was among the most brutal crimes committed by the Government of the Soviet Union at any time in its history.

For the first time, the IRD's brief[20] contained the history of what actually happened. It described Soviet duplicity, the evidence of the Polish Red Cross working committee and the inconsistency in the Soviet report. It contained evidence from the surviving inmates of Kozelsk camp and the US Congress Select Committee's report and its findings. IRD's brief was qualified by the Northern Department as late as November 1960, as 'an independent research study, which had no official status'.

This supercilious attitude of the senior officers, their reluctance to admit the truth in public because they did not see 'what purpose would be served by appearing to blackguard the Russians' was incomprehensible to those who were dealing with Katyn at the lower levels of the FCO in 1956.

Notes

1 TNA FO 371/86679 NP 1661/6, confidential air courier despatch from the British Embassy in Washington enclosing Bliss Lane's copies of letters and newspaper cuttings of two articles published in the *New York Herald Tribune* on 3 and 4 July 1949, written by Julius Epstein, a

journalist who had served in the Office of War Information. 'Murder of 10,000 Polish PoWs in Katyn Forest still unsolved – Germans and Russians accuse each other – Writer urges Inquiry into wartime slayings'; and 'Soviet guilt for Katyn murders indicated by mass of evidence – Neutral enquiry under UN is urged to verify fate of thousands of Polish officers'.

2 TNA FO 371/100719 NP 1661/1, note dated 6 February 1952.

3 TNA FO 371/86679 NP1661/6 comments by FORD staff: A. F. Maddocks, D.S. Watson, J.Grant Purves, G. W. Shaw, on a despatch from the British Embassy in Washington dated 29 June 1950.

4 TNA FO 371/94780 NP 1661/3.

5 TNA FO 371/100719 N 1661/9 *The Katyn Forest Massacre: Hearings before the Select Committee to conduct an investigation of the facts, evidence and circumstances of the Katyn Forest massacre*, Part 2, 4, 7 February 1952, United States Government Printing Office, Washington 1952.

6 TNA FO 371 /100719 NP 1661/4, inward saving telegram No 324, 28th March 1952, annotated in red ink by Sir Anthony Eden.

7 TNA LCO 2/5172, note No. 5310, 3 April 1952.

8 TNA PREM 11/311 annex, draft of third person note to United States Ambassador regarding Katyn massacre, 7 April 1952.

9 TNA FO 371/97631 U 1661/13, inward saving telegram No 376 of 10 April 1952 from Ambassador Oliver Franks to the FO and Whitehall distribution.

10 *Hearings before the Select Committee to conduct an Investigation of the Facts, Evidence and Circumstances of the Katyn Forest Massacre Eighty-Second Congress, Second Session on Investigation of the Murder of thousands of Polish officers in the Katyn Forest near Smolensk, Russia.* Part 4, held in London, April 16–19 1952. Published in Washington 1952.

11 TNA FO 371/97632 U1661/22, 18 April 1952.

12 TNA LCO 2 /5172 AU 1661/23, confidential note No.507 by Robert Cecil, head of American Department FO to Sir Oliver Franks, British ambassador in Washington, dated 5 May 1952.

13 TNA FO 371/97632 U1661/22, briefs by R. Cecil, R. Barclay, Sir William Strang and Sir Anthony Eden, all April 1952.

14 TNA FO 371/97632 U 1661/25, WO (branch minutes) 1937 / MI 11 (L), 13 May 1952.

15 TNA FO 371/100719 NP 1661/11 and 12, notes on German war film on Katyn, from 25 April 1952.

16 TNA FO 371/100719 NP 1661/9, a copy of the report, part II on the Hearings in Washington of the Katyn Murders on 4–7 February 1952. Includes comments by N. Statham, T. S. Tull and Geoffrey W. Shaw.

17 TNA FO 371/100719, NP 1661/20 confidential despatch via air courier No. 535, dated 20 November 1952 from Sir Oliver Franks, British Ambassador in Washington, to Sir Anthony Eden, Secretary of State at the Foreign Office; and Statham's views on Roosevelt's administration.

18 Hubert Miles Gladwyn Jebb (1900–1996) entered Diplomatic Service in 1924, served in Tehran and Rome. Private Secretary to Permanent Under Secretary of State 1937–1940; onetime Private Secretary of Lord Cadogan and chief executive of SOE. Counsellor in the FO and in that capacity attended the Conferences of Tehran, Yalta and Potsdam; Executive Secretary of Preparatory Commission of the United Nations 1945; Assistant Under Secretary of State and United Nations Adviser 1946–1947; Permanent Representative of the UK to the United Nations 1950–1954, GCMG; Ambassador to France 1954–1960.

19 TNA FO 371/100719 1662/17/52, 30 July 1952, NP 1661/15 28, 25 August 1952.

20 TNA FCO 28 / 714 B 334, The Katyn Wood Murders, 4-page typescript with footnotes, unsigned, [13] April 1956.

chapter nine

PUBLICATIONS

The exiled Poles would not and could not submit to the Soviet lies. With each succeeding anniversary, a fresh wave of agitation would begin and although the British government would keep its distance, some MPs would actively support any Polish initiative. The Anglo-Scottish and Anglo-Polish Societies and some British writers would bring Katyn to the government's and the world's attention. One of the lesser known but extremely well edited publications was a'Press Bulletin' of the League for European Freedom, under the chairmanship of the Duchess of Atholl with the Dean of Chichester as her deputy. The January 1949 issue was devoted to the Burdenko report on Katyn at Nuremberg. Exasperated officials at the now renamed Foreign and Commonwealth Office considered these articles 'a scourge, which only opens an old wound'.

Professor Hudson's *A Polish Challenge*

The unsatisfactory outcome of the Nuremberg trials prompted people of conscience to write about the injustice suffered by the Poles. A Cambridge scholar, Professor George Hudson, during the war a member of FORD who had left the Department for academia in 1946, gave a barely publicised lecture at the Royal Institute of International Affairs at Chatham House, entitled *A Polish Challenge,* which was subsequently published in *International Affairs,* the journal of the Institute, in April 1950. A short section is quoted here; his analysis would be picked up during the 1972 parliamentary debate, as will be seen later.

> … As Russian advocacy made such a poor showing at Nuremberg, it is *a fortiori* probable that it would be less effective if confronted in a court of law with the massive evidence, which the Poles in exile have now assembled and published. At Nuremberg the German defence counsel conducted his case with ability, but he was unaware of the Polish evidence and had no access to it. He was unaware,

for example, that between September 1941 and August 1942, in the period of Polish-Russian *rapprochement*, the Polish Government addressed eight enquiries about the missing officers to the Soviet Commissariat of Foreign Affairs, that the question was taken up three times with Stalin personally, once by the Polish Ambassador Kot, once by the Polish Prime Minister, General Sikorski, on his visit to Moscow in December 1941, and once by General Anders, and that the British Ambassador, Sir Stafford Cripps, also made enquiries in the matter. On no occasion did Stalin, Molotov, or Vyshinsky even hint that the Germans had captured the prisoners.

... The British and American Governments at this point [1943] definitely sided with Russia against Poland, both diplomatically and through officially inspired publicity. It was indeed obvious that a neutral enquiry which assigned Russia responsibility for the massacre would be morally disastrous for the common cause of the Allies against Hitler; the Polish Government itself subsequently recognised that the request for an International Red Cross enquiry was inexpedient, and had in fact only made it to allay the agitation in the Polish army, which contained large numbers of relatives and friends of the prisoners missing in Russia. But the adverse attitude of the British and American Governments was due not to a simple faith in Russian innocence or to doubts about the International Red Cross – this was the first and last time that either its impartiality or its competence for an investigation concerning prisoners of was called in question by the Western Allies – but to the information in their possession, not then available to the public, showing how strong was the *prima facie* against Russia.

The British and American policies were therefore necessary in terms of *raison d'état*, but they had far reaching political consequences. From the Russian point of view a breach of relations with the Polish Government in London was in any case required sooner or later, if Russia was to have a free hand to set up a puppet administration in Poland after driving out the Germans, but it was difficult for Russia to find a pretext for such a break which would put Poland in the wrong in the eyes of the world, and it was only the British and American reaction to the Katyn disclosures which enabled Russia to isolate Poland diplomatically and pose as the aggrieved party in what was fundamentally a policy of aggression. Relations between the Kremlin and the Polish Government, once broken off, were never resumed, and Britain and America, having once endorsed the Russian case against the Polish Government, found no firm ground on which to stand until they were driven to their final betrayal of the Polish national cause at Yalta.

Thus the Katyn case was decisive for the whole course of events concerning Poland from 1943 onwards, and Poland suffered a double disaster, first in having had several thousands of officers and other prisoners of war massacred, and secondly in being universally condemned for suggesting that the matter called for impartial investigation. Now that the war is over, however, the question of responsibility for the massacre still remains, and it is hardly decent to argue that the truth which it was in 1943 too dangerous to seek is today of too little importance to be worth discussing.

Janusz Zawodny and Louis FitzGibbon

In the 1960s, the most popular of the books on Katyn was Janusz K. Zawodny's *Death in the Forest.* Published in 1962 in English, it was based entirely on Polish sources and the US Congressional Committee's findings and remains the most quoted book in bibliographies on Katyn. There were four books written by an Englishman, Louis Fitzgibbon, which drew more publicity: *Katyn – a Crime without Parallel* 1971; *The Katyn cover-up* 1972; *Katyn – Triumph of Evil,* 1975; and *Unpitied and Unknown – Katyn,* 1975. All were based largely on the Polish government-in-exile's documentation gathered between 1941 and 1946, as well as the Foreign Office files opened in 1972.

Miesięcznik Literacki

A note, *Inconvenient Memories*, written by Richard O. Miles of the EE&S (East European and Soviet) Department on 2 October 1969, drew the attention of his colleagues to an article written by Wojciech Żukrowski in the September issue of *Miesięcznik Literacki* (Monthly Literary) in Poland. For the first time since the communists took power in Poland, a Polish writer stated in print that the Soviet army had invaded Poland on 17 September 1939. It was baffling to all who read it, how had it managed to bypass the censor? The only explanation could have been a comradeship between the author and General Mieczysław Moczar, member of both the Secretariat and the Politburo. It became clear to most of the IRD staff that people in Poland generally accepted Russian responsibility for Katyn.

British Foreign Policy in the Second World War

The impending publication of Sir Llewellyn Woodward's *British Foreign Policy in the Second World War*, (official history series) caused a stir within the FCO corridors. It was printed by HMSO in December 1971 after Woodward's death. The text on Katyn was taken from the FO documents; to be precise, from Ambassador O'Malley's report, which declared: 'It may be said that the victims were Polish and that these were killed in the spring of 1940, almost certainly about March and April of that year.' In May 1971, when the book was already printed but not yet published, Robin Hankey of SSRD, the Soviet Section Research Department, spotted the controversial reference not picked up previously by the FO, and reacted immediately. A sharp interchange followed with the Library and Records Department. Hankey pointed out that 'No judicial enquiry with satisfactory claims to objectivity has ever been held on the Katyn massacre and Ambassador O'Malley's despatch in May 1943 represented his own conclusions only.' The common-sense reply was that since O'Malley's documents on which Woodward's statement was based would be available at the Public Record Office in 1972; it would be pointless to deny it, as historians would see the truth for themselves.[1]

The *Daily Telegraph* and *The Sunday Times*

The other two notable authors who focused very much on O'Malley's two despatches of 1943 were journalist Ian Colvin of the *Daily Telegraph* in his 'Katyn Wood Report' (July 1972) and Lord Nicholas Bethell for *The Sunday Times* Magazine, 'Britain Stays Silent on Stalin's Massacre', (May 1972). Full of blistering words of condemnation, Bethell challenged Lord Avon (Sir Anthony Eden) to speak up – 'If he wanted to, he could wipe the slate just a little bit cleaner with a minimum of embarrassment.' Lord Bethell, before publishing the text, sent a copy of the draft to Eden for comments. In prior communication with Sir Denis Allen and Sir Frank Roberts, the two most experienced diplomats on the Katyn issue in the FO, Eden replied curtly that having read the debate in the House of Lords last June, he agreed with the line taken by Lord Aberdare the government spokesman that 'to seek to give further publicity to this episode could have no effect except that of reopening old wounds.'

Frank Roberts, who was at the British Embassy in Moscow, complained that relations with the Soviet Union were ruined each time Katyn was brought back into the spotlight by the exiled Poles.

Julian L. Bullard of the EE&SD spoke to Sir Owen O'Malley, who by now was quite elderly and out of the diplomatic limelight. He said that he appreciated the British government's position and would agree with any statement they might make as a result of Bethell's article. It was evident that the Department expected some sort of pressure from the press for a statement to be made, intending to put right the injustice done by the wartime hushing-up of the crime, even if it meant associating the British government directly with the charge that the massacre was carried out by the Soviets. It was a perfect opportunity to disclose the shame. This, of course, the Government refused to do. Nothing was to be gained by changing its tune now, and in consequence, a neither affirm nor deny attitude was adopted by Whitehall, irrespective of who was in government at the time.[2]

The BBC Documentary

The Soviet Political Bureau – Leonid Breznev, Aleksei Kosygin, Mikhail Suslov, Yuri Andropov, Konstantin Katushev, Borys Panomarov, Konstantin Rusakov and Andrei Gromyko – once again supported the monumental structure of the lie. They approved Gromyko the Foreign Affairs Commissar sending instructions to Mikhail Smernovsky, the Russian Ambassador in London, to present a démarche to the British with regard to the Katyn monument proposed for West London. He was to express indignation because Britain was well aware that the Military Tribunal at Nuremberg had acknowledged the offence to be German. On 16 April 1971, Ivan Ippolitov of the Soviet Embassy called upon Wynn Hugh-Jones of the Russian Department of the FCO with a complaint about a forthcoming programme on BBC 2, a drama documentary based on the diary of Major Adam Solski, entitled *The Issue Should be Avoided*. Ippolitov called it an unfriendly act that would damage the good relations between the two countries and would create ill will towards the Soviet Union and Poland. He demanded that the BBC be persuaded to abandon the film. Hugh-Jones replied that the BBC was autonomous and it was not within the power of the FCO to prevent them from transmitting a programme. However, he agreed that the Russian representations would be brought to the BBC's attention: 'The BBC needs to co-ordinate their multifarious foreign activities a little more closely.' As a result, the programme shown on 19 April was extremely carefully presented so as not to incriminate the Russians overtly. Nonetheless, the Polish communist government in collusion with the Soviets called off the planned visit to Warsaw by the BBC Director General Charles Curran in protest.[3]

The incident had reverberations in Moscow, Warsaw and Bonn because it resurrected the story of an alleged conversation on Katyn between Nikita Khrushchev and Władysław Gomułka during the de-stalinization period in 1956. The story lacked proof but was recorded in 1971 by Richard T. Jenkins of the East European and Soviet Section; apparently, while in Warsaw in 1965, he was told by a Soviet history student Yuri Poliakov that Khrushchev disclosed to Gomułka the Polish communist leader that Stalin was to blame for the Katyn massacre. Gomułka allegedly refused to go public for fear of inflaming further anti-Soviet feelings in Poland. This report was despatched to the Embassies in Moscow and in Bonn after an article on the same subject appeared in April 1971 in the *Neue Zurcher Zeitung*, indicating that Prime Minister Edward Gierek neglected the matter after the Poznań riots of 1956.[4]

Notes

1 TNA FCO 28/1475 ENP 10/1, correspondence between R. Hankey, Soviet Section Research Department of the FO and Rohan Butler Library and Records Department, dated between 18 May and 18 November 1971.

2 TNA FCO 28/1945, ENP 10/1.

3 TNA FCO 28/1475, ENP 10/1, correspondences between 20 April and 17 May 1971; *Katyn Dokumenty Ludobójstwa,* Institute of Political Studies PAN, letter by Gromyko 12 April 1971.

4 Ibid.

chapter ten

FAILURE AT THE UN – SUCCESS WITH THE MEMORIAL

Very little is known about the attempt to bring Katyn to the attention of the United Nations General Assembly. The Polish government-in-exile was still functioning in London, but had no power or any recognition from Western governments. It had to rely entirely on British friends, influential or otherwise, who would take up their cause – clandestinely or openly. Many of them sympathised with the Poles, some even fought tirelessly on their behalf, amongst them Lord Barnby, Lord St. Oswald and Airey Neave MP; others joined in when the question of raising a monument to the dead became such a problem. After the war, Sir Owen O'Malley, who steadfastly stood his ground for so many years, was strangely silent. In his autobiography *The Phantom Caravan*, published in 1954, he does not even mention Katyn, as though it never happened in his wartime diplomatic career.

Airey Neave MP

Airey Neave,[1] who was at Nuremberg as an official investigating officer, felt uneasy with the result on Katyn and supported the Polish idea to present the case at the UN General Assembly. He looked for advice and guidance from Merrick S. Baker-Bates, head of the UN (E & S) Department of the FCO. He was told that according to the rules, a private individual or even a group of MPs could not put an item on the agenda of the Assembly because they did not represent the British government, who would very likely resist the idea. There was no procedural reason why the British government or any other member state of the United Nations should not seek to put Katyn on the General Assembly's agenda. But the British government had avoided ascertaining the truth for nearly 30 years – changing now they might be ridiculed. Neave, like O'Malley, also had to abandon the idea of taking the matter to the ICRC (International Committee of the Red Cross) in the context of treatment of PoWs. Baker-Bates, who anticipated that the ICRC would not want to be involved in a politically contentious question, dissuaded him.[2]

The Polish Diaspora, especially in Britain and the US, had organised meetings and petitions in support of the motion. The Federation of Poles in Great Britain, embracing some 54 organisations, made representation to the British government requesting condemnation of the perpetrators 'in the interest of humanity, truth, justice and history'.[3] A letter addressed to the British government written by the Secretary of the Worcester Branch of the Polish Ex-Combatants Association, Mieczysław Jarkowski (the Honorary Chairman of the Association in Great Britain), also indicated that an attempt was being made to bring Katyn to the attention of the United Nations. It simply read:

> My committee, which represents the Polish community in Worcester, begs you to sign the appeal of Mr Neave MP, calling for investigation by the International Court of the Katyn murders. We feel that this matter has been shrouded in secrecy for far too long.

Lord Barnby's Brave Efforts

Lord Barnby[4] was to raise the all-important parliamentary question on 17 June 1971, while Lord St Oswald's supplementary questions were to follow. The House of Lords were to consider

> ... whether Her Majesty's Government will now support an effect to secure pronouncement establishing beyond contention the authorship of the mass murder of over 4,000 Polish officer prisoners of war in the Katyn Forest near Smolensk, Russia, in the spring of 1940, and bring to light the disappearance without trace of a further 10,000 Polish officers interned in 1939 in the Soviet camps of Ostaszkow and Starobielsk.

Lord Barnby's presentation was preceded by an aide-mémoire, which he wrote in a questionnaire format and sent to Maurice, Lord Aberdare, for presentation at the Despatch Box in the House of Lords. The note was analysed and commented on on 16 June 1971 at the East European and Soviet Department of the FCO by Lord Robin Hankey, long-serving First Under Secretary of State, who considered Barnby's presentation rather weak and not at all original. He compared it to the prefaces of FitzGibbon's four books, not considering it material for a serious debate on policy. The style apparently did not appeal to him as he paraphrased Barnby's text:

Why should we, in Britain, be concerned with this?

– Because Poland was our ally, for whom we went to war. Poland contributed magnificently to victory, but because of Yalta, Poland herself achieved no freedom for herself. Because of Russia, we did not allow the Poles to take part in the Victory March. If we accepted Poland's sacrifices in time of war, we must help them now over an elucidation of the crime at Katyn.

What object will all this serve?

– If nothing else, it will show our gallant ex-allies that they are not forgotten and if a judgement can be achieved on an international forum, it will at least provide some kind of 'moral indemnification for the thousands of surviving widows and other relatives and brother officers of the victims.

Lord Hankey's Brief

Lord Hankey, perhaps the oldest and most knowledgeable authority on Katyn, knocked down almost all of Barnby's arguments; first, one of the reasons why the British government did not pay much attention to the US Select Committee was that its members apparently subscribed to the principles of Macarthyism and that was why the conclusions of the Select Committee were not officially adopted. More to the point, he considered Barnby naive not to realise that an admission to 30 years of lies by the Russians would have an explosive effect in Poland and Eastern Europe. On the question of the international 'conspiracy of silence', a taboo subject in political and diplomatic circles, he retorted with truly British pragmatism:[5]

> Fear of offending Russia is not the only reason for the hushing up of the matter; the question is whether an International Inquiry, (which would in fact certainly exclude countries in the Soviet bloc and perhaps be entirely a 'Western' inquiry), could amass any new facts (there are a good many publications already available after all) and come to any decisive 'judgement' in the absence of Soviet and communist Polish co-operation. Probably such an inquiry would be just a public repetition of evidence already in print. In fact the crime has very likely been elucidated as much as it ever will be.
>
> The subject is presumably 'taboo' in the Soviet bloc. Western diplomats presumably in turn feel that there is nothing to gain by striking quixotic attitudes. Given the facts of power, how can Britain be responsible for Poland's tragedy (especially Katyn)? Or is it, as seems to me implied in 'because of Yalta', where Churchill did about as much as he could for Poland in the circumstances, given the facts of power and Roosevelt's credulity.

According to Hankey's brief, Aberdare was to refute Barnby's arguments and declare the matter to be a moral issue, rather than a legal one. He was to point out that the British were not associated with any of the three investigations carried out by the Germans, the Russians and the Americans. Since the truth was not established in 1941, 1944, 1946 or 1952, what chance would the new enquiry have to establish guilt 'beyond contention'? The debate ended with by now well-worn Katyn cliché: 'the only result of a new enquiry would be to re-open old wounds.'[6]

Parliamentary Debate

On 17 June 1971, Hansard recorded the proceedings at the House of Lords' question time, under the heading: *Polish War Prisoners: Mass Murder in Russia.*[7] After presenting the question, Lord Barnby began his speech:

> My Lords, it is a curious coincidence of Parliamentary Orders that two consecutive matters of business should each refer to countries, which are alleged to be in the unfortunate position of being oppressed. With the indulgence of the House, I would say that having heard the discussion on the previous Bill I am reminded that I happen to be among the few in this House who actually sat in another place with the Irish, and tonight I heard the familiar talk of the 'oppression' by Britain of another country. Perhaps I might tell the House with regard to my Motion that the first time I visited Poland was when she was under the oppression of a foreign country, as the Congress of Poland was still under the subjection of Russia.
>
> To turn to my Question, it has of course no Party partisan aspect. In that way, it is the more pleasing to put forward. I seek to report a gap in history, in the hope that there might be put in motion an exploration through some recognised international authority, which will correct the omission …
>
> There has been a complete conspiracy of silence. There is a blank in history as to the authorship of this odious crime. There has been much talk in other circles of our obligation, the British obligation for the respect of international morality. There are other concurrent contemporary topics. I feel this is one, which justifies ourselves and the other Allies examining our consciences.
>
> If I may be pardoned for striking a personal note. I speak on this matter because between the wars I visited the then Polish Independent Republic four or five times a year and travelled widely. I knew at that time a good deal about Poland and I was astonished, as all noble Lords would have been had they been there, at the achievements of Poland in the integration in a short time of the currency, weights and measures and legal system. Those three systems were merged into one as a result of the fusing together of the areas occupied by Russia, Austria and Germany.
>
> A similar Motion to this one, with over 180 signatures to it, is down for debate in another place. I understand that steps are being taken to put this matter on the

> agenda of the United Nations Human Rights Committee, or before the General Assembly of the United Nations, which next meets in September. It will be thought by many: why raise this subject now so long after its occurrence? My Lords, what are the thoughts of the relatives of those murdered men and all the other Poles who died in the Allied cause in the last war? No indemnification was ever received by any of them. Now the relatives of those living in our country, ageing, many in dire poverty, believe that their feelings would receive some balm if they could only be assured as to what has happened and what was the fate of these people. Many of them are living with us in an alien country without normal contact with their own people …
>
> I would urge that the Minister in reply not only offers sympathy, but also the prospect of some action of an effective character. I beg to ask the Question.

In the absence of an accredited spokesman Peter, Marquis of Lothian, the Minister of State for Health and Social Services Lord Aberdare, was asked to take the questions and hold a debate on Katyn in the House of Lords, on 17 June 1971.

A key brief from Sir Thomas Brimelow, Parliamentary Under Secretary of State, was prepared for Lord Aberdare – to resist the parliamentary pressure to allow a fresh enquiry, which would pin the blame on the Soviets. He admitted that personally, he believed that this was where the blame lies, but the British government had a lot to lose by becoming involved in an international wrangle. He did not think it would succeed, since no co-operation from the Soviets or the Polish government would be forthcoming. The whole subject was horrible to him and the best course was to 'let the dead bury the dead'. Sir Thomas knew very well the difference between a letter and a statement in Parliament, which, once recorded in Hansard, would cause a fierce reaction from the Polish (Warsaw) and Soviet governments. He advised accordingly:[8]

> It is true that both Houses of Parliament would like HMG to attribute responsibility for the Katyn massacres to the Soviet Government. But I do not think that it would be in the interest of HMG to make any statement in the House, which might be held to have this implication. It is a controversy in which we have nothing to gain, but in which our relations with the Soviet and Polish Governments could be harmed. No one expects HMG as a Government to act as an arbiter on historical debates in general, though individual members of the Government may hold personal views on such debates. This is a subject best left to historical researches and personal conclusions of private individuals. The Noble Lord [Lord Barnby] is fully justified in pointing out that at the time of the Katyn murders, Poland was an active, loyal and valued ally of this country; but it does not in 1971 give to HMG a 'locus standi' for calling for a further investigation into this crime.

Lord Aberdare followed the FCO briefs and stood his ground, but soon realised that the debate had not been handled satisfactorily as complaints were coming in thick and fast to the office, demanding satisfaction from the Government – or at least an expression of their view.

Sir Alec Douglas Home and EE&SD Brief

An Early Day Motion on Katyn was going to be put before the House of Commons on 12 July 1971, by Airey Neave. He was instrumental in persuading 193 members of the House of Commons to sign a petition in support of the Motion. Extremely dissatisfied with futile debate in the House of Lords, where the 'old wounds' mantra returned, Neave reacted angrily – 'Whose wounds are these?' It was imperative for him and Lord St Oswald to see Secretary of State Sir Alec Douglas-Home. Neave was persistent in arguing that this most atrocious crime committed against PoWs, was a case worthy of bringing before the Human Rights Conference in Vienna.[9] A meeting was arranged for 19 July 1971, and John P. Weston of the East European and Soviet Department offered to prepare a brief. It consisted of carefully selected comments and arguments as expressed by senior officials of the Foreign Office over a number of years. Most is background history, which need not be repeated here, only points regarding 'HMG attitudes' and 'defensive arguments' as underlined by Douglas-Home are highlighted.[10]

> We welcome the chance to speak frankly about HMG's attitude towards Katyn.
>
> It is true that there has been a working assumption in the Foreign Office for many years that the Russians were responsible for Katyn. But that does not mean that HMG as a Government should now make a public pronouncement as to where the guilt lies. There are nevertheless certain constraints, which make it difficult for HMG to avoid comment altogether on this subject, if we are to appear inconsistent or disingenuous.
>
> HMG cannot be expected to act as an arbiter of historical debates. It may be true that both Houses of Parliament would like HMG to attribute responsibility for the Katyn massacre to the Soviet Government. But it is difficult to see that it would be in the interest of HMG to make any statement which might be held to have this implication. No one expects HMG to act as an arbiter on historical debates in general, though individual members of the Government may hold personal views on such debates; the Department do not consider that HMG should be expected to depart from this principle in the case of Katyn.
>
> If the facts about Katyn are known, why the need for further action? If the facts are not sufficiently established, why should HMG be expected to express a view, and what good would a new enquiry do without the help of the Polish and Soviet Governments?

> There is in fact an inherent weakness in the position of Lord St. Oswald and Mr Airey Neave, to which the Secretary of State might wish to draw attention. In pressing for a new effort to 'secure pronouncement establishing beyond contention' the authorship of the Katyn massacre, they are compelled to argue either (a) that the facts about Katyn are well known, i.e. the Soviet Government is guilty, in which case no further effort to establish the authorship of the crime would appear to be necessary; or (b) that some new enquiry is first necessary to establish the facts to universal satisfaction; in which case it must be asked why HMG should now be expected to express a public view if the evidence is still incomplete, and whether any new enquiry would be likely to succeed without the cooperation of the Polish and Soviet Governments, which is not to be expected in the circumstances. Lord St. Oswald's case therefore comes down to a request for public condemnation of the Soviet Government by Britain (and others) without further ado, which is not a course of action likely to advance HMG's interests in any way whatever. But we see no advantage in breaking the silence that we have preserved for nearly 30 years on the Katyn massacre.
>
> HMG does not shrink from criticising Soviet actions where British interests require it e.g. the Soviet threat in the Indian Ocean.
> Defensive point 12
> HMG will not take an initiative to raise Katyn at the UN, because as Lord Salisbury said in the House of Lords this would be useless without Soviet cooperation.

Sir Alec must have convinced the two politicians, as the parliamentary debate was not picked up again. Lord Aberdare dropped the case with a final statement:

> My Lords, as I told the House on 29 June, I meant that we are speaking of the murder and disappearance of Polish officers on Soviet territory.

The Katyn Memorial Fund

Undaunted by failure in both Houses of Parliament, Airey Neave wrote on 28 February 1972 to the Secretary of State Sir Alec Douglas-Home, asking whether there would be any objection to the erection of a monument to the dead of Katyn in one of the Royal Parks in London. The idea, conceived some time before, was chiefly to help the families who wanted to have a place to grieve for their husbands and fathers murdered 'on Soviet territory'. A Memorial Fund was launched and a Committee was formed under the chairmanship of Lord Barnby, Airey Neave and Lord St Oswald deputising; the task of Honorary Secretary was given to Louis FitzGibbon and Honorary Treasurer to Helen Marcinek, English wife of a Polish officer. The patrons of the Memorial included a number of prominent Polish émigré and British personalities.[11]

On 28 May, an article was to appear in the *Sunday Times* by Lord Bethell and EE&SD was busy telephoning war-time diplomats (Lord Avon – Anthony Eden – Sir Frank Roberts, Sir Dennis Allen and Sir Owen O' Malley), to warn them of the official policy on Katyn and that they must stick to the official line if the press were to quiz them. At 87 years of age Sir Owen was probably not too concerned about the FCO's admonitons but he towed the line anyway. In his article, Bethel refers to these gentlemen who were no longer in government, and asks them to do the decent thing and admit the truth of what they personally, secretly believed.

Urged by Julian Bullard, Douglas-Home, the Secretary of State, agreed to see Neave and Lord Barnby on 6 June, with a view to persuading them to drop the project, as Warsaw and Moscow interpreted it as a 'calculated political act'. Douglas-Home argued that it would not help the dead or the living and would be regarded only as 'a salve to one's conscience'. But there was a hidden agenda regarding relations with Russia and Poland, which at that time were fragile and the bilateral talks in the pipe line might have been affected. Douglas-Home advised Neave to look for a private place – a Polish church or a cemetery would be eminently suitable. During further discussions, Neave retracted his original pledge that there would be no inscriptions on the monument or any statement attributing responsibility to the Russians. It was a difficult pledge to honour, as an appeal for funds was already printed and distributed with the forbidden text. By that time a sum of £8,000 had been collected, a good part of it from Members of Parliament. Encouraged by this response, Count Stefan Zamoyski had the courage and audacity to invite the Secretary of State to contribute; he did not.[12]

The first location chosen was Thurloe Place, on Cromwell Road, jointly controlled by the Victoria and Albert Museum and the Department of Education (DOE). Permission was refused. Ironically, some years later at that particular spot a monument was erected and dedicated to the victims of another wretched act of Soviet violence, the pro-German Cossacks who were deported by force from occupied post-war Germany back to Russia by the disingenuous British government, where Stalin's reprisal awaited them.

Another position was sought, this time in St Luke's disused churchyard gardens in Chelsea. The local council was willing to give permission, but discreet pressure by Whitehall on Church authorities together with organised opposition from the residents, who feared public demonstrations on their doorstep, put an end to the project. The Committee fought but lost on appeal to the Diocesan Consistory Court.

With the change in government, Lord Barnby wrote to the Labour Party Minister Goronwy Roberts for his understanding and support. Roy Hattersley, the Minister's Parliamentary Private Secretary, answered on his behalf in a predictable manner.[13]

> It would be wrong for me to give you the impression that the present administration would be any readier than their predecessors either to be associated with the plan to erect a memorial in this country or to promote a new enquiry into

> the circumstances of the massacre. HMG have absolutely no standing in this matter and that the only result of a new enquiry would be to open old wounds.

Julian Bullard's brief[14] for Douglas-Home included some of his personal views, which were bordering on the cynical. He could not see the reason why HMG should authorise a monument to the victims of Katyn, rather than to those of any other atrocity that occurred in a foreign country during the war. He advised the government to stop this 'gratuitous irritant' and tell the sponsors that they could erect a monument inside one of the Polish churches or cemeteries, or play for time and steer the Poles to a less conspicuous site. Either way, the FCO had to approve any inscription.

Airey Neave had another meeting, this time with Anthony Royle, the Permanent Under Secretary of State, on the subject of the inscription, repeating almost the same arguments as Bullard. Neave this time stood his ground. Having visible support from an all-party committee, amongst them Peter Archer, Lord Barnby, Sir George Sinclair, Winston Churchill, Sir Tufton Beamish and William Hamling, he would not bow to Royle's wishes and asked him to face the committee himself. He rejected the notion that Anglo-Polish relations were at stake; the heart of the matter was 'the recognition of a serious injustice'. He asked the Under Secretary how long HMG 'should submit to covering up Soviet responsibility'.[15]

In 1975, a 20-foot black granite obelisk was erected with a large engraving of the year '1940' and the words: 'The conscience of the world cries out for a testimony to the truth.' Hidden among the trees in the tranquillity of Kensington & Chelsea Cemetery next to Gunnersbury Park in west London, the monument was unveiled by Mrs Maria Chełmecka, widow of an officer murdered in Katyn. With dignity and prayers, completely unacknowledged by the British authorities, the monument became a symbol of the truth. It is known that those who attended unofficially were forbidden to wear uniforms, but Sir Frederic Bennett, Major John Gouriet and Air Marshal Sir Walter Merton turned out in full dress. Also present were the representatives of the British Legion and some 20 MPs. Two Scottish pipers played a moving lament, in the absence of the Royal Artillery Band, who had previously been criticised for playing at an Anglo-Polish function. The FCO did not want to be seen condoning the association of the Band with a 'political forum' or to associate British military personnel, even indirectly, 'in any way that might have implications for relations with Poland and ultimately the Soviet Union'.[16]

Notes

1 Airey Neave, (1916–1979) MP, officer of the Territorial Army, sent to France 1940, wounded and taken prisoner Oflag IX and Stalag IXa in Toruń, Poland. Escaped, caught and imprisoned in Colditz, escaped again, reached London 1942. Capt. recruited for MI 9 escape and evasion operations as intelligence officer. After the war served on BWCE at Nuremberg, empathised with the Polish cause. Assassinated, probably by the INLA (Irish National Liberation Army).

2 TNA FCO 28 /1475 ENP10/1, M. S. Baker-Bates' brief UN (E & S) Department of the FCO to G. Walden Eastern European and Soviet Department (E&SD), 14 June 1971.
3 TNA FCO 28 / 1475 ENP 10/1, correspondence between 16 May and 24 May 1971, signed by the chairman Franciszek Miszczak, Czesław Kolarczyk and Józef Płoski.
4 Lord Barnby, Colonel, CMG, CBE, Chairman of the Katyn Memorial Fund.
5 TNA FCO 28 / 1475 ENP 10/1, analysis of Lord Barnby's aide memoir by Lord Hankey, 16 June 1971.
6 TNA FCO 28/ 1476 ENP 10/1, 22 June 1971, also in FCO 28 /1945 ENP 10/1, 17 June 1971.
7 TNA FCO 28/ 1475, copy of Hansard from17 June 1971, 5.17 pm, covering Lord Barnby's Motion on Katyn.
8 TNA FCO 28/1476 ENP 10/1, note by Sir Thomas Brimelow for Lord Aberdare intended as a reply to Lord St. Oswald's question about Katyn in the House of Lords, 6 July 1971.
9 TNA FCO 28 / 1945, minutes of the meeting taken by J.A.N. Graham, Private Secretary of Sir Alec, between Airey Neave MP, Lord St. Oswald and Sir Alec Douglas-Home, typed on 19 July 1971, marked confidential for Mr Weston (EE&S Department), copies sent to Sir Thomas Brimelow and David Logan, private secretary to PUS.
10 TNA FCO 28 / 1476 ENP 10/1 Part A, brief prepared by the EE&SD of the FCO for Sir Alec Douglas- Home's meeting with Lord St Oswald and Airey Neave on 19 July 1971.
11 Members of the Anglo-Polish Memorial Committee: the Marquis of Salisbury, the Earl of Arran, Viscount Monkton, Lord Barnby, Lord St Oswald, MPs Sir George St Clair, Sir Tufton Beamish, Winston Churchill (grandson of Sir Winston), Airey Neave and Peter Archer; among the Poles: President A. Zaleski, Ambassador E. Raczyński, Generals S. Kopański, L. Ząbkowski, K. Ziemski and Dr Z. Stahl; from the USA A. Mazewski, S. Korboński, S. Kolańczyk.
12 TNA FCO 28/ 1945 ENP 10/1, confidential briefs from EE&SD to Private Secretary from 24 May to July 1972.
13 TNA FCO 28/ 2533 ENP 10/3, letter dated 3 April 1974.
14 TNA FCO 28/ 1945 ENP 10/1 Part A, brief by Julian L. Bullard head of the EE&SD, 11 July 1972.
15 TNA FCO 28/ 1947 ENP 10/1, minutes of the meeting held by A. Royle, PUS and A. Neave MP on 17 October 1972
16 TNA FCO 28/1947 report by Derek Tonkin, EE&SD, 28 November 1972.

chapter eleven

GATHERING OF DOCUMENTS BY THE FCO

In the light of this unprecedented exposure of Katyn in Parliament and in the media, the public became aware of the divergence of opinion within Whitehall. It was considered prudent to prepare a summary of documents on Katyn, in case some British researchers or investigators from abroad challenged the sources.

This task was passed to the Historical Adviser of the FCO, who in his preamble to a memorandum wrote: 'It is like being forewarned of a possible future inflow of archival documentation from Russia and perhaps the Russians might just be forthcoming about Katyn in the future.' Prophetic words! The memorandum was to be the first attempt at compiling Katyn documents and looking afresh at some of the Russian evidence of 1943. It was to be a concise dossier of information for the newcomers at the FCO, who had limited knowledge of the subject and tended to rely on the dated briefs. The collation revealed that some civil servants expressed a different judgement on Katyn to that of British government policy down through the years.

Rohan Butler's Memorandum

Dr Rohan D'Olier Butler was the Historical Adviser to the Secretary of State at the FCO who would organise the work. A Fellow of All Souls Oxford, he was a senior editor of the Foreign Office series *Documents on British Foreign Policy.* Butler's intention was not to present evidence, but to record the reactions of Foreign Office officials to the Katyn story. The interim memorandum contained 35 paragraphs of extracts from documents and confidential papers from various departments, designed only for internal circulation, entitled *Reactions in the Foreign Office to the Katyn Massacre.*[1] It included the material from 1943 onwards; anything prior to it was considered to be already covered by the Research Department - which was an oversight on Butler's part, as evidence despatched by the British Military Mission in Moscow 1940–42 was of some significance. The memo covered the Nuremberg Trials of 1946 and the Congressional Enquiry of 1952. Butler's selection was occasionally surprising. Writing on the Congressional Hearings, he chose to describe the hooded witness, whilst completely ignoring Van Vliet's statements, and more important, he did not disclose the silence kept about Gilder's report. He also accepted and quoted one of Denis Allen's derisive explanations, that the Soviets could not have known the whereabouts of the Polish officers because of a massive administrative breakdown of the Soviet PoW system.

The first draft of the memorandum was ready by 4 September 1972, and Butler passed it onto his colleagues of the EE&SD and IRD (Information Research Department) for appraisal. For the first time since 1944 Professor Sumner's critique of the Burdenko report was to be scrutinised by new people at Whitehall. Butler summed the situation up rather prettily: 'Historical evidence may coincide with political convenience - but the latter does not dictate the former.'

Critical Appraisal of Butler's Report

Mervyn Jones of the IRD, who wrote a topical commentary about *Miesięcznik Literacki* in 1969, was first to express his thoughts on the memorandum. He concentrated particularly on the analysis of the contents of the Russian report and found many discrepancies. He considered Butler's case against the Russians to be understated.[2]

It is not known if Mervyn Jones had read a report of April 1948, which was sent from the British Embassy in Ankara to Sir Anthony Meyer of the IRD. The report was a summary of evidence collected by a Commission of Enquiry set up by General Anders. After the inconclusive verdict at the Nuremberg Trials and the beginning of cooling of Soviet-British relations, the report was intended as a piece of anti-Soviet propaganda. The IRD was very much opposed to the use of the report for this purpose. The British did not want to take a stand in support of General Anders that would elicit criticism in the UK and thereby negate any propaganda value anyway.[3]

Mervyn Jones continued his critical appraisal of Butler's report, by alluding to some 'blurring of distinction' between the assessment of the evidence and the British desire to believe the best of the Russians. Jones felt that Butler should have clearly stated the basic facts at the outset, that up to 1973 no survivors from other camps Starobelsk or Ostashkov had ever appeared alive. He insisted on the importance of a meeting in October 1940 of Merkulov, Deputy head of the *NKVD* in Moscow, with a group of Polish officers, among them Lt Colonel Zygmunt Berling. When it was suggested to him that the Polish Army in the USSR would be reinforced with officers from the PoW camps of Ostashkov, Starobelsk and Kozelsk, Merkulov had replied 'No, not those, we have made a great mistake with them.' There is another reported version of this statement – 'We gave most of them to the Germans' – referring to the agreement between Hitler and Stalin regarding the exchange of PoWs in December 1939 at

Zakopane. The chief administrator of the NKVD dealing with prisoners of war Major Pyotr Soprunenko reported on 25 October 1940 that according to a decision of the Central Committee, 33,000 PoWs of the Polish Army from the German-occupied zone of Poland, plus civilian workers, 42,440 men in total, were deported to Germany. This figure excluded 8,403 men engaged on building project No.1 and a further 3,619 on forced labour at Narkomchermet.[4]

Major Kenneth H. Duke, 1st Secretary of the East European Section of the Research Department, had been a member of the British War Crimes Executive in 1946 and head of the British team at Whaddon Hall cipher centre. He had helped the inquiry by collating the captured German documents, and even after 25 years he still considered them to be of some importance. He challenged Butler for lightly dismissing the conclusions of the Congressional Investigation Committee of 1952.

Different comments were expressed by Julian L. Bullard, son of Sir Reader Bullard, British wartime Ambassador in Teheran, who had witnessed the exodus of Poles from the USSR in 1942 with their tales of Russian brutality and disappearances. He was almost alone in the FO in supporting the indefatigable Ambassador O'Malley in his accusations against the Russians. 'Not for reason of filial piety' wrote Julian Bullard, did he disbelieve the Russians. He pointed out some peculiar factors in the Soviet report, such as its propagandistic, accusatory title. He flagged the unreliability of witnesses alleged to have seen the Germans extracting letters with dates after May 1940, or who claimed to have seen the Germans bringing lorry loads of corpses to Katyn at night. In spite of these serious and belated findings, young Bullard found nothing in Butler's memorandum to suggest the need for revision of the long-standing official attitude of 'suspension of judgement'.

Anthony Royle, PUS (Permanent Under Secretary) read the report and reached the following conclusion.[5]

> 1. Whilst responsibility of either nation for this dreadful massacre is not proven in the legal sense, it is clear that most distinguished and middle level officials in this office over the years 'sense' from both records or talks or involvement in some way that the Soviets were responsible – I am not convinced by the argument that the Germans are more likely to have done the deed because of their record of manslaughter. The Soviets deeds over the past 50 years may well equal or excel the Nazi record – nor am I convinced by letters/documents on the corpses used as evidence because they date from 1941: the unchallenged evidence of no news after 1940 such as letters etc is interesting and tends to influence my view that the murders took place in 1940. Though in spite of these comments I am much impressed by Mr T. Brimelow's view, Para 17.
>
> 2. If reasons of State and our alliance with Russia at the time had not been paramount – if we had no Foreign Policy influence bearing upon us – an impossible

scenario! I feel certain that we would in 1945 and should now in 1972 put the finger of shame on the Soviet Union.'

On 1 November, the final, most critical comments on the Burdenko report came from Derek Tonkin[6] of the EE&SD. There is no record of how Butler reacted to these criticisms but in his amended and extended report of 10 April 1973, paragraph 65, Butler acknowledged Tonkin's grave doubts about the validity of the Burdenko report.

By 13 November 1972, Julian Bullard submitted all appraisals of the memorandum to Rohan Butler, in anticipation of the final report. Tonkin, by now a Counsellor in the Permanent Under Secretary's department, and a representative member at the JIS (Joint Intelligence Service), was producing ministerial weekly digests of intelligence as well as any special assessments that were needed; Burdenko's report for Butler's memorandum was one of them:

Katyn

1. In your submission of 16 October, you concluded that nothing in this memorandum by the Historical Adviser suggested to you that there was any need to revise or that there would be any advantage in revising our present and long-standing official attitude of suspension of judgement as regards the facts of the Katyn massacre.

2. I have recently been studying some of the original background material to Katyn, including the report by Mr Kazimierz Skarżynski, Secretary-General of the Polish Red Cross, who was compelled by the Germans to go to Katyn and who passed to us in the strictest confidence in 1946 his account of the two months stay of the Polish Red Cross representatives at Katyn. Although my studies have brought to my attention some very passionate and eloquent expressions of opinion, I do not consider that any of the events described in Mr Skarżynski's report, or any of the other papers I have read, throw any new light on the circumstances of the Katyn massacre and those responsible.

3. I think however that I should record that I have been struck by several very evident inaccuracies and contradictions in the Soviet Report. I am not speaking here of the value of the scientific evidence (origin of the bullets, rope, age of the saplings, medical evidence etc) but of illogicality and errors of fact evident in the Soviet Report itself. It seems to me that a journalist of Mr Bernard Levin's calibre would have little difficulty in making mincemeat out of the Soviet Report, if he cared to turn his mind to it. It may well be that Soviet awareness of the weakness of their case has made them so nervous.

4. In this minute, I would therefore like to do two things:

a. Firstly, to point to what appeared to me to be very evident weaknesses of logic in the Soviet Report.

b. To draw attention to the purely personal conclusions of Mr Skarżyński in his 1945 report [FO 371/ 56476] (N 5269/G of 1946) which have not hitherto been translated.

5. As regards the Soviet Report, the weaknesses of the Soviet case are I think best illustrated in the following four items. The quotations given are drawn directly from the Report.

a. 'The total number of corpses as counted by the medico-legal experts was 11,000'. This is quite untrue. As the Report makes clear, the Soviet Commission in fact exhumed only 925 bodies. Even the Germans admitted recovering only about 4,300. '11,000' is clearly a figure clutched at by the Soviet authorities to explain away the disappearance of this number of Polish Officers from the three camps at Kozelsk, Starobelsk, and Ostashkov.

b. The Polish war prisoners were housed in three special camps – camps Nos 1-ON, 2-ON and 3-ON, located 25 to 45 kilometres west of Smolensk" – these three camps, geographically, bear no relation at all to the three camps described in (a) above. Only Kozelsk was situated anywhere near Smolensk. The two other camps were hundreds of miles away. Nonetheless the Soviet Report would have us believe that these camps really existed. It is almost incredible that no one has ever appeared who had ever heard of these 'ON' camps; no letters were ever received or sent to them; no one has ever appeared who had ever been there; no actual place names are given to the camps. The indications, in short, are that they are completely fictitious.

c. 'The Germans staged numerous round-ups of those war prisoners who had escaped from the camps'. – The Soviet Report admits that numerous PoWs escaped into the forests as the Germans overran Katyn. If we bear in mind that these were principally officers, desperately anxious to avoid capture; that the area was in a state of intense confusion; that the neighbouring forests offered ideal conditions for survival undetected; is it not incredible that not a single Pole appears to have remained at large?

d. 'Of the documents discovered by the experts in forensic medicine, the following deserve special attention'. – The Soviet report makes much of the discovery of nine documents dating to the summer of 1941. If genuine, these documents would seem to indicate that the victims were still alive in late 1940, even 1941, when the Germans were in control of Katyn.

The first point about the description of the documents in both the Russian and the English versions of the Soviet Report is that the Russian draft of the English translation were prepared by persons who had only a very vague knowledge of Polish names. We are supposed to believe that there are Poles with names like 'Edward Adamovich Lewandowsky', 'Jadwijna' and 'Irene Kuczinskaya'. There are no patronymics in Polish; on the other hand I imagine it is just possible that some Russian camp official insisted that Poles invent patronymics simply because Russians have them. The spelling of the English version is curious. For example, the Russian version of items Nos 3 and 8 of the name 'Lewandowski' is identical. In the English version, item 3 is almost Polish – 'Lewandowsky', as is item 8 – 'Lewandowski', but neither of them achieves the correct Polish version 'Lewandowski'. The Russian version of No 8 is E Lewandowsky, but the English version is Z Levandowsky. The paper ikon No 5 may perhaps be a corruption of 'Jadwiga' which to a Russian observer, not fluent in Polish, might appear to be 'Jadwinja', that is, the 'g' in Jadwiga has been misinterpreted as 'nj', No 9 is alleged in the English version to be a postcard in Polish to 'Irena Kuczinskaya'. This seems to be a primitive attempt to transpose into Polish 'Irena Kuczyńska'.

6. It seems more likely that the so-called 'documents' have been described (in rather unintelligent fashion) by propagandists who were neither interested in correct translation nor even in making the names credible. But perhaps I could go even further and hazard a guess as to the origin of each of the nine.

i. The letter in Russian from Warsaw is probably quite genuine. The Moscow Post Office stamp and the note in red ink in Russian are credible. The point is, however, that this document could quite easily have been placed with the corpses as though it had been found on a body, whereas in fact it could have been kept simply among items not deliverable because the address had been liquidated.

ii. The postcard from Tarnopol is almost certainly a doctored document. We are told:– 'The manuscript text and the address have been lost.' This means presumably that they are illegible.

iii. and iv. These two camp receipts dated late 1939 were probably quite genuine, but it is doubtful whether the two recipients were Poles at all, since their names appear to be more Russian than Polish. What is probably quite spurious are the comments on the backs of the receipts – annotations dated 14 March 1941 and 25 March 1941, to the effect that the objects concerned (both watches) had been sold to some individual called 'Yuvelirtorg' [Glaviuvelirtorg, Main Jewellery Trade Commission]. This gentleman's name is certainly not Polish.

v. This paper ikon may be genuine and the name 'Jadwiga' perhaps has been misrepresented as 'Jadwinja'. The date '1941' has almost certainly been added on.

vi. vii viii. Probably quite fraudulent or at the very least doctored receipts from the non-existent camp numbered 1-ON, all relating to sums of money allegedly deposited.

ix. This postcard is possibly genuine. Critics have pointed out that of the very few 'Polish' names actually mentioned in the Soviet Report, only that of Stanislaw Kuczinsky bears any relation to any known Polish prisoner of war at the three known Polish PoW camps. In correct Polish, his name would be

'Stanisław Kuczyński'. There was a Captain Kuczyński; he was at Starobielsk. He was however removed by the NKVD in December 1939 and was never heard of again. The probability is that the postcard is genuine, but the date has been forged.

7. Against these nine documents which the Soviet report believes to be so important, it should be borne in mind that the Germans have produced several hundred names, which they published in the (German controlled) Polish press, as well as large quantities of documents, including nine cases containing several hundred pieces of documentation which were sent to the Institute of Forensic Medicine in Krakow for study by Polish scientists (under strict German control) over a period of months. None of these documents, which included diaries, letters and other official papers, contained references or dates beyond May 1940.

8. My conclusion from all this is that the evidence in the Soviet Report is:
a. simply incredible,
b. of pretty shoddy and inept propaganda production.

9. I mentioned above the hitherto un-translated report by Mr Skarżynski, Secretary General of the Polish Red Cross, I attach a translation of his purely personal conclusions. Generally, Mr Skarżynski's report is a very eloquent and at the same time very scrupulously objective account of the two months stay of the ten members team of the Polish Red Cross Society at Katyn. I do not know whether this report has been published in another context or not. If it were to be released in the public records, although it does not appear to contain any new facts, it is a very moving document.

10. In the light of the above, it does not surprise me that the Russians seem so desperately keen to suppress the whole affair.[7]

Notes

1 TNA FCO 28/1946 ENP 10/1, first draft of a memorandum 'Reactions in the Foreign Office to the Katyn Massacre', compiled by Dr Rohan D'Olier Butler, assisted by Miss J. Roskill and Miss C. Gray, for the attention of Julian L. Bullard and Sir Thomas Brimelow, Parliamentary Under Secretary of State, 4 September 1972.

2 TNA FCO 28/1946 ENP 10/1, appraisals of Butler's memorandum dated between 15 September and 13 November 1972 by: D. Mervyn Jones (IRD), K.H. Duke (East European Section Research Department), Julian L. Bullard (EE & Soviet Department), Anthony Royale (PUS) and Derek Tonkin (East European & Soviet Departmento.

3 TNA FO 371/71707B N4297, British Embassy in Ankara, 3 April 1948, an account of Katyn massacre, probably based on Supplementary Report written in 1946 by the Poles. Handwritten memo instructs no stand to be taken in support of General Anders or any use of it for propaganda purposes.

4 *Katyn Dokumenty Zbrodni, losy ocalałych* (Katyn Documents of Crime, the fate of survivors), NKVD documents edited by Wojciech Materski, Natalia Lebedeva and others. Warsaw 2001, Vol III, p.186, document No. 68.

5 TNA FCO 28/ 1946 ENP 10/1, Anthony Royle PUS on Butler's memorandum, 20 October 1972.

6 Derek Tonkin (b. 1929) studied modern languages including Polish, joined the FO in 1952, served mostly in the Far East and posted to Poland in 1955 and 1966. At the FCO in 1972 as Counsellor at PUS Department, representing it at the JIS, experienced in assessments, involved with Butler's memoranda on Katyn and the memorial issue.

7 TNA FCO 28/1947 ENP 10/1, comments on Butler's report by D. Tonkin (EE&SD), sent to Julian Bullard 1 November 1972. Copies were sent to: Sir Thomas Brimelow and Bernard Cheesman, Thomas Barker, head of the Information and Research Department, George Walden, Clive Rose and Rohan Butler.

chapter twelve

ACTIONS AND REACTIONS IN POLAND

In Poland, the word 'Katyn' could not be spoken in public, but there were churches where families and others would gather for prayers and lay flowers under secretly erected plaques dedicated to the dead officers. Attempts were also made to erect a symbolic cross at Warsaw's Powązki Cemetery, which was dismantled overnight on the order of the *UB*, the security police. In spite of these restrictions, an unofficial 'Katyn Institute' began its activities in Kraków in April 1979. Set up by nameless delegates from Gdańsk, Katowice, Lublin, Łódz, Poznań and Warsaw, the Institute received moral support from the newly formed resistance movements, the forerunners of the *Solidarność* such as *KOR* (*Komitet Obrony Robotników* – The Committee in Defence of Workers) and *ROBCiO* (The Committee in Defence of Human Rights). Their activities were co-ordinated through an independent periodical called *Spotkania* (Meetings) and in spite of censorship, which was strictly applied, somehow a book was published in 1980 under the pseudonym Leopold Jerzewski; written by a young historian Jerzy Łojek, entitled *Dzieje Sprawy Katynia* (A Historical Account of the Katyn Affair). It contained all the post-war material, the US Select Committee deliberations as well as the attempt by the communist authorities in 1945 to prepare a lawsuit against Germany accusing them of murder. Apparently a Polish prosecutor, Dr Roman Martini, was burdened with this task and when he had studied all the documents, he came to a different conclusion. The case was abandoned – but this did not save Martini who was found murdered, allegedly by burglars, in March 1946. Łojek and other opposition speakers such as Adam Wojciechowski, Wojciech Ziembiński and Wanda Ferens, who made public denunciations of the government's silence on Katyn, had shown tremendous courage. Others patiently waited for a further ten years.[1]

On the 40th anniversary of the Katyn massacre, 'The Coordinating Council of Poles in the Free World' proclaimed 1980 as 'Katyn Year', to remind the nation that Katyn woods, where Poland's best sons are buried, still lay unattended and forgotten by their own government – still afraid to challenge the mighty Soviet apparatus.

Russia's Response

In the same year of 1980, a group of Russian dissidents, among them Vladimir Bukovsky, Natalia Gorbaniavska and Aleksandr Ginzburg and others, published an article in a periodical *Kontinient* suggesting that soon it would be time for the Russian people to pass judgement on the murderers of Katyn. Little did they realise that with the birth of the *Solidarność* movement in Poland, which inspired *perestroika* and *glasnost* in Russia, in consequence the 'white spots' in Polish-Soviet relations were bound to be closely scrutinised.

In 1985 the two Presidents Mikhail Gorbachev and Wojciech Jaruzelski signed a declaration of 'Cooperation in the Sphere of Culture, Learning and Ideology' – with the aim that nothing should burden the future generations of Soviets or Poles with the deeds of their forefathers. This was a striking ratification, which enabled both sides to set up a joint committee of historians from the party political faithful. Lord Glenarthur in the House of Lords on 11 July 1988 declared: 'There is indeed a substantial circumstantial evidence pointing to Soviet responsibility for the killings. We look to the Soviet-Polish Commission to settle the question once and for all.'

The Russian intention was to emphasise political, rather than academic co-operation between the Poles, led by Professor Jerema Maciszewski and the Russians under Professor Georgi Smirnov, the Director of the Lenin-Marx Institute of the Central Committee. Maciszewski, in a book written ten years later, describes Smirnov as an Adviser to the First Secretary Mikhail Gorbachev. Smirnov was not an historian, and tended to follow the contemporary anticommunist feeling abroad, yet he continued to assume that the Soviet 'Special Commission' under Nikolai Burdenko had already resolved the '*katynskij vopros*' in January 1944.

Throughout the post-war years, a select few Russians were privileged to read about Katyn.[2] A young, inquisitive historian, Natalia Lebedeva, was one of them. In the 1970s, she studied the records of the Nuremberg trials and this was the first time that she came across the name 'Katyn'. She was intrigued by Burdenko's acceptance of the main argument, that the method of shooting of the Polish officers was comparable to those used by the Germans in Orle. Lebedeva's supervisor, Professor A. J. Poltorak, tried to stop her, advising her that the case was not clear and it was better not to touch it. In 1988, an investigative journalist of *Litieraturnaja Gazieta*, Vladimir Abarinov, received a letter from A. A. Lukin, the former commander of 136 Signals Battalion, which in 1939 was in charge of PoW movements including the Kozelsk camp. Abarinov contacted Lebedeva for advice, as to how this letter could be utilised, as his search for information in the Central Military Archives had proved fruitless. Lebedeva knew the difficulties of getting access to several important archives, where the word Katyn was so secret that it was undocumented. But she followed her instinct not to search for operational documents that were out of her reach, but for the written records of the movements and assignments of 136 Battalion, which listed their journeys to Gnezdovo, Ostashkov and other destinations. This was the key.

Lebedeva was determined to delve deeper; through her academic contacts at the Historical Institute, she was recommended to Georgi Smirnov, head of the Historical Committee, who could help with general research in the Russian National Central Archives known as 'Special' *CGOA* (*Centalny Gosudarstvenny Otiel Archiv*). Two of her colleagues, Valentina A. Parsadonova and Yuri N. Zoria, were also engaged and together they collected enough material for a series of papers on the subject of Katyn.[3]

The Polish–Russian Historical Committee

Katyn was not the only subject on the agenda of the Historical Committee,[4] there were other issues to be discussed, such as the 1920 Bolshevik war and its aftermath, the death of Soviet PoWs, Polish-Soviet relations, the execution of Polish communists by Stalin in 1930s, and the deportation of about a million Poles in 1939-1942 to the USSR. But Katyn still loomed large, and the aim was to present an expert commentary on the 1944 Burdenko report, to disprove Burdenko's false evidence presented at Nuremberg.

The strategy was promising, but it did not bring immediate results. The Poles had to wait another four years for the Russians to disgorge their infamous Top Secret archives. The report, which has been paraphrased below, should be read in conjunction with the FORD report of 1944 written by Professor Sumner and the EE&S's report of 1972. None of the British or Poles involved in the analysis of the Burdenko report was an expert in the field of forensic medicine or law, but they could analyse it from a logistics point of view and found the document to be fraudulent.

The leading Polish members of the Polish-Soviet Historical Committee of 1988 – Jerema Maciszewski, Czesław Madajczyk, Ryszard Nazarewicz and Marian Wojciechowski – were totally unaware of the FCO's foursome from the East European and Information Research Departments, Mervyn Jones, Anthony Royle, Kenneth Duke and Derek Tonkin, and their 1972 unrestrained reassessment.

1. Out of 100 witnesses called by Burdenko; none came from the Polish group of internees, allegedly in the unidentified camps No.1-ON, No.2-ON, No.3-ON, or from the spared group at Griazovets camp. There were no witnesses called who were on Russian staff duties in all three camps, and nobody knew the fictitious Major Vetoshnikov, who was supposed to have been the camp commandant.

2. It would have been natural for Burdenko to include Poles from the Union of the Polish Patriots (Communists) who were in the USSR at the time, but he did not.

3. The Burdenko report stated that 11,000 officers lived in camps near Smolensk, yet the international group of journalists and press reporters were not shown any of the buildings, administration documents or any other proof. The question of

prisoner evacuation when the Germans approached Smolensk also came under scrutiny and was found to be not believable.

4. The report presented at Nuremberg was at odds with the dates of the massacre. While witnesses stated that the Poles were shot in August–September 1941, at the International Military Trials, the Russian prosecutor changed it to September–December 1941, undoubtedly due to a remark made by the American journalist, that the bodies wore winter clothing.

5. The German unit accused of shooting the Polish officers was wrongly identified. *Oberstleutnant* Friederich Ahrens arrived in Smolensk in November 1941, his predecessor *Oberstleutnant* Albert Bedenck in charge of *537 Nachrichten Abteilung*, (Divisional Signals unit 537), which reached Katyn in September 1941. Lt Ahrens testified at Nuremberg, that there was no construction unit (*Bauabteilung*) in Koze Gory. The same was true for the German operational group B (*Einsatzgruppe B*), which was also accused of the murder, this could not be proven and the Russian Prosecutor had to abandon the case.

6. The question of the nine documents were of trivial importance in comparison with the huge documentation held by the Germans, including diaries and hundreds of cards and correspondence, which stopped in spring 1940. The Burdenko report stated that 'some' of these documents had been found on six bodies of the first batch of 101, out of a total of 925, which had previously been exhumed by the Germans and had *PCK* metal tags on them. The Russians failed to produce the 'rest' of the documentation as evidence at the Trials.

Having presented these arguments before their Soviet counterparts, Maciszewski's team subtly argued that to sustain the credibility of Burdenko's report in the 1980s, further documentation was required to back up the original evidence and this should be released from the Russian archives. The Politburo knew of the existence of the Katyn papers, but the Central Committee was not, as yet, ready for such a bold step and decided to play for time. After four years of procrastination, the Historical Committee was disbanded, but a protocol regarding the construction of a cemetery went ahead. Gorbachev's instruction to search Soviet archives for Katyn files continued. Fortunately for the Poles, Natalia Lebedeva, who was doing research on the movement of prisoners of war including the Polish officers from the Kozelsk camp, found papers amongst the *NKVD* files. This Top Secret material, called 'Packet 1', was located in the archives of the National Council of Ministers. This would indicate that all successive heads of state since Stalin knew of its whereabouts, but adopted a delaying tactic.

Once Pandora's box had opened, *Tass*, the official organ of the Soviet government accused the *NKVD* of the wrongdoing and declared publicly that it was 'the atrocity of the Stalinist period'. On 13 April 1990, the first batch of hundreds of documents was handed over by Gorbachev during the presidential visit to Moscow of Wojciech Jaruzelski. They consisted of lists of names from the Kozelsk and Ostashkov camps and included such information as rank and place of domicile. It was a highly selective and incomplete set of documents, but for the Poles this was an unheard of precedent, an opening of communications, at long last, between the Russo-Polish teams of researchers and scholars. They had to wait until April 1992 for the Archival Military Committee to be set up and begin work.

Lt Col Anatoly Yablokov, the first Russian Military Prosecutor in charge of the Katyn case, began his investigation in 1990. He called upon an independent historical committee. It contained Professors Boris Topornin, Aleksandr Yakovlev, Inessa Yazdborovskaia, Doctors Valentina Parsadanova, Lev Belayev (Forensic Medicine) and Yuri Zoria. He was the son of Nikolai Zoria, assistant to Rudenko at the Nuremberg Trials, whose unsuccessful task was to stop Ribbentrop speaking about the Secret Protocol to the German-Soviet Non-Aggression Pact of 23 August 1939; he was found dead the following day.

After three years of gathering evidence, Yablokov presented a motion under Russian criminal law, proposing that Stalin and members of the Politburo be judged guilty of the crime, based on Article 6 of the International Military Tribunal at Nuremberg. Creators of the Burdenko report and those who gave false testimony at Nuremberg were to be guilty of abuse of power. While those who perpetrated the murder were subject to the death penalty under the 1926 Criminal Code, without limitation of time. This obviously would have required new legislation in the Russian Duma, which was unattainable and the whole of Yablokov's proposition was flatly rejected by the Main Military Prosecutor's Office. It was on the insistence of the Polish Deputy Attorney General, Stefan Śnieżko that the investigation continued in Belarus and the Ukraine Prosecutor's Offices to search for further documents on those from other camps. Grim exhumations of the dead at Mednoe (Ostashkov camp) and Kharkov (Starobelsk camp) were to proceed.[5]

The 1940 Soviet Politburo Document

In 1992, after Boris Yeltsin's rise to power, not to be outshone by the now deposed Gorbachev, he released the two most important documents from the Presidential Archives of the Russian Federation. The first, dated 5 March 1940, was a motion presented to the Politburo by the People's Commissar of the USSR for Internal Affairs, Lavrenty Beria, arguing for the liquidation of 25,700 Polish internees who had 'transgressed against the Soviet State' and who should face 'justice of the highest order – death by shooting'. Beria accused the Polish officers of being 'hardened, unrepentant enemies of Soviet authority, who, while in internment, continued their anti-revolutionary activities causing agitations against the Soviet State'. The verdict was a state secret and was to be overseen by the '*Troika*': Vsevolod Merkulov, Bohdan Kobulov and Leonid Bashtakov.

The second document was an extract from the minutes of a meeting held on 5 March 1940 by the Political Bureau of the Central Committee, accepting the motion and signed by Stalin, Kliment Voroshilov, Molotov and Mikoyan; in the margin, annotated by the secretary, two additional names had been added, that of the absent Mikhail Kalinin and Lazar Kaganovich, both 'for' the resolution. (At the same meeting, the Central Committee approved the building a new sarcophagus for Lenin.) This time the bearer of truth for the Poles was the Director of *GARF*, The National Archives of the Russian Federation, Professor Rudolf Pikhoia, who in Warsaw on 14 October 1992 handed the document to Lech Wałęsa, the first non-communist President of a newly restored sovereign Poland.[6]

Among the documents passed to Lech Wałęsa was an important, handwritten draft by *KGB* chairman Aleksandr Shelepin, intended for Nikita Khrushchev in 1959. Based on the decision by the Special Troika of the *NKVD*, Shelepin advised that according to the evidence, the total number of Polish officers shot in 1940 was 21,857: 4,421 were shot at Katyn; 3,820 at Kharkov; 6,311 in the Kalinin region and 7,305 in Western Ukraine. In his opinion the sealed archives kept in the Committee of State Security of the Council of Ministers had 'no further operational or historical value to the Soviet organs or our Polish friends'. Mindful of some indiscretion that might arise through western interest in Katyn, he strongly recommended their destruction. After all, he argued, the official document prepared by academician Burdenko was 'sufficient proof to indicate that the Germans were responsible for the deed'.[7]

British Policy on Katyn in the 1990s

The response of surviving members of the Katyn families was muted. It was felt that the Soviet admission and Britain's cool acceptance of the truth, which they had avoided for over half a century, was inadequate. The relatives of the dead were waiting for some kind of justice – a condemnation of those responsible for the genocide. The suffering of widows who lived through the trauma of Katyn has never been fully acknowledged by any of the wartime allies.

Likewise, the Polish Diaspora accepted the British government's public denunciation of the Soviets with a marked indifference. William Waldegrave, the then Foreign Minister, called it a 'mealy-mouthed diplomacy', which actually did not pay dividends in terms of relations with the Soviets or the Poles. Knowing full well that the Russians were forced by public opinion to examine their own documents on Katyn, the FCO was inclined to accept that 'the time has come to point the finger more clearly at the Russians'.[8] But still, these were empty words, of which the public were unaware.

It took the late Robin Cook, the Foreign Secretary, to acknowledge that previous administrations could have been more candid much earlier about Soviet guilt; he duly instructed the FCO historians to revise the existing History Note and lay bare the reasons for the British policy towards Katyn.

Behind closed doors, the search for the Katyn documents began, just in case the speculation by Rohan Butler about 'the Russians [becoming] more forthcoming about Katyn in he future … than in the past' became a reality. Butler's report of 1973 was dusted off and furnished with 37 pages of updated notes with annexes by the present-day historians of the Records and Historical Department of the FCO, with a short foreword by Denis MacShane (Minister for Europe, 2003). *British Reactions to the Katyn Massacre 1943-2003* was printed in a limited edition for distribution to commemorate the 60th Anniversary of the discovery of the Katyn massacre on 13 April 1943.[9] The general public had to be satisfied with the FCO website.

'The Unquiet Dead of Katyn Still Walk the Earth' (G.F. Hudson)

In August 2004 the representatives of the *Instytut Pamięci Narodowej IPN* (Institute of National Remembrance) in Warsaw, which is responsible for tracing all crimes committed against the Polish nation, informed the Russian Prosecutor that after their abandonment of the case, the Institute would like to investigate the case afresh. The response was positive at first but after initial negotiations, the Russians informed the *IPN*'s authorities that certain files were still non-disclosable and would not be available until the government decided to release them. The Russians confirmed that out of 183 files of documents, 116 would remain closed and only 67 would be accessible for inspection but not for copying. This was an unexpected blow as such conditions were not part of the August deal.[10]

Things went from bad to worse when in March 2005, the Russian Military Court announced that the inquest on the dead at Katyn was to be terminated, owing to 'lack of presumptive evidence of crime'. The Poles believed that at least 2,000 perpetrators should have been accused; not only those who issued orders or physically took part in the killings, but also those who assisted in the convoys. It is worth mentioning that in 1990 when the case started, at least five alleged perpetrators of the Katyn crime were still alive. These were Pyotr Soprunenko, Leonid Reikhman and Ivan Serov, who were allegedly involved with 'clearing out', that is, shooting the PoWs; plus Kaganovich, a member of the Politburo who approved it, and Shelepin, head of *KGB*, who was in charge of the Katyn documents and tried to dispose of them.

The word genocide was absent from Russian criminal legislation until it was enshrined in Article 357 of the new criminal code, to be in line with international law which came into force in 1997. Article 357 also dealt with inhumane treatment of PoWs. Article 358 condemned deportations of civilians. However, Article 10 of the new code disallowed charges for those crimes committed before the code came into force – that meant Katyn, Mednoe and Kharkov were out of bounds. Article 10 follows the Russian legal tradition of not prosecuting the dead. Owing to the protracted investigation, lasting until 2005, the last perpetrator responsible for the crime at Katyn was no longer alive.

Yeltsin's successor Vladimir Putin failed to resolve the situation, even after the opening of Polish war cemeteries at Katyn, Kharkov and Mednoe, which was considered to be a stepping-stone to reconciliation. Presently the matter is at a standstill, no dialogue and no apology for the Polish Families Association, let alone a Russian confession to genocide. Years go by while 'The unquiet dead of Katyn still walk the earth.'

Notes

1 Zdzisław Jagodziński, *A groby katyńskie wciąż jeszcze wołają* (The Katyn graves are still calling), *Tydzień Polski* London 19 April 1980.
2 *Katyn. Dokumenty Zbrodni, Echa Katynia,* Vol IV, Warsaw 2006, Introduction pp.28-36.
3 Natalia Lebedeva *Katyn: preiestuplenije protiv chlovechenstva*, (Katyn: a massacre against mankind), *Katyn zbrodnia przeciwko ludzkości*, translated by K. Bidakowski, published by The Council for Defence of Memory, Strife and Martyrdom, Warsaw 1997.
4 *Katyń. Dokumenty zbrodni Echa Katynia* (Katyn. Documents of the crime) Vol IV, Warsaw 2006, chapter 102, p.459, a report of the Polish side of the Polish-Soviet Historical Committee of April 1988: Professors: J. Maciszewski, C. Madajczyk, R. Nazarewicz, M. Wojciechowski analysing the Soviet Report of 1944 (the Burdenko report).
5 *Katyń. Dokumenty Zbrodni Echa Katynia* (Katyn, Documents of the crime), executive editorship: Wojciech Materski, Bolesław Woszczyński, Ewa Rosowska, Natalia S. Lebediewa, Nelli A. Petrosova. Naczelna Dyrekcja Archiwów Państwowych w Warszawie (Polish National Archives in Warsaw) and *Państwowa Służba Archiwalna Rosji w Moskwie* (National Archives of the Russian Federation in Moscow *GARF*), Warsaw 2006, Vol IV, document 135, 2 August 1993, p.525-563; *Katyn Crime Without Punishment*, edited by Anna Cienciala, Natalia Lebedeva and Wojciech Materski, Obstacles to Reconciliation pp. 259-264, Yale University Press 2007.
6 *Katyn Dokumenty Zbrodni, Jency nie wypowiedzianej wojny* (Katyn. Documents of the crime), Vol. I, documents 216 and 217, 5 March 1940.
7 *Echa Katynia* Vol. IV, document 93, 9 March 1959.
8 *Katyn: British reaction to the Katyn Massacre 1943-2003,* published FCO 2003, footnote 107, FCO ENP/331/1.
9 *Katyn: British reaction to the Katyn Massacre 1943-2003,* includes a Memorandum by Rohan Butler of 10 April 1973, annexes and selected documents, published in 2003 by FCO Historians to commemorate the 60th Anniversary of the discovery of the Katyn Massacre; www.fco.gov.uk
10 *Biuletyn Instytutu Pamięci Narodowej* IPN No. 5-6, May-June 2005, (Bulletin, Institute of National Remembrance), *Rozmowy Biuletynu Komentarze Historyczne*, (Discussions and Historical Comments).

INDEX TO PEOPLE

130
13 144 оп
СОВ. СЕКРЕТНО
от 5.III-40 г.

СССР
НАРОДНЫЙ КОМИССАРИАТ ВНУТРЕННИХ ДЕЛ

„ .... “ марта 1940 г.
№ 794/Б
г. МОСКВА

ЦК ВКП(б)

товарищу С Т А Л И Н У

За

т. Калинин - за
т. Каганович - за

В лагерях для военнопленных НКВД СССР и в тюрьмах западных областей Украины и Белоруссии в настоящее время содержится большое количество бывших офицеров польской армии, бывших работников польской полиции и разведывательных органов, членов польских националистических к-р партий, участников вскрытых к-р повстанческих организаций, перебежчиков и др. Все они являются заклятыми врагами советской власти, преисполненными ненависти к советскому строю.

Военнопленные офицеры и полицейские, находясь в лагерях, пытаются продолжать к-р работу, ведут антисоветскую агитацию. Каждый из них только и ждет освобождения, чтобы иметь возможность активно включиться в борьбу против советской власти.

Органами НКВД в западных областях Украины и Белоруссии вскрыт ряд к-р повстанческих организаций. Во всех этих к-р организациях активную руководящую роль играли бывшие офицеры бывшей польской армии, бывшие полицейские и жандармы.

Среди задержанных перебежчиков и нарушителей гос-

Beria's memorandum to Stalin proposing the execution of the Polish officers, accepted by the Politburo, Moscow, 5 March 1940.